INSTRUCTION

AS A

HUMANIZING SCIENCE

A series of three volumes to be used to increase learning by increasing the effectiveness, efficiency, and productivity in designed instruction.

Volume I

THE CHANGING ROLE

OF THE EDUCATOR:

THE INSTRUCTIONEER

by

DON STEWART

SLATE Services, Publishers
Post Office Box 8796
Fountain Valley, California 92708

iii

Library of Congress Card Number 75-13470
Cloth Cover ISBN 0-913448-08-7
Paperback ISBN 0-913448-09-5
Manufactured in the United States of America

First Printing July, 1975

DEDICATION

I want to dedicate this series to the thousands of teachers who during the past decade or more have indirectly helped me to develop the concepts presented in this book by challenging them and making me justify and defend these concepts over and over again.

I also want to dedicate this series to my deceased Aunt and Uncle, Birdie and Frank Christopher of Wichita, Kansas, who indirectly provided the financial resources necessary to take the time to write the series.

I want to dedicate Volume I to the thousands and perhaps millions of teachers who will use it to help guide them in the performance of their new role as an Instructioneer and who will reap the benefits of becoming a truly professional teacher.

Don Stewart

Series Philosophy — "The Socratic Oath"

Most educational institutions in their charters or constitutions have stated a philosophy that is probably very much in agreement with the goals of our society. All too often these statements are so general in nature that they cannot be put into practice by the teachers and other educators whose job it is to develop a curriculum in support of the philosophy. Because the teacher's role is so critical in preparing the learner for life and even throughout life, there are many comparisons that can be made between the role of the teacher and the role of a doctor. Consequently the philosophy of the author can be succinctly stated in the following "Socratic Oath" which parallels the "Hippocratic Oath" which is taken by doctors in the performance of their role with their patients.

THE SOCRATIC OATH

You do solemnly swear, each person by whatever he holds most sacred, that you will be loyal to the profession of teaching and just and generous to its members; that you will lead your lives and practice your art in uprightness and honor; that into whatsoever educational institution you shall enter, it shall be for the good of the learner to the utmost of your power, you will set yourself up as an example to your students by constant efforts to keep abreast of the changes in your field of study, adding what is new and dropping what is obsolete; that you will endeavor to determine the knowledge level of new students and adjust the course to their needs and, if appropriate, remedial studies for some and advanced placement for others; that you will exercise your art in such a manner that every student in your classes regardless of race, creed, or economic status will progress positively through the content of your course; that you will exhaust all available methods, media, and instructional materials if necessary in order to help the student learn all of the objectives of your course; that within your power you will not allow any student in your classes to proceed to subsequent courses without achieving all of the prerequisite behaviors available in your course and necessary for a successful progress in the subsequent courses. These things do you swear. And if you will be true to this, your oath, may prosperity and good repute be ever yours; the opposite if you shall prove yourselves forsworn.

Copyright 1966 - Donald K. Stewart - all rights reserved

Parchment copies of "The Socratic Oath" ready for framing are available for purchase from SLATE Services, Publishers, P.O. Box 8796, Fountain Valley, California 92708.

TABLE OF CONTENTS*

Because the three volumes represent a series and are strongly interrelated, the Table of Contents in each volume contains the chapter and unit headings from all three volumes.

---

*It is customary to place the Table of Contents after the front material (Preface, Foreword, etc.) and usually just before the first chapter. However, in this series, the Table of Contents is placed before most of the front material for three reasons: first, it is recognized that most potential readers skim through the Table of Contents as a preliminary appraisal of the contents of the book; second, in this book, the front material is longer than in most other books and if the Table of Contents was placed in the customary location, it could be difficult to locate; and third, the front material is considered to be important enough that it should be placed after the Table of Contents along with the rest of the book and it should be included in the Table of Contents for ease of identification and location.

Volume II — A Behavioral Learning Systems Approach to
   Instruction: Analysis and Synthesis

Chapter VI — Determining the Purpose of the Instructional Event:
   Objectives and Evaluation
A. Introduction
B. Instructional Specifications
   1. What is Learning
   2. Reasons for Specifying Objectives
      a. Identifies the Subject Matter Focus
      b. The Nature of the Behavior is Revealed
      c. Behaviors to be Modified are Identified
      d. Facilitates Instructional Planning
      e. The Objective can be Communicated
      f. Helps Students Plan their Learning Time
      g. Achievement Can be Measured
      h. Teacher Accountability is Possible
      i. Facilitates the Development of Common
         Expectations
      j. Increasing specificity, Increases Chances for
         Learning
         (1) Interaction between SO's and teachers
            Role in Maximizing Learning
   3. Reasons for General Objectives
   4. Other categories of Objectives
      a. Educational Objectives
   5. What is a Specific Objective?
      a. The analysis of a specific objective
         (1) Specifying the Learning Environment
         (2) Specifying the Behavior
         (3) Specifying the Object of the Behavior

PREFACE

or

Why Be Concerned About the Role of the Educator?

Almost one out of every three people in the United States is either a full or part-time student, a teacher, or an educational administrator and at some time in every person's life in the United States, they are directly involved and affected by the educational process. Although the 1974-75 enrollment of almost 59 million students gave evidence of a continued slight decline of less than one percent, the total cost of education of almost $108 billion gave evidence of a continued increase of over eleven percent and accounts for eight percent of our gross national product. There is no other facet of our society that involves so many people and has such a critical affect on the future lives of the people (students) who are the consumers of these educational services. Therefore, the purveyors of these services take on a very critical role in our society. Ideally, this role should be performed in such a manner that the consumers are positively affected by these services. In fact, this is not the case. That is why I wrote my first book *Educational Malpractices: The Big Gamble in our Schools* in which I identified forty-one (41) educational malpractices that are commonly found in most educational institutions and being practiced by a majority of the teachers and administrators. This first book was primarily written for students and parents of students to make them aware of the malpractices being perpetrated on them and to give them some practical suggestions (including actual dialogues) which can be used to alleviate or eliminate these malpractices. Secondarily, this book was also written for teachers as a summary of the solutions to the problems as presented in this three volume series. Ironically, the very same educators who are performing the malpractices against students basically want students to have success in learning. The major problem is the strength of the loyalty that most educators hold for the traditions of education which have been handed down through generations of teachers. The strength of these traditions, even though they are malpractices, gathers support from two areas. Since *teachers tend to teach the way they are taught not the way they are taught to teach*, as long as most of the teachers at all levels of education carry on most of the malpractices, their students who become teachers will tend to do the same. However, the major support for the continuation of these malpractices comes from most of

xxi

the teacher-training institutions which not only practice the malpractices, but they preach them and demand that their students also perform these malpractices in order to graduate.

If education is a critical aspect of our society and the teachers and administrators in education perform a critical role in the educational process, I can't possibly imagine a more critical role in our society than those faculty in higher education who are teachers of students who are planning to be teachers. In any other discipline at a college or university, the faculty members may affect hundreds of students each semester or quarter and over a lifetime they may affect thousands of students, but teachers of students who are planning to be teachers, indirectly affect millions of students. Because of this, it is critical that teacher-training institutions make the necessary changes to eliminate the malpractices in their own teaching and in how they teach others to teach. As a result, the major motivation behind the writing of this book is to prepare a text that could be used by students who are preparing to teach. *Notice though*, at the present time, only teachers who are planning to teach at the elementary or secondary level are required to take any special training in *how to teach*. All that is needed at most institutions of higher education is an advanced degree. The assumption is made that to require graduate students or non-education faculty to take some education courses or training on *how to teach* and/or *how to test* would not be of much value because it can be easily pointed out that teachers who have had these education courses and the faculty who teach the courses typically don't actually behave much differently in the classroom than teachers who have never had any of these courses.*

Consider for a moment the seriousness of the existing problem in which thousands of higher education faculty are involved in the teaching and testing of millions of students and they are not in the least qualified to perform this critical role of *teaching* and *testing*. Yet, their actions and decisions are permanently affecting the future lives of their students. Therefore, a secondary audience for this book are the teachers who have never had any courses or formal training on *how to teach* and/or *how to test*, but would like to help more of their students learn more and would like to be more honest with students in their instructional evaluation situations. A third group for which this book could be of value are the administrators and teachers who have been trained through the traditional education courses to carry on the malpractices

---

* A recent study funded by the U. S. Office of Education as part of its Targeted Research and Development Program found little research evidence to show that teachers having teacher preparation courses have any greater effect on students' performance than teachers who haven't had these courses.

described in my first book.

Although the titles of the series and each volume were selected to communicate to potential readers the emphasis which I have placed in the series and within each volume, it is possible because of differences in the prior experiences of the reader to misinterpret this emphasis. To minimize possible misinterpretation, the primary emphasis throughout the series is on increasing learning — student learning! In changing the emphasis in the instructional setting from *what teachers do* to *increasing student learning*, two traditional concepts become obsolete: the classroom itself and the teacher's role as a presenter of content in that classroom. Almost every educational institution has somewhere in its charter or constitution the statement *to develop each student to the maximum of his or her ability*. Notice, the statement does not say to develop the *average* student or *most* students or a *curve's worth* of students. The statement specifies EACH student. In other words, the majority of educational institutions are legally committed to the concept and practice of individualized instruction. Since it is practically impossible to have a class of students who are all at the same level and who all learn at the same rate, it is also impossible to individualize instruction on a mass or class basis. Hence, the concept of classes of students is obsolete and since under the concept of individualized instruction it would be rare to gather a group of students together for an instructional experience, the concept of the teacher's role as a presenter of course content to a group of students also becomes obsolete.

As pointed out in my first book, the two major problems in traditional education are the evaluation process throughout education (from evaluating students all the way up to the evaluation of the U.S. Office of Education) and the teacher-training institutions. The reasons that the teacher-training institutions have become a major part of the problem in education instead of being a part of the solution are that most of them are practicing the malpractices, are teaching the teachers-to-be to practice the malpractices, and are training the students for an obsolete role as presenters of course content. Although some of the schools of education think they are being very modern by individualizing their instructional program, the content of the individualized program still emphasizes the traditional role of the teacher as a presenter of course content rather than teaching the teachers-to-be on how to individualize instruction for their students. The new role of the teacher as an instructioneer is the one that should be taught by the teacher-training institutions and should be *practiced by teachers at all levels of education.*

Among traditional educators, there has been a belief for decades that elementary school teachers teach differently and should be trained differently than either secondary school teachers or higher education faculty and that secondary school teachers teach differently and should be trained differently than either elementary school teachers or higher education faculty. The new role of the teacher and the process of designing instruction as described in this series is essentially the same role and involves the same basic behaviors for teachers at all levels of education from pre-school to graduate or continuing education.

The National Field Task Force on the Improvement and Reform of American Education has called for a new leadership to bring about increased effectiveness and inefficiency. In their report, the Task Force states that:

The welfare of this nation requires that schools attain new levels of success, and that this attainment be more inclusive of the population. Although a larger proportion of American youth is enrolled in school than at any other time in our national history, many thousands leave school with inadequate sustaining learning skills — and with insufficient preparation for the transition from school to the work force and effective participation in other aspects of the society.

Although their report calls for administrators to take on the leadership role, I believe successful change can best be brought about by cooperative leadership on the part of both teachers and administrators. Teachers should take the lead in accepting and performing their new role and encourage administrators to accept and perform their new role. Administrators should take the lead in accepting and performing their new role and encourage teachers to accept and perform their new role. Because of the transposition of authority as discussed in Chapter IX, Volume No. 3, it is actually more important that teachers be the first to institute changes which increase student learning. Whereas it is possible for teachers to improve student learning without administrative leadership and cooperation, it is almost impossible for administrators to improve student learning without the leadership and cooperation of teachers.

An important point to remember is that regardless of the teacher's feelings towards behavioral objectives, systems approaches, humanism, etc., practically every teacher evaluates their students and assigns some kind of evaluation mark. Realizing that not all desirable objectives lend themselves to measurement, the intent of this series is to maximize the learning of whatever it is that teachers are presently using as a basis to evaluate students and then to improve the quality, quantity and relevance of the learning objectives for each course.

INTRODUCTION

I expect to hear repeatedly three particular comments about this series. First, I expect to hear comments about the reading level of this series or that it is not very *scholarly*. Second, I expect some traditional oriented educators to be upset because I haven't quoted from or referred to the works of the many *big wheels* in education often enough (name-dropping) or at all. Third, in looking at this series in its present form, some readers will charge that I have not practiced what I am preaching.

With reference to the use of *scholarly* language, I would like to describe an experience which I had about five years ago. I had just completed a two-day seminar at a university when one of the faculty participants approached me and said, *I really liked the Seminar, but one thing has bothered me throughout the Seminar. What is that?*, I asked. *Your language,* said the professor. I asked him, *What is wrong with my language?* He replied, *It was not very scholarly.* I asked him, *What do you mean by saying that my language was not very scholarly?* The participant replied, *I understood everything you said!!!* Particularly in higher education, there is a tendency among faculty to select textbooks that will impress members of an accrediting team or most visiting colleagues even though the textbook may be so *scholarly* that even the teacher has trouble understanding what the author is saying (not to mention the fact that many of the students can't read or learn from it).

The name-dropping syndrome which is found in most *acceptable* papers, articles, and books is supposed to indicate that the author is acquainted with the work done by others in the field. By careful selection of references and quotes from the publications of *big wheels* in almost any major field of study, it is possible to support almost any point of view via inference. This is because in the process of developing a particular point-of-view, many of the *big wheels* have changed their ways of looking at certain concepts. As a partial result of the *publish or perish* dictum in higher education, a trend has developed which at best is questionable. This trend is the writing of articles and books which are primarily built on quotations and references from other writers with little, if any, new contributions actually being made by the person writing the article or book except the collecting of the quotations and references. Under certain conditions, this type of article or book could be of value particularly when it is one of the first in its field. After that, most of the articles and books in this category are just a rehash of one another. Since I have been conducting seminars and classes for over a decade on the topic of this series, the vast majority of the material in this series is original. In fact, the beginning of this series goes back to a 74-page paper entitled *A Behavioral Learning Systems Concept as Applied to Courses in Education and Training* which I wrote in 1964. Over 5,000 copies of this paper and revised editions of this paper have been sold. I have also written a number of articles during the past decade on various aspects of the same basic concept and these have been published in a wide variety of journals, magazines, and books.

There have been a number of publications which have been written about various aspects of developing objectives or developing instructional units which have been written in a format which would illustrate that the author was *practicing what he was preaching.* This would be very laudable if all the readers of the publications had the same needs. Rarely is this a realistic assumption. Although it is possible that some publications will only be read by one type of reader, the majority of publications are read by readers with differing needs. Therefore, the design of this series has been based on an analysis of reader needs and hopefully has built in sufficient flexibility that most of the many reader needs can be satisfied.

A majority of the initial users of this series will probably use this book as a reference source and many of the learners who use this series as textbooks for formal courses will probably also want to use this series as reference sources after they have completed the courses. Since most reference books are of the traditional format, I decided to write this series in the traditional format except for the following:

1. The general objectives (GO) and some of the specific objectives (SO) for each chapter will be listed at the beginning of each chapter.
    NOTE: The GO's and SO's at the beginning of each chapter are those which I believe are particularly important. A teacher who may want to use one or more of the volumes as a textbook for a course, may want to add more GO's and SO's and/or may want to delete some of the GO's and SO's which I have listed.
2. Following this Introduction, there is a list of six categories of readers who might read this book with directed guidelines for each type as to how they might locate what is most relevant for them.
3. Following the list of potential readers and their prescriptions is a list of fifty-one critical new concepts which are suggested in this book with the page numbers where these concepts are discussed in more detail.
4. For those learners who have problems in reading this series because of the reading level and for those learners who learn better from an audio-visual source or like an audio-visual reinforcement, films

covering most of the major topics and accompanying Active-Involvement Forms will be available by late 1975 or in 1976.

As mentioned in the Preface, the primary purpose of my first book, *Educational Malpractices: The Big Gamble in Our Schools,* was to point out to students, parents and educators, specific problems in the traditional approach to the instructional process which interfere with learning and to present a summary of the solutions to these problems which is presented in this series in much greater detail and are designed to eliminate the educational malpractices and to maximize student learning. To accomplish this task, I have divided the series into three volumes.

Volume I   Changing Role of the Educator: The Instructioneer
Volume II   A Behavioral Learning Systems Approach to Instruction: Analysis and Synthesis
Volume III   Creating an Emphasis on Learning: Quality Control, Productivity, and Accountability

In order to help most educators to accept the changes suggested in this series, I have found that it is necessary to present the rationale or reasons which support the need for the changes. Chapters I-III, Volume I, have been written with this view in mind. Chapter I, *Education vs. Instruction: Which is the Profession,* points out some of the major problems in education today and how they conflict with the alleged functions of education in our society. Chapter II, *Instruction or Education: Which is Humanizing,* takes a very critical problem which is of concern to educators, students, parents, and almost every citizen in our country and points out how the present instructional approach in most schools is not very humane and how by changing the teacher's role and by instituting a Behavioral Learning Systems Approach in the instructional process not only makes the process more humane, but can contribute significantly towards developing students who are more humane in their relationships with other people. Chapter III, *Why a Behavioral Learning Systems Approach (BLSA) to Instruction?,* describes various definitions of *systems* and how the application of the systems concept can help to eliminate many of the problems found in the present educational process without being as rigid and inhumane. Chapter IV, *Identification and Development of a Philosophy of Instruction and Theories of Instruction,* describes the six steps to be taken in achieving excellence in instruction and then continues on to develop the first step, identification of a philosophy of instruction and the theories of instruction. Chapter V, *The Changing Role of the Teacher from Educator to Instructioneer,* is the major and last chapter of the first volume and describes the second step in the process of designing effective and efficient instruction. A comparison is made of the new role with the traditional role of the teacher with an emphasis on how the new role helps the teacher and the whole instructional process become more humane in dealing with students. Major differences between the traditional philosophy and the philosophy of the Behavioral Learning Systems Approach (BLSA) to instruction are pointed out particularly as these differences affect the role of the teacher, i.e., whereas tradition considers student errors as a normal student or genetic problem which requires little, if any, follow up, the philosophy of the BLSA considers student errors as a learning problem brought about by student learning differences or problems in the learning environment, both of which can be solved. The Chapter ends with a description of a number of supportive roles which can help the teacher be more effective and efficient.

Volume II, *A Behavioral Learning Systems Approach to Instruction: Analysis and Synthesis,* concerns the next two steps in the process of designed instruction: the identification and specification of learning objectives and matching test items and the development of the instructional environment such that it will facilitate the achievement of the desired objectives. Chapter VI, *Determining the Purpose of the Instructional Event: Objectives and Evaluation,* is the first chapter in Volume II and is primarily concerned with the specifying and evaluation of instructional objectives in all three domains of learning: cognitive, sensory, and affective. In addition, reasons for specifying objectives, and guidelines for writing specific objectives, and the questions to be asked to justify the students' need to learn the objectives are discussed in detail. One of the most important concepts covered in this chapter is the need for and how to identify the minimum common core specific objectives in each course. Another important concept presented in this chapter concerns the need for a high correlation between the statements of what should be learned (specific objectives) and the test items or criteria for evaluation used to evaluate whether or not the desired learning has been achieved. As discussed in the chapter, this need for a high correlation between objectives and evaluation makes most traditional evaluation procedures and formats inappropriate and obsolete including standardized and normed tests and the so-called objective type test items (multiple-choice, true-false, and matching).

Chapter VII, *A Behavioral Learning Systems Approach to the Design of the Instructional Environment,* is the other chapter in Volume II of the series. The Chapter starts out with a comparison between the development of learning environments with and without specific objectives. Next, the development and selection of instructional software and hardware is discussed in detail.

Volume III, *Creating an Emphasis on Learning: Quality Control, Productivity, and Accountability,* concerns the necessity for making learning the major emphasis in our schools rather than the traditional emphasis which may have little relationship with learning. Chapter VIII, *Quality Control, Productivity, and Accountability,* starts out by discussing three important concepts: a critical principle of evaluation, the effects of a problem called *entropic drift,* and an evolutionary (some might call it revolutionary) transposition of authority which takes student learning from the bottom of the authority pyramid and puts it at the top of an inverted pyramid of support functions. Then the evaluation of students, teachers, administrators, etc., are discussed from the point of view of their affect on student learning. Of particular importance is the discussion of the evaluation of teachers as professionals rather than as artists or laborers.

Chapter IX, *Instructional Research: A New Role,* describes the last step in the designing of effective and efficient instruction. Traditionally, educational research has had little, if any, affect on what actually happens in the classrooms of our schools. The reasons for this waste of energy, time, and educational dollars are identified and then, the chapter concerns itself with methods by which instructional research can become a critical partner in designed instruction.

Chapter X, *Changing From Traditional (Chance) Education to Designed Instruction,* concerns the various steps that can be taken to bring about the change in the instructional environment. Included are comments on the implications of the Behavioral Learning Systems Approach on a variety of contemporary innovations in education.

By the time many readers reach this point in the last volume of the series, they will have questions which they want answered. For other readers who want to implement some of the suggestions I have made in this book, their colleagues may have challenged them with some questions about various aspects of the systems concept or about the imagined results of implementing some or all of the systems concepts. Therefore, the last part of Chapter X consists of a number of questions (and my answers to these questions) which typically arise at the Seminars which I have conducted with faculty from a variety of schools, colleges, and universities throughout the United States and Canada.

GUIDELINES TO READERS

In order to minimize the learning time involved in going through this book, I will identify six categories of readers. Categories II and III are further divided into sub-categories. After each grouping there are brief guidelines as to how readers in that grouping can get the most out of this series in the shortest time. (Those readers who have already read my book, *Educational Malpractices,* or have attended one of my seminars, see footnote below.)

I. *Description:* Learners who are planning to be teachers in preschool, elementary, secondary, higher education, or continuing adult education (this also includes people who are planning to teach in training programs in business and industry, military programs, and private schools).

Prescription: In reading through this series, pay particular attention to the general objectives (GO's) and specific objectives (SO's) found at the beginning of each chapter. If one or more of these volumes are being used as a textbook for a course, it would be particularly helpful if the teacher of the course followed some of the guidelines suggested in the series. Although most of the SO's are rote memory, the major process objective is described in Chapter X, Volume III, under pre-service training. It is very important that you get involved in solving a learning problem such that 90 percent or more of the students learn 100 percent of your SO's as the process will convince you of the practicality of the instructional design process. Also, be sure to use a pretest and post-test of your attitudes towards the four basic concepts of the whole series. This attitudinal instrument is described under the affective domain in Chapter VI, Volume II.

II. *Description:* Teachers who are already teaching and would be

---

My book, *Educational Malpractices,* and my seminars have both emphasized the problems to be found in traditional education and have presented a summary in 68 pages of the book or in two days or more of the seminars what is contained in about 1000 pages in this series. Consequently there is an overlap which is spread throughout the series. Therefore, in addition to the guidelines suggested for the reader category that you fit into, try to program yourself through the reading. Every time you come to a familiar concept, section, paragraph, or sentence which you recognize comes from *Educational Malpractices* or from one of my seminars, skip ahead by skim reading until you encounter new material and then slow down your reading speed to your usual level.

interested in trying out some new ideas and/or approaches to the instructional process. This category can be divided into six subgroups.

A. *Description:* Teachers who are already trying some aspects of the systems concepts and want to either double check their present approach or expand their application of the systems concept to their instructional activities.

Prescription: Before reading any of this book, readers in this group should read through the list of fifty-one critical new concepts which follows this section. Any concept which is of interest can be pursued by reading the reference pages listed at the end of each concept. In addition to these specific references, here are some general guidelines. For this group, the first three chapters of Volume I can probably be skipped. You should read through Chapter IV and those parts of Chapter V dealing with learning problems and individual differences. In Volume II, depending upon your experience in specifying objectives and developing matching test items, you may find it best to skim read over those parts you already know and practice and read a little more carefully those parts that are new. You may also find that Volume II will be a very good reference source as you develop and/or select instructional materials. In Volume III, that part of Chapter VIII dealing with the evaluation of students should be of interest and you might want your administrators to read that part of Chapter VIII dealing with teacher evaluation. If your use of various systems concepts is being challenged by your colleagues, you may find the last part of Chapter X useful as it concerns questions and answers about various systems concepts.

B. *Description:* New teachers who have not had any formal training on *how to teach* or *how to test* and also haven't been teaching long enough that they are committed to a particular technique or approach to instruction.*

Prescription: Readers in this group can probably skim over the first three chapters in Volume I. Because teachers in this group

---

* Quite often, teachers in this group feel guilty about not having any special training or courses on *how to teach and test.* Since few education courses are relevant to the needs of teachers-to-be, not having any formal training actually becomes a benefit. In other words, they haven't been tainted yet!

will have a tendency to teach *as they were taught*, Chapter IV and particularly Chapter V will be very important. All of Volume II will also be very important. That part of Chapter VIII in Volume III dealing with student evaluation is of importance, but the rest of Volume III may not be appropriate at the moment.

C. *Description:* New teachers who have had formal training on *how to teach and test*, but haven't been teaching long enough to be considered as being in the traditional teaching rut.

Prescription: The first three chapters in Volume I will probably be very important for these readers as they may have difficulty in accepting the rationale for the need to change the teacher's role and in accepting the new role itself. Chapters IV and V and all of Volume II will also be of importance to this group of readers. Again, only that part of Chapter VIII dealing with student evaluation is of particular importance; however, all of Volume III could be of value in helping the reader to accept and put into action the Behavioral Learing System Approach (BLSA) to instruction.

D. *Description:* Teachers who have been teaching for a long enough period of time to develop a pattern or style of teaching that is fairly consistent, but haven't had any formal training on *how to teach or test.*

Prescription: Teachers in this group will generally take a little longer to make the transition from the traditional approach to the Behavioral Learning Systems Approach. Because of this, readers in this group should pay particular attention to Chapters I—III in Volume I. Depending upon how traditional your pattern of teaching is (if you fit into this group), it may be useful to read Volume III before finishing Volume I or starting Volume II. The more traditional you are, the more important it may be to read Volume III. After Volume III, it may be best to read through Volume II and then come back to read Chapter IV and V in Volume I. After reading Chapter V on the new role of the teacher, it may be useful to review those sections in the rest of the series which you found most difficult to accept. It would also be useful if you could follow up the reading by attending a seminar dealing with these concepts in order to meet and talk with other teachers who are in a similar situation and some person(s) who is well acquainted with the systems concept.

E. *Description:* Teachers who have been teaching for a long enough period of time to develop a pattern or style of teaching that is fairly consistent and have had formal training on *how to teach and test.*

Prescription: The more traditional the teacher's pattern of teaching the more difficult it may be to make the transition from the traditional approach to the Behavioral Learning Systems Approach. However, an ameliorative factor is that many or maybe even most traditional teachers basically want students to have successes in learning and want to be at least partially involved in helping the students achieve their successes. I sincerely believe that once the traditional teacher is convinced that the concepts suggested in this series will actually help more students learn more that the teacher will be motivated to make the change and will try to be as loyal to the systems approach as the teacher was to the traditional approach. Given this situation, readers from this group should read Chapters I—III in Volume I, skip over Chapter IV, read Chapter V and then read Chapters VIII and X in Volume III. If, at this point, the reader is convinced of the need for specific objectives and matching test items in designed instruction, read Chapter IV and then all of Volume II. If the reader still has doubts about the need for specific objectives and matching test items, it may be best to try to attend a seminar on the systems concepts; to try to meet with some fellow teachers who are applying some of the systems concepts in their courses; and/or identify a learning problem in one of the reader's own courses and while trying to develop a solution to the problem read through Chapter IV in Volume I and all of Volume II.

III. *Description:* This category of readers are involved in trying to help teachers to make the changes and/or to implement some of the suggestions made in this book through in-service sessions which probably include large and small group meetings and individual conferences.

A. *Description:* This subgroup of readers are ones whose primary task is the conducting of in-service professional development sessions.

Prescription: For this group, Chapter X of Volume III will probably be the most important preparation and should be read first. In addition, Chapters I—III in Volume I and the malpractice dialogues at the end of my book, *Educational Malpractices,* should be very useful in answering the faculty questions of the type *Why I shouldn't change!* I assume that if the in-service sessions are to be about the systems concepts, that Chapters IV through VIII will be read very thoroughly. It would be very useful for this person if before any in-service sessions he or she worked with an interested teacher and identified a learning problem and solved it in accordance with the systems concepts. This would not only be a good experience for the in-service trainer, but the problem and solution could be used as a model for similar efforts by other teachers attending the in-service session.

B. *Description:* This subgroup are administrators who have responsibilities for the instructional program but have never had any formal training on *how to teach or test.*

   Prescription: During the past decade, this group has been trying to think of themselves as *instructional leaders.* At the present time, this particular group of readers may be hesitant to lead in a direction in which they have not had any formal training. Since most formal courses on *How to Teach and Test* are irrelevant, not having them can actually be considered a benefit. For this group it would probably be best to read Chapters I—III in Volume I and all of Volume III. Before trying to encourage teachers to change, it might be very useful to read through the malpractice dialogues at the end of my book, *Educational Malpractices,* and then to read Chapters IV and V of Volume I. Because the administrator will probably not be as involved in the instructional process as the teacher, it isn't as necessary that he or she knows the contents of Volume II as well as the teachers. However, administrators should be acquainted with the concepts if only to be in a better position to understand what the teachers are doing. Those administrators who want to think of themselves as *instructional leaders,* should know Volume II as well or better than the teachers and since these administrators usually don't have classes of students upon which they could practice the application of the systems concepts, they should work frequently with teachers in their efforts to identify and solve learning problems and to develop instructional materials in accordance with the systems concepts (as presented in Volume II).

C. *Description:* This subgroup are administrators who have responsibilities for the instructional program and have had formal training on *How to Teach and Test.*

Prescription: The main difference between the last subgroup and this one is that the administrators who have been trained as traditional teachers will have a greater tendency to evaluate teachers in accordance with traditional criteria which in turn will tend to keep teachers in their traditional role despite efforts by the administrators to get them to change. As a result, readers in this group may have to pay particular attention to Chapter VIII in Volume III. Otherwise, the prescription would be the same as the last group. If you are a reader in this group and you feel that you are quite progressive and that your faculty have been and are involved in many instructional innovations, you may find that the Exhibits (pp. 143–244) in Part II of my book, *Educational Malpractices: The Big Gamble in Our Schools,* and Chapter X in Volume III of this series may be important in evaluating prior and present innovations. In case your time for reading is limited and particularly if you feel your faculty are already using some aspects of the learning systems concept, you may want to look through the following section on the *Summary of New Concepts* (as suggested in this series) and pick out the concepts which you feel most relevant for you and your faculty and read up on those.

IV. *Description:* This category of readers are in many ways the most important because they are the teachers of students who are learning to be teachers and what they do or don't do with these students will indirectly affect millions of other students that these students will be teaching.

Prescription: This category breaks into two subgroups. The largest of the two subgroups concerns those teachers of teachers-to-be that are teaching any of the subjects these students might take *but not* actually courses on *How to Teach and/or Test.* These readers can follow the prescriptions outlined for them under category II with the following added reminder: students will go out as teachers and they will teach the way they were taught not necessarily the way they were taught to teach (particularly when the way they were taught to teach doesn't match the way they were actually taught)!

The other subgroup, although smaller, is the most critical group of all. These readers are the ones who will decide whether or not to use this book as a textbook in their course(s) on *How to Teach and/or Test.* In previewing this book, look through the following section on the *Summary of New Concepts* (as suggested in this series). Then, you should read Chapter X, Chapter V, and Chapter VIII. If you can accept the concepts and particularly the new teacher's role as an instructioneer, then you might read Chapters I—IV, skim read through Chapter V again, and then read Chapters VI and VII. Of critical importance in the design of a successful course involving the concepts presented in this series, would be the practicing of what is preached and the course project in which each student identifies and solves one or more learning problem units.

V. *Description:* This particular group of readers are primarily interested in doing research which might affect what happens in instructional situations.

Prescription: For this group, Chapters IV and IX will be the most important. Then the reader may want to look through the following section on the *Summary of New Concepts* (as suggested in this series) and also Chapter V for some ideas on what research they might want to do. The balance of the book could be read in any sequence desired.

VI. *Description:* This last category of readers consists of parents of students and students themselves who want to find out in more detail how to go about improving the instructional process so as to be more conversant on the topic when talking with professional educators or when trying to evaluate teachers or schools as to their effectiveness and efficiency.

Prescription: The readers in this group should first read my other book, *Educational Malpractices: The Big Gamble in Our Schools.* Having read that book, these readers might want to read Chapters IV, V, VIII, and X in this series and then whatever concepts in the following section, *Summary of New Concepts* (as suggested in this series, which are of interest to them.

SUMMARY OF NEW CONCEPTS

I consider the following 51 concepts to be essentially new and different from instructional concepts found in most other books of a similar nature. Not all of these concepts are new from the point-of-view that no one has ever heard or thought of them before; but they are new in that most educators, particularly traditional educators, have not come in contact with them before. Even though some of the more innovative educators have thought of and maybe even practiced some of these concepts, the major contribution I think I can make in addition to the concepts themselves, which may be new to even these innovative educators, is that all of these 51 concepts fit together in a package and constitute the Behavioral Learning Systems Approach to Instruction.

Volume I. *The Changing Role of the Educator: The Instructioneer.*

1. As a profession, education is the only one that commits malpractices on its clients by design and tradition. (See pages 27-36).

2. Actually education, as traditionally practiced, is not a profession in accordance with the three primary criteria for evaluating a profession: the existence of a specialized knowledge and skills; high standards of achievement and conduct; and a prime purpose of public service. (See pages 7-20).

3. Although the humanization or dehumanization of the instructional process is a critical issue in our society, most of the teachers of the courses which are claimed to be the major vehicles for humanization actually teach and test in a manner which is not very humane! (See pages 26, 29-31).

4. Given that humanism is concerned with positive interrelationships with other people and the respect for the rights of others, to interpret humanism as the freedom to *do your own thing* is to develop selfism, an emphasis on self regardless of effects on others, which is anti-humanism. (See pages 57-60).

5. Regardless of whether or not a teacher likes the concept of a *system's approach to instruction*, each teacher and each student is already an integral part of one or more systems and these systems

will continue to exist and function as systems. Therefore, the question *is not* do we or don't we want to use a systems approach, but given we are already in an instructional system, do we want to maximize the potential positive benefits and minimize any negative aspects. (See pages 69-78).

6. Although many educators, psychologists, and others have written about and tried to develop a theory of instruction, there hasn't been one which has proved itself in application. There is a theory of instruction, in fact, two theories of instruction: one for teaching and learning in the affective domain and one for teaching and learning in the other domains of learning. (See pages 101-120).

7. Once an educator accepts the concept and need for actually individualizing instruction instead of just talking about it, the classroom concept becomes obsolete along with all of the teacher behaviors associated with the classroom concept, i.e., the teacher as a presenter of content, the topic of classroom management, micro-teaching, practice-teaching (as practiced in most teacher-training institutions, etc. (See pages 129-136).

8. The humanistic role is that of an Instructioneer who helps each student achieve success by identifying his or her learning problems and solving them. (See pages 136-144).

9. Most teachers already practice this role but not in the right place. Notice the following conflict in most traditional teachers' behavior. If a student came up to a teacher in the hallway and said, *I don't understand what you were just saying in class*, not a single teacher in the tens of thousands that I have ever talked with would even think of taking out their gradebook and grade the student down for asking that question. Almost all of the teachers I know would try to solve the student's learning problem. However, in the classroom, when most traditional teachers give tests and students make mistakes which indicate that *they don't know or understand*, most teachers will mark the mistake as wrong and record the score in the gradebook without solving the learning problems. The instructional process can be significantly improved, if teachers will only bring their behavior in the hallways of *trying to solve learning problems* into the classroom and solve learners' learning problems instead of recording grades. (See pages 304-306).

10. In almost all areas of our society, it is an accepted common sense practice to diagnose first and design the appropriate treatment

second. Only in the traditional approach to education is this process reversed. The treatment is given to the students first and then the students are given the test. Not only is the common sense sequence reversed, but the data revealed in the diagnosis (test) is usually ignored except for some kind of score which is recorded. I refer to this behavior of the traditional educators as evidence of the *Backwards Ostrich Philosophy*. Tests should be given first and the treatments designed to fit the needs of the learner as evidenced by the results of the tests. At the end of the treatment, a duplicate test should be given and depending upon the results of that test, subsequent treatments should be revised to facilitate the learning of whatever was missed. (See pages 88,187-188).

11. A learning problem is basically any situation in which a student is expected to learn, but for one reason or another the student hasn't achieved the desired learning (student errors on tests, essays, etc.) As a learning problem, it is something to be solved, not just recorded in a gradebook. (See pages 144-196).

12. When a student leaves a unit of a course or a course not knowing some of the objectives of that unit or course which are a prerequisite for success in subsequent units or courses, his or her chances for success are significantly reduced. This condition is referred to as *cumulative ignornace.* It is not the fault of the learner. The teacher and our present system were the ones that allowed the student to leave the unit or course not knowing the critical objectives. *Cumulative ignorance* is a malignant disease associated with the traditional teacher-oriented educational system and it should be eliminated or at least reduced. (See pages 36-39, 42-43, 64,73).

13. A very common and hence popular misconception among educators and psychologists is the use of the words *ability* and *capacity* as synonyms when referring to intelligence. As a result, evidence of differences in ability and particularly evidence of different levels of ability are reported in such a manner as to indicate that these same differences apply to *capacity* (limits) as well. Most research that is used to suggest or prove that one race or culture has more intelligence than another is based on this popular misconception. As far as I have been able to find out, no one has ever identified the 100 percent full capacity (limits) of the human mind. Therefore, at this point in time, it is not valid to even hypothesize, let alone prove, that there are differences in capacity (limits). Probably the most acceptable hypothesis of the capacity (limits) of the human mind is that it has infinite capacity (limits). Can you imagine a situation in

which the healthy mind stops accepting any further input because it is full? On the other hand, I can't imagine anyone not agreeing that there are individual differences in ability of which part of this difference is genetic and part of it is environmental or learned. Just because there are differences in ability does not in any way affect the concept of capacity (limits). Ability may very well affect how the capacity *is filled* given certain situations but not the capacity (limits) itself. Differences in ability are clues which indicate the need for different learning materials, techniques, and pathways in order for the same learning to occur. For example, most IQ tests tend to be based on verbal ability. Therefore, students who score low on IQ tests have low verbal ability at that point in time. In order to bring about learning, a teacher could either teach verbal ability or use learning techniques that are less verbal and more appropriate for the learner's abilities. You do not have to compromise or change what they learn only how they learn. (See pages 31-35, 75, 88, 92-100).

14. Intelligence is frequently equated to *rate of learning* such that the slower learner is considered to be not as *intelligent* as the faster learner. Given that students learn best in different ways, to compare students intelligence (rate of learning) in a situation where these differences are ignored is unfair and the student's *apparent* rate of learning is not equal to the student's *real* rate of learning. (See pages 204-279).

15. Given that a teacher performs the role of the Instructioneer such that students' learning problems are identified and solved, at least 90 percent or more of the students can learn 100 percent of specified learning objectives. (See pages 111-120).

Volume II. *A Behavioral Learning Systems Approach to Instruction: Analysis and Synthesis*

16. An addition to the two domains of learning, cognitive and affective, the third domain is not the psychomotor domain as is popularly believed. The third domain of learning is the *sensory* domain.

17. All cognitive, sensory, and affective domain objectives are non-measurable on a direct basis and, as such, they are all general objectives.

18. When one specifies a specific behavior which is supposed to signify

indirectly the achievement or existence of a cognitive, sensory, or affective domain objective, the achievement is by inference only and, as such, the specific measurable objective is only a part of the more general non-measurable objective.

19. The measurement of the achievement of specific learning objectives in the three domains of learning refers to different student behaviors: cognitive learning is inferred from psychomotor behavior, sensory learning is inferred from sensomotor behavior, and affective learning is inferred from emotive behavior.

20. Instead of hiding from students what they should be learning which is traditional, students should know at the beginning of a unit or course what cognitive and sensory learning they will be expected to achieve.

21. Affective domain objectives are not generally given to the learners ahead of time nor would the achievement or non-achievement of affective domain objectives be used to arrive at grades for learners. The achievement or non-achievement of affective domain objectives by learners is primarily a measure of the effectiveness of the teaching design rather than being a measure of learning.

22. In contrast to the teaching and learning of cognitive and sensory learning which is done directly, the teaching and learning of affective learning has to be done indirectly. You cannot demand the achievement of an affective objective. If you do, you are liable to develop beliefs, attitudes, and values which are opposite from what you want.

23. In contrast to cognitive and senosry learning which is achieved best when it is done intentionally and is achieved least when ignored, affective learning goes on all the time regardless of whether or not teachers want to do anything about the development of beliefs, attitudes, and values through the use of a designed systematic approach to instruction. At the present time, most beliefs, attitudes, and values are developing by chance and, as such, some of these emotional tendencies are not necessarily in the best interests of the students, the schools, the community, or our country.

24. Despite the fact that some educators are against the concept of

behavioral objectives, almost every teacher depends on *behavioral test items* for evaluation. In other words, almost every teacher evaluates their students and bases their evaluation on something the student is doing (behavior) or has done (the result of a behavior).

25. The learner behaviors which are required to indicate achievement of an objective have to match as close as possible the behavior specified in the unit or course objectives, i.e., objective type test items are inappropriate because rarely does an objective specify the exact behaviors which take place in the objective type test situation.

26. The purpose of most tests which are given in traditional educational settings is to obtain a score of some kind which later can be used as a basis for assigning a grade or can be manipulated in a variety of ways using various statistical instruments in order to generate more data. The purpose of tests under the learning systems concept is to identify student learning problems. If any score is given to a student, it would be when the student has achieved 100 percent of the test.

27. The test items, papers, performances or whatever else a teacher uses to evaluate students' achievement are actually the real objectives of a course or instructional unit. If there is any difference between the learner behaviors described in the professed objectives for the course and the learner behaviors necessary to successfully pass the evaluation instrument (test, paper, etc.), students will generally try to learn whatever is on the evaluation instrument and will ignore the stated objectives. As a result, if there are stupid or irrelevant test items and/or criteria in the evaluation instrument, students end up learning stupid and irrelevant things.

28. It is good to *teach to the test*. In fact, that is what teachers should be doing! If a test actually tests for the achievement of something a teacher wants students to learn, then why not teach what you want the students to learn (the test). If a test doesn't test for the achievement of something a teacher wants students to learn then of course a teacher shouldn't teach to *that* test nor should the teacher use *that* test.

29. There is no place in designed instruction for *normal* or standardized tests because they are not based on a standardized list of specific objectives and the distribution of scores is built into the tests, i.e., a

professional test item writer can take any multiple-choice item and by holding the stem and the correct choice constant and by varying the distractors in the wrong choices can get almost any percentage the writer wants of the people who are answering the test item to answer it correctly or incorrectly. In addition, in *normed* tests, test items are selected primarily because they are good discriminators rather than because they measure the achievement of important learning. A good discriminator is a test item that 50 percent of the students will miss whereas a good test item should be one that is first considered important and desirable.

30. When dealing with rote memory objectives and test items, 100 percent achievement of the objectives is equal to 100 percent achievement of the matching test items because they are on a one to one basis. However, when dealing with process objectives and test items where almost every objective is tested by more than one test item, the percentage achievement of the objective is rarely equal to the percentage achievement of process test items. 100 percent achievement of process objective may be equal to 80 percent achievement of process test items.

31. Most innovations in education and instruction are concerned with different methods of doing something. As long as teachers don't know specifically what they want their students to learn, any method should be acceptable. However, once a goal is defined, there may be certain methods which will be more successful in facilitating learning in certain students than other methods.

32. Similarly, as long as teachers don't know specifically what their students should be learning, almost any materials can be selected, particularly for a learning resource center and open classrooms. Under these conditions, learning is by chance and is biased in the direction of the person(s) who selects the materials. Once the desired objectives are specified, there will be certain materials which will be more successful in facilitating learning for certain students than other materials.

33. Instead of having every teacher reinvent their course objectives as if no one else had ever taught the course before and given that the vast majority of students are going to live in the same society, there has got to be something in common in every course with the same name that is considered desirable to learn, regardless of where in the country the course is taught. These minimum common core

objectives can be identified.

34. Students may know best how they learn and what they are interested in, but they do not know best *what* they should learn.

Volume III. *Creating an Emphasis on Learning: Quality Control, Productivity, and Accountability*

35. In all evaluation of humans, there is a psychological principle in operation. *Human beings tend to do those things that the person whom they allow to evaluate them wants them to do!* What this means is that as long as teachers are evaluated on a variety of things not including learning, then teachers will tend to be concerned about a variety of things not including learning. When teachers are at least partially evaluated on the basis of the student learning they have helped facilitate, then they will tend to be concerned about facilitating learning.

36. Whenever the goals are unknown or fuzzy, there is a tendency to make the means to the goals the objective or goal. This situation can be referred to as *Entropic Drift.* As long as we don't really know what students should be learning, the process or method becomes the most important. When a teacher doesn't know what students should be learning from reading a book, reading the book (the vehicle for learning) becomes the objective, rather than learning.

37. When identified student learning becomes the focus of schools, there can and will be a transposition of control. Whereas at the present time student learning is at the bottom of the authority pyramid and important (often critical) decisions concerning student learning are being made by people who rarely work with or even see the students, under the Behavioral Learning Systems Approach (BLSA), student learning is at the top of an inverted support pyramid, and everyone's role is designed to support the one above and indirectly to help facilitate student learning.

38. Whereas quality control is a familiar concept in many fields, it is long overdue in the instructional process. Whereas the traditional approach is satisfied with a normal curve's worth of achievement wherein the average student learns about "C" worth or about 75 percent which causes designed cumulative ignorance, under the

Behavioral Learning Systems Approach (BLSA), 90 percent or more of the students have to learn 100 percent of the required specific objectives. Whereas in the traditional approach, time, methods, and materials are constant and learning is a variable, under the BLSA, learning is kept as constant as possible and time, methods, and materials are all variables.

39. In talking with thousands of teachers, I find that they want quality control such that all students should be learning 100 percent of the specified objectives and/or test items instead of the 80-90 percent suggested by many *systems* consultants or the 65-75 percent (or less) which has been considered *normal* under the traditional approach to instruction. If you are a teacher or plan to be a teacher, consider the following situation, the question and your answer to the question:

> You have given your class a test in which there were 50 points possible and 40 points (80 percent) was identified as passing. The question is *If 40 points is passing, which 10 points are not important?* If your answer is that you think all 50 points are important, then you actually want the students to achieve 100 percent. If your answer is that there are 10 points that aren't important, then why are you testing for student achievement of unimportant things and why are you grading a student down for not learning something you now admit is not important!

40. Just as teacher organizations and other employee groups demand the right to have a grievance committee to give them recourse as protection against administrative decisions which are unjust and capricious, and with negative effects on the teachers; students need and should have the same right as protection against teacher decisions, grading, and educational procedures which are unjust and capricious and with negative effects on the students.

41. Once teacher training institutions accept the concept of individual differences in bringing about quality control in student learning, and that tests are diagnostic in nature, the present test and measurement course as offered in most teacher training institutions becomes obsolete. Unless a student is going into research, there is no need for the teacher-to-be to learn how to do statistical gymnastics with students' scores. Even if a student may plan to do educational research, there is no need to teach the student how to

use *distractors* in order to trick students into answering tests in such a way that the test maker obtains the curve of results he wants regardless of what students actually know or don't know. The emphasis in test and measurement courses from the systems point-of-view will be how to write objectives and test items that have a 100 percent correlation and on how to solve learning problems. Whereas in the traditional test and measurement course the best test items are ones that 50 percent of the students who are answering them will answer them wrong, under the learning systems concept the best test items are ones that are first considered important and secondly the ideal situation would be where 100 percent of the learners learn 100 percent of these important items.

42. Since the traditional courses in test and measurement are essentially useless, a critical condition exists in that not only are those teachers who have not had any training in testing not qualified to do testing and evaluation (about 50 percent of elementary and secondary teachers and almost 90 percent of higher education faculty), but even those teachers who have had training in tests and measurement are also not qualified to perform such a critical task in education and particularly in designed instruction.

43. Given an educational situation in which the average student only has to learn 75 percent of the course and a normal or *chance* distribution of learning is acceptable, it is not very necessary for the teacher to know much about teaching and/or testing. In addition, given that the teachers role is to present course content rather than to facilitate learning and that tests can be manipulated to give almost any desired results without affecting student learning, there is even less reason to know anything about teaching and testing. In contrast, in a society where learning has become very important, teaching-learning effectiveness also becomes important. As the costs of education increase, efficiency also becomes a critical issue. Under the BLSA where 90 percent or more of the students have to achieve 100 percent of the required SO's, it is necessary for teachers to know what they are doing. It takes specialized knowledge to be an effective and efficient teacher not only at the elementary and secondary levels, but also in higher education.

44. Individual differences as a concept applies to teachers as well as to students. Teacher negotiations and/or contracts which ignore indi-

vidual differences among teachers are unreal, and inappropriate, i.e., all teachers in a given institution should have the same size class, same teaching load, and paid about the same amount of money.

45. Given that the individual differences in teachers can be recognized and the teachers are performing the role of an instructioneer, teachers will be able to teach multiple levels of the same course and/or multiple courses simultaneously. This would be very similar to the old one-room school concept. No one ever heard of a teacher in a one-room school canceling fourth grade because there wasn't enough students enrolled. This concept becomes more important in view of decreasing enrollments.

46. Given that most teachers have not been taught how to teach as defined in terms of facilitating student learning, nor on how to develop and use diagnostic tests and that very few teachers have ever been hired on the basis of their ability to facilitate student learning, then it is not fair to hold a teacher accountable for student learning unless schools and administrative bodies provide appropriate systematic in-service training first.

47. Given a situation where a teacher is having trouble solving student learning problems, the administrative structure should include an *Instructional Crisis Squad* that could work with the teacher and help solve learning problems such that both the students and the teacher have success.

48. Although teacher salaries were in need of improvement and the teacher union movement has done a great deal to increase teacher salaries and to improve other working conditions, continued emphasis of teacher organizations on the teacher as a laborer rather than as a professional will be at the detriment of the teaching-learning situation. Professionalism and unionism are almost antithetical in their goals and concepts and teachers will have to decide which way they want to go.

49. Educational research has also been affected by entropic drift in that since we don't know what students should be learning (the goals of education), the emphasis of educational research has been on the process of education, i.e., methods, materials, techniques, etc. As such, educational research is a non-science because it deals with man-made phenomenon. In contrast, instructional research is primarily concerned with learning and is a science becuase learning

is a natural phenomenon.

50. Given that there is little commonality in what is being learned in courses with the same title, that tests can be manipulated to give any desired results, and that standardized tests don't match any known lists of specific learning objectives, not only is most educational research irrelevent and useless, most of it is invalid because the data is invalid. Regardless of the power of the statistical instruments used and the validity of the methods used, if the data is *garbage* to begin with, the results are still *garbage*. (GIGO — garbage in — garbage out!)

51. There is a method of evaluating the design of an instructional situation on the basis of three factors: potential boredom factor, the instructional effectiveness factor, and the instructional efficiency factor. Using this technique, it can be shown that *Seasame Street*, which has been heralded as the model for future instructional television, although entertaining, has a high potential for boredom and is not very effective nor efficient from the point-of-view of learning.

CHAPTER I

EDUCATION OR INSTRUCTION: WHICH IS THE PROFESSION?

General and Specific Objectives

GO — To have an understanding of the purposes for schools and why these purposes have not been achieved.

    SO — List the four basic purposes of schools.

    SO — Define *education* and *instruction* and point out their differences with reference to measurability.

    SO — Define *profession* in terms of the three primary criteria cited in Webster's Dictionary.

    SO — List the five reasons why traditional education has not achieved its basic purposes and give at least one example of each.

    SO — Defend the importance of teachers of teachers-to-be in terms of the numbers of students they affect directly or indirectly.

GO — To understand that designed instruction is more able to satisfy the needs for learning and the purposes for schools than traditional education.

    SO — List ten or more of the 39 comparisons between instruction and education and give an example from your own experience which supports the existence of the stated condition in education.

There has been and still is a continuous discussion (sometimes heated debates) over whether schools should be concerned with education or instruction. If it can be agreed on that both education and instruction exist in a school, then as a general rule, those teachers who think that they are primarily concerned with education usually feel that education is on a higher plane or level than instruction and as a consequence they look down on courses and teachers who are primarily concerned with instruction. Quite typically the term *education* is usually used in reference to the so-called *academic* subjects and the term *instruction* is usually used in reference to the courses which are vocational, occupational, or career oriented. Sometimes the difference between the two areas, education and instruction, is dependent upon whether or not the major emphases are on mental skills or sensory skills. Consider for a moment, don't most or all of the various forms of

1

student evaluation in the so-called academic courses involve physical or sensory behaviors also: writing papers, giving oral presentations, class or group discussion, writing answers in tests, etc? Sometimes the difference between the two areas is based on levels of intellectual effort in which those teachers in the so-called academic areas are supposed to be dealing with higher level and more complex mental tasks than the teachers in the vocational-technical areas. Consider for a moment, how many of the teachers in the so-called academic areas repair their own cars, television sets, or computers? Very few. Why, because they feel these machines are too *complex*. Isn't it odd that the student who supposedly doesn't have enough intelligence to build a proper sentence or paragraph may be able to build an extremely complex machine!

There are other stated differences between the two terms which could be discussed, but first I want to go back to why we have formal learning activities in our society, then I will try to identify the needs of our society that these formal learning activities are supposed to accomplish, then I will come back to the discussion of education vs. instruction.

Learning can occur under almost any set of circumstances. In fact, a great deal of learning takes place in a wide variety of informal situations without the assistance of any formalized instructional activities. The experiences that one encounters just in everyday living are in themselves learning situations. Because it is very difficult to predict ahead of time what will happen in life, learning experiences resulting from the interaction between the learners and life occur by *chance*. In other words, one never knows when the learning experience will occur or if it will occur at all in a specific individual's living experiences. This type of informal education is also often referred to as *trial and error* education, because in the efforts of a person to obtain something, go someplace, or satisfy some desire, the person will try some method, technique, or pathway, thinking to the best of his ability at that time that this particular method should be successful. If that particular method turns out *not* to be successful, then the person is faced with the decision, *Is what I want really worth a second try?* If the person decides that it is worthwhile, then the person will select a second method keeping in mind his previous effort and his perceived errors or mistakes. This process is continued until either the person succeeds in gaining his goal or objective or he makes the decision that further attempts to achieve this goal are really not worthwhile, and abandons either temporarily or permanently any further efforts to achieve the goal. Quite often when people are unable to succeed in achieving a particular goal they will compromise on a lesser goal, so at least they achieve a partial success. The *errors* in the trail and error type of informal education could very easily result in the loss of many lives (primitive people trying to kill

2

certain animals, centuries of military people trying to win wars, modern-day drivers trying to learn what to do in emergency situations, or any other of a variety of activities where errors can be fatal). The *errors* could also result in physical, mental and/or spiritual injuries. In an effort to alleviate at least to a degree the loss of life, injuries, or heartaches, each generation tries to pass on to succeeding generations the knowledge that was passed down to them, plus whatever additional knowledge they have gained in their trial and error informal educational activities. In their efforts to increase the effectiveness in the transference of this trial and error learning from one generation to another, situations were contrived or established so that necessary learning could happen on purpose, rather than waiting for the learning experience to occur by chance, or possibly not even at all. Efforts in this direction began to formalize the learning experiences of the young people. Even at the present time, some of the most successful teaching-learning situations in which the teacher is also the parent occurs when the teaching is carried out or demonstrated in a living situation. This transference of trail and error learning from one generation to the next generation by parents and/or other relatives, when carried out in a situation other than the life situation may not be as effective as when the teaching-learning situation is the real thing. This is because the parents or relatives may not be able to communicate as well to the learner using verbal and visual symbols for the real life situation as they are able to do in the actual real life situation.

Since most parents were probably not as effective in a teaching-learning situation which relied on verbal and visual symbols, they looked for other parents or people in the social group who were more successful in communicating to the learners through verbal and visual means. Success in this instance was measured by the learners being able to take advantage of trial and error learning of former generations without actually going through the living experiences themselves. Therefore, the contribution of formal instruction was designed to affect the student's learning in such a manner that the experiences considered to be necessary or desirable by the teacher occurred on purpose and by choice instead of by chance.

Originally, this formal education was accomplished in two separate teaching-learning situations. One situation concerned the practical learning in order to participate in life. In this situation, the parents or relatives still carried on the task of teaching. The second situation concerned the passing on of customs, folklore, classic education, etc., much of which was taught through verbal and visual symbols. In this situation, a special person or persons carried on the task of teaching and eventually this activity took place in specific locations or buildings which were referred to as schools. It is important to point out that in

3

both of these situations what was passed on to the young was confined to what parents, relatives, and teachers knew. It was also confined to what parents, relatives, and teachers thought the young should know and at what age they should know it.

Until the present century, most formalized education with someone other than parents or relatives was considered to be a luxury, and as such, these learning experiences were reserved for the social elite who could afford such a luxury. In the United States, however, during the past three hundred years there has been a growing commitment to an education for everyone. Although this commitment existed on paper, the interpretation of the word *everyone* varied considerably along with variations in the interpretation of just how much education *everyone* should have. The last hundred years has seen the emergence, due to modern technology, of many new human tasks which have demanded new kinds of complex skills. During this same time, the opportunities were rapidly decreasing for people to engage in gainful employment with only limited educational background. Both of these trends, increasing commitment to education for all and decreasing opportunities for the uneducated, can be traced to the expansion of the employment needs in fields which require increasingly greater educational backgrounds for employment.

Although many workers may not need a high school or post high school education to perform adequately on the present job, they may need this level of education in order to perform adequately on other jobs to which they may be eventually promoted. The fact that having a high school or post high school education does not improve a person's performance on his job does not necessarily mean that the person didn't need the extra education; it may mean that the traditional curriculum in the high school or institution of higher education is irrelevant with respect to the needs of the real world and should be changed accordingly. In view of the fact that we may not even be able to describe the needs of our youth as they go out to work in jobs which have never existed before, our emphasis will have to change from having a curriculum designed to satisfy identified needs in technical and professional areas to a curriculum designed to help the youth identify the needs once the new job is identified and to be able to learn on their own the needs they have identified. In other words, to fit into a constantly changing world, schools have to develop students who are independent self-learners.

A. EDUCATIONAL NEEDS, PURPOSES FOR SCHOOLS, AND WHY PURPOSES HAVE NOT BEEN ACHIEVED

The educational needs of our country in the coming years are not

4

only going to be in the technical and professional areas, but in the development of programs concerned with helping people to get along better with one another and improved utilization of their increased leisure time. The conflicts between various segments of our society which are described daily in newspapers and on radio and television point out the critical problems of our interpersonal and intergroup relationships. In the past, churches and homes have attempted to teach our young people how to get along with their neighbors. Because most church leaders and parents have not been taught how to teach humanity, it has been a hit and miss situation.

Even though the needs of our society are much different, the functions which our schools are to accomplish are not that different. Schools are supported by taxpayers and other funding resources to accomplish the following purposes in regard to their students:

1. To prepare the students in such a way that they will be able to take maximum advantage of the opportunities available in our society and to enjoy the tangible items and the intangible benefits representative of the high standard of living in our country.
2. To prepare the student in such a way that he will not only be self-supporting, but will become a taxpaying and contributing member of the society.
3. To be sure that the experiences necessary for each student to achieve the first two purposes happen by design, rather than by chance.
4. *To develop each child to the maximum of his capability* (this function will be found written into the charter or constitution of almost every school district, college, and university in the country).

These four functions have been stated in many ways by many different people but the goals implied by these four statements are not being achieved. There are at least five major reasons for this lack of achievement. The most fundamental and basic reason why educational institutions are not able to achieve these goals is because the goals implied by the first function have never been specified specifically enough to allow absolute measurement, communication, teaching, and learning by design. Various state departments of public instruction have tried to define the content of each course at each grade level in the form of guidelines for the teachers. Most of these guidelines describe activities for the teacher or for the students. Quite typically, the objectives that are listed in the state departments' course guidelines are so general that the interpretation of any one objective varies widely from one teacher to another.

A second very fundamental reason concerns the meanings which educators have for words which are used to describe the teaching-learning process. For example: what kind of meanings do people have for the word *education?* I have asked thousands of educators at all levels of education to define the word *education*. Of primary interest is the fact that most educators have great difficulty in verbalizing their definition and are reluctant to even try. Ultimately, partial agreement can be obtained as to the following definition:

> *Education* is the totality of experience that a person goes through while living, including both formal and informal experiences, useful and useless experiences, relevant and irrelevant experiences, and positive and negative experiences which result in a change regardless of whether or not this change is measurable or even observable.

The dictionary defines:

> *Education* is the act or process of educating or being educated.

The fact that educators find it difficult to define *education* and even the fact that the dictionary defines the word in terms of other forms of the base word *educate* should indicate the ambiguity and generality of the term *education*. The dictionary definitions of the words *educate* and *educated* also provide some interesting points.

> *Educate* is to develop a person by fostering to varying *degrees* the growth or expansion of knowledge, wisdom, etc.

> *Educated* is the possessing of an education; having information or knowledge *beyond average*.

The definition of the base word *educate* suggests that education should result in *differences in achievement* and the definition of *educated* suggests that only a minority of the population can attain whatever *educated* refers to.

The last and most important point to bring out in discussing the word *education* or any of the other forms of the base word *educate*, is their complete absence in the dictionary definitions of *learning* or *teaching*. If a person is concerned with *learning* and *teaching* then according to the dictionary, the person will have to be concerned with *instruction* and *training*. An examination of the definitions of *instruction* and *training* indicates a much greater degree of specificity of what is learned, taught, achieved, etc., than is suggested in the definition of *education*. When educators are asked to define *instruction* or *training*, most of their replies converge on the concept of a planned or designed teaching-learning situation.

As might be expected then, at the present time, under the label of *education*, relatively few *educators* in any subject matter area or at any level have specified their course objectives and/or have designed the teaching-learning situation to maximize learning for *all* students.

In view of the foregoing, *education* represents a situation in which neither learning nor teaching is defined or specified, yet in the schools,

6

students are penalized by the results of tests which test for the achievement of specific learning tasks which they have never been specifically made aware that they were supposed to learn. Following this traditional education pattern, learning takes place by chance and it is possible to correlate students' *ability to learn* with their *ability to guess* what they are supposed to learn. Almost every student has had the experience of studying very hard for a test, but when he or she got into the testing situation, the student discovered that he or she had studied the wrong things. This does not mean that the student's parents are divorced or provide the wrong environment for learning, or that the genetic ability of the student is inadequate for the learning task. It just means that the student didn't guess very well. Sad to say, in too many teaching-learning situations at the present time, the letter grades which students receive are actually indications of the correlation between the teacher's guess of what to test and the student's guess of what to study.

In contrast, *instruction* represents learning by design where the results of tests indicate potential need for additional learning and it is possible to correlate students' *successful achievement* with a teacher's *ability to teach.* If these definitions of *education* and *instruction* can be accepted, then it may very well be that one of our basic concepts is in error. For decades, most people have referred to *education* as a profession. Many of the educators across the country, when making demands upon school boards, administrators, and taxpayers, ask to be treated as *professionals.*

In order to decide for sure whether or not *education* or *instruction* can be considered as a *profession*, it is necessary to also examine the word *profession.*

A *profession* is a calling requiring *specialized knowledge* and often long and intensive preparation, including instruction in skills and methods, as well as the scientific, historical, or scholarly principles underlining such skills and methods, maintained by force of organization or concerted opinion, high standards of *achievement and conduct,* and committing its members to continued study and to a kind of work which has for its *prime purpose the rendering of a public service.*

In reference to the above definition of a *profession* as described in Webster's Dictionary, there are three items of particular interest. The first one refers to a *specialized knowledge.* If the person calling himself a professional is an engineer, then of course the specialized knowledge would be in engineering. If the person was a professional doctor, the specialized knowledge would be in some field of medicine or surgery. If the professional person is a lawyer, then the specialized knowledge should be in law. Consequently, if the professional person is a teacher, then the specialized knowledge should be in *teaching and learning.*

7

This brings up the third reason why schools are not achieving their goals in our society and this reason concerns the general role of the teacher in the teaching-learning situation. In most professions there are two major roles: the practitioner and the researcher. The practitioner is the one who practices or exercises the profession. The researcher is the one who studies and does research within the profession in order to provide information to the practitioner such that the practitioner's professional role will be more successful, effective, and efficient in achieving the prime purpose of a profession: the rendering of public service. For example, in the medical profession (see Diagram A — Figure 1), the goal of the practitioner is to take patients who have varying degrees of sickness (line cd) and get them well (line ab) by design, by intuition, by trial and error, etc. The goal of the researcher is to study various critical medical problems and experiment with new diagnostic or treatment concepts which will help the practitioner do less of his or her practice based on guessing and more based on design. To do this, the researcher finds a group of patients who have a similar physical problem and then gives them a specific treatment for a specific length of time. Then, the researcher can as a result of the treatment identify how close to good physical health (line ab) the patients can get as a result of the treatment.

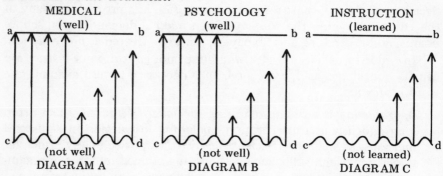

Figure 1 — Practitioner—Researcher Model

In a similar manner, in psychology (see Diagram B — Figure 1), the goal of the practitioner is to take patients who have varying degrees of sickness (line cd) and get them well (line ab) by design, by intuition, by trial and error, etc. The goal of the researcher is to study various critical psychological problems and experiment with new diagnostic or treatment concepts which will help the practitioner do less of his or her practice based on guessing and more based on design. Again, to do this, the researcher finds a group of patients who have a similar mental problem and gives them a specific treatment for a specific length of time. Then, the researcher can identify how close to good mental health the patients can get as a result of the treatment.

Notice the similarities between the two professional fields. The practitioner in both fields is concerned with taking patients at varying levels of physical or mental sickness and getting them all the way up to well (line ab) using whatever treatments and whatever length of time necessary to achieve this goal. The only constant for the practitioner (for each patient) is getting the patients well! However, the researcher in both fields is concerned with experimenting with specific treatments for specific lengths of time. The major dependent variable for the research (in each experiment) is how well the patients were able to get. What should be obvious now is that practitioners are concerned with individuals (human beings) and researchers are concerned with treatments (regardless of whether the treatment is used on human beings or some other sub-human animals).

In instruction (see Diagram C, Figure 1), researchers perform in a similar manner. They find a group of students who don't know something and then they put the students through a specific treatment for a specific length of time and measure how much the students learned. The problem is that when the researcher tries to give the information he or she has learned from the experiment to the *practitioner*, it is difficult to find instructional practitioners who will take students from wherever they are intellectually and help them learn all of whatever it is the students are supposed to learn with an emphasis on each individual. In education, as it is practiced in most schools today, the teachers who are supposed to be the practitioners are acting out the role of the researcher instead of that of the practitioner. In most classrooms, the treatment and the length of time is constant for most students and learning is left as the dependent variable instead of letting the treatments and time vary as necessary in order to have all students be successful and learn all of each course. In other words, the instructional role of the *practitioner* is a missing link in the achievement of the goals which society has assigned to our schools. However, under the concept of education, this situation (no instructional practitioners) may be appropriate because in *education* there is supposed to be varying degrees of achievement and only a minority of students are able to achieve the *educated* status!

Since students already have different levels of learning when they start school, it is relatively simple to maintain or increase these differences. In fact, a teacher may have to be careful not to teach the students who have lower levels of learning because they are liable to catch up to the other students and then everyone would be educated.

This brings into focus the fourth reason why schools have not been able to achieve the functions which society expects them to fulfill. This reason concerns the passing on of the specialized knowledge which is supposed to be a characteristic of a *profession*. If the results of

9

education is to end up with students achieving varying degrees of learning and only a minority of the students become educated, then the *specialized knowledge* tends to concentrate on the teaching of the researcher's role where the treatment and time is a constant and learning is the dependent variable. What makes the *specialized knowledge* rather empty, is that almost anyone without the *specialized knowledge* can achieve the same results in a classroom — differences in achievement and a minority of the students achieving the top levels of achievement or becoming *educated*. It can be readily observed that teachers in elementary and secondary schools who are teaching a specific subject and have had four or more years of *education* courses do not teach very differently than teachers in a college or university who teach the same subject and have never had any *education* courses. In other words, the actual behavior of a teacher in a classroom is not affected very much by whether or not he or she has had any *education* courses. As further evidence of the lack of value of *education* courses in the eyes of non-education faculty and administrators in higher education, is the fact that to my knowledge, no four-year college or university requires that their faculty have any training or courses in teaching or testing in order to teach at that college or university (except in the college or schools of education). It is assumed that having an advanced degree is all that is necessary to qualify the faculty member for teaching and testing. This is a very unrealistic assumption and results in wide variations in teaching effectiveness and efficiency in higher education — from the disastrous teacher who not only can not teach but enjoys making students feel miserable and at the other extreme the great master teacher who through years of trial and error has finally found techniques of maximizing teaching effectiveness and efficiency.

On almost every college and university campus throughout our country, the faculty in the schools and departments of education are considered by the faculty in other colleges, schools, and departments as being somewhat lower in *professional quality*. Although the majority of education faculty are aware of this negative attitude, there are a few education faculty members who have never been exposed to situations in which this attitude becomes apparent. As viewed by education faculty who are aware of this attitude: some feel that this negative attitude held by non-education faculty is a result of psychological defense mechanisms developed from guilt feelings about their role as a teacher without ever having any formal courses or training in *how to teach;* some feel that there may be a basis in fact for this attitude and tend to avoid meeting or mixing with faculty from the other subject areas; but the majority of education faculty who are aware of the existence of this attitude try to ignore it.

From the point of view of our society in reference to the relative importance of education faculty vs. other faculty, the comparison would be highly in favor of the education faculty. Besides being directly responsible for the teaching and learning of students who are majoring in education which make up a significant percentage of the almost seven million college students, education faculty are indirectly responsible for the teaching and learning of over 55 million students in elementary and secondary schools. The results of the education faculty's effectiveness or ineffectiveness has affected, is affecting, or will affect every person born and raised in our country. What the teachers in our elementary and secondary schools do or do not do to their students will to a great degree affect the success of college or university students in all subject matter areas, and even more basic, what these teachers do or do not do to their students may affect whether or not the students will even go on to a college or university. Since these teachers in the elementary and secondary schools are products of the education faculty, it is difficult to imagine a more important and critical role in our modern society than that of the teachers of *teachers-to-be* such as the education faculty of our colleges and universities.

If the role of education faculty in our modern society is really that important, what is the reason for the existence of the negative attitude held by their colleagues in other subject areas? Theoretically, education faculty should be considered specialists in the teaching-learning situations and as such, faculty members in other subject matter areas who identify learning problems should be able to get help from the *teaching-learning expert*. Let us assume that this should happen on a campus and a faculty member who has identified a learning problem goes to the School of Education for help. After inquiring at the main office, he is directed to see a particular professor who happens to be teaching a class at the moment but will be out of class in about 15 minutes. Instead of waiting in the office, the faculty member decides to go up to the professor's classroom thinking that while he is waiting maybe he can pick up some good teaching ideas by observing the *teaching-learning expert* in action. After watching the education professor in action for about ten minutes, the disappointed faculty member leaves thinking to himself, *after 15 or more years as a teaching-learning specialist, this education professor doesn't teach any different than I do and I have never had one formal course on how to teach. Of what value can those education courses be? Besides, he did not even practice what he was preaching.*

Although some teacher-training institutions are trying to *practice what they preach*, five to ten schools out of the almost 1600 teacher-training institutions in this country are not enough to say that this action indicates a trend. Almost every school district superintendent will agree that graduating teachers need in-service training before they

11

can go into classrooms as effective teachers.

On most college and university campuses throughout our country, the schools or departments of education represent the most traditional and conservative group of faculty on the campus.

If the majority of college and university faculty learn how to teach as well by chance as the education faculty do by years of undergraduate and graduate education courses, then maybe the output of our schools should be of no surprise to society. It is possible to take *The Big Gamble* out of education and have learning happen by design rather than by chance. In an age of mass education at all levels, we can not continue to consider *teaching* as an art with master and good teachers a rare experience in the educational life of our students.

Education may not be a profession, but *instruction* can be a profession and also a science. If this is true, then courses on *instruction* offered by colleges, schools, and departments of *instruction* would be designed to teach teachers how to teach by design and all students would learn, rather than have only a minority who can become *educated*.

These schools or departments of instruction should be rampant with innovations in teaching and learning and unrecognizable as being copies of other schools and departments on campus. As specialists in teaching and learning, schools and departments of instruction should be able to establish minimum learning standards wherein 90 percent or more of their instruction majors learn 100 percent of the specified objectives of every instruction course regardless of the time or learning modes necessary to achieve this minimum level. This assumes that the teachers of these courses know or can define specific measurable objectives for each of these courses. If the non-graded concept is good enough for elementary and secondary schools, why isn't it good enough for the teacher-training institutions? Isn't it time to put the verbal lectures on instructional innovation into practice — not in the campus laboratory school or only in the audio-visual courses — but throughout the instructional curriculum? The methodology and technology is available today to create REAL teaching-learning specialists.

With reference to the existing *educational* system, Philip Coombs in his book *The World Educational Crisis* said:

An educational system can lose the power to see itself clearly. If it clings to conventional practices merely because they are traditional, if it lashes itself to inherited dogmas in order to stay afloat in a sea of uncertainty, if it invests folklore with the dignity of science and exalts inertia to the plane of first principles — that system is a satire on education itself. Individuals showing authentic gifts may still emerge from such a system. But they will not have been produced by it; they will merely have revived it. Moreover, from the

12

standpoint of society, the resources invested in perpetuating such a system are ill-fitted to serve well either themselves or their society.

In *Time* magazine, September 23, 1966, Ronald C. Nairn, President of Prescott College, when asked why the college didn't offer any courses in education, replied, *We would love to teach education if we could find anyone who knew anything about it. This would be the greatest breakthrough since the time of the Greeks.*

The fifth reason why our schools have failed to achieve the goals set forth for them by our society is the whole process of evaluation as it is practiced in *education*. This major barrier to change in education is also largely a result of tradition and is handed down from one generation of teachers to another. Just as teachers teach the way they were taught, teachers also test the way they were tested. The problem of evaluation extends throughout the educational system and at all levels. Students are evaluated by their teachers. Teachers are evaluated by their administrators. Administrators are evaluated by school boards or boards of regents. School districts and colleges are evaluated by the state departments of education, and regional or national accrediting associations, and indirectly, by the U. S. Office of Education. The state departments of education and in some ways, the U. S. Office of Education are evaluated by our society and in particular by legislators who indirectly are evaluated by the voters.

If education or instruction is a profession, the primary purpose of the profession should be one of public service and the prime responsibility of this public service should be to facilitate learning. If these assumptions were correct, then it would be reasonable that the major evaluation through the line from the students to the U. S. Office of Education should be based on learning. But this is not the case. As long as most teachers have not really specified what it is that they want their students to learn, it will be difficult to evaluate whether or not students have learned this vague thing called *education* which they were supposed to learn while in school. Therefore, a set of *education* courses has been and are concerned with the measurement of the achievement of something which has not been defined. Of course, this makes it much easier to carry on the role of a researcher rather than the role of a practitioner because tests can be designed to give any desired results. The present problems in the testing of students will be more thoroughly discussed in Chapter VI. It is sufficient to say at this time that rarely do tests actually test what teachers want students to learn.

The same problem concerns the evaluation of teachers. Although learning is supposed to be the major emphasis in education, it is a rare event when a teacher is evaluated on his or her ability to help students learn (as measured by student achievement). Most teachers are evaluated on a wide variety of potentially irrelevant criteria such as their degrees, how they look, how they act in the classroom, etc. Almost all of the criteria are in terms of what the teacher does regardless of how it affects students' learning.

Administrators, school board members, etc. all the way up to the U. S. Office of Education are in a similar situation. Although *learning* is supposed to be our major product in schools, whether or not it is achieved by students is not one of the criteria used to evaluate administrators, etc. In changing from *education* to *instruction*, the process of evaluation will have to be changed such that learning is in *fact* (by actions) the major emphasis of our schools rather than just an emphasis in words only.

Once the learning objectives that the students are supposed to learn in schools have been specified and the evaluation process has been designed to evaluate the achievement of those objectives, then in keeping with the definition of a *profession*, teachers will have to become concerned about *high standards of achievement and conduct*. With reference to high standards of achievement, the professional practitioners can not accept anything less than "A" or "B" achievement of their course objectives. Oddly enough, the very professions which claim high standards of achievement in their profession accept mediocre achievement in learning. Almost all professional schools, (medical, dental, nursing, etc.) allow students to progress through their courses without having to learn everything that is tested in the tests which the students take. Learning only a "C's" worth is considered *normal!!!* If all the test items in professional courses are important, then the students taking these courses should achieve ALL of the items. If some of the test items are not important, then why put them in the test and why grade a student down for not learning something that the teacher says is not important? As an example, most professional examinations (national, state boards, etc.) allow a person to be licensed as a professional if they can *pass* the test by answering 50-75 percent of the test items right. If all of the items are important, then the students should be required to learn ALL of them.[1] As a basic minimum, the schools of *instruction* should require their students to achieve "A" or "B" worth of every course before going on to subsequent courses.

In order to have high standards of professional *conduct*, it is necessary to identify *conduct* in doing what? The end of the definition of a *profession* states that the prime purpose is the rendering of a *public service*. If it can be assumed that high standards of conduct is in

---

[1] Of interest, is the fact that most professional examinations are not only kept hidden from the students, but also from the teachers who are teaching the professional courses. This secretive procedure insures *chance* learning and *chance* success. After all, if the students and teachers saw the examinations, all of the students might learn what they need to know and nobody could be failed!!

14

reference to this performing of the public service, then is it for the good of public service that we design tests so that we purposely fail a certain percentage of students? Is it for the good of the public that we expose the students to a learning situation in which we know they cannot learn? If education is a profession, then it is the only profession in which *disservice* to the public is part of the high standards of conduct.

B. INSTRUCTION vs. EDUCATION

To further emphasize the need for designed learning or instruction in contrast to the present situation of chance learning or education, the remaining pages of this chapter consist of paired statements which point out the differences between the teaching-learning situation as it is found in most schools under the name of *education* in contrast with a teaching-learning situation as it would be found in a school under the name of *instruction*.

Instruction	Education
1. In view of the mobility of our population, curriculum emphasis is on learning objectives which are relevant for application in state, regional, national, and even international situations with less emphasis on local application.	1. Regardless of the mobility of our population, curriculum emphasis is on learning objectives which are for local application if relevant at all.
2. Funding of the schools is primarily based on student learning regardless of attendance.	2. Funding of the schools is primarily based on student attendance regardless of learning.
3. Negative student attitudes and values are in part a result of internal (in the school) environment and as such, can be changed.	3. Negative student attitudes and values are a result of external (outside the school) environment and as such, can not be changed.
4. School activities are only specified when they will directly or indirectly affect learning and the effects are observable, measurable, and positive.	4. School activities are specified and performed regardless of whether or not they affect learning, and whether or not the effect, if any, is positive or negative.

15

Instruction (cont.)

5. Learning events are never used as punishment.

6. Learning is considered as a constant and time and treatments (methods and materials) are considered as variables.

7. Non-learning is primarily attributed to controllable factors and secondarily to non-controllable factors, i.e. genetics, home environment, etc.

8. Equal opportunity is defined as equal opportunity for *achievement* which probably will necessitate unequal schools, funding, teachers, and learning experiences for unequal students in order to equalize results.

9. Courses are scheduled when and where students want them (even if only for one student). Remember, students can learn without teachers and out of schools!

10. Students stop their courses whenever they have finished learning whatever is important in the courses.

11. The physical presence of the student in school and in front of a live teacher is *not* critical for learning to take place.

Education (cont.)

5. Learning events are used as punishment.

6. Time and treatments (methods and materials) are considered as a constant and learning is considered as a variable.

7. Non-learning is primarily attributed to non-controllable factors and secondarily to controllable factors.

8. Equal opportunity is defined as providing equal schools, funding, teachers, and learning experiences to unequal students which guarantees unequal results.

9. Courses are scheduled when and where convenient for teachers and available space.

10. Students have to stop courses and learning at specified times regardless of whether or not they have learned what is important in the courses.

11. The physical presence of the student in a school and in front of a live teacher is critical for learning.

16

Instruction (cont.)

12. Learning is measured in terms of specified learning objectives which the student has achieved.

13. The design of the learning situation is such that all students have success.

14. The system design allows each student to make his or her own career decisions.

15. Students are not allowed to start courses without first learning whatever is necessary in order to successfully learn the objectives of the courses.

16. Students learn humanity towards their fellow man by design.

17. *Capacity to learn* is treated as an unknown and *ability to learn* is treated as a variable in which the necessary abilities are either taught to the student or methods using other abilities are used.

Education (cont.)

12. Learning is measured in terms of the time a student spends in a classroom and/or in a course, i.e., credits, semesters, years (regardless of the actual learning that takes place).

13. The design of the learning situation is such that there is differential success (curve grading).

14. The system design channels students into certain educational or occupational areas and some students into a future of unemployment and welfare.

15. Students are allowed to start courses even though it is known their lack of prerequisite knowledge predetermines failure.

16. Students learn *about* humanity towards their fellow man by trail and error and maybe not at all. (In fact, students may learn inhumanity towards their fellow man by design).

17. *Capacity to learn* and *ability to learn* are equated and thought of as synonyms for each other, i.e., if a student doesn't have the ability to learn via a certain method, it is assumed that the student's innate capacity to learn is likewise limited.

17

Instruction (cont.)

18. Individual differences in students and teachers are taken into consideration in designing instruction.

19. Teachers and administrators are primarily evaluated on their ability to facilitate student learning.

20. Instructional emphasis is on student learning regardless of the teachers' role.

21. Each teacher is expected to teach students objectives from a curriculum which has been cooperatively identified with other teachers.

22. Each teacher spends a major part of his or her teaching time working with small groups and individual students and less time preparing to teach and presenting course content or information to students.

23. Test item analysis is done to identify learner problems and instructional problems.

24. Test items are included in tests because they are considered important regardless of how many students can or can't answer the item correctly.

25. Good results of a test is when

Education (cont.)

18. Individual differences in students and teachers are ignored and the educational design assumes equal ability.

19. Teachers and administrators are evaluated on the basis of a variety of criteria *except* their ability to facilitate learning.

20. Educational emphasis is on the teachers' role regardless of student learning.

21. Each teacher is expected to *reinvent* his or her own curriculum wheel and then teach it to students.

22. Each teacher spends a major part of his or her teaching time preparing to teach and then presenting course content or information to the students with less time spent working with small groups and individual students.

23. Test item analysis is done to identify good and bad test items.

24. Test items are included in tests which are good descriminators, usually resulting in 35%—65% of the students answering the item correctly — regardless of whether or not the item is important.

25. Good results of a test is when

Instruction (cont.)

all or almost all of the students achieve all or almost all of the items on the test.

26. Student errors are looked on as learning problems and opportunities for teaching.

27. Test scores are not recorded because eventually all students will achieve 100%.

28. Teacher-made tests are made up *before* the instructional event begins because it is critical to identify what students should learn and teachers should teach.

29. Tests are diagnostic in nature so they are given first and the treatments given to the students reflect the results of the tests (diagnose first — treat second).

30. It is good to teach to the test because the test items are all important.

31. Standardized tests are seen beforehand by students and teachers.

32. Only a high correlation be-

Education (cont.)

the students' scores fit a normal curve with only a few students achieving all or almost all of the items on the test.

26. Student errors are looked on as normal and a problem for the student.

27. Test scores are recorded and are used in determining grades.

28. Teacher-made tests are made up *after* the instructional event or towards the end of it so that it is easier to construct items which will result in a normal curve.

29. Tests are used to determine grades so the treatment is given first and the tests afterwards (treat first — diagnose second).

30. It is bad to teach to the test because the test items are selected because they are good discriminators, not because they represent important learning, and in teaching to the test, the ability of the item to discriminate is diminished.

31. Standardized tests are hidden from students and teachers.

32. Low correlation between

Instruction (cont.)

tween test items and specific learning objectives is acceptable.

33. Students are given the specific learning objectives of a course at the beginning of the course.

34. Both general objectives and specific objectives are used, but the test items are taken only from the specific objectives.

35. Criterion tests are the rule and there is no purpose or value for normative tests.

36. Instructional technology (hardware, software) used only for the sake of learning.

37. Instructional research directly applicable and useful for actual learning events.

38. It is critical in teaching to know how to teach, test, set objectives, and solve learning problems and it is also critical to know course content.

39. The most commonly used definition of *discipline* is in terms of teaching and learning.

Education (cont.)

course objectives and test items is acceptable.

33. Students only find out exactly what they should have learned when they are tested (when it is too late to learn).

34. Only general objectives are used and the test items are selected from a vague and ambiguous population of items (the guessing game).

35. Normative tests are the rule and criterion tests are the exception.

36. Educational technology (hardware, software) used for the sake of the technology.

37. Educational research not usually applied or useful for actual learning events.

38. It is not cirtical in teaching to know anything about teaching, testing, setting objectives, and solving learning problems, but is critical to know course content (degrees in subject matter).

39. The most commonly used definition of *discipline* is in terms of punishment.

CHAPTER II

INSTRUCTION OR EDUCATION: WHICH IS HUMANIZING?

General and Specific Objectives

GO — To understand the need for humanism.
    SO — List the three general principles about the teaching and learning of humanism.
    SO — Identify one or more examples from your own experience which demonstrates each of the three principles and explain how the example demonstrates the principle.
GO — To realize that many traditional educational practices are inhumane.
    SO — Define malpractice as defined in this Chapter or in any dictionary.
    SO — Given the definition of malpractice and the concepts of curve grading so-called *objective* type tests, and essay tests, make a statement about each concept which will support that it involves an educational malpractice.
    SO — Describe two or more experiences in your own life where individual learning differences in students were ignored and you developed negative feelings.
    SO — Differentiate between the two definitions of the word *capacity* and make a statement concerning the effect on student learning when the two definitions are treated as only one definition.
    SO — To make a statement concerning the validity of I.Q. scores as they relate to mental *limits*.
    SO — Describe two or more experiences in your own life where you observed individual differences among teachers and where the ignoring of these differences had negative effects on student learning.
GO — To understand that these traditional inhumane practices have tragic results.
    SO — Define *cumulative ignorance* and describe two or more experiences in your own life where cumulative ignorance had negative effects on subsequent learning.
    SO — List at least three or more negative affects of academic failure on the student.
    SO — Given a class of students graduating from high school,

explain how they can have different levels of cumulative knowledge.

SO — List the two basic problems with traditional education as identified in this chapter.

GO — To recognize that treating the symptoms of educational problems doesn't often affect the causes of the problems.

GO — To know that designed instruction is more humane from the students point-of-view than traditional education.

SO — List at least five out of the 21 comparative situations in which designed instruction is more humane than traditional education.

SO — In reference to the five or more situations used in the last SO, describe how in two or more of these situations you have personally found them to be inhumane.

Because of the length of this Chapter (41 pages) and as an aid to the reader, I am including that part of the Table of Contents that covers this Chapter.

SUBTABLE OF CONTENTS

INSTRUCTION OR EDUCATION: WHICH IS HUMANIZING?

Although there have been a number of articles written and presentations made in past decades concerning the need for *humanism* in education, during the past five years there has been an ever increasing flow of these articles, books, and presentations. This clamor for humanism in education over the decades is in part a result of many educators who have *sensed* some of the same educational problems which I have identified in this series and my book *Educational Malpractices: The Big Gamble in Our Schools.*

In general, the demands for increased humanism fall into two categories: those which are asking for a reordering of priorities in the school curriculum such that certain areas which foster humanism are given more emphasis than at present and those which are just asking for more freedoms.

I am in agreement with the real humanists in their cry for a greater emphasis in the area of the humanities (literature, arts, philosophy, psychology, sociology, etc.) because our greatest problems today are not technological problems or vocational problems — these are being solved. Our greatest problems today in our own society and around the world are PEOPLE PROBLEMS! If we have not learned how to get along with our own blood relations or neighbors, then how can we expect to get along with different racial, cultural, and national groups. We will never be able to eliminate war as a solution to world problems when nations find that they cannot get along with one another if we are not able to first eliminate the fighting and bickering in the interpersonal and intergro p relations in our own society. Although many religious groups claim to be devoted towards helping man get along better with his fellow neighbors, their actual emphases as identified by their actions are much more on the individual's relationship with God and/or Christ, the particular religious group's unique mode of worship, and the observance of a set of man-made rules governing the social behavior of the members of the religious group. As a result, very few members of our society have been formally taught or aided in learning *how to get along better with your fellow-man.* As a society, we have worked harder at expanding areas of freedom for greater numbers of people than we have worked at helping people learn how to use these freedoms with appropriate compassion and intelligence such that increased humanism parallels increased freedoms.

Invariably, at every seminar which I have conducted and at every gathering of educators in which I have been a member, the problem or issue of humanism has come up. In order to present the case of *Instruction or Education: Which is Humanizing?*, I would like to use the following sequence of topics.

A. Need for Humanism;
B. Traditional Inhumanities in Our Schools;
C. The Tragic Results of The Traditional Inhumanities;
D. Breeding Ground of the Traditional Inhumanities;
E. Humanistic Solutions with Potential Inhumane Results; and
F. Instruction vs. Education

In order to discuss these demands for humanism, it is best to start by identifying the common meanings for the word *humanism* as reported in Webster's Dictionary.

— a devotion to the humanities
— a devotion to human welfare
— a way of life centered upon human interests
— a philosophy that regards man as a natural object and asserts the essential dignity and worth of man and his capacity to achieve self-realization through the use of *reason and scientific method.*

Another word that is often included in the demands for humanism is *humane* which is defined in Webster's Dictionary as:

— marked by compassion, sympathy, or consideration for *other* human beings or animals.

A. NEED FOR HUMANISM

To put the matter in a nutshell, there are three main grounds on which our education system rests: first, the right of every man to the completest education the nation can give him on his own account, as necessary to his enjoyment of himself; second, the right of his fellow-citizens to have him educated, as necessary to their enjoyment of his society; third, the right of the unborn to be guaranteed an intelligent and refined parentage.

In Edward Bellamy's story *Looking Backward*, which was written in 1887, Julian West fell asleep and slept until the year 2000, and as he examined the educational system of that time, a Dr. Laete described to him these three main purposes for education. Although this was written almost one hundred years ago, the humanistic needs expressed are relevant today. The first two purposes (grounds) are very similar to the reasons given by most psychology teachers as to why a person should study basic psychology, i.e., to have a better understanding of one's self and to have a better understanding of your fellow man.

Philip Coombs, in his book *The World Educational Crisis,* made this comment about humanization.

24

When we send children to school, we expect that the experience will make a desirable difference in their lives. They are also moulded, of course, by their families, friends, church, and other environmental forces, each in its own distinctive way. But we expect the school to give them things they cannot get elsewhere. Among others, we expect the school to endow children with the means to lead fuller, more satisfying lives and to enjoy the *humanistic* aspect of education as an end in itself. All this comprises what may be called the *consumption* dimension of education. We also expect the school to endow children with the means to be better citizens, to get a better job, and to contribute more to society's welfare — this comprises what may be called the *investment* dimension of education. The two dimensions are not mutually exclusive.

Ralph Tyler in his book, *Basic Principles of Curriculum and Instruction,* suggests the following curriculum rationale: identify what children and youth need to learn to live personally satisfying and socially significant lives in a constantly changing world, select learning opportunities that enable students to learn what they need to learn, organize these learnings in such a way that they are both effective and efficient, and then carefully appraise the program to see how effective it has been and to what extent students have learned what they needed to learn.

William Menninger, in his *Living in a Troubled World: Selections from the Writings of William C. Menninger,* lists eight characteristics he thinks education might nuture:

the capacity to change; the abandonment of solutions learned in childhood; the ability to accept frustration for future gain — compromising rather than fleeing or fighting; the ability to meet stress without acquiring disabling symptoms; the ability to find more satisfaction in giving than in receiving — a reversal of the infant role, which was only demands; the ability to relate to people in a consistent manner rather than switching from friendliness today to hostility tomorrow; the ability to direct one's hostile energy into constructive outlets; the capacity to love, which is the only neutralizer of hate.

Arthur Foshay in *Curriculum for the 70's: An Agenda for Invention* states that:

The time has come to change the central function of the school, which was stated by the Educational Policies Commission in 1961 to be the development of rational powers. The central function of the school is to provide legitimate grounds for self-respect. For one cannot be a private individual without self-respect; one cannot relate to others without self-respect. What is legitimate about self-respect is to be determined not only by one's private sense of well-being, but also by one's ability to relate to other people successfully and respectfully.

Arthur Coombs in the ASCD 1970 yearbook, *To Nuture Humaneness,* states that:

Vital questions of values, beliefs, feelings, emotions, and human interrelationships in all forms must be integral parts of the curriculum. To achieve this end, it is not enough that we simply teach the humanities. Instruction in English, social studies, art, music, and drama is not enough. Humanism and the humanities are by no means synonymous. *As a matter of fact, such subjects are often taught in the most inhuman fashion.* It is fascinating that the human qualities of love, compassion, concern, caring, responsibility, honor, indignation, and the like are largely left to accident in our schools.

Although psychology began as a scientific discipline in 1879, it has still not found its way into the curriculum of most American schools. The same could be said of sociology, anthropology, and political science. These are the sciences of the new era expressly developed to help human beings to understand themselves and their relationships with other people, the most pressing problems of our time. Where they exist in the curriculum at all, it is usually somewhere on the periphery. They are *elective* subjects to be studied only by those students who have successfully acquired the traditional subject matter. But if humanism is truly important, these matters must not be merely peripheral; they must lie at the very center of the curriculum. After all, the most important problems deserve the most important place.

Jack Frymier in the April, 1971 issue of *Motivation Quarterly* identified what I would consider a very critical problem in utilizing the quality of humaneness.

It was Jefferson who argued that no people could be both ignorant and free. We have dealt with that idea for almost 200 years. Now we are confronted with the reality itself. And the fact of the matter is, we have not prepared young people to make intelligent, compassionate decisions. We have been negligent, and, in fact, have contributed to the problem. We must examine our practices and our assumptions, our philosophy and our programs, to see where we can change. And change we must.

In the *good old days* when people grew up, lived, worked, and died within a few miles from where they were born, the number of new people encountered were minimal. Learning how to get along with them could be extended over a period of years and the learning could even be of the trial and error type because there was lots of time.

26

Today is not the *good old days.* Our society in particular has become very mobil which increases the number of people we meet and at the same time decreases the amount of time to learn how to get along with them. On top of this, there are also increasing varieties of life styles encountered. As a result of this, the decision making with reference to interpersonal relationships has increased considerably and has become increasingly critical for successful living.

To be against the teaching and learning of humanism would be like being against motherhood, God, and country. There can be no doubt that an increasing emphasis in our instructional efforts has to be in the area of humanism. It has been proved beyond a doubt that we can teach most cognitive and physical skills to most students and trainees. What hasn't been proved is that we can teach humaneness. However, three general principles can be stated with a fair degree of confidence. First, lecturing about being humane, does not necessarily help a person to become humane. Second, humane qualities can be transmitted by setting examples in a humane environment. Third, it will be more difficult to produce humane qualities in an environment in which the students frequently encounter examples of inhumanity.

B. TRADITIONAL INHUMANITIES IN OUR SCHOOLS

In my book, *Educational Malpractices: The Big Gamble in Our Schools,* I made the assumption that most educators believe that they are professionals. As such, educators have to accept some responsibilities along with the privileges of the professional. One of these responsibilities includes the potential of being sued for malpractice. There have been sufficient cases of professional malpractice brought to court that malpractice has been legally defined as follows:

Malpractice is a dereliction from professional duty, whether intentional, criminal, or merely negligent by one rendering Professional services that result in injury, *loss* or damage to the recipient of these services or to those entitled to rely upon them or that *affects the public interests adversely.*

As an aid in understanding the concept of malpractice, it is useful to also define gross negligence:

Gross negligence is negligence marked by total or nearly total disregard for the *rights of others* and by *total or nearly total indifference to the consequences of an act* (on the client).

With reference to the definition of gross negligence, notice how the term is defined in terms of a disregard or indifference to humanistic concepts. Therefore, malpractices also show a disregard or indifference towards humaneness. Listed in my book, *Educational Malpractices: The Big Gamble in Our Schools,* and in Chapter VIII, Volume III, are forty-

27

one such malpractices which are found in most schools at all levels of education. Many of these malpractices are concerned with the traditional educational practices in testing and grading.

The most critical one concerns the fact that although the majority of teachers at all levels give tests[1] and assign grades[2] which generally indicate levels of achievement, very few of these very same teachers have specified what it is they want students to learn. As a result, the levels of achievement (as measured by tests) are very much affected by how good the students are at guessing what the teacher is going to put on a test. Almost every one who has been a student has had the experience of studying very hard for a test and discovering while taking the test that he or she had studied the wrong things. Low grades or failure resulting from this common traditional educational situation are often blamed on genetics, home environment, natural endowment, or many other factors outside of the school. Rarely are the negative results attributed to the inhumane *educational* guessing game.

In addition to this inhumane guessing game, many school districts, colleges, and universities utilize and encourage some form of curve grading. In fact, based on data from the tens of thousands of teachers (at all levels) that I have worked with, probably 80 to 90 percent of the teachers use some form of curve grading in their evaluation procedures. Although most curve grading refers, at least in part, to the normal probability curve, there are so many variations from the actual normal curve that the term *curve grading* as it is used in most classes is best defined as follows:

> Curve grading relates to the practice of evaluating students with a major emphasis on what a student learns relative to his classmates, and a minor, if any emphasis on what a student learns in comparison to the defined content of the course.

What makes this particular traditional practice inhumane is that by design only a minority of students can have success and in many situations, a certain percentage of students have to fail regardless of the level of achievement.

By not knowing specifically what students should be learning in a particular course, a teacher is very free to do whatever he or she wants. By the design of the test, teachers who have not specified their course objectives can pass or fail any number of students they wish. Therefore, any teacher who does not have specific objectives for his or her course

---

[1] Throughout this series, the word *tests* is used in reference to paper and pencil tests (objective, problem solving, essays, etc.), performance tests, production or process tests, and product tests.

[2] Throughout this series, the word *grades* is used in reference to any form of grading, i.e., letter grades, percentage grades, pass-fail, etc.

but in the same course gives tests or any other type of evaluation instrument and assigns grades on the results of these tests (essays, etc.) are being inhumane towards the students who are graded down from an "A" and particularly those students who are failed. Even worse, are those teachers who have taken the time and effort to specify their course objectives but use tests or other forms of evaluation which do not match the objectives. What makes this lack of correlation so inhumane is that it purposely misleads the students. For example, in a history course, few objectives will be stated in terms of the student memorizing names, dates, and places of historical significance; yet in the tests, all too often, the students are tested on their memory of names, dates, and places. In a introductory psychology course, one or more of the following three objectives are generally given: to have a better understanding of yourself; to have a better understanding of others, and to improve interpersonal communication. Yet in most psychology courses, the tests are of the objective type in which the key behavior to learn is to *out-psych* the teacher or author of the test rather than to *out-psych* yourself or others in the world outside the classroom.

Teachers who use objective type tests (multiple-choice, true-false, and matching) are involved in an insidious form of inhumanity against students. Although this form of testing is very wide spread and is called *objective* because the scoring or correcting is objective, the actual writing of these tests is very subjective. In fact, a professional test item writer can take any multiple-choice item and by holding the stem and the correct choice constant and by varying the wrong answers the writer can get almost any percentage of students he or she wants to answer an item wrong or right. This flexibility is built into the so-called *objective* type test items by using what is called distractors in which students are purposely distracted from selecting the correct answer or from selecting any of the wrong answers. If, as teachers or teachers-to-be, we believe in humanism in instruction then there is no place in instruction for tests which purposely trick students particularly when the cumulative effect of the tricks (distractors) is to cause some students to score lower than others (designed discrimination).

In many of the courses which fall into the category of *people* courses, they may not use objective tests, but they do use essays or term papers for evaluation. The criteria used to evaluate the essays or term papers are generally not disclosed to the students ahead of time. As a result, the students have to guess and quite often they are wrong. In most of these writing assignments, the major objective is to complete the assignment not necessarily to complete it at some level of quality. In grading these writing assignments, few teachers actually communicate to the students what is wrong and as a result, there are remedial writing courses offered in junior high schools, senior high schools, and in colleges and universities. Another result is that in the United States and Canada, one of the courses with the highest *flunk-out* rate is freshman composition. To make matters worse, answer the following multiple-choice opinion item based on your previous experience as a student and as a teacher (if you are one or have ever been one):[3]

If a student' essay was given to a group of teachers and each of them was to grade the essay independently, the grades would be:

a — all the same   c — mostly different
b — mostly the same   d — all different

I have asked over 150,000 teachers this question. If your choice agrees with the vast majority (over 90%) of these teachers, then you picked either choice (c) or choice (d). Try to imagine the significance of this response. What you (if you picked choice c or d) and the vast majority of teachers are really saying is that the letter grade a student receives on an essay or term paper reflects more about the teacher who graded the essay than about the student who wrote it!!! Can you even conceive of the number of students whose present and future lives are being affected negatively by this extremely subjective and inhumane process. Although some of the students' essays would obviously be graded higher than they maybe should have been, this is not as positive a situation as one might think at first. The higher grades falsely build up the students' self-image on a foundation of make-believe quality. Sooner or later the students whose grades were inflated will identify the truth and the fall from the greater heights will be more destructive of the self-image than those students whose grades were correct or deflated.

Although there are still many teachers that do not have specific objectives for their courses, almost all teachers are involved with the evaluation of student achievement. Since the objectives represent the answer to the question, *Achievement of what?* and the test items represent the answer to the question *How do you know the students achieved it?*, then the writing and preparation of objectives and test items become a very critical behavior for anyone that wants to be or is a teacher. At the present time, as high as 50 percent of the teachers in elementary and secondary schools in most states admit that they have not had any training in testing and in higher education as high as 90 percent of the faculty have not had any training in testing.

Those who have had courses in testing are not trained in the sense necessary for a humane testing program as most courses and texts on test and measurement are more concerned with teaching statistics and

---

[3] As discussed in Chapter 4, there are three forms of multiple-choice items which are acceptable. In this case, since the item is asking for an opinion, there is no such thing as a right answer. Therefore, multiple-choice items in this category are not really test items which can be graded or used to *punish students.*

on how to identify and change non-discriminating tests items than on how to honestly test for the achievement of an objective. Therefore, most teachers, who are teaching at the present time, are perpetrating inhumane acts on their students during the evaluation portions of their courses. For this very reason, Chapter VI, in Volume II, deals with the problem of setting objectives and preparing test items.

Another common traditional educational inhumanity concerns the definitions of the word *discipline*. At first, the primary definition (according to Webster) concerned teacher, instruction, tutoring; a subject that is taught, a branch of learning, a field of study; training or experience that corrects, molds, strengthens, or perfects especially the mental faculties or moral character. A secondary definition concerns punishment and the control gained by enforcing obedience or order. At the present time, although the word discipline is still used to refer to a field of study, most people on the street would think of the secondary definition. Among educators, who haven't identified what it is specifically that learners should be learning, it would obviously be difficult if not impossible to set up training or an experience that corrects *(correct has not been identified)*, molds (the pattern for the mold has not been identified), strengthens (haven't identified what is to be strengthened), or perfects (what *perfect* is hasn't been identified). As a result, most educators also think of *discipline* in terms of the secondary definition. Even most teacher training institutions are more concerned with *classroom control or management* than with *learning*.[4] In most traditional schools at all levels, students are more apt to be *disciplined* because they didn't follow certain rules of attendance and behavior in class rather than if they didn't learn. Of course, in the traditional school, non-learning can always be blamed on outside factors (genetics, home environment, etc.) What makes this inhumane, is that the actions of the traditional educators communicate to the students that it is more important *how you act* than *whether or not you learn* and makes the purposes of education a hypocrisy and the educators themselves hypocrites. The tragic result is that many students and teachers *tune-out* of school discipline (in the form of teaching and learning) because of the image of school discipline (in the form of punishment and control). Even at the present time, there is a lot of discussion concerning banning or increasing corporal punishment in our schools. To remedy this particular form of inhumanity, I would like to suggest the reestablishment of the primary definition of the word discipline not only in our rhetoric but also in our actions. Chapter VIII in Volume III is concern-

---

[4] In evaluating teachers-to-be during their practice teaching, a common criteria concerns classroom control whereas rarely does any supervisor check to see if the students who are being taught are actually learning.

ed with *discipline or quality control in learning.*

Another very serious inhumanity has become so traditional that it has become an accepted part of the educational scene. In the early part of this century Dewey and others started talking about individual differences in students. Since then many books, conferences, and courses have been devoted to individual differences in students. Yet today, in most schools, individual differences are ignored. For example, every educator would subscribe to the belief that students learn at different rates, yet in almost every school time limits for learning are established: one and two week units, quarters, semesters and years. Not only is this hypocrisy, it is a design for non-learning for the slower students. The *traditional* inhumane solution to this problem of differences in rate of learning is not to allow more or less time for learning, but to increase the course for the faster student and decrease the course for the slower student (commonly called *ability grouping*[5]). What makes this practice inhumane is that what is cut out for the slower student may predestine the student for non-achievement in subsequent courses or for permanent enrollment in classes for slow students if the students stay in school. Chapter VII, in Volume II, is concerned with putting into practice our beliefs in individual differences.

One of the most serious inhumanities committed against students by educators at all levels again concerns the definition of two words. The critical words in this instance are *ability* and *capacity. Ability* is easily defined as the quality or state of being able to perform (physically or mentally) or the natural talent or acquired proficiency (learning) to perform. The problem comes in the definitions of *capacity.* The primary definition concerns the concepts of limit and volume. The secondary definition tends to make *capacity* a synonym for *ability.* As a result, in many situations, *ability* and *capacity* are used interchangeable because of the similarity in the general definition for *ability* and the secondary definition for *capacity.* But in reading these words and also in using these words, most people tend to think of the two words as synonyms from the point of view of the primary definition of *capacity.* In other words, whereas *ability* refers to a natural or *learned* quality (level of ability can be increased by learning), *capacity* refers to a limit (a point beyond which it is impossible to go — can't put six gallons in a five gallon can). As a result of this confusion, once educators, psychologists, and others identify that certain students have or don't have certain abilities, this is interpreted as indicating different capacities (limits) not different capacities (abilities). Under the concept of different capacities (limits), it is assumed that it would be impossible

---

[5] This practice has been declared unconstitutional in the Hobson-Hansen case in Washington, D.C., 1968.

to change the capacity because it is heredity. Under the concept of different capacities (abilities), it is possible to teach or to help the student increase his or her ability. To help clarify this problem, think of *ability* as referring to how children learn and *capacity* as referring to how *much* children can learn. With reference to the latter, it will also be helpful to know that I do not know of anyone in our world that has succeeded in identifying the 100 percent full capacity of the human mind nor anyone who is conscious and who has reached the limit of *zero learning* (can't learn anything), and neither does anyone of the over 150,000 educators I have talked to. In short, educators, psychologists, or anyone else in using the word *capacity* has to be referring to abilities because no one knows what the capacity of the human mind is and since we don't know what it is, no one can say and defend that any one person or group (racial or otherwise) has less capacity (limits) than someone else. What educators, psychologists, and others have been identifying is differences in capacities (abilities) which are in part natural talent and in part learned.

As an example of an extension of this confusion in definitions, consider the *nature-nurture* controversy which has been debated for decades. The *nature-nurture* theory states that heredity sets the absolute *limits* as to what it is possible for one to do or become, while the environment sets the *limits* as to what one actually does with the inborn equipment that he or she received through biological inheritance. Obviously, this theory is based on the primary definition of capacity (limits) and as such indicates that it is possible to reach a static state mentally and physically in which no more learning can take place — an extremely inhumane point of view. From the point of view of the secondary definition of capacity (abilities) the nature-nurture theory sounds dynamic, exciting, and humane, i.e., the theory states that heredity gives a person certain natural talents or *abilities,* while the environment controls which of these *abilities* are developed and utilized and which other abilities are learned and developed.

Intelligence tests are often defined as mental capacity (limits) tests, yet in actuality, these tests are only testing the individual's capacity (ability) to answer or perform the intelligence test at that particular time. Many intelligence tests are primarily testing verbal ability (not limits) and as long as schools don't really teach verbal ability by design, the I.Q. scores will remain essentially constant (when corrected for chronological age) and consequently were believed to represent natures contribution. During the late 1950's and throughout the 1960's many different projects have been conducted in which verbal ability was taught directly or indirectly and I.Q. scores for individual student participants have been raised as high as 30 points. Obviously, the verbal ability which is being tested includes not only nature's contribution but

33

also nurture's contribution. In line with the definition of capacity (limits) in I.Q. testing, notice the titles: genius, superior, average, educable, trainable, high-grade moron, etc. Using the definition of capacity (ability), regardless of whether it is ability based on nature, nurture, or both, the concept of limits will have to be deleted from the achievement categories. The new categories might be genius ability (can help others learn), superior ability (independent learner), average ability (needs some help from teacher), below average ability (needs frequent help from teacher), low ability (needs constant help from teacher), etc.

In almost every school and in almost every classroom, instances can be identified in which the confusion in the meanings for the word capacity has caused one or more students to be treated in an inhumane manner. Most teachers make statements concerning whether or not students are learning to capacity. Are these teachers talking about *limits* or *abilities?* If they are referring to limits, remember no one knows what these limits are, so in a way, no one is working or learning up to his or her limit. If they are referring to abilities, are these nature, nurture, or both? If nurture or both, maybe the reason why a student isn't learning to capacity (ability) is because the teacher isn't nurturing (teaching)!

This same confusion in definitions also has put Arthur Jensen of University of California at Berkeley and William Shockly of Stanford University in the newspaper headlines. Both of these men are claiming that there are racial differences in intelligence and these claims are backed up by tests that supposedly measure capacity (limits). What is interesting, but very sad and inhumane in its effects, is that Jensen and Shockly are saying publicly what a majority of educators and psychologists also believe by their actions with students. In many schools throughout the United States and Canada, there are efforts to group students according to ability in which the educators are equating ability to capacity (limits). In addition, at every single seminar, conference, workshop, or class which I have conducted or attended, sooner or later one or more educators have made statements regarding their students which indicate a belief in difference in mental capacity (limits). The slight difference between Jensen and Shockly is that they use the word *racial* in talking about these differences whereas educators don't use the word *racial* but somehow in setting up the various *ability* groupings based on test results, these groupings all too often follow *racial* lines. Almost anyone who has been exposed to other cultures beyond a brief glimpse, should be willing to attest to the fact that different cultures *nurture* different abilities. It should follow then that on intelligence tests which test capacities (abilities) that certain cultural or racial groups would score consistently higher or lower than other groups. If the identified abilities could be defended as desirable and necessary to be successful in our society, then it also follows that arrangements should be made to *nurture* by design the inadequate ability until it is adequate. One should keep in mind that almost every cultural or radical group have nurtured certain abilities which may be very useful to everyone in our society. If anyone in reading or listening to Jensen's or Shockly's statements would substitute the word *ability* every time they use the word capacity (limit), then what they are saying is not so radical.

From the point of view of educators, it is so much easier on their conscience to believe that a student's inability to learn is a problem of capacity (limits) because there is nothing that they or anyone else could do. To accept that a student's inability to learn is a problem of capacity (ability), then conscientious educators would be bothered by the possibilities that maybe they didn't *nurture* the inadequate abilities sufficiently for learning to take place or that maybe they should have tried other instructional methods and materials that were more in tune with the learner's abilities such that the same objectives could have been learned. In order to confront this problem, Chapter V will deal with the concept of learning problems and how to solve them such that all or most[6] students learn all or most[6] of the course or unit learning objectives.

Another traditional inhumanity concerns the ignoring of individual differences among teachers. At least with students, educators talk about individual differences even if they don't do much about it. In reference to individual differences among teachers, not only is not very much done about it, but the concept isn't even discussed. Although some school districts are using differentiated staffing and higher education has had different teaching ranks for decades, these differences in ranking and responsibility are rarely based on individual differences among teachers in their ability to facilitate student learning. All too often, changes in rank or position in education depend on a wide variety of criteria *except* the primary purpose for education and educators — to facilitate student learning. Notice, in teacher contract negotiations throughout United States and Canada, the contracts generally state the class size and number of classes for most teachers which assumes teachers are the same. What makes this traditional practice inhumane, is that the poorer teachers have just as many students and classes as the master teachers and even everyday common sense can identify that the students in the poorer teachers' classes are not going to have as many learning problems solved as the students in the master teachers' classes. To make it even worse, it is traditional in most schools

---

[6]The percentage of students that learn and the percentage of objectives that the students learn is determined by the willingness, persistence, and capacity (ability) of the teacher to solve students' learning problems. (It is assumed that teachers don't have a problem with capacity (limits) in solving learning problems.)

that most of the supposedly *better* teachers (as measured by degrees, length of service, etc. not by their ability to facilitate learning) are given fewer classes and fewer students in their classes. To compound the problem, very few teachers at any level are evaluated partially, if at all, on the basis of whether or not their students are learning. Since teachers, their roles, and their training for these roles constitute another critical factor in the developing of a humane instructional situation, Chapter V will be primarily concerned with teachers role in instruction.

Two closing comments concerning the traditional inhumanities found in most of our schools at the present time. First, concerns why we need to teach humanism. Not only is it important for every individual to learn by design how to get along with his or her fellow human, but it is critical that teachers and teachers-to-be learn how to deal compassionately with students and parents. Consider the following: in the 1970's and here in the most modern country in the world, parents are reluctant and many just plain fearful of complaining to their children's teachers or school administrators for fear of *retaliation against their children!!* Second, have you ever wondered why many students' attitudes towards learning become less and less positive and some students become very negative towards learning? Remember in elementary school how teachers used *learning as punishment* for doing something wrong, i.e., *Do 20 extra homework problems!*, *Write 200 times*, *I won't chew gum*, *Write two punishment essays*.

C. THE TRAGIC RESULTS OF THE TRADITIONAL INHUMANITIES

The most obvious results of the traditional inhumanities are the effects on achievement, but the most tragic are the effects on the minds of the students and their families. With reference to achievement, the most serious effect of several of the traditional inhumanities is a concept I call *cumulative ignorance*. In every course or sequence of courses in which what a student learns or doesn't learn in earlier units or courses affects the student's success in subsequent units or courses, there is the possibility of *cumulative ignorance*.

> Cumulative ignorance is the cumulative effect on non-learning which affects subsequent learning, and is created in a situation where a learner is permitted to leave a course or unit without achieving the critical objectives which are necessary in order for the student to have success in subsequent units or courses (or out in the real world).

If students are not learning everything they are supposed to learn at each grade level (represented by students getting "C's" "D's" and "F's") as they proceed from kindergarten through college, it should not be the least bit surprising when we identify students who are one or two years behind their classmates in elementary school and they never seem to be able to catch up with their classmates; in fact, they get further and further behind. It is very possible that years of cumulative ignorance can build up to the point where a learner is unable to perform adequately in the learning situation. Presently, students' inability to learn is blamed on a variety of causes, such as genetics, home environment, motivation, etc., rather than on the fault of an ineffective and inefficient teaching-learning situation which cumulatively makes it impossible for the students to learn.

Although cumulative ignorance may be a problem in all subject matter areas, it is of particular significance in course sequences in which the achievement of basic course content is necessary in order for satisfactory achievement in subsequent courses. Cumulative ignorance can be most easily demonstrated in courses such as mathematics, English, foreign languages, and science. Consider Table I. The columns represent all of the objectives in third, fourth, fifth, sixth, and seventh grade mathematics. If a student achieved all of the course goals, he would be at the top of the column. To demonstrate cumulative ignorance, let's take a student who received a "C" in third grade and was passed on to fourth grade.

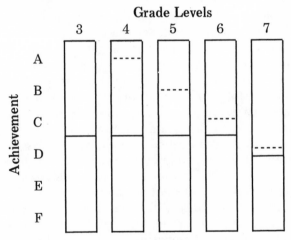

TABLE I — CUMULATIVE IGNORANCE

It should be reasonable to expect that the objectives in addition and subtraction which the student *did not learn* in third grade will lower the ceiling of what the student *could learn* in multiplication and division in the fourth grade (the ceiling for what the student *could learn* is represented by the broken line near the top of the fourth-grade column). If in the fourth grade, this student is again a "C" student and is passed on to fifth grade, the cumulative effect of what he *did not learn* in third and fourth grade will lower even further the ceiling of what the student *could learn* in fifth grade. If again the student achieves "C" worth of the course and is passed on to sixth grade, the cumulative effect of what he *did not learn* in third, fourth, and fifth grades now may lower the ceiling of what the student *could learn* almost equal to "C" achievement. At this point, the student is well aware of the fact that he is working harder for his "C" grade then he was before. This is because the student is actually learning a greater percentage of what he could learn with his degree of cumulative ignorance. Now if this student goes on into seventh grade, the cumulative effect of what he *did not learn* in third, fourth, fifth, and sixth grades may very well lower the ceiling of what he *could learn* to below that of "C" achievement. Depending on the number of courses in the sequence, this process of *cumulative ignorance* may continue until either the student drops out of the course sequence because he feels uncomfortable in a situation where he does not understand what is being presented, or the student is forced out of the sequence because of failing grades, e.g., very few of "C", "D", and "F" students in ninth grade algebra complete four years of high school mathematics.

The effects of cumulative ignorance are very easily observed in foreign language, in that almost any student who is a "C" student in the first year of a foreign language will experience a great deal of difficulty during the second year of a foreign language, because the "C" achievement in the first year indicates that there were a number of learning objectives which were not learned during the first year, but are very necessary for successful achievement during the second year of the foreign language. All teachers are very familiar with the effects of cumulative ignorance in English grammar, in which students, during the very early years of elementary school are allowed to pass on with "C" and "D" achievement in English grammar, spelling, vocabulary, essays, etc., and as a result, English grammar is taught almost every year all through the twelve grades of elementary and secondary education, and when the students start college, the freshman year at college also devotes a certain amount of time to English grammar and writing essays. At many colleges and universities, remedial basic (bone-head) English has become a common course. In spite of this, a National Health Survey found that over a million teenagers were illiterate and couldn't read at the fourth grade level. In another report by the National Advisory Council on Adult Education, they found that there are 54 million adults in our country who have not graduated from high school and many can neither read or write.

Because the cumulative ignorance for each student is slightly different, what all of the students in a given class don't learn collectively

38

includes most of the objectives in a course. As a result, repeated courses such as history and particularly English end up being rather redundant and boring whereas they should be among the most exciting and relevant courses in the curriculum. Cumulative ignorance is also very apparent in reference to the disadvantaged students who start school anywhere from one to three years behind the average advantaged student. Because this difference is never really eliminated, the difference affects the ceiling of what the disadvantaged student can learn in each of the subsequent grade levels such that, if they go on to high school, they will be five and six years behind the average advantaged student.

If cumulative ignorance can develop when students receive a grade of "C" consider how quickly the cumulative ignorance can develop when students are only achieving "D" or "F" worth of a unit or course. Of course, when the concept of cumulative ignorance is associated with concept of curve grading, it is very possible for students who are even achieving "A" or "B" worth of a course to be developing cumulative ignorance. Almost every student had had the experience of being in the class where the results of a test were so low that even the "A" or "B" student achieved only half or less of the test items. Students who are suffering from cumulative ignorance are generally referred to as potential dropouts or non-college material. A number of educators around the country are beginning to recognize the existence of cumulative ignorance, and in recognizing the causes, refer to these students as potential *pushouts*.

One particular aspect of this same concept which appears on the outside to be a very positive concept, but underneath, it has very negative consequences. This is in reference to the situation in which teachers know that the student has not learned what he needs to know to be successful in subsequent courses, but they are trying to be nice to the student, and so they give the student what is called a *soft* "D" or they may just like the student and may give the student a "B" or a "C" when actually the student didn't learn that much of the course. A slightly different situation, but with the same effects, occurs in many classrooms in which there are *disadvantaged* or minority group students and a teacher who either does not like the students or doesn't believe that they are capable of learning the course objectives. It is common for these teachers to give *disadvantaged* students passing grades so as not to be identified as being discriminatory, even though the teachers know that the students have not learned the course objectives. The common result of both of these situations is that the student is passed on with varying degrees of cumulative ignorance. Over a period of time, what may have been intended as an act of friendship actually reduces the student's chances for success. As far as cumulative ignorance is concerned, it is just as bad for a student to progress to the course with a "C" or a "D" as it is for the student to progress to the next course with an "A" or a "B", but still knowing only a "C" or "D" or "F" worth of the objectives.

Edward Bellamy, in his *Looking Backward* published in 1887, commented on the results of the traditional approach in which only a few students learn all of a course and the rest leave the course with varying degrees of cumulative ignorance.

> To educate some to the highest degree, and leave the mass wholly uncultivated, as you did, made the gap between them almost like that between different natural species, which have no means of communication. What could be more inhumane than this consequence of a partial enjoyment of education!

In a situation where students have cumulative ignorance and they continue in the course or sequence of courses, sooner or later they may fail.

One of the most serious aspects of the evaluation of students by teachers is the failing grade, regardless of the letter used to indicate this failure, "F", or "E", or "U", or the word *Fail*. All of these symbols indicate a rather terminal situation, and when these grades are placed on a student's record, they remain there throughout his lifetime.

Teachers have the right and obligation to indicate to students that they have not learned everything important in their courses by giving the student an "I" (incomplete), but teachers do not have the right to fail students, nor is the giving of an "F" in accordance with the concepts of professionalism.

Although millions of students throughout the country will receive one or more "F's" every time grades are reported, the grade "F" tells more about their teachers and the philosophy of the system than it does about the students. Just as easily as teachers can say that the students *are not able to learn or will not learn*, others could say that the teachers *are not able to teach or will not teach*.

Very few teachers will state that they want their students to learn facts, yet an examination of the tests these teachers are giving will reveal that students are being failed for not learning what the teachers say are not important — FACTS. This is because teachers have not specified what they want students to learn and do not know how to specifically test for the achievement of desired behaviors which they can't identify or specify. Therefore, in order to have some kind of tests upon which to base a grade, many teachers test for the easiest things to make up test items for — FACTS!

Teachers should not be permitted to fail students for not learning something that the teacher is not able to specify or identify what it was the student did not learn. Testing and grading situations which exem-

40

plify this statement can be found in almost all teaching-learning situations, in which the teacher is unable to specify what it is exactly the students were supposed to learn, yet they are able to assign some kind of grade which is supposed to indicate the student's achievement or lack of achievement of something which has never been defined or identified.

If a student who is given an "I" decides not to complete the work and leaves the "I" on his record, *that is the student's decision* and any time he wants to complete the course the opportunity should be open. When a teacher or school gives a student an "F", *that is the teacher's or school's decision* and that decision may drastically change the students future life by:

— affecting whether or not the student can stay in school,
— affecting the educational or vocational goals of the student,
— predetermining the types of education and employment the student can go into,
— affecting the success of the student in subsequent courses because of the influence on future teachers' subjective judgment,
— affecting whether or not the student will get a job because of the influence on future employers,
— affecting the students' self-image and subsequent relationship with the rest of society, and
— alienating the student sufficiently from the majority of society that the student becomes a social misfit, delinquent, and potential criminal.

Nothing breeds success like success and nothing breeds failure like failure!

The concept of being a *failure* is not acceptable to the healthy human mind. Therefore, a student who receives a series of "F's" and "D's" will sooner or later reject the concept of being a *failure* and in doing so will have a tendency to reject the society that supports the point of view that he or she is a *failure*. In rejecting the majority of society, the student too often finds the only alternatives open are to join a segment of society which also has rejected the majority of society or a group which the majority of society has rejected. In either case, the results tend to lead eventually into juvenile delinquency and crime. This conclusion has been supported by a number of committees, commissions, research projects, individuals, etc. Somerset Maugham stated:

> *The common idea that success spoils people by making them vain, egotistical and self-complacent is erroneous; on the contrary; it makes them for the most part, humble, tolerant and kind. Failure makes people bitter and cruel.*

Clyde Campbell, in his article, *The Effect of Failure on Learning,* states that . . . *failure is the germ bed for arson, pillaging, looting, and not the surface reasons frequently stated,* (for arson, pillaging, and looting).

Some people claim that there are positive aspects of failure in school because in real life there may also be failure. If our educational goal is to help learners face the concept of *failure* and somehow benefit from the experience, then the teaching-learning situation should be designed accordingly — to be able to derive benefits from failure. In other words, if the concept of *failure* is important, then lets teach all students "A" or "B" worth of how to cope with and benefit from *failure.*

In spite of failures and cumulative ignorance, most students in elementary school are promoted anyway because of the traditional policy of *social promotion.* This policy fits the Peter's Principle in which (in business and industry) people are promoted until they reach a level of incompetent performance such that they can't be promoted any further. Due to cumulative ignorance, students who are promoted regardless of learning until they reach a level in which they are considered incompetent (artificial limits not innate limits) to learn, are then pushed-out or they quit. Ellen Lurie, in her book *How to Change the Schools* states that,

> Every year 95 percent of all the children (in New York City schools) are promoted, whether or not they have learned the subject matter which was supposed to be covered and whether or not they have passed any of the tests. Although the board claims that it has adopted this policy because to do otherwise would be *psychologically harmful* to the children, it is more likely that they have done so because the schools would become so terribly over-crowded they could not function if the children who did not learn were left back. In any event, by promoting most of the children, the parents are given the illusion of progress; as my grandmother used to say, the children grow older, but they don't grow up. By the time a child is ready to graduate from sixth grade, at the end of elementary school, he should be reading on the sixth-grade level. But if he is reading one year and eight months behind grade level, he is still promoted to seventh grade. One-third of the city's sixth graders were reading below this minimal requirement in April 1968 and yet only 5 percent of these students were left back. The remainder, over 20,000 children, who could not read, were promoted into junior high school. The professionals know enough to demand minimum salary standards for themselves, but they refuse to set minimum performance standards for the pupils — or for themselves.

Some students who are suffering from a large amount of cumulative ignorance and still manage to graduate from high school take advantage

42

of the widely advertised *open (front) door policy* in most community colleges and some four-year colleges and universities. Rather quickly, many of these students are forced or voluntarily make use of the not so widely advertised *open (back) door policy*. It is bad enough that many young people, particularly from the minority groups, were unable to get into higher education, but now, under the guise of being humane, any student can enroll and then most of those which normally wouldn't have been admitted before are flunked out. At least before, the non-admitted students could get angry with the establishment. Now, convinced by teachers that they don't have the capacity (limits), the ex-students can only get mad at themselves and their parents — a very inhumane result.

Of course, at the present time, in the large urban ghetto high schools, one out of three students drop out before graduation. Dr. Webb, Executive Director of the National School Boards Association, states that:

> The ghettos are teaching us that the cost of neglect comes high and demands payment from suburbs and small towns far away. We now know that today's child uneducated in one town or one distant rural area is tomorrow's adult on welfare in a city, or a desperate man in a prison far from his home town.

In view of the many traditional inhumane educational practices, let's take a look at what the output of our educational institutions actually is at the present time. On a national average as of 1966, only *71 percent* of the students who started first grade completed twelfth grade. This figure is 24 percent below the estimate of national needs for high school graduates made by the educators themselves. This figure also indicates a national dropout rate of 29 percent.[7] The actual dropout rate varies from state to state and from school to school; some schools will have as low as 4 or 5 percent dropout, while some schools may have as low as 4 or 5 percent dropout, while some schools may have as high as 60 percent dropout.[8]

On a national average as of 1968, only 50 percent of our high school graduates started college, and only 50 percent of this group will graduate from college. Therefore, only *18 percent* of our first-grade

---

[7] A survey of 140,000 unemployed people in Chicago revealed that almost two-thirds of them had never completed high school. Therefore, a person who does not have a high school education, or one who does not have some kind of skills or training to offer, is destined to a life of unemployment, welfare and nonparticipation in the fruits of our society.

[8] Frank Brown, Principal of Melbourne High School, Melbourne, Florida, states that since his school has become nongraded in an attempt to accommodate individual differences, his teachers have not *pushed out* (by using some of the malpractices listed in Appendix I) their first high school dropout.

students are graduating from four-year college programs. The present output of 18 percent is about 37 percent below the estimate of national needs indicated by the educators themselves. Although official figures are not available for the percentage of first-grade students who complete a two-year college program or two years of a four-year college program, an estimate can be made. If 71 percent of the first-grade students complete high school and 50 percent of this group starts college, this would indicate that about 36 percent of entering first-grade students start some type of a two-year or four-year college program. If only 18 percent of entering first-grade students complete a four-year college program, then about 27 percent (halfway between 36 percent and 18 percent) probably complete two-year college programs or two years of a four-year college program. This percentage is about 48 percent below the estimate of national needs indicated by the educators themselves. A recent survey indicated that only four percent of our entering first-grade students were able to go on to complete graduate studies for appropriate degrees.

Most educators will agree that the dropout problem is serious and needs attention. But consider for a moment, even though students do graduate from high schools, two-year post high school programs, and four-year post high school programs — are these students really taking with them 12, 14, or 16 years of cumulative knowledge and course content: Assuming that there is some kind of correlation between what students learn and the grades that they receive, the vast majority of graduating students will take with them significantly less than the 12, 14, or 16 years of cumulative content.

As an investor, would you be interested in investing in a company in which only 71 percent of the products of the company reached the end of the production line, and of those, the majority are in various stages of development or deterioration depending on a person's point of view? Since most of the students will be forgetting more and more of what they did learn in school, the word *deterioration* seems more appropriate.

In order to better understand the following percentages in Table II, let's look at some actual numbers. There are approximately 50 million students in elementary and secondary education in the United States, which averages approximately four million students in each grade. Using the national average of 29 percent dropout, this would indicate that in excess of one million students drop out of our junior high and senior high schools every year, contributing to unemployment and welfare problems, and even more important, contributing to a growing segment of our population that is unhappy with their share of opportunities and benefits available in our country. Of the three to four million who do graduate from high school, only about one-half of them

44

will go on to college, and less than one million will graduate from college. In contrast to elementary and secondary education where the greatest dropout is during the last three or four years of the twelve-year sequence, in higher education, the greatest dropout is during the first year, about 600,000 freshmen students.

TABLE II — CUMULATIVE YEARS OF CONTENT REPRESENTED BY THE GRADES OF STUDENTS COMPLETING TWELVE, FOURTEEN, OR SIXTEEN YEARS OF SCHOOL

	Estimated Cumulative Content[9]		
	High School 12 Years	Two-Year College Program 14 Years	Four Year College Program 16 Years
"A" students, about 12% of the graduates ("A" equals 95% or more of content learned)	11.4	13.3	15.2
"B" students, about 17% of the graduates ("B" equals 85% or more of content learned)	10.2	11.9	13.6
"C" students, about 54% of the graduates ("C" equals 75% or more of content learned)	9.0	10.5	12.0
"D" students, about 17% of the graduates ("D" equals 65% or more of content learned)[10]	7.8	9.1	10.4

[9] These statements are hypothetical because to learn 85 percent of the content of a course assumes that at least the person assigning the grade knows what 100 percent of the course content is. Since few, if any, teachers have specified 100 percent of the learning objectives of their courses, the 95 percent, 85 percent, 75 percent, and 65 percent are percentages of a vague content that is not specifically definable at this time. Also, if a curve is used in assigning grades, the grades are determined more by the comparative amount the students' classmates learned rather than by how much of the actual course content the students learned.

[10] Some of the "D" students are students who have gone through a certain amount of social promotion during their years in educational institutions, and as such, the high school diploma is really a gift from the high school and merely represents 12 years or more of attendance in an education institution. The cumulative years of content learned could be even as low as four or five years.

It should be obvious that if a student is unable to complete high school or to successfully complete at least one or more years of post high school education or training that his lifetime earning power is going to be drastically affected. In fact, according to government statistics a high school dropout will earn about $100,000 less during his lifetime than a high school graduate. A college dropout, particularly if the student becomes a dropout during the first year, will earn about $200,000 less during his lifetime than a four-year college or university graduate. Although the students and their subsequent families are directly affected by these losses, society is indirectly affected by the loss of tax revenue from the students' loss of potential higher earnings and the loss of complex potential benefits which might have been gained by the increased spending power over the lifetimes of the students. Actually, society is also directly affected by the loss of their investment in the education of these dropouts and the increased costs of unemployment and welfare programs. The suffering, mental anguish, humiliation, and frustration of students and parents which is associated with the development of conditions that lead to the decision to drop out of school cannot be measured and tabulated, but the losses mentioned above can be estimated (see Table III). In order to make these numbers in Table III more meaningful and relevant, fill in the appropriate numbers of your state and local community in the blanks provided or on a separate piece of paper.

As a result of these negative educational practices, millions of our fellow citizens who have gone through our educational systems are not able to obtain work which is more appropriate to their real potential, and to enjoy a higher standard of living, which would have accompanied the upgrading of their vocations. In addition, these inhumane educational practices directly affect the effectiveness and efficiency of the teaching-learning process, such that billions of dollars invested in education are being wasted. More serious than the financial losses are the detrimental and inhumane effects of many of these practices on the minds and self-images of millions of our students and ex-students who have been convinced that they are incapable of learning anything successfully in our schools. Urban Task Force on Education concluded that, generally, as school vandalism rates have increased, school officials have failed to heed the message of vandalism. That message is clear when targets are systematically analyzed, *The highest rates of school vandalism tend to occur in schools with obsolete facilities and equipment, low staff morale and high dissatisfaction and boredom among the pupils.*

Most important of all, are the students who are still in our schools, or who will be going through our schools during the years ahead. Can we really afford to perpetuate these inhumane educational practices at the expense of these students' futures?

46

TABLE III — POTENTIAL COSTS OF PRESENT INEFFECTIVENESS AND INEFFICIENCY IN EDUCATIONAL INSTITUTIONS

A. Elementary and Secondary Schools	National	State	Local
1. Total number of students	50,000,000		
2. Number of students per grade	4,170,000		
3. Average number of dropouts per year[11]	1,210,000		
4. Average investment per student per year	$625		
5. Average investment per student for ten years[12]	$6,250		
6. Potential annual loss of society's investment in education[13],[14]	$7.56 billion		
7. Potential annual loss of unearned income to the student and society[15]	$42.4 billion		
B. Colleges and Universities			
1. Number of freshmen students per year	2,000,000		
2. Number of dropouts during first year[16]	500,000		
3. Society's investment in each student's education[17]	$1,000		
4. Potential annual loss of society's investment in higher education[18]	$500 million		
5. Potential annual loss of unearned income to the student and society[19]	$72.5 billion		

---

[11] This figure is based on 29 percent of the number of students per grade.

[12] Since the average dropout leaves school during the tenth grade, society has paid for his education for ten years.

[13] This is only a potential loss. Some of the dropouts are able to be successful (contribute to the system by paying taxes) in spite of their educational handicap. Many of the dropouts may be able to earn enough so as not to be a continued liability for society, but they do not earn enough to contribute to the system by paying taxes.

[14] This figure is a result of multiplying the number of dropouts by the amount of the average investment per student for ten years.

[15] This figure is a result of multiplying the number of dropouts by the amount of lost potential unearned lifetime income ($35,000).

[16] The national average in 1967 was 25 percent. This percentage varies from state to state and from school to school. It is quite common for some institutions of higher education to lose 50 percent of their freshman class.

[17] This figure is above and beyond the direct costs paid by the student.

[18] This figure is a result of multiplying the number of dropouts in higher education times the average investment of society in their education.

[19] This figure is a result of multiplying the number of dropouts in higher education times the amount of lost potential unearned lifetime income ($145,000).

47

D. BREEDING GROUND OF THE TRADITIONAL INHUMANITIES

In analyzing or trouble shooting most complex problems, it is necessary to separate the symptoms of the problems from the causes of the problems and then try to identify what conditions breed, generate, develop, or cause the causes! A very common mistake is to treat the symptom rather than the cause. For example, in reference to the Vietnam War, the solution suggested by many people was to stop the war and bring all the soldiers home. Since the war was just a symptom of a critical social problem, stopping the war is no doubt a good thing, but it not only doesn't begin to treat the real problem, it has actually aggravated the problem. The major problem is that people in our society can't get along with one another. In the absence of humanistic understanding, when one group imposes their views and actions on other groups who hold different views then our inability to get along with our fellow man is aggravated.

The results of the traditional inhumanities are also symptoms and it is very possible to not even connect these symptoms with the traditional inhumanities. Based on surveys of educators and many articles written by educators it is apparent that many educators are trying to treat the symptoms not the causes of the symptoms. For example, since letter grades cause problems for students, then the cause is identified as the letter grades and the tests from which the letter grades are derived. By eliminating grades and tests, the problem is supposed to be solved. Of course, the real problem is that the students didn't learn what they were supposed to and eliminating grades and tests still hasn't helped the students learn. Some writers will even go further and suggest that grades, tests, and objectives be eliminated. In that way, there is nothing that really has to be learned, no tests or grades to be given and hence no chance of failure for the student and consequently no problems. This rationale might work, if what happened in schools was so completely irrelevant and isolated from the rest of the world and each course was isolated and non-dependent on any other courses. But this is not the case, there are things that should be learned in order to live a successful humane life and most courses do not exist out in limbo. There are interdisciplinary relationships and dependencies that exist. Therefore, treating the symptoms will not solve the problems.

Sad to say, but there are some educators who in treating the symptoms are not really trying to solve the problems. They see the elimination of the symptoms as an easy way out of doing their job because the elimination of grades, tests, and objectives, also eliminates any chance of being held accountable for any lack of learning. These teachers, under the guise of humanism, are creating pockets of cumulative ignorance which sooner or later affects the learner negatively in subsequent courses and in life. As such, these teachers are being very inhumane towards their students.

In recognizing that the results or symptoms indicated previously are directly related to the many traditional inhumane educational malpractices found in our schools at all levels, it is important to identify their breeding place. Since many other writers have identified many of these same malpractices in past decades, why are they still used? What perpetuates their use in our schools? Probably the most influential factor and the hardest to control concerns the loyalty of educators to these very same traditions and a problem identified by an old adage, *Teachers teach the way they were taught not the way they were taught to teach.* Teachers also test the way they were tested not necessarily the way they were taught to test!

The real basic root of the problem comes down to the fact that most teachers haven't specified what it is that students should be learning. As a result, it is also very difficult to identify what a teacher's role should be and how to evaluate both the student and the teachers performance. This brings into focus the two major problems in education as I identified them in my book, *Educational Malpractices.* These two problems have sort of a *chicken and egg* relationship. It is difficult to say which is more important, which one is first, or which one caused the other. One of these problems concerns the whole problem of evaluation from evaluating the student and the teacher all the way up to evaluating the state and national offices of education. What makes it a problem is that learning is not the emphasis in these evaluations. Obviously, without identified specific objectives, it is very difficult to evaluate the achievement of something when we don't know what it is we are trying to evaluate the achievement of.

The other problem is the teacher-training institutions. There are the ones that pass on these traditional inhumanities from one generation of teachers to another. Richard Graham, Director of the Teacher Corps, had envisioned that the Teacher Corps would help bring about massive changes in educational practice but it didn't work that way. He reported in the December, 1970, issue of CHANGE:

> When the Teacher Corps began, the feeling was that you could learn to be a teacher out there, where the action is, in the schools. Instead we found that these programs were not internships but apprenticeships, and very often to the worst of practices. The attitudes of many would-be teachers changed from openness and flexibility to the rigidity and conventional attitudes that too many teachers exhibit.

Nor did the new courses added to the traditional teachers college curriculum make much difference. They usually were offered in the same inflexible pattern that is imposed on too much of higher education—

lectures, texts, semester-long courses, and all the rest.

The concept of practice teaching in which the student is working with teachers and supervised by teachers who are using the inhumane educational malpractices is probably about as bad a way as possible to help teachers-to-be to do the right thing with their future students. It is like the blind leading the blind. To illustrate the *chicken and egg* relationship between the two problems, for decades test and measurement courses taught the concept of the norm referenced testing wherein a curve of achievement scores is the desired result.

Since students already have different levels of achievement when they start school, it is relatively simple to maintain or increase these differences. In fact, a teacher may have to be careful not to teach the students who have lower levels of achievement because they are liable to catch up to the other students and then everyone would be educated. Therefore, the most successful way to run a school or department of *education* charged with training teachers is to have a series of courses which are vague, ambiguous, and general enough so that students don't learn how to teach. Of interest, there is evidence to support this last statement. Almost all teachers in elementary and secondary education will verify that few if any of the *education* courses they took as students have been helpful in teaching. Most in-service sessions have a similar reputation. Almost anyone can observe that teachers in elementary and secondary schools who are teaching a specific subject and have had four or more years of *education* courses do not teach very differently and the results are not that much different than teachers in a college or university who teach the same or similar subject and have never had any *education courses.* In other words, the actual behavior of a teacher in a classroom and the learning of the students is not affected very much by whether or not he or she has had any *education* courses. As further evidence of the lack of value of *education* courses, is the fact that to my knowledge, no four-year college or university requires that their faculty have any training or courses in teaching or testing in order to teach at that college or university (except in the college or schools of education). It is assumed that having an advanced degree is all that is necessary to qualify the faculty member for teaching and testing. This is a very unrealistic assumption and results in wide variations in teaching effectiveness and efficiency in higher education — from the disastrous teacher who not only can not teach but enjoys making students feel miserable to the great master who through years of trial and error finally found techniques of maximizing teaching effectiveness and efficiency.

Of special concern for college students is the evaluation of their performance by graduate students or teaching assistants. Generally speaking, most graduate students who are teaching assistants in colleges

50

and universities have had even less preparation in how to teach or how to evaluate students than the rest of the college or university faculty. Usually, they are placed in the role of a teacher with minimum, if any, guidelines and information on how to handle the job. As a consequence, thousands and thousands of students are not only failed in courses taught by graduate students, but are given such low grades that they may be forced to change their major area of study, or drop out of college entirely. Occasionally, some graduate students intuitively are better teachers than some of the faculty in the colleges and universities. Graduate teaching assistants can be used very effectively in the teaching-learning situation, but they should only be used in situations where specific learning objectives are defined and/or tests which have been developed by competent faculty have been given to the students and the graduate teaching assistants are instructed to teach what the students don't know, as revealed by these tests.

Under the concept of humanism in instruction, the goals are to help *all* students learn *all* of the objectives of any course plus whatever else the students want to learn. From this point of view, norm referenced tests are obsolete and not appropriate and the teacher's role as a presenter of course content regardless of learning is also obsolete. Therefore, most teacher-training institutions which operate in the traditional manner are also obsolete. Arthur Coombs in his article on *Training Humane Teachers* states that:

Humanness is learned from the quality of an individual's interaction with significant others. Humanistic goals, therefore, demand careful attention to the kinds of teachers being produced by our teachers, colleges and our in-service programs.

E. HUMANISTIC SOLUTIONS WITH POTENTIAL INHUMANE RESULTS

A number of solutions have been suggested in attempts to solve the problems represented by the results of the traditional inhumanities. As pointed out, most of the suggestions deal with treating or eliminating the symptoms rather than dealing directly with the problems. Most of the significant suggestions fall into seven categories.

1. What's the hurry for change?
2. Hide the schools' failures!
3. Equal opportunity for all!
4. Career education for all!
5. Do your own thing!
6. Success without success!
7. Emphasis on the humanities!

1. WHAT'S THE HURRY FOR CHANGE? Educators whose sugges-

tions fall into this category recognize the need for some changes, but they are so comfortable in their traditional inhumane ruts that it is difficult to give them up all at once. Their suggestions are generally concerned with taking small steps in the right direction. An example which illustrates this category of solutions involves a professor of education from California State University in Los Angeles. In response to an issue of my DAIRS Newsletter concerning educational malpractices in teacher-training institutions, this professor of education wrote the following letter to me:

November 19, 1970

Slate Services
P.O. Box 456
Westminster, California 92683

Dear Sir:

I read your statement concerning teacher trainers and teacher training. And, I might add, I agree with many of your statements. But, I wonder if the harsh damning tones are going to win many converts. Actually, an increasing number of our professors are teaching and using behavioral objectives. It is still far from universal but an impressive start has been made.

In short, I think your generalizations to the entire profession are somewhat unfair. We too are very much aware of the need for improvement and we are looking for help. Nor do we fear being held accountable. Most of us welcome it, whatever you might have read about the positions of organizations such as the N.E.A. and the A.F.T.

I wish you well in your efforts to improve classroom teaching and teacher-training. And, most of us look forward to working together with groups such as yours. But, few teacher trainers are going to be eager to join hands with one who has just clobbered them with a sledgehammer.

Consider the last two sentences in the first paragraph *Actually, an increasing number of our professors are teaching and using behavioral objectives. It is still far from universal but an impressive start has been made.* The concept of using behavioral objectives has been given a variety of beginning dates, but at least by 1960, along with programmed instructional materials, the concept of using behavioral objectives in teaching should have been integrated into departments of education (assuming that they should be leaders in the teaching field — not followers). At the time of the writing of the above letter, ten years had gone by and still the use of behavioral objectives was *far* from universal! During those ten years and during the next ten to twenty years before the use of behavioral objectives might become universal, think of the tens of thousands of students who will receive failing grades. Think of the tens of thousands of students who will be passed on to other courses with "C" and "D" grades not knowing what they should know to have success in those subsequent courses and when the students falter academically, it'll be blamed on genetics, home environment, or motivation! Consider the middle line in the second paragraph, *Nor do we fear being held accountable. Most of us welcome it.* As long as *being accountable* is just another one of those educational phrases without meaning that educators throw around, I'm sure this professor and his colleagues would welcome *being held accountable;* but when *being held accountable* refers to the millions of dollars and unmeasurable mental suffering that their inhumane educational malpractices have caused, I wonder how they would welcome paying out millions of dollars in court settlements! Consider the last sentence, *But, few teacher trainers are going to be eager to join hands with one who has just clobbered them with a sledgehammer.* In checking on the enrollment figures for the past ten years and using the average *flunk-out* rate for institutions of higher learning in California, as high as 10,000 students may have been washed out of California State University, taking approximately two billion dollars out of the ex-students future lives. How many more thousands of students have to be treated in this inhumane manner before the faculty causing the trouble should be *clobbered!* (These figures are not unique with California State University. In fact, the same figures or worse could be said about almost every institution of higher education as of the date of the letter.)

2. HIDE THE SCHOOLS' FAILURES! Under the capacity (ability) and capacity (limit) confusion, it has been so easy for decades to fail students out of school and blame it on genetics, home environment, motivation, etc. (anything but the teachers). Hopefully, in this era of emphasis on being humane, teachers will *nurture* rather than blame failure on *nature.* Yet, some of the old traditional beliefs still sneak in. For example, the Carnegie Commission on Higher Education in its report, *More Effective Use of Resources: An Imperative for Higher Education,* suggests that the *reluctant* learner or poorly motivated students should be dropped out of colleges and universities to save money! One of the greatest *resources* we have in our country are people. Does it make sense that in a report on the *more effective use of resources* that a Commission should suggest degrading a significant group of students by failing them out of school? It costs a lot more to

53

support a group of people on welfare and unemployment for the rest of their lives than it does to solve their learning problems and find out how to motivate them. The costs in mental anguish and losses in self-respect are much more expensive for our country than helping the students have successes and increased self confidence which could well have been an asset for our country.

Amazing as it may seem, Robert L. Ebel, President of the American Educational Research Association suggests that the *unwilling learner should be taken out of the public schools.* He says that efforts should be made to change the student not the teachers or the schools. Ebel's version of the word *change* doesn't mean change the materials, time, or motivation in order to facilitate learning by recognizing individual differences. His version of the word *change* means to change their physical location out of the schools!! This would be analogous to a president of an American Medical Research Association suggesting that patients who are not getting well on schedule should be taken out of the hospitals because their not getting well is the patients fault not that of the hospitals and the medical staff. How about a president of an American Legal Research Association suggesting that clients whose cases are being lost in court should have their cases dropped because its their fault for not bringing better cases to their lawyers. It's certainly not the fault of the lawyers. If Ebel and other *educational* researchers like him would reassess their role from the point of view of *instructional* research, then when they identified *unwilling learners*, they would be tempted to research *why* the learners are unwilling to learn in order that they could provide this information as an aid to the teacher practitioners. This would be the humane role. Because this change in the role of the researcher is very important, Chapter IX, Volume III will be devoted to the new directions and roles in instructional research.

Another way to hide the schools' failures is to treat the symptoms of failure by not giving numerical or letter grades which indicate failure or comparative low achievement. It should be obvious that what is needed is to change the learning situation and solve the learning problems such that the students have success in learning. To stop giving failing letter or number grades doesn't change the learning situation. In fact, in not letting the students know whether or not they are having success may very well delude the students into thinking they are doing alright. Then at some point later in the same course, in subsequent courses, or out in life some of the students will discover the bitter truth of failure because the necessary prerequisite learning didn't take place. When these students then blame themselves for failures and their self respect is damaged if not destroyed, how humane is the elimination of letter and number grades? It may be humane for the teachers because they won't know about the failures they've caused, but the concept is

54

very inhumane for the students (learners). I guess the former reason is why in the report of the United Federation of Teachers' Committee for Restructure in Junior High School, they suggested that grades should be eliminated to remove the stigma of failure from students. Why not be humane and TEACH to remove the failure not only in the symptom (grades), but also in the cause (the learning situation), by teaching what the students need to know.

3. EQUAL OPPORTUNITY FOR ALL! Prior to about 1965, it was a very common situation to find the advantaged students in advantaged learning environments and the disadvantaged students in disadvantaged learning environments. As a result, the advantaged became more advantaged and the disadvantaged became more disadvantaged. These results are obvious even to the least rational educator. During the past decade, there has been a big emphasis on *equal opportunity* for all. The way in which the term *equal opportunity* is defined concerns both the advantaged and disadvantaged having equal school facilities, equal learning materials, equal teachers, and equal financing. In using this definition of *equal opportunity*, it should also be obvious that it is a design for *unequal learning* which although humane in comparison to the previous unequal learning environments is still inhumane. *Equal opportunity* should be defined in terms of *equal opportunity*. When equal opportunity for *learning* is desired, this means that the disadvantaged students will have to have enough more of learning facilities, materials, and teachers such that their learning is equal to that of the advantaged students (this is in reference to the learning minimums discussed in Chapter VI, Volume II. Of course, this has been the philosophy behind compensatory programs for disadvantaged students. The problem with almost all of these programs is that until the schools identify what the students are supposed to be learning, it is extremely difficult to compensate for the right things and in the right direction. What is needed in order to do the humane thing, is to first identify what should be learned and then have unequal opportunities (facilities, materials, and teachers) for all such that the students have equal opportunity for learning![20]

4. CAREER EDUCATION FOR ALL! The recent emphasis on career education has some very good points in its favor, but built into it is a basic flaw which makes the whole concept slightly inhumane. If one considers the number of students who don't finish high school and the

---

[20] As an example, a student who enters a course with cumulative ignorance does not have an equal opportunity for learning in comparison to students who do not have the same cumulative ignorance until the cumulative ignorance is eliminated. Another example might concern rate of learning. A student who learns half as fast as another student does not have equal opportunity for learning unless the student has twice *as much time to learn.*

number of students who graduate from high school but don't go on to a post high school education or training, the concept of career education for all is good. If one recognizes that a lot of what is being taught in our schools today is non-utilitarian, then the concept of career education for all is good. But whenever something new is added to the curriculum, something else is slighted. Hopefully the decrease is not in critical areas. If the career education curriculum is taught in the same manner and with all the educational malpractices that the other courses are taught, then maybe career education is just more of the same inhumane *educational* effort. The basic flaw, however, is a problem which is directly or indirectly involved in establishing any vocational or technical curriculum. Students who are directed into the career fields are ones that have had trouble in the so-called academic courses. Their inability to learn is attributed to limited mental capacity rather than to unsolved learning problems. Because of this negative bias against vocational and technical careers, the emphasis on career education starting even in elementary school may be used as a channeling device to direct the non-achieving students into vocational-technical careers at even an earlier age than is occurring at present rather than attempting to solve their learning problems. In addition, in a society where change is a way of life, to even think of selecting a career for students or to have them select a career in elementary or junior high school has got to be about as irrelevant as the present curriculum. Many of the jobs and positions available today may be obsolete in ten years and there are many jobs and positions which will be available in ten years that we don't even know now! A much more humane approach would be to teach the students how to be independent learners not only in academic areas, but also in career fields and to help both students and parents develop a positive attitude towards vocational-technical careers. In this way, whenever a student did identify a career of interest, the student would know how to go about learning the necessary skills, knowledge, etc. Another aspect of the emphasis on career education is that this reinforces the belief that the main function of schools is to prepare students for work. As pointed out in the beginning of this chapter, the problems in our society are not generally career or work oriented, most of them are *people problems.* If the schools are to reflect the needs of our society, then students should be learning how to solve *people problems.* Recent data indicates that as many or more people are relieved from their jobs because they can't get along with fellow workers than because they are incompetent. This is partially because training programs emphasize job skills not human relations. In looking toward 20 hour or less work weeks where the working hours constitute a minority of our time, educators who are concerned with a stable society must also be concerned with not only the human relationships

56

on the job, but the human relationships off the job. Communities, states, and nations are presently involved with inner and outer conflicts caused, maintained, and heightened by ineffective human relationships. Even more critical then career education should be *living education* in which the emphasis is not on how to *do your own thing in isolation and the hell with anyone else*, but on how to live and enjoy life with other human beings. Every person in our society who expects to live with one or more other people should learn how to understand and get along with others. In fact, even if a person wanted to live alone and actually *do his or her own thing*, they should learn how to understand themselves.

5. DO YOUR OWN THING! The contemporary theme of *let the students be free to do their own thing* has roots that go back to interpretations of the *progressive education* movement. As I have encountered this philosophy in reading and while conducting in-service seminars throughout the United States and Canada, there appears to be four different factions all of which are for academic freedom for the teachers to do their own thing and all of which are against the specifying of learning objectives for students: the first faction consists of educators who are primarily concerned with maintaining the status quo (which in most courses does not include the use of specific objectives); a second faction wants to place the student in an environment which will facilitate learning but the student is still free to do what he or she wants; a third faction consists of writers and speakers who advocate freedom for students but really don't mean what they say or write; and a fourth group who advocate complete freedom for the learners and do mean it.

Academic freedom is usually defined in terms of freedom for the teacher and freedom for the learner. Assuming that schools are primarily established for students, then freedom for the teachers should not be regardless of its effects on students. In other words, when the teachers use of freedom has negative effects on students then certain limitations should be set up in order to minimize or eliminate the inhumane effects. For over two thousand years, education and learning has been looked on as a vehicle for obtaining mental and sometimes physical freedom and ignorance has been considered as a barrier of limitation of freedom. When teachers in their exercise of freedom do not help students learn, they are limiting the students chances for freedom. What students should be learning concerns the use of specific objectives. In an attempt to be contemporary, many teachers feel that the students should be setting their own specific learning objectives. If the subject matter specialists, the teachers, have trouble in preparing specific learning objectives, how can the students (who are naive learners) be expected to specify the necessary learning objectives? Can it

57

really be assumed as Dwight Allen does, that children are born smart and then slowly regress intellectually until they die.[21] Can we really assume that as a society there is nothing that we have learned that is valuable enough to pass on to the next generation? Can we really assume that reinventing *intellectual and skill wheels* by trial and error learning is the best way to learn? To accept these two statements as valid assumptions for schools is to place students in jails of frustration surrounded by bars of ignorance — a very inhumane situation. There are things that as a society and as individuals in our society that we have learned that will be also of value in helping the next generation to have even more freedom than we have had. Critical objectives which are specified and *learned* in prerequisite courses give the students not only greater freedom in learning objectives of subsequent courses, but allow the student to have greater freedom in learning related objectives which may not even be a part of subsequent courses, and may not be specified. Critical objectives which are not specified and are not learned by chance in prerequisite courses, severely restrict the students freedom in learning the objectives of subsequent courses and any related objectives not in subsequent courses. Some educators who resist specifying objectives are asking for the privileges of the professional teacher (money, respect, working hours) but are rejecting the responsibilities of the professional teacher (accountability for student learning) and in the process are placing their freedom above that of the students. Some other educators who resist specifying objectives are doing so because the specific objectives they have seen are not very important and may even be trivia. In their ignorance of the different types and levels of objectives and how they should be used in instruction, these teachers are restricted in their freedom of viewing the concept of learning objectives and how they affect learning. This ignorance of the teachers in turn causes these same teachers to treat their students in inhumane ways (educational malpractices).

With reference to the *do your own thing* factions, the first faction who want to maintain the status quo includes educators from both groups just described with primary emphasis on freedom for the teacher not to change regardless of the effects on students. The second faction who are concerned with putting the student in an environment which will facilitate learning, if they haven't specified objectives to be learned, then it becomes difficult if not impossible, to set up an appropriate environment. This is similar to the situation in *Alice in Wonderland*

---

[21] Dwight Allen, Dean of the School of Education, University of Massachusetts, wrote in the March, 1971, issue of *Psychology Today*, about seven myths in education. One of these myths is *that children are stupid until the teacher makes them smart* or what Allen calls *Original Stupidity*. If Allen believes this statement to be a myth, then he must believe in the opposite.

when Alice asked the Cheshire Cat which road she should take. The Cheshire Cat told Alice that if she didn't know where she was going, any road would be alright. The teacher's role in this faction is to capitalize on the student's random interest behaviors or activities to facilitate learning. Again, if the teacher hasn't specified what the desired learning objectives are, then the teacher won't know which student behaviors to reinforce in order to facilitate learning. As a result, the teachers' actual role consists of providing an environment which keeps the students busy regardless of learning.

The third faction is the best known of the four factions because so many well known educators write about the *do your own thing* concept for students and most of these don't really mean what they say.

Charles Silberman in his *Crisis in the Classroom* attacks the concept of Individually Prescribed Instruction (IPI) because of the use of specific objectives and then makes this comment, *What students may need to learn most is that some questions have more than one answer and others may have no answer at all.* In making this comment, Silberman has actually suggested two objectives: first, the student should be able to identify questions which have more than one answer; and second, the student should be able to identify questions which have no answer at all.

Jerry Walker, Program Chairman of the 1968 National Humanities Conference, in *Humanities Programs Today* states that *students should be the ones who select the topics, problems, or ideas that they are going to study.* In the same article, Walker also states that he would teach a humanities course *by leading students to an identification of our present culture — its institutions, its art, its social customs, its patterns and means of work and recreation, its religious, its human relationships, and its technology.*

Postman and Weingartner in their *Teaching as a Subversive Activity* ridicule Bruner's statements that *the task of teaching a subject to a child is to make the child perceive objects and relationships the way authorities perceive them,* yet, a few pages later they say that *the process of becoming an effective social being is contingent upon seeing the other's point of view.* In another statement, Postman and Weingartner state that *you would certainly not expect that the same knowledge is to be learned by every student;* yet, they want every student to become an effective social being.

John Holt in his *How Children Learn* states that *What is essential is to realize that children learn independently, not in bunches, that they learn out of interest and curiosity, not to please or appease adults in power; and that they ought to be in control of their own learning, deciding for themselves what they want to learn and how they want to learn it.* Later on in the same book he states

It is good that they are allowed and encouraged to paint big, sloppy, colorful pictures with poster paint, without anyone leaning over their shoulder telling them to do this this way or that way or that what they have done is wrong. But there are possibilities in art that they can hardly have dreamed of, as I would never have dreamed of anyone being able to make that knight (an artist drew a knight in full armor on paper for Holt when he was a child). They ought to be exposed to the idea that art can be, not just a diversion, but a powerful way of getting in touch with and expressing reality. In short, they should meet some people who can make real things appear on paper.

Eula Cutt in **Humanities Programs Today** states that *there are no definite measurable skills that students must attain;* yet, just prior to this statement she lists seven objectives, one of which is *to develop the student's sense of achievement.* If there are no measurable objectives, how are the students going to know whether or not they have achieved anything?!

Most educators in the fourth faction are actually a subgroup of the third faction because those who really believe that the students should *do their own thing* and that there should be no objectives, no tests, no administrators, etc. are actually also saying that there should be no teachers and no schools. I would be glad to believe these people, but after making these statements, they keep on teaching. If they would quit, I would believe them. Many of these same people define *doing their own thing* as students being able to set their own goals and to know how to set up the means to get there. Setting goals and identifying means are not innate behaviors, they are learned behaviors and if these two objectives are important then they should be taught by a humane design such that all students learn them.

The only group that really belongs in this fourth faction is the free school movement. Within the movement itself, however, there are great differences in how a free school should be operated. At the moment, since few public or private traditional schools can guarantee any common learning among all of their graduates, the free schools can't do any worse than nothing.

6. SUCCESS WITHOUT SUCCESS! William Glasser in his book *Schools Without Failure* makes a big issue of how critical it is for students to have success in school. Of interest is the fact that many of his suggestions don't actually facilitate success. For example, he suggests that students spend 30 minutes or more each day in discussion groups in which the students learn to talk freely about any topic. If the student is failing, to take another 30 minutes away from school work may help the student fail faster. What the students may really need is

30 minutes of concentrated study or tutoring in the subject or topic they are failing in so that they can have success. Glasser suggests that all students pass (regardless of learning) which is the same as social promotion which is already practiced in almost every school to the detriment of most students. The concept of cumulative ignorance and the ignoring of individual differences makes Glasser's suggestions and social promotion a design for failure. Glasser suggests a grading system of superior (s), passing (p) and no grade. He also suggests that a student be restricted to only one "S" per semester. Since "S" represents basic achievement plus increased initiative and responsibility according to Glasser, this means that he only wants students to learn initiative and responsibility in one course each semester which then becomes a design for non-success. Glasser states that *children should have a voice in determining the curriculum and the rules of their school. Democracy is best learned by living it.* Later on in his book, he says *If we can do nothing more, we should explain to children that what they are learning is a part of general knowledge that has been found to be valuable; that if they do not see its immediate importance, they must accept on faith its importance to their general education.* Forcing the students to *accept on faith its importance*, is this a democratic way of letting students decide what to learn? In another passage, Glasser states that *Critical thinking should be taught through discussions from elementary school on.* What if the students democratically decide not to learn critical thinking? In commenting on the Upward Bound Program, Glasser suggests that all students sign an agreement to attend classes and tutoring sessions and if any student misses five classes and/or tutoring sessions they should be removed from the program. What is so magic about attending classes or the number five? What if a student learns better on his or her own rather than in a class and isn't removing a student from the program a form of failure?

7. EMPHASIS ON THE HUMANITIES. Most teachers in the humanities believe their courses contain many of the necessary answers for the problems of our society. They are probably right, but not in the humanities courses as most of them are taught at the present time. This criticism is particularly true in courses in which the teachers resist specifying learning objectives. In being vague with respect to learning, humanities courses are subject to most of the 41 educational malpractices.

Many teachers of humanities courses look down on vocational-technical courses as being beneath them in importance and quality because the students that are failed out of the humanities courses often end up in the vocational-technical courses and have success. If helping students have a success is humane and good for the self-image and failing students is inhumane and damages the students self-image, then vocational-technical courses must be more humane than the humanities courses!

Grace Graham in *Toward a Humane School* claims that in too many school systems the students have become things which are processed in an assembly line to ensure a uniform product. The only thing uniform is the twelve years the students stay in elementary and secondary schools and the years and hours in front of teachers in order to get the various degrees. Because of individual differences and varying amounts of cumulative ignorance, the learning product is extremely heterogeneous. Whenever a humanities course is taught in a class situation, for a specific length of time, and different grades are given to students at the end of the course, you will find a humanities course taught in an inhumane manner.

As the concepts of specifying objectives, accountability, and performance contracts become more and more accepted as an important part of the instructional process, those educators who are resisting these concepts will clamor even more that these concepts are dehumanizing education. Obviously, their resistance is related to the fact that specifying objectives takes extra effort and to be accountable takes extra effort. In fact, if being *humane* is to be considerate of your fellow man, then by specifying objectives so that the students know what they have to learn and to be accountable such that at least 90 percent or more of the students learn these objectives is being much more considerate than the teacher who *cops out* of his responsibility to the students and society by letting the students *do their own thing* such that the students don't learn what they need to know in order to *do their own thing* successfully and then this self-professed *humane* teacher blames the students' lack of achievement on genetics, home environment, national or international pressures, etc.!

F. INSTRUCTION vs. EDUCATION

In discussions concerning humanism, the debates often revolve around three issues: reason versus humaneness, science versus humanities, and rational versus emotional. These issues should not be debated. They should be discussed and analyzed from the point-of-view of how in using reason we can be more humane; since the humanities are so critical, how can we use a scientific or systematic approach in the teaching and learning of the humanities and how can we use a more humanistic approach in the teaching and learning of the sciences; and how can we use sufficient emotion in our rational decisions in order to be humane and how can we be sufficiently rational in our emotional decisions in order to be humane. In order to make intelligent and yet compassionate decisions, people need to have the proper balance of cognitive, affective, and sensory learning. Ineffective learning in one or more of these three areas may very well cause a person to make inhumane decisions. Because being humane is so critical, everyone and particularly educators should want instruction in these areas to be taught and learned by some systematic design and for the teachers and students in these areas to be willing to be held accountable for the achievement of such critical humane behaviors.

WHICH IS HUMANIZING?

Traditional Education	or	Designed Instruction

Is it humane to let learning occur by chance such that only a few students have success and by design some fail?

Is it humane to design learning situations such that all or almost all students have success?

Is it humane to let over half of the children who leave elementary school leave not achieving sixth grade skills in reading and arithmetic?

or Is it humane to design learning stiuations such that all or almost all students leaving elementary school have achieved sixth grade skills in reading and arithmetic?

Is it humane to hide from students what it is they are supposed to learn until they are tested when it is too late to learn?

or Is it humane to be honest and let students know what it is they are supposed to learn and give them a chance to learn it before testing them?

Is it humane to select test items which by design place students' grades on a curve regardless of whether or not the test items match the course objectives?

or Is it humane to select test items which match the course objectives?

Is it humane to use objective-type test items in which distractors are purposely used to trick students into missing the right answer or to select the right answer regardless of whether or not the students know the answer?

or Is it humane to avoid any tricks in testing such that the test results indicate what the students know and can do rather than how good the test designer is at designing tests?

WHICH IS HUMANIZING? (continued)

Traditional Education	Designed Instruction
Is it humane to force students to take courses and attend classes in order to learn when neither the teachers or these courses nor the administrators supervising the courses are able to identify what it is the students should be learning?	or Is it humane to allow students to take courses and attend classes on a voluntary basis in courses where neither the teachers of these courses nor the administrators supervising the courses are able to identify what it is the students should be learning?
Is it humane to use data from standardized tests for grading, placement, or in any other way affecting the student when the tests are based on trickery and are seldom correlated very highly with critical specific objectives?	or Is it humane to reject all data from standardized tests which are based on trickery and/or are not highly correlated with critical specific objectives?
Is it humane to blame non-achievement on factors outside of the teaching-learning environment (genetics, parents, home, etc.) and hence non-changeable when the teaching-learning situation itself is not very effective or efficient?	or Is it humane to look on non-achievement as a problem of the teaching-learning environment and hence potentially correctable until such time as the teaching-learning environment has achieved maximum effectiveness and efficiency.
Is it humane to ignore individual differences in rate and mode of learning and set up courses and career programs in terms of time exposed and content covered rather than in terms of achievement of necessary learning objectives?	or Is it humane to recognize individual differences in rate and mode of learning and set up courses and career programs in terms of achievement of necessary learning objectives regardless of time, content, and method of presentations?
Is it humane to allow students to go on to subsequent units and courses knowing the student has not learned the prerequisite objectives necessary for success?	or Is it humane to require achievement of all necessary prerequisite objectives before going on to subsequent units or courses in order to insure success?

64

Traditional Education	Designed Instruction
Is it humane to lower the learning requirements of a unit or course in order to pass a student within a set period of time knowing that the compromise also lowers the student's chances for success in subsequent courses and decreases the student's career and employment options?	or Is it humane to solve the learning problems such that the student maintains maximum chances for success in subsequent courses and maximum options for career and employment decisions?
Is it humane to let teachers make up and give tests for the purposes of evaluating student achievement when the teachers haven't been trained on how to make up tests which actually test for achievement of specified objectives?	or Is it humane to require that all teachers who make up and give tests for the purposes of evaluating student achievement have been trained and have achieved this critical behavior?
Is it humane to ignore individual differences in teachers regardless of the negative effects this practice has on student learning?	or Is it humane to take advantage of individual differences in teachers such that these differences facilitate learning?
Is it humane to make education students take courses and learn inhumane behaviors which they are to use with their students?	or Is it humane to require instruction students to take courses and learn humane behaviors which they are to use with their students?
Is it humane to use educational materials which the teachers know will keep some students from learning?	or Is it humane to use instructional materials which the teachers know will facilitate learning for all students?
Is it humane to tell students to learn certain objectives and then test the students on their achievement of other hidden objectives?	or Is it humane to tell students to learn certain objectives and then test for the achievement of those certain objectives?

65

WHICH IS HUMANIZING? (continued)

Traditional Education	Designed Instruction
Is it humane to grade students down and especially to fail students for not learning something which even the teacher can't specify what it is the students didn't learn?	or Is it humane to grade only those things that are measurable both from the teacher's and the student's point-of-view and anything important enough to grade students down for not learning is considered important enough to teach such that students are not graded down at all?
Is it humane to punish students with learning activities such that the students develop negative attitudes towards those learning activities?	or Is it humane to use learning activities only in potentially positive situations such that students develop positive attitudes towards learning?
Is it humane to teach critical humanizing courses in inhumane ways such that the students don't learn critical humane attitudes and behaviors?	or Is it humane to teach critical humanizing courses in such a way that students learn critical humane attitudes and behaviors?
Is it humane to give the educational treatments first and the test (diagnosis) second and then ignore the diagnostic information, assign grades, and go on to the next educational treatment?	or Is it humane to test (diagnose) first and then design and give an instructional treatment second such that the treatment is based on the diagnostic information gained from the test?
Is it humane to interpret non-learning after only one or two attempts as a genetic problem and non-changeable?	or Is it humane to interpret non-learning as a learning problem which can be potentially solved even if it takes numerous attempts?

CHAPTER III

WHY A BEHAVIORAL LEARNING SYSTEMS APPROACH TO INSTRUCTION

General and Specific Objectives

GO — To understand that educational institutions, their personnel, and students are already part of a system.

    SO — Define *system* as used in this Chapter, book, and series.

GO — To understand that the effectiveness and efficiency of a system are affected by the degree of commonality and clarity of its goals.

    SO — Describe one or more problems which occur when the goals of a system are unclear and/or when different parts of the system have different goals.

    SO — List and describe at least four advantages of applying the system concept to the instruction process.

GO — To understand that most criticisms of the system concept are based on emotion and misunderstanding.

WHY A BEHAVIORAL LEARNING SYSTEMS APPROACH TO INSTRUCTION

System — a complex unity or organized procedure made up of many interrelated and yet often diverse parts or sub-systems which is subject to a common plan or serves a common purpose.

Learning — the process of acquisition of new knowledge, attitudes, and skills and the modification of existing knowledge, attitudes and skills.

Behavior — an observable and measurable activity arising from an internal or external stimulus.

A Behavioral Learning System — a system in which the common purpose of all the parts or sub-systems is to bring about in learners the observable acquisition of new knowledge, attitudes, and skills and the observable modification of existing knowledge, attitudes, and skills.

Systems Analysis — the process of the identification, separation, and study of the many parts of sub-systems and their interrelationships in a larger system in order to improve the effectiveness and efficiency in achieving the common purpose of the larger system. Systems Synthesis — the process of combining often varied and diverse parts or sub-systems into a larger system based on a network design of interrelationships which tends to maximize the effectiveness and efficiency in the achievement of the common purpose of the larger system.

The term *system* can be applied to many things and has been used by many of us to refer to such things as a telephone system, payroll system, transportation system, school system, etc. During and after World War II, researchers in the military and industry developed a special meaning for the term *system*. This new meaning concerned man-machine relationships such that as a particular machine was designed, developed, and completed, the necessary training of personnel to operate and work with the particular machine was designed, developed and completed simultaneously. The utilization of this type of system resulted in greater efficiency and effectiveness of the process leading from the design stage to the operational stage of hardware and software. A critical part in this type of system was the specification of the operational objectives or purposes of the machine, of the man or men working with the machine, and their interrelationships. It was not until after the advent of programmed instruction that this system concept could be applied to education with a meaning similar to that just described. Programmed instruction introduced the need for specifying educational objectives and the techniques for making general and ambiguous objectives into specific objectives. Because of this specification, it became possible to make the learning of these objectives the common purpose of the instructional activities or system. Although education has been concerned with stating educational objectives for decades, these objectives were not specific and measurable. As a result, educators stated objectives, described educational activities, and then designed tests almost as if they were three separate functions with little if any correlation between them. Traditionally, because of the lack of any specified common purpose, it would be very difficult to adapt the systems concept to education.

In adapting the system concept to instruction, several differences must be noted. In the military and in industry, the end product or goal is a machine of some kind with the trained people to operate and work with the machine; consequently, this system is often referred to as a man-machine system. In instruction, the end product or goal is learning; consequently, this will be referred to as learning system. Machines are the major emphasis throughout the man-machine system, whereas in the learning systems concept, the importance of machines, if any, is dependent upon the machines' contribution to the learning process.

68

Although the man-machine system and the learning system differ in several respects, there are also similarities. In the military and in industry, quality control is built into the man-machine system to increase the effectiveness and efficiency of the developmental processes of the man-machine system. In instruction, quality control can be built into the learning system to increase the effectiveness and efficiency of the learning system. In both the man-machine system and the learning system, all activities should be based on verifiable or measurable specific objectives not on guesses, opinions, or other nebulous or ambiguous statements.

To many professional educators, this notion of a systems approach which has been borrowed from engineering and industry may seem harsh and even ominous in its implications for the management of instructional processes. But instructional planning in modern educational institutions cannot be conducted on a piecemeal basis without some effort toward a rational and efficient deployment of human and technical resources. Consequently, the use of the systems concept is intellectually and practically inescapable.

Actually the concept of a system should be very familiar to educators if they are at all aware of the world around them. Education in itself is a part of the system represented by our society. Education as a sub-system has instruction as one of its major elements. Instruction as a sub-system has many elements of its own, i.e., administrators, teachers, schools, students, instructional materials, etc. A very important aspect of the systems concept are the interrelationships among the various elements of the system. This very same aspect is also the major source of problems in any system. Whenever an element in a system stops working towards the common purpose or starts working towards some other purpose, or whenever the interrelationships among the elements in a system are ignored or affected negatively, the system is in trouble.

John Gardner pointed out that *many independent elements in a system may find it impossible to work together in achieving any common purpose and a system that cannot pursue its common purpose cannot long survive. Sooner or later it will lose coherence, all sense of purpose, all sense of direction and all capacity to achieve the shared goals of its members.*

As can be easily observed, the systems concept thrives on dependent interrelationships which would appear to be in conflict with the concept of *academic freedom*. If *academic freedom* is defined as the freedom to do anything the teacher wants regardless of how it affects others, then this view of academic freedom could not exist very long in a system. If, however, academic freedom is defined as the freedom to do anything the teacher wants as long as the results of the teacher's actions contribute positively towards the achievement of the common goal, then this view of academic freedom can very easily co-exist within a systems framework.

When teaching is the emphasis as in *education*, it is a simple matter for the teacher to overlook the interrelationships with other elements (other teachers, students, etc.) in the system because seldom do these other elements affect the teaching etc. As a result, the teacher can operate in the classroom as if in isolation. When learning is made the common purpose as in *instruction*, it will be very difficult to overlook the interrelationships with other elements in the system because almost all elements of the system can affect learning. As a result, the teacher has to become aware of his or her role in the system.

A. ADVANTAGES OF APPLYING THE "BLSA" TO THE INSTRUCTIONAL PROCESS

The greatest advantage will be in the identification of learning as the common purpose of the system. As it is now, where the common goals of education are vague and ambiguous, it is difficult for the various elements in the system to cooperate in the achievement of any one or more of these vague goals. As a result, it is not uncommon to find in a school district, college, or university the teachers, students, administrators, parents, and taxpayers at odds with one another and expending large amounts of energy trying to achieve each group's goals at the expense of the other groups. An impasse is developing between educators, administrators, and taxpayers. Each year, more and more school tax and school bond issues are being defeated at the ballot box. Each year, the costs of education are increasing without accompanying increases in the effectiveness and/or efficiency of the educational process.[22] The greatest deterrent in identifying learning as the common purpose of the instructional system has not been the acceptance or rejection of the system's concept but the identification of what specifically should be learned by students in a variety of courses and at various levels of instruction. Since the majority of teachers have not identified specifically what they want students to learn, it would be impossible to apply the systems concept to the learning element of the instructional process until the desired learning is identified. However, there have been numerous attempts to apply the systems concept to the teaching element (presentation of course content) of the instructional process. Because most presentations of course content ignore individual differences among students and most evaluations of presenters ignore individual differences among teachers, applications of the systems con-

---

[22] American Institutes for Reasearch (AIR) reached similar conclusions as a result of their survey *Progress in Education: A Sample Survey (1960-1970).*

cept to the presenting element of the instructional process are doomed to failure once the *newness* of the application wears off. Applying the system concept to the learning element of the instructional process is a very different approach from what has been tried in the past. Teachers, administrators, students, parents, and taxpayers will realize that all groups really do have a common purpose — learning!

Another advantage in viewing the instructional process as a system within a system, is that it will be possible to examine critical relationships within a system, across systems, and even over time. For example, at the present time, since there have been very little change in the schools for several decades, then there has probably also been very little change in the output of the schools with reference to the knowledge, attitudes, and skills the graduating students have taken with them. In a changing society, it is critical that the schools reflect these changes by turning out students who have the necessary knowledge, attitudes, and skills to be successful in the society they are entering. There should be constant feedback to the schools from the real world such that the schools can make the appropriate changes in their curriculum. This feedback could contain employment availability information such as the surplus of teachers and engineers and a continuing shortage of nurses during the early 1970's. This does not mean that the surpluses and shortages will remain that way and that students shouldn't try to study for a career in a field where there is a surplus of applicants. By viewing our society as a system, it should be possible to make predictions as to future employment changes and then in viewing the schools as a part of the system to let the students know what the opportunities might be at the time of their graduation — a sort of supply and demand index. For example, if a student wanted to study for a career in which there was going to be a predicted surplus and only seven out of ten graduates could expect to follow that career, the student might change his or her mind and choose another career where the chances for employment would be higher. The student could also choose a secondary career to study simultaneously with the primary choice and plan to work in the secondary career until he or she could obtain work in the primary field.

In realizing the interconnection between systems, it may become more obvious that when the schools are ineffective and inefficient, that unemployment, rehabilitation and welfare costs increase. By application of the system concept to the instructional process and by viewing the school system as a part of a larger system, it might be possible to make the schools and the instructional process responsive enough to the needs of our society that the costs of unemployment, rehabilitation, and welfare could be reduced.

Almost as important as preparing and getting the right job and to some people even more important is the problem of learning how to get along with other people regardless of race, religion, culture, economic status, political beliefs, etc. The fourth annual Gallup Poll of Public Attitudes toward Education (1972) revealed that 44 percent of those surveyed felt that children should get an education in order to get better jobs and 43 percent felt that children should get an education in order to learn how to get along better with people at all levels of society. Although our schools concentrate a lot of energy and courses on careers and preparation for careers,[23] there is not much effort or courses specifically designed to help students get along better with other people (see page 23). Just as it is possible to take advantage of the systems concept to facilitate the selection and preparation for needed careers in our society, it is also possible to use the systems concept to help students learn by design *how to get along with other people.* Because this particular goal of our society and of our school system is deeply involved with attitudes and values, it is critical that everyone in our society, especially teachers, become aware of the interrelationships among the systems and how these interrelationships affect the development, modification, and extinction of attitudes and values. It is also important to recognize that attitudes and values are not static and directly teachable and learnable like most knowledge and skills. Attitudes and values are dynamic and can only be indirectly created and acquired and as such are much more affected by the interrelationships within a system and among systems than is the teaching and learning of most knowledge and skills.

The advantages in applying the systems concept to the instructional process are even more critical because it is in the instructional process where all of the educational malpractices are found. In looking at the school as a system, each grade level and each course at each grade level became elements in the system and in turn these elements became sub-systems. Almost every course assumes that the student has learned some things previous to the course and in many courses what a student learns is a foundation for subsequent courses or life experiences. Although there is some communication between teachers as to what a particular course *covers* (what teachers present), there is seldom communications between teachers as to what *each* student has learned in a particular course. The very fact that at the present time a majority of the students in most classes learn "C", "D", or "F" worth of their courses indicate that from 25 percent to 50 percent of the content of most courses is not being learned by most students. Under the present traditional educational approach, very little — if anything — will happen

---

[23] As of the writing of this book, the emphasis on career education is being introduced into elementary education.

to a teacher who allows most of their students to leave his or her course knowing "C" worth or less of the course. Yet, for the students what they didn't learn in one course could very well cause them serious trouble in subsequent units or courses (cumulative ignorance). If a school is going to be learner-oriented, the school has to be considered as a system in which what students learn or don't learn in one course may very well affect them in other courses.

A similar advantage, but one where the concern is not with under-learning but with overlearning is in looking at the school as a system when considering preschool. At the present time, as more and more states start offering preschools, more and more children are learning more earlier; but, since the rest of the school ignores the fact that the school is a system and any change in one part also affects the other parts, the other grades and courses are not changed accordingly and just like in Head Start Programs, the advantage of having preschool disappears within a year or two. Once educators recognize that the school is a system and by adding preschool at one end of the system that changes should be made in almost every grade and course up to 12th grade at the other end. Without identifying and building in these changes, the millions of dollars spent in preschool will be wasted in addition to creating more bored and under achieving students in first grade because they already learned many of the first grade objectives while in pre-school.

One of the greatest advantages in applying the systems concept to instruction will be in the savings in energy and dollars which are spent on educational innovations which have little if any affect on learning. At the present time in education where *presenting course content* is the emphasis and relatively few teachers have specified their student learning objectives, most innovations have to do with new ways of *presenting course content* and the evaluation of the innovation is based on a variety of criteria except increased learning (specific objectives and tests to test the achievement of these objectives are *not usually* available). Under the systems concept where learning will be the emphasis (learning objectives and the tests to test for the achievement of these objectives will have to be available), innovations will only be used if they can directly or indirectly affect learning and the evaluation of the innovations will be based on whether or not the innovation actually did increase learning.

Many writers who have criticized education have commented that education, as it is presently structured, is a labor intensive or cottage type industry. Under this point-of-view, hoped for increased effectiveness is almost always attached to requests to decrease the teachers' productivity by decreasing the size of the classes and/or decreasing the teachers teaching load (number of classes). Quite typically the hoped for increased effectiveness doesn't occur because primarily the specific learning objectives haven't been specified so any increases in learning couldn't be measured anyway and secondarily because with an emphasis on *presenting course content*, the size of the class doesn't really matter or affect learning levels anyway. As presently structured, schools and classes are set up on the basis of at least two assumptions — *BOTH FALSE!*

1. Students can only learn in a school environment (campus, building, etc.).
2. Students can only learn in front of a live teacher.

Under the systems concept, it will be possible to allow students to learn any place (including homes) that facilitates learning better than other places and it will be recognized that learning can take place with or without the physical presence of teachers. Actually, in almost every class of twenty or more students, if the teacher has specified what it is the students are supposed to learn, there are five or more students who could and would learn on their own if the teachers would allow it and thereby essentially reducing the class size that the teacher has to teach. (At this time, there are over four million students in the United States and Canada who are learning by correspondence instruction — away from teachers and out of schools!)

B. CRITICISMS OF THE APPLICATION OF SYSTEMS CONCEPTS TO THE INSTRUCTIONAL PROCESS

Since the systems concept is a very logical and pragmatic approach towards instruction, the arguments against the use of the systems concepts are often illogical, emotional, and bordering on fanaticism and desperation. I have had several participants in my seminars become so upset over the logic of the systems concept that in order to maintain the status quo have said to me, *I can't accept what you are saying because there just has to be something wrong with it. I don't know what it is, but to be that logical, its got to be wrong!*

The most common criticism of the systems concept is that it is mechanistic. Depending on the person using the term, the criticism could be taken in two different ways. The first involves connotations of mechanical, machinery, etc. This criticism is made by people who associate the systems concept with television systems, computer systems, film and slide systems, etc. and this hardware or equipment emphasis is equated to dehumanization. In refuting this criticism, it is necessary to point out a common error with respect to the word *dehumanization.* To many people, to decrease the number of humans involved in a process or to decrease the involvement of humans in a process is to automatically *dehumanize* the process. If to *humanize* is to

74

be responsive to the needs and desires of the individual and the humans involved in a process are not concerned about the individual, then to take away these humans and replace them with any machine that does facilitate the satisfaction of individual needs and desires, then the replacement of the humans by the machines is actually *humanizing* the process. Under the present educational approach to instruction with the emphasis on *presenting course content*, to replace the human *presenters* with mechanical *presenters* neither humanizes or dehumanizes the process. If the teachers use the release time from presenting to work with individual students who aren't learning and solves their needs such that they do learn, then the replacement of the present teachers role with something else and the change in the teacher's role actually *humanizes* the instructional processes — this is what the application of a behavioral learning systems approach to instruction would do. The behavioral learning systems concept may or may not involve any hardware or equipment. It is not a method such as programmed instruction, televised instruction, team teaching, etc., it is a process within which any method can be used as long as it is effective in helping more students learn more of whatever it is the teachers want the students to learn.

The second view of the criticism that the systems concept is mechanistic is actually a compliment. Under the philosophical concept of mechanism, it is believed that things can be ordered or arranged such that certain things happen (such as learning) as opposed to teleology or vitalism in which it is believed that most events are predetermined and there isn't much that can be done. The concept of IQ as representing a student's natural capacity (limit) fits very well into the philosophical concept of teleology. Given a student who is having trouble learning a particular concept. The believer in IQ and teleology would view the student's learning problem as a problem in natural capacity (limit) and wouldn't attempt to solve the student's needs, would recommend that the student try some other concept more within his capacity (limit), and as a consequence of not satisfying the students needs would actually dehumanize the situation. The believer in mechanism would probably use the systems concept and would view the student's learning problem as a problem which can be solved by taking into consideration the student's capacity (abilities) and needs. In solving the learning problem and meeting the student's needs, the mechanist is actually *humanizing* the situation. If being mechanistic means applying the behavioral learning systems concept such that individual student's needs are satisfied and each one has success in learning, then as a teacher, I want to be mechanistic and humane rather than teleologistic and inhumane.

A similar objection is made by educators who claim that the outputs of school aren't measurable and as such doesn't lend itself to the economist's production model or any mechanistic view. In one way, I would have to agree because at the present time very few teachers have specific measurable learning objectives; so applying the systems concept without knowing what is to be learned by the students would be inappropriate and impossible. However, in almost every classroom, teachers are giving tests and/or grading students. They are measuring something and therefore, the systems concept can very easily be applied to those things that are already being measured. There are millions of students that are presently getting "C's", "D's", and "F's". At that time when educators have helped all of these students achieve "A's" and "B's" worth of their courses by applying the behavioral learning systems approach to the students' learning problems, then there will be time enough to worry about whether or not the systems concept or any other approach is useful in helping students learn those things which no one is able to measure whether or not the something exists! J. Myron Atkin, University of Illinois, in attempting to refute, delay, retard, or hopefully destroy the movement towards the use of a systems approach towards instruction and in particular the use of behavioral objectives,[24] uses a similar argument. Not only does he state that the objectives are difficult to measure, if at all, but that there are hundreds of these non-measurable objectives available in almost any learning event and to narrow all of these down to a few measurable objectives would be a disservice to the learner. Yet, when Atkin and others with like arguments give tests, they also narrow all of those non-measurable objectives down to a few test items which become so important that if the students don't answer them correctly, they are graded down accordingly. It seems odd that the measurable test items are important enough to punish students for not learning them, yet the measurable objectives which the test items represent are not important enough to teach, to identify ahead of time, or to be communicated to the students.

Several other criticisms of the systems concept made by Atkin are quite typical of the illogical reasoning used by educators who try to resist the logic of the systems concept. For example, Atkins states that *one of the major shortcomings of the engineering model when it is applied to the field of education centers on the question of societal values.* Atkins goes on to point out that in business and industry the decision making process is more centralized whereas in education it is diffuse and there is no *concensus on specific ends.* In analyzing Atkin's criticism, note that he says the problem concerns *societal values* then he goes on to discuss decision making and ends up making the same point

---

[24] Atkin, J. Myron, *Research Styles in Science Education* pp. 33-41, and *Behavioral Objectives in Curriculum Design, A Cautionary Note,* pp. 60-65, *Current Research on Instruction,* Edited by Anderson, Faust, et al, Prentice-Hall, Inc., Englewood, Cliffs, 1969.

that I and others have made that there is a need to identify *specific ends* and then to identify any concensus on as many of these *specific ends* as possible.

For another example of Atkin's criticisms of the systems concept, consider the following:

> Another difficulty inherent to the systems approach is the fact that values and social outcomes are difficult to quantify. How does one determine quantitatively the usefulness of five hours per week of physical education in grade four in limiting crime? Make no mistake. Precisely this type of calculation must be made to utilize the engineering model.

This statement is about as far fetched a delusion of what the systems concept is as if one were to claim that the only true christians were those who bled regularly from the hands and feet. Note again Atkins reference to values and social outcomes. Although Atkins criticisms against the systems concept tend to concern the affective domain (attitudes and values), what the vast majority of students are being graded down and failed for in their schools and classrooms is the non-learning or lack of learning in the cognitive (knowledge) and sensory (skills) domains.

By the time the application of the systems concept has helped eliminate or at least greatly reduced the negative educational malpractices being carried on in most schools today, that will be a good time to look at the long range goals of instruction. At least under the systems concept there is a better chance of identifying the interrelationships among various systems which can help schools ultimately reduce crime or at least by giving all students success and challenge in schools instead of giving many failure and boredom, the systems concept can reduce or eliminate the direct contribution that some schools make in channeling some students into crime.

Another criticism by Atkin and others is that the use of the systems concept will discourage innovations by demanding specific objectives, i.e., particularly the ability of the teacher to capitalize on opportune moments for effectively teaching an idea or a concept. First, in order to capitalize on an opportune moment for effectively teaching an idea or concept, a teacher has to know specifically what the idea or concept is that the students are supposed to be learning. If the specific objectives haven't been identified, then it becomes extremely difficult to capitalize on an opportune moment for effectively teaching something the teacher doesn't know what it is he or she wants the students to learn. Second, in reference to the discouraging of the innovative teacher, under the traditional approach to instruction and when teachers haven't specified what it is they want their students to learn, innovations are primarily concerned with different ways of presenting the course content or in structuring the class. Since the teacher doesn't know what the students are supposed to learn anyway, it is very difficult to evaluate innovations or to defend the costs of the innovation — particularly as the innovation may contribute to the teaching-learning process. Once teachers have specified their course learning objectives, innovations can be concerned with new ways of solving learning problems. Since more students will be learning measurable things, it becomes much easier to evaluate and defend the costs of innovations. If schools are really built and staffed to help students learn, then the most important innovations should be concerned with helping more students learn more rather than with helping teachers present course content regardless of any measurable learning!

CHAPTER IV

IDENTIFICATION AND DEVELOPMENT OF A PHILOSOPHY OF INSTRUCTION AND THEORIES OF INSTRUCTION

General and Specific Objectives

GO — To understand the need for keeping the three functions of instructional institutions separated.

SO — List the three basic functions.

SO — Describe how the second and third functions negatively affect the first function in a traditional educational institution.

GO — To know that excellence in instruction can be achieved.

SO — Given the chart comparing the six steps towards the development of designed instruction and traditional education, state the primary problem associated with each step in the traditional approach and describe how that problem is solved under the Behavioral Learning Systems Approach.

GO — To understand the need for a philosophy of instruction and its affect on instruction.

SO — State the philosophy of the Behavioral Learning Systems Approach.

SO — State how a person's point-of-view can affect what they do and give at least one example from your own personal experience.

GO — To understand the need for a theory of instruction and its affect on instruction.

SO — List the three domains of learning and define the type of learning each domain is concerned with.

SO — Given a blank chart of the similarities and differences between the two theories of instruction, fill in the missing similarities and differences.

SO — Describe the major difference between the teaching and learning in the cognitive and sensory domains and in the affective domain and describe at least two personal experiences of learning in the affective domain which support that this difference exists.

SO — List the five elements in the instructional event.

SO — List the six strategies for effectiveness and efficiency in cognitive and sensory learning in an instructional event.

79

SO — List the nine strategies for effectiveness and efficiency in affective learning in an instructional event.

Because of the length of this Chapter (36 pages) and as an aid to the reader, I am including that part of the Table of Contents that covers this Chapter.

SUBTABLE OF CONTENTS

IDENTIFICATION AND DEVELOPMENT OF A PHILOSOPHY OF INSTRUCTION AND THEORIES OF INSTRUCTION

There are three basic functions which instructional institutions should concern themselves (placed in order of importance):

First — The planning, development, and carrying out of instructional programs in which the major emphasis is on the consumer of the programs and in which measurable learning takes place by design in the most effective and efficient manner for *each* individual student;

Second — The planning, development, and carrying out of scholarly programs in which the major emphasis is on the producer or presenter of the programs; and

Third — The record keeping, body counting, money raising, and other measurable things (not learning) which are necessary to facilitate and support the first two functions.

At the present time, these three functions of our instructional institutions are so entangled that they are hardly identifiable as separate functions. In the absence of the concept of learning by design, the second and third functions have taken precedence over instruction and learning. The record keeping function determines when learning starts and stops (class schedules, semesters, and years) and in between these time limits, the second function lock-steps the learning process because the producer needs a captive audience to present to. In support of the second function, most teacher training institutions presently emphasize the teacher as a presenter of course content, teacher work loads are based on a certain number of presentation hours per week (higher education) or per day (elementary and secondary schools), preparation time or periods are given to prepare presentations, almost all teachers are evaluated in part on their ability to present, and even most state and many school district curriculum guidelines are based on what teachers should be doing as producers rather than on what students should be learning. The crime in skipping classes or school is not measured in terms of losses in learning, but in terms of financial losses for the school because of a lower *average daily attendance*, which affects the budget of most public schools.

Since the major emphasis of these three volumes concerns the first function (learning by design), it may help to eliminate some of the overlapping of the three functions and thereby indirectly clarify the first function by defining in more detail the second and third functions.

The second function concerns the teachers and students in a school and even people in the community as producers of original data, concepts, materials, etc., and also as presenters of topics which are of interest to the teachers, the students, and to the community. This function is not directly related to the instructional program of a school and not all teachers or students have to be involved in this function. Presentations made by teachers or students under this function would be open to any other teachers or students and anyone in the community. Since students will be primarily learning as individuals under the first function, there will be few, if any, classes as they are known at the present time. Since there would be no class schedules, the presentations could be scheduled whenever a teacher, student, or someone in the community developed a presentation that they felt would be of interest to the students, other teachers, and the community. There would be no time limits imposed and a presentation could last for 30 minutes or a week. One of the benefits of having the presentations in an open-ended format is to eliminate a problem almost every teacher has had with reference to group discussions. Just as the discussion group is about to reach the real *meat* of the discussion, the bell usually rings and the class breaks up. In subsequent classes, it is almost impossible to rekindle the excitement and heat of discussion of the previous class. Because the presentations under the second function are not concerned with designed instruction, it would not be necessary for the teacher to specify any objectives or give any tests. On the other hand, *because learning by design is not a part of these presentations, no one should be required to attend them and no letter grades or credit should be given for attending them.* Attendance would be voluntary. The major interaction between the first and the second functions would be where events in the second function provided motivation and excitement for learning course material (objectives) under the first function.

Teachers at several colleges who have tried this approach have found that at first it is very devastating to end up with only a few people who are willing to take the time to listen rather than the usual *captive audience* of students who are required to take the course. Once the teachers get accustomed to this new situation, the challenge of the role becomes exciting and their presentations almost automatically improve in order to increase the number of listeners and the quality of the discussions. One teacher of a science course, who had developed his laboratory sessions into a continuous progress arrangement such that students could complete the course at any time, decided to use the general lecture sessions not as a vehicle for transmitting important course content (which was available on audio tapes in the laboratory) but purely as a motivational device. If he had an exciting film that lasted 40 minutes, that is all the longer the lecture class lasted. If a student had prepared an exciting presentation and it only lasted 35 minutes, that was the end of the class. If the teacher couldn't find anything exciting to present to the class, he cancelled the session. As a result, by the middle of that semester, there were more students attending his lecture sessions than were enrolled in his course. The word had gotten out to other students that what was happening in that lecture session was exciting.

Under the present overlapping of the first and second functions, the first function (learning) is negatively affected because in order to have classes for the second function (scholarship), teachers tend to lockstep the learning process and to ignore individual student differences. On the other hand, the second function (scholarship) is also negatively affected by the overlapping of the two functions in that the time schedules, instructional objectives, testing, and grades associated with the first function (learning) tends to limit or restrict the creativeness and range of topics, the time involved, who does the presenting, and the freedom of expression by the participants. It would be so much simpler to separate the two functions such that each could be made more effective and efficient and without having negative affects on the other function. The separation of functions would be easiest in higher education, but with a little effort in breaking with traditions, the separation of functions could occur just as easily at all levels of instruction.

The third function is primarily concerned with record keeping, financing, etc. and should not determine the beginning and ending of learning (units, quarters, semesters, and years) and should be subservient to the other two functions. In view of all the acknowledged learning differences between individuals, it is inconceivable that learning should be defined in terms of time and scheduled accordingly, i.e., two years of English, three years of mathematics, 180 days in a school year, three credit courses generally meet three times each week. It is not necessary that the dates for counting bodies and charging fees have to also control the instructional process. In an instructional system where learning by design is the major emphasis, individual differences between students and the concept of quality control (almost all of the students learning all of the objectives of their courses) would dictate the need to allow students to start courses at any time and to finish courses at any time. Under this type of system, fees, tuition and other costs charged to the student, parents, or taxpayers for instruction would be looked on as rental of faculty and facilities for a period of time. The students who can learn more of what they need to know and want to know than some other students will get through their instructional programs faster and at a lower cost *(without sacrificing learning)*. Students who need more time to learn what they need to know and want to know than some other students will take longer to get through their instructional programs and at a higher cost *(without sacrificing learning)*.

A. A DESIGN FOR EXCELLENCE IN INSTRUCTION

In reference to the first function, designed learning or instruction, if the goal is to make this function as effective, efficient, and humane as possible, then it will be necessary to recognize that the needs of society are much different now than even a few decades ago. As such, the assumptions which define the relationship between the instructional process and society have also changed. The assumptions which will facilitate excellence in instruction are:

1. Taxpayers and the majority of other financial resources which support our instructional institutions do so in the belief that the instructional institutions are there for the benefit of the learners and not for the benefit of educators;

2. The primary benefits which our society derives from instructional institutions are the effects which these institutions have had on the students going through these institutions, as measured by:

a. The student's ability to not only be self-supporting, but to become a taxpayer who financially contributes to the progress of our society.

b. The student's ability to contribute towards the progress and achievements of our society through his education and efforts to help his fellow man (other than financial).

c. The student's ability to take advantage of the *fruits* of our society in terms of the intellectual, spiritual, emotional and physical possession of material items which altogether constitute the high standard of living available in our society, which is for the most part envied throughout the world.

3. An educator's primary purpose is to facilitate learning by establishing the appropriate instructional environment that is conducive to learning.

4. A less important purpose of an educator in the instructional function is to present information, since the mere presentation of information does not guarantee learning.

5. If learning does not take place, it is possible to obtain the desired learning through appropriate changes in the instructional environment based on the identification and solving of the learners' learning problems.

6. It is important in an effective and efficient instructional system to find out where the student is on the ladder of learning and proceed from that point without gaps or unnecessary overlaps.

7. If the learning objectives of a particular course could be definitely stated and if all of the learners achieved these objectives, they would all receive "A" or some equivalent symbol indicating 100 percent achievement.

8. Learning objectives cannot be directly defined in specific behavioral terms but can be described indirectly as a result of other specific observable and measurable behaviors.

9. Undefinable learning objectives which cannot be tested for existence or cannot be described in terms of other observable and measurable behaviors should not be included as course requirement for grading procedures.[1]

10. Grades based on undefinable objectives and the temperment of the grader do not contribute to an effective and efficient instructional system.

11. In order for society to continue on from its present level (eliminating the need for each person to invent the wheel by trial and error) and in view of the high mobility of our society, not only within a state, but between states, there must be a common core of basic behaviors which every person in our society should have as a minimum. The sooner that the students are able to achieve this basic minimum core of behaviors in order to participate in our society, the more time the person will have to develop individual interests and activities.

12. The local emphasis in instructional institutions should not be so much concerned with having a unique curriculum and the development of local standards which are meaningless outside of the local area, but should be concerned with the development and maintenance of a maximum effective and efficient instructional system which will facilitate the learning of the basic minimum core of behaviors identified as necessary for success at the national, regional, state, and local levels and at the same time have resources available for the individual student to learn whatever else he or she may want to learn in addition to the minimum core without the limitations of time. (The starting and finishing of an instructional unit is determined by when the individual student wants to start a unit and when the student has completed the unit, not when scheduled to be convenient for teachers, registrars, administrators, etc.)

13. Part of the national emphasis in instructional institutions should be on the development of learners who are capable of continued self-learning throughout the rest of their lives away from formal instructional situations in order to adapt efficiently to a constantly changing society. In other words, instead of having intellectual growth stop when formal classes stop, one of the instructional system's goals would be to eliminate the need for the learner's dependence on formal classes and teachers — a truly independent learner by design.

---

[1] This does not mean that undefinable learning objectives are any less important. It is just that if the achievement of an indefinable objective is required, the learner can never prove that he or she has learned it nor can the teacher prove that the learner hasn't learned it!

14. A less important function of instructional institutions are research activities, which may not result in direct or even indirect benefits for society (particularly in higher education, where research may be carried on for the major purpose of obtaining something to publish — with or without quality — rather than to solve some real problems which may sooner or later actually benefit the instructional process and/or society as a whole).

Using these assumptions as a base, the following six factors and sub-steps will enable and facilitate the development of excellence in our instructional systems. All six factors operating together constitute my view of a *Behavioral Learning Systems Approach to Instruction.* In order to imporve the effectiveness and efficiency of almost any traditional instructional situation, it is not necessary to utilize all six factors and all of their many components. Any one component in any one factor can be applied to most traditional instructional events with a resultant increase in effectiveness and efficiency. This increase is because the traditional approach to education is so filled with malpractices that almost any effort to change the traditional approach into more of a designed learning approach can't help but result in increases in student learning.

In order to emphasize the differences between the Behavioral Learning Systems Approach to Instruction and the Traditional Educational Approach to Instruction, Chart I compares the six major steps in the development of an instructional (or educational) unit or course under both approaches. Note the following fundamental problems in the sequence of the Traditional Educational Approach which subsequently directly or indirectly resulted in most of the educational malpractices identified in my book *Educational Malpractices: The Big Gamble In Our Schools* (Chapter VIII, Vol. III). As you may notice in the sequence of the Behavioral Learning Systems Approach, these fundamental problems have either been corrected or eliminated.

1.0   The philosophy that some students can't learn is not actually stated in writing, but is evident by the fact that the vast majority of teachers at all levels grade their students' achievement on a curve (even though many of them will deny that they do). This philosophy is in direct conflict with the statement in every school's charter or constitution, *To raise each student to the maximum of his ability.*

2.0   The role of the teacher under the traditional approach is rarely concerned with learning. This is primarily because the objectives under the traditional approach are non-measurable and it would be very difficult to evaluate the teacher's ability to facilitate something that is not observable. Oddly enough however, these same teachers with the traditional non-measurable objectives give tests and grade (measure) their students on their achievement of the non-measurable objectives!

2.1 Traditionally, school buildings are built and various educational equipment systems are installed without knowing what students are going to be learning in or with them and whether or not the buildings or equipment systems will facilitate the desired learning.

3.0 Of course, the real core of the problem in the traditional approach is the lack of measurable learning goals. Without any observable and measurable learning objectives, every other aspect of the traditional approach has to be developed around other criteria which in most cases actually end up interferring with student learning.

4.0 Without specific objectives for students to learn, the developers of educational materials can only be concerned with *covering the course content* with the assigned time interval which results in about as many different versions of the same course as there are people or groups developing them. Although it may be good to have some differences, it also should be good to have some common elements between courses with the same name. Particularly when these courses are required as a basis for success in subsequent courses.

5.0 In most areas of our society, no one would think of building or developing something without knowing ahead of time the specifications for the end product. In education, it is very normal to make up the tests towards the end of the educational event. Given that the objectives are general and non-measurable, it would be impossible to make up tests which would test exactly what the learners are supposed to learn. Therefore, tests can be made up to fit almost any criteria. The tests could be designed to fail as many students as desired and to pass as many as desired (regardless of student learning). This critical area is treated very casually in education as evidenced by the fact that teachers are not required to know anything about testing. Although about half of the elementary and secondary school teachers have had training in the making of the traditional type tests, (multiple choice, true-false, and matching), the other half and almost all of the present teachers in higher education are not qualified to make tests of any kind. In some ways, those teachers that haven't had the traditional educational training in making tests are better off because they haven't learned the malpractices associated with the traditional testing approach, i.e., the designed use of distractors to make a certain percentage of students miss a particular test item (regardless of whether or not the students have learned the concept of the test item) in order to increase the discriminating power of the test item.

5.1   Since it is generally believed among traditional educators and most psychologists that the normal probability curve represents the distribution of innate intelligence in terms of capacity (limits) of a random selection of students, tests are often designed to give a distribution of results which fits the normal curve. Therefore, when the results of a test approximate a normal curve distribution, the situation is looked on as *normal!*

5.2   If tests can be considered as identifying what students know and don't know, then the tests can and should be considered diagnostic. If they are diagnostic in nature, then education is the only field in our society which practices what I call the *Backwards Ostrich Philosophy* or gives the treatment first and the diagnosis last. If this backwards approach is not bad enough, consider the fact that instead of doing something about what has just been diagnosed with a test, the majority of the teachers will probably just assign a grade and forget the diagnosis.

6.0   Normally researchers in most fields tend to work on problems which the practitioners in the field have identified as being troublesome. In turn, when the researchers have arrived at one or more solutions, the practitioners are eager to utilize them. However, in education, researchers rarely work on learning problems identified by the teachers (in order to identify a learning problem, it is necessary to know what should have been learned) and in turn, teachers rarely utilize the results of educational researchers.

Six Steps in the Behavioral Learning Systems Approach Towards Instruction	Six Steps in the Traditional Educational Approach Towards Education
1.0 Philosophy — all students can learn.	1.0 Philosophy — some students can't learn.
1.1 A theory of instruction to be used as a guideline to help all students learn.	1.1 Theories of learning and education serve as guidelines to make sure some students can't learn.
2.0 The primary role of the instructor is as a diagnostician and solver of learning problems and as	2.0 The primary role of the instructor is to present course content and to be effective in class-

2.0 (cont.)
a coordinator of the instructional environment such that at least 90 percent or more of the students learn 100 percent of the specified objectives of the instructional units or courses.

2.0 (cont.)
room management, i.e., keep attendance, keep students busy and the room orderly.

2.1 Build school buildings which appear modern and possibly represent particular methods of education, i.e., schools without walls, etc.

2.2 Install various equipment systems of technology depending on what is considered up-to-date, i.e., television, learning resource centers, dial-access systems, computers, etc.

3.0 Write general and specific objectives. The general objectives serve as guidelines in the development of the specific objectives and in the course materials. The specific objectives serve as measurable criteria to make up tests for student achievement and to design instructional materials.

3.1 Develop tests which match on a one-to-one basis the specific objectives of the unit or course.

3.0 Write general objectives to serve as guidelines, but since none of the objectives are measurable, they are usually filed away and brought out only when accrediting teams or other visiting educators come to the school. (Although many teacher training schools are teaching their students about writing objectives, most teachers can still only write general, non-measurable objectives — particularly teachers in higher education.)

4.0 Try out the tests on students to find out which objectives the students don't know and what materials have to be developed to facilitate the learning of those objectives.

4.1 Develop the appropriate instructional environment which will help students learn the desired objectives.

4.2 School building design re-

4.0 Develop sufficient materials according to any one of a number of different methods in order to cover the course content and keep the students busy for a set amount of time, i.e., 2 week unit, quarter, semester, etc. Since the objectives are non-measurable, different teachers will develop materials which will teach different things.

4.1 Use the materials with students in an environment where

4.2 (cont.)

flects the Philosophy, theory of Instruction, and needs of learners in order to learn all of the instructional objectives and to maximize scholarship for students and instructors.

4.3 Any instructional technology installed and used in the schools or community will be selected because of its contribution in helping students learn all of the instructional objectives.

4.1 (cont.)

the emphasis is on time and individual differences are ignored and often more materials are given to the faster students who might finish early and some materials are cut out for the slower students by teachers who think that the slower students probably couldn't learn from the materials anyway.

5.0 Try out the materials on students in an environment where the emphasis is on learning and students, teachers, administrators, etc. are held accountable for student learning.

5.1 Tests are used to identify learning problems and non-learning is looked on as indications of the student's learning capacity (abilities) to learn from the given instructional environment.

5.2 Depending on the learning problem, the instructional environment is changed as often as necessary to solve the problem such that 90 percent or more of the students learn 100 percent of the specified objectives.

5.0 Develop teacher made tests or use standardized tests. Since the course or unit objectives are non-measurable, the test items may or may not measure what the educational materials helped students learn, but they are designed to give results that fit the philosophy such that there are only a few "A" and "F" students, about twice as many "B" and "D" students, and the rest or a majority are "C" students. Although about half of the elementary and secondary school teachers have had training in making tests of this type, the other half and almost all teachers in higher education are not qualified to make tests of any kind.

5.1 Assign grades based on the results of the tests.

6.0 Conduct research on improving the effectiveness and efficiency of the instructional environment. Given specific objectives of an instructional unit to be learned and certain types of stu-

6.0 Conduct research on improving the educational environment. Since unit and course objectives are non-measurable and tests and/or materials used by researchers may not match the tests and/

6.0 (cont.)

dents (which makes this research practical for use by instructors using the same objectives and students), the goal is to find what combination of materials, media, learning consequences, etc., will bring about the desired learning (a natural phenomena which makes this scientific research and instruction a science).

6.1 Also conduct specific research on bringing about the desired learning of a specific instructional unit or part of a unit which specific types of students are having trouble learning (a learning problem identified by teachers).

6.0 (cont.)

or materials used by teachers (which makes the research of little value for use by teachers), the goal is to research methods, equipment, teacher behaviors, etc. (man-made phenomena which keeps this from being scientific research and education as a science).

B. A PHILOSOPHY OF INSTRUCTION

Regardless of what anyone that is *in* or *out* of the field of education or instruction says, writes, and/or does, one thing that is almost as sure as sunrise and sunset is that one generation will continue to want the next generation to be educated and instructed. There are many different ways that have been and will be attempted to achieve this end.

Regardless of the methods used, there will also always be attempts to achieve the end goal more effectively and more efficiently. The purpose of this book is not to sell a particular vehicle for instruction, but to describe a process within which an unlimited varieties of vehicles could be used for instructional purposes. Because there are an infinite number of vehicles which could be used, the *trial and error* approach which characterizes the traditional educators' efforts becomes extremely time consuming and expensive with almost random increases in effectiveness and efficiency. What is needed, are some basic guidelines to follow in order to reduce the time and expense of the *trial and error* approach.

Obviously, the ultimate measure is whether or not the vehicle or vehicles achieve the objectives of the instructional event. It is conceivable that someone may come up with a vehicle for instruction which is in conflict with all of the guidelines I will suggest, but if all of the learners learn all of the desired objectives without the learners experiencing any negative side effects, then I would have to accept the use of that vehicle in that or similar learning events regardless of the conflict with the guidelines.

In identifying the appropriate guidelines, it is important to view the instructional sequence as consisting of three parts: the learning environment, the learning event, and the consequences of the learning event. In past decades, educational researchers have concentrated on the psychobiological aspects of learning which concerns the learning event and on descriptive studies of what teachers and/or instructional vehicles do in the instructional sequence. Research concerning the psychobiological aspects of learning (which includes most learning theories) was considered more scientific than the research on what teachers or instructional vehicles do in the instructional sequence because science has been defined as the *systematic study of natural phenomena*, and whereas learning is considered a natural phenomena, what teachers and instructional vehicles do is considered man-made and man-organized. A common problem with both of these areas of research, is that the goals or objectives of the instructional sequence were not identified so it has been very difficult to validate any of the theories in terms of making the instructional sequence more effective and/or more efficient. In addition, the psychobiological theories of learning attempted to describe happenings occurring inside of the learner and hence very difficult, if not almost impossible, to measure and the descriptive studies of the teacher and/or instructional vehicles generally ignored the learning event entirely and in holding the treatment (teacher and/or instructional vehicle) constant also ignored individual learning and teacher differences.

Another complicating factor which seriously affected the descriptive studies of the teacher and/or instructional vehicles even when the learner was taken into consideration, was the problem described earlier concerning the definition of the word *capacity*. Most educational researchers defined capacity in terms of learning *limits* rather than in terms of learning *abilities*. In order to achieve excellence in instruction in accordance with the assumptions listed earlier, it is very necessary to have a particular POINT OF VIEW or PHILOSOPHY. In order to gain an understanding of the concept *point-of-view*, look at Figure 2. Are

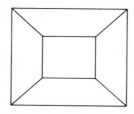

Figure 2.

92

you looking at an elevator shaft or are you looking down on the top of a truncated pyramid? While looking at the visual, if you imagine that you are looking down an elevator shaft, the inner square has a tendency to recede. If you imagine that you are looking down upon the top of a truncated pyramid, the inner square has a tendency to protrude. Consider Figure 3. Are you looking at an open book with the printed pages

Figure 3.

towards you and the binding bent away from you or are you looking at the front and back cover with the binding bent towards you? As in Figure 2, what you see depends on your *point-of-view*. If you imagine you are looking at the open pages of the book in Figure 3, the center line representing the spine of the book recedes. If you imagine you are looking at the front and back covers of the book, the center line tends to protrude. Consider Figure 4. If you imagine that you are looking up at

Figure 4.

this glass from beneath it, the front of the bottom rim of the glass (B) appears to be closest to you and the back part of the top rim (A) appears to be the farthest away. If you can imagine that you are looking down on the glass from above it, the front of the top rim (A) appears to be closest to you and the back part of the bottom rim (B) appears to be farthest away. Consider Figure 5. In this visual, I would like to find

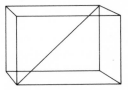

Figure 5.

93

out if you can actually see two different *points-of-view*. Imagine that you are looking up at the cube. Line AB should appear to be the closest edge of the cube. Now imagine that you are looking down on the cube. Line CD should appear to be the closest edge of the cube. Repeat these two points-of-view situations several times. In the process of switching point-of-view, do you notice anything else happen in the visual? Did you notice that the diagonal of the cube seemed to change corners? If you didn't see the diagonal change corners, repeat the process of switching between the two points-of-view several more times, remember, don't watch the diagonal — concentrate on the point-of-view. Observe the diagonal only in the periphery of your vision. If you cannot see the diagonal change corners, you are also probably having trouble seeing clearly the two different points-of-view in Figure 2, 3, 4, and 5. Where this could be a problem in instruction, is that if you have problems in seeing two points-of-view you may also tend to be close-minded in learning situations where students have a different point-of-view than you have. This could result in the students being graded down for being impertinent, argumentative, or just because they can't learn. Where this concept becomes important is that in an instructional situation that is teacher oriented, the materials and experiences are usually selected because the teacher views them as appropriate and traditionally if the students can't learn from these materials, it is assumed that the students have limited (genetic) *capacities* for learning. However, if a teacher can accept that there are other ways of viewing the situation, then the teacher may want to consider alternate paths in the achievement of the same objectives based on the point-of-view that non-learning may be more a problem of finding the right materials and experiences for each student than it is a genetic problem of mental limitations.

Because of the present patterns of *education*, students, parents, teachers, and educational administrators are tempted to say in situations of non-learning that certain students CAN'T learn. Quite often this comment is supported on the basis of *genetic differences* which affect the *capacity* of students for learning. The meaning many people have for the word *capacity* tends to suggest the concept of a limit such that some students CAN'T learn. There is some evidence to indicate that as human beings, we are using only a very small portion of the full capacity of our minds which in itself has never been identified. If we don't know what the full capacity of the human mind actually is, how can anyone state as a fact that some students have less capacity than others. All that can really be said is that some students have more trouble learning than others (particularly when students have to learn from the same materials and learning experiences in spite of their individual human differences).

94

Whenever a teacher comments about certain students who *can't learn*, these comments indicate that there must also be some students who *can learn*. Although this tends to suggest that all students can be placed into two groups, those who *can't learn* and those who *can learn*, the actual differences between these two groups is a matter of degree and in reality there is probably no such thing as a student who 100 percent *can't learn*. The student would have to be dead or unconscious in order not to be able to learn something. At the other extreme, it is doubtful if there are any students who are 100 percent instantaneous learners. All learning takes time and effort. In a typical continuum, whatever or whoever is at the extreme ends of the continuum are so uncommon as to be referred to as hypothetical or even nonexistent. The difference between these two types of students can be graphically represented by Figure 6, which represents the learning continuum (range) from a hypothetical student who is at one extreme and 100 percent *can't learn* to a hypothetical student at the other end of the continuum who 100 percent *can learn*.

100 percent
Can't Learn

100 percent
Can Learn

Figure 6 — Learning as a Continuum

A student's place on the continuum depends on a wide variety of variables, and may vary from subject to subject and from one learning environment to another learning environment. The teacher who says that he or she has students who *can't learn* is not referring to the extreme end of the continuum (Figure 6), but has actually made a dichotomy (divided into two parts) out of the continuum (see Figure 7).

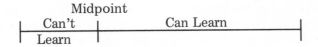

Midpoint
Can't
Learn

Can Learn

Figure 7 — Learning as a Dichotomy

When a teacher looks on the learning continuum (Figure 6) as a dichotomy, the placement of the midpoint tells more about the teacher than it does about the students. As an illustration, consider the concept of disadvantaged-advantaged. Since it is possible to always find some-one who is more disadvantaged than you are and there are very few, if any, 100 percent disadvantaged people, and it is also possible to always find someone who is more advantaged than you are and there are few,

95

if any, 100 percent advantaged people, then the concept of disadvantaged-advantaged must also be a continuum (see Figure 8).

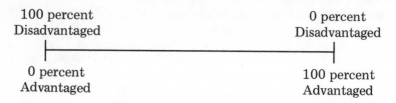

Figure 8 — Disadvantaged-Advantaged as a Continuum

In the case of dollar income, the Government at one time changed the continuum into a dichotomy, which means that there are two classes, illustrated by Figure 9. A person who earned $2,999 per year was classified as disadvantaged and a person who earned $3,001 per year was classified as advantaged. For about $2 difference, a person could change from one group to the other. Changing a continuum into a dichotomy for many concepts is very unrealistic.

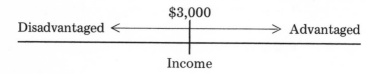

Figure 9 — Disadvantaged-Advantaged as a Dichotomy

When people make a dichotomy out of a continuum the neutral point of the dichotomy usually tells more about the person making the dichotomy out of the continuum than it tells about the differences between the two groups of the dichotomy. For example, the placement of the midpoint on the disadvantaged-advantaged continuum at $3,000 tells more about the point-of-view of the legislators who set the midpoint than it actually tells about people who earn $3,000. I personally knew people who earned less than $3,000 per year. Some of them were shocked to find out that they were disadvantaged, as they thought they were doing pretty well. I also knew people who were earning a lot more than $3,000 per year and they were convinced that they were disadvantaged. It should be obvious to most readers that there is a lot of difference between earning $3,000 per year and living in New York City and earning $3,000 per year and living in some rural area of our country.

Consider a third continuum. The next time you get any group of people together, ask them to think of the concept of *middle age* and then have each person write down on a piece of paper that number that each one thinks is the midpoint of the range each one thinks of as *middle age* (see Figure 10).

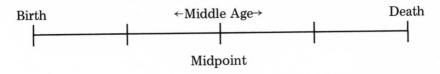

Figure 10 — Age Continuum

I have asked tens of thousands of people this question in numerous seminars and institutes which I have conducted and according to the numbers these people wrote down, the midpoint varies all the way from 30 years to 65 years. Generally, the number or age that people write down will vary considerably depending upon their own age. People who are older generally put the midpoint higher. People who are younger generally put the midpoint lower. The results also depend on the kinds of people whom they know or are acquainted with. Again, the placement of the midpoint tells more about the person making the placement than it does about the people in each of the two groups divided by the midpoint.

When teachers have the point of view that there are students in their classrooms who can't learn, then it makes a lot of difference who the teacher is. For example (see Figure 11).

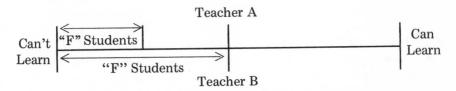

Figure 11 — Learning Continuum as a Dichotomy

Teacher A on the top part of the continuum may have come from a poor environment and had to study very hard for everything that he or she was able to learn, and has experienced not only many successes, but also some failures. But because this teacher was able to learn, his or her minimum level of expectations (midpoint) is rather low towards the *can't learn* extreme. Teacher B may come from an environment which was conducive to learning, found learning very easy, and experienced a majority of successful experiences in his or her learning career. As a result, Teacher B is liable to put the mid point of the dichotomy much higher and closer to the *can learn* extreme of the learning continuum. The point to stress is that the students who happen to fail in between

97

Teacher A's midpoint and Teacher B's midpoint will be classified by Teacher A as *can learn* students and they probably would learn if taught by Teacher A, while the same students would be classified by Teacher B as *can't learn* students and they probably wouldn't learn if taught by Teacher B. This has been supported by a variety of research projects which have essentially discovered that if a teacher believes that the students can't learn, they don't learn, and students whose teachers believe they can learn, do learn.

This type of situation formed the basis for Robert K. Merton's theory of the *self-fulfilling prophecy* which he described in 1948. Essentially his theory asserts that in many, if not most, situations, people tend to do whatever is expected of them to the degree that even a false expectation may elecit behaviors such that the false expectation appears true.

From this point of view, minority groups who are insisting that the teachers in their schools be teachers from the same group or from a minority group with similar background experiences, are actually right as long as the teachers who are being compared (majority group teachers vs. minority group teachers) both look at the teaching-learning situation as a dichotomy. When the teacher has a background similar to that of his or her students, more students fall into the *can learn* category and will have success. The problem is that as long as teachers (minority group or majority group) looks on the teaching-learning situation as a dichotomy, some students are in the *can't learn* category and are not going to learn and will probably fail. If not with a letter grade of "F", the student may be convinced he is a failure with the resultant effect on the student's self-image, which may ultimately be worse than getting a letter grade of "F". Parents and students have found, either through trial and error or personal experience, that the degree of similarity of backgrounds of teachers and their students does affect learning. With teachers who are from the same minority group environment, more learners learn. BUT, the problem is not whether or not you need minority group teachers, the problem is that both groups of teachers are looking on learning as a dichotomy, rather than a continuum.

Consider another continuum (see Figure 12) with *sane* at one end and *insane* at the other end.

Figure 12 — Sanity as a Continuum

As with most continuums, there are very few people, if any, that

98

are 100 percent sane and there are very few people, if any, that are 100 percent insane. Almost everyone is somewhere between the two extremes. Notice however that very few people claim to be 10 percent insane. If anything, a person would want to be positive and say *I'm 90 percent sane.* In most societies, there is a critical point in the continuum beyond which people are committed to some place away from the rest of the society. This critical point varies from one society to another and as such, the placement of the critical point reflects the views of that society which sets the critical point. Over past centuries, once a person went over the line in this dichotomy, it was assumed that it was permanent and the person was placed in custodial care. In the late 1800's and early 1900's, psychologists and psychiatrists made a very interesting observation. They noticed that there were people who were close to the critical point on both sides of the point and they were not that much different from one another, yet they were quite different from people who were closer to the extreme ends of the continuum. In other words, they finally recognized that the varying degrees of sanity identified sanity as a continuum rather than as a dichotomy. As a result, the handling of the mentally ill changed from a situation where custodial care was the emphasis to a situation where diagnosis and treatment became the emphasis. The guiding philosophy changed from one that said if a patient is past the critical point, there is no hope and the patient *can't* be expected to get well, to a philosophy that says that patients who are past the critical point *can* get well and the placement of a patient on the continuum is a tentative indication of how much help the patient will need. If a patient doesn't get well, it is not necessarily a problem of the patient, it is a problem of the inadequacy and limitations of the available diagnostic tools and available treatments.

Similarly, in education, for decades educators have believed that IQ scores were indicators of genetic *limits* and the intelligence categories of genius, superior, average, educable, trainable, high grade moron, low grade moron, and idiot made the learning continuum into eight groups instead of just a dichotomy. In the late 1950's and throughout the 1960's, a number of projects resulted in changing the IQ scores of the participants. Consequently, more and more educators are accepting the point-of-view that IQ scores are merely indicators of *abilities* which can be changed via instruction. The guiding philosophy is changing from the belief that each of us has certain mental limits and nothing can be done to change them, to a philosophy that everyone can learn. It may take some longer than others. It may involve a wide variety of methods, materials, and equipment, but all learners *can learn.* If a learner doesn't learn, it is not necessarily a problem of the learner, it is a problem of the inadequacy and limitations of the available diagnostic tools and available methods, materials, and equipment.

If a teacher has the traditional point-of-view or philosophy, then who the teacher is ethnically and the kinds of experiences that the teacher has had in his or her own education affects which students learn and the limits of the students' learning. If a teacher can accept the point-of-view or philosophy which I have stated, then who the teacher is ethnically and the kinds of experiences that the teacher has had in his or her own education will not affect which students learn because they will all learn and any limits encountered are not the genetic *limits* of the students, but the limits of methods, materials, time, etc. which are appropriate to the students *abilities*. In hiring teachers for students who have known learning problems, the philosophy or point-of-view of the teacher is much more important than his or her ethnic origin, educational degrees or certificates, or the number of years of teaching experience. Given a teacher with the right humanitarian philosophy, the teacher at least can pick up the right methods, materials, etc., in the process of solving learning problems. Given a teacher with the wrong non-humanitarian philosophy, even if the teacher has all the right methods and materials to choose from, certain students will end up in the *can't learn* category. What makes for a very sad and inhumane situation is when a teacher from an ethnic origin that is believed by many educators to have genetic limits in learning is teaching a class of students from the same ethnic origin and the teacher accepts as fact that the majority of the students can't learn because of the genetic limits. This teacher and others in similar situations typically view the fact that they broke through the supposed genetic limits as rare exceptions of which they hope there will be a *few* in their classes. Students from an ethnic origin which generally have negative experiences in the typical traditional school would be better off to have a teacher of a different ethnic origin but with the right philosophy than a teacher from the same ethnic origin, but the wrong philosophy.

The philosophy that *all students can learn* is a belief, an attitude, a value, and a guiding principle which will keep the teacher searching for solutions to learning problems rather than accept defeat after only one or two attempted solutions. Having this philosophy does not guarantee that every student will learn every objective, but it does guarantee that under this philosophy more students will be learning more and each year as more solutions to learning problems are identified, more students will be learning more.

If given the right philosophy in which any genetic differences are concerned with different abilities which affect how students learn not how much they can learn (limits), then it is possible to view the instructional sequence in such a way that the study of *instruction* is a science. As suggested earlier, the instructional sequence consists of

100

three parts: the learning environment, the learning event, and the consequences of the learning event. To make the study of *instruction* a science, several changes should be made in the instructional sequence. Assuming that one might ask the questions about any instructional sequence, *What is being instructed?* and *How do you know it was successful?*, then the instructional environment, the learning event, the evaluation of instruction, and the consequences of the evaluation or of the learning event. Since the consequences of the evaluation or of the learning event are actually a part of the design of the instructional environment, the instructional situation is made up of at least four elements:

Instructional	Instructional	Learning	Instructional
Objectives	Environment	Event	Evaluation

If given the objectives of an instructional situation, and an instructor whose concern is to find the right combinations of materials, methods, equipment, and consequences such that all of his or her students will learn *all of the objectives*, then this represents a scientific activity because the learning which is occurring is a natural phenomenon. The emphasis of the instructor is on bringing about the desired learning in the learner as measured by the instructional evaluation instrument not on how the teacher behaves, not on any specific method, materials, or equipment, and not on the non-measurable things that are thought to be happening inside the learner. This emphasis and the philosophy that all learners can learn, describes the missing role in traditional education, that of the PRACTITIONER (see page 8).

C. THE THEORIES OF INSTRUCTION

In trying to develop a theory of instruction within which learning is going to be the emphasis, it is necessary to examine what is being instructed. Obviously, what is being instructed are the objectives of the instructional situation, but not all objectives are the same. In 1948, a group of psychologists who were interested in achievment testing met to discuss the difficulties of communicating about their work on educational evaluation in the absence of a common frame of reference. They decided that what was needed was a theoretical framework consisting of a system for classifying the goals or objectives of the educational process. As a result of this meeting and many subsequent meetings, Bloom, Krathwahl, etc., in 1956 had published a *Taxonomy of Educational Objectives: Handbook I — Cognitive Domain* and in 1964 they had published the *Taxonomy of Educational Objectives: Handbook II — Affective Domain*. The *cognitive domain* includes those

101

objectives which vary from simple recall of materials learned to highly original and creative ways of combining and synthesizing new ideas as well as the development of other intellectual abilities and skills. The *affective domain* includes those objectives which concern changes in interest, attitudes, values, emotions, and can vary from simple attention to selected phenomena to complex but internally consistent qualities of character and conscience. A third domain was identified at that time as the *psychomotor domain* which included objectives which emphasize some muscular or motor skill, some manipulation of material and objects, or some act which required a neuro-muscular coordination.

Although Bloom, Krathwahl, and the rest of the group felt it was important to develop a taxonomy for the cognitive and affective domains, they had this to say in *Handbook I* about the psychomotor domain:

> A third domain is the manipulative or motor-skill area. Although we recognize the existence of this domain, we find so little done about it in secondary schools or colleges, that we do not believe the development of a classification of these objectives would be very useful at present.

Of interest, is another paragraph in the same *Handbook I* and only a few pages away from the above statement:

> One of the first problems raised in our discussions was whether or not educational objectives could be classified. It was pointed out that we were attempting to classify phenomena which could not be observed or manipulated in the same concrete form as the phenomena of such fields as the physical and biological sciences, where taxonomies of a very high order have already been developed. Nevertheless, it was the view of the group that educational objectives stated in behavioral form have their counterparts in the behavior of individuals. Such behavior can be observed and described, and these descriptive statements can be classified.

The conflict that Bloom, Krathwahl, and others have overlooked in these two statements is that in the second statement, they are saying that one cannot observe and manipulate objectives in the cognitive and affective domains, but that it can be done indirectly by stating the objectives in behavioral form which then does allow observation and measurement. However, in the first statement, they are saying that the development of a classification of objectives dealing with observable behaviors (manipulative, motors skill, writing, speaking, etc.) would not be very useful. The critical point that they missed is that in classifying the behaviors which indirectly measure cognitive and affective learning they were also developing a listing of motor skills. No matter what domain is involved, if the objectives are measurable, then the objectives are behavioral objectives and describe motor skills. Since all measurable objectives are behavioral objectives, the necessary concepts to remember are how to differentiate between the behavioral objectives which reassure cognitive domain learning *indirectly,* behavioral objectives which measure affective domain learning *indirectly,* and behavioral objectives which measure learning in the third domain *directly* or *indirectly.*

NOTE: Whereas Bloom, Krathwahl and others have referred to the third domain as the psychomotor domain, most dictionaries define *psychomotor* as relating to muscular action believed to be the result of *previous conscious mental activity.* This definition would be much more appropriate in describing the behaviors which are used to indirectly measure cognitive learning rather than a distinct third domain. Therefore, the term *psychomotor behaviors* will be used to refer to those observable and measurable behaviors from which one infers that cognitive learning has or has not taken place.

In examining different types of learning, it can be readily identified that the term *cognitive learning* is also inappropriate in describing learning in the cognitive domain. A more appropriate term should indicate what teachers are trying to develop in the learner. In the cognitive domain, teachers are trying to develop *intellectual skills.* In a similar manner, what teachers are trying to develop in learners with reference to the affective domain are *emotional tendencies.* In other words, as a result of designed instruction, when the learners are in certain situations, we want them to be able to use appropriate intellectual skills which will be demonstrated by certain psychomotor behaviors and to react with appropriate emotional tendencies which will be demonstrated by certain *emotive behaviors.*

This leaves the third domain still unidentified. In the case of intellectual skills and emotional tendencies, both of these distinct types of learning use the body to express thinking and feeling. If the body is just a vehicle to express these two types of learning, then to think of the third domain as representing manual skills is to limit the description of the domain to the vehicle for its expression. In examining a manual skill like typing, a majority of the early learning actually reflects conscious mental activity and as such is expressed in psychomotor behaviors. Once a typist can type 60 words a minute, additional conscious mental activity will not improve the typist's rate of typing. So as the typist improves his or her typing speed to 80 words or more per minute, this cannot be psychomotor behavior. What is happening is that the senses of the body are developing higher levels of coordination. In this case, the senses of the skin (tactile), visual sense, and the kinesthetic sense in the muscles of the arms, hands, and fingers work together to improve the typing speed. In order to have a type of learning that is distinct from the other two domains, the concept of

103

manual skills cannot be used because up to the point where additional conscious mental activity affects the manual skill, this is really just a psychomotor behavior. From that point on, in the development of the manual skills, it is a result of increased skills of the various senses working together. I will refer to these skills as *sensory skills.* The behaviors to be measured will be called *sensomotor behaviors* and the third domain should be the *sensory* domain.

NOTE: Many educators become agitated about the use of the word *behavior.* Almost every teacher who evaluates students are evaluating something that the students are doing or observable evidence of something that the students have done. The very same teacher that condemns the term *behavior* or *behavioral* as in *behavioral objectives* turns around and evaluates their students on some of their behaviors, i.e., answering on objective type test *by circling* letters or numbers, *by writing* an essay or report, by *performing* in some way, by *making* a product, etc. By slightly altering Dewey's comment *Children learn what they do,* it could be stated, *students should do what they are supposed to learn.* In order to find out what students should do, one would have to first identify what learning should take place and then identify the observable and measurable behaviors related to the desired learning.

Since cognitive, sensory, and affective domain learning is not directly measurable, all cognitive, sensory, and affective learning objectives are general objectives. There is nothing wrong with using words like to understand, to know, to be aware, to sense, to feel, or to value. These words represent good *general* cognitive, sensory, and affective learning characteristics.

In being general, the only problem with objectives using these terms is that they are not measurable.

TABLE IV — LEARNING DOMAIN DIFFERENCES

	Cognitive	Sensory	Affective
Types of Learning	Intellectual Skills	Sensoria Skills	Emotional Tendencies
Types of Objectives	General Only	General Only	General Only
How Measured	Indirect	Indirect	Indirect
What Behavior Measured	Psychomotor Behaviors	Sensomotor Behaviors	Emotive Behaviors

With reference to the three domains, there are some differences

104

which directly affect the learner in the instructional situation.

In learning cognitive and sensory objectives, it is best if the learner knows at the beginning of the instructional event what these objectives are and how the achievement of the objectives will be measured because cognitive and sensory objectives are instructed and learned directly.

However, in the development of affective objectives, to tell learners ahead of time that your goal is to change their attitudes and values may actually interfere or at least delay the development or change in attitudes and values because you cannot demand or legislate an attitude or value, i.e., *Love your fellow man!*, *Pay attention!*, *Honesty is the best policy and you had better believe it!*, etc.[2]

Depending on the situation, it is possible to force someone to exhibit behaviors while under observation that my indicate the achievement of the affective objectives, but that does not mean that the affective objectives have been developed or changed internally. For this reason, it is very critical in evaluating for the achievement of affective objectives that the learner has to be confident that the consequences of not achieving the affective objectives will not affect the learner in any negative manner.

TABLE V — LEARNING DOMAIN DIFFERENCES

	Cognitive	Sensory	Affective
Purpose of Behaviors	To Communicate Mental Thoughts	To Communicate the Degree of Sensoria Skills	To Communicate the Intensity and Direction of an Emotion
Objectives Given to Learner at Beginning of Instruction	Yes	Yes	No
Learner Identified in Evaluation	Yes	Yes	No

---

[2] This is why most of the drug abuse, cigarette smoking, forest fire, etc. educational campaigns or programs are not very successful. Most of these programs contain some cognitive information which can be taught directly, but the major desired emphasis concerns attitudes and values and the achievement of these objectives seldom occurs when taught directly and particularly if authorities (parents, instructors, administrators, police, etc.) demand achievement.

These differences as indicated in Table V result in some additional differences. Since an instructor cannot demand achievement of affective objectives, an instructor will have to be satisfied with the best achievement he or she can design into the instructional environment. As a result, (with reference to the affective domain) any evaluation of the achievement of affective objectives actually is evaluating primarily the ability of the instructor to design instructional environments which will achieve the desired attitudes and values even though secondarily the evaluation data does give data about the achievement of the learner. Because it may not be possible for an instructor to be successful in helping all learners achieve the affective objectives and because the evaluation is actually evaluating the instructor's design of the instructional environment, the emphasis in evaluation is on increasing the percentage of learners in a *group* that do achieve the affective objectives. The results of the evaluation, are viewed as diagnostic information indicating changes to be made in the design of the instructional environment such that more learners in the next group will achieve the affective objectives.

The treatment of evaluation of learning in the affective domain is in contrast to the treatment of evaluation of learning in the cognitive and sensory domains. Since psychomotor (indirect cognitive) behaviors and sensomotor behaviors are taught and learned directly, the instructor can demand 100 percent achievement and any evaluation of achievement primarily evaluates the achievement of the individual learner even though when viewed as a group, the achievement levels secondarily evaluate the instructor's design of the instructional environment. The results of the evaluation of cognitive and sensory objectives are used as diagnostic information indicating what the learners have left to learn in the instructional event.

The attitudes and values of the instructors and the learners also affect learning and bring out two additional differences between the three domains. In the teaching of cognitive and sensory objectives, whether or not the teacher has positive or negative attitudes and values concerning the cognitive and sensory objectives, only has minor effects on student learning. If the students know that the accountability for learning the cognitive and sensory objectives is their responsibility, students will learn in spite of the teachers attitudes or values. However, in teaching affective objectives, the instructor will find it very difficult to help students achieve an attitude or value which is in conflict with the instructor's own attitudes or values. Even though the instructor may be able to claim that he already has the desired affective objectives, if his observable emotional behaviors indicate otherwise, the conflict between what the instructor *preaches* and what he or she practices will interfere with the achievement of the desired objectives

106

TABLE VI — LEARNING DOMAIN DIFFERENCES (Cont.)

	Cognitive	Sensory	Affective
Quality Control	100% Achievement	100% Achievement	Best Possible Achievement
How Taught and Learned	Directly	Directly	Indirectly
Instructional Emphasis	Individual	Individual	Group
Primary Purpose of Evaluation	Diagnose Student Learning	Identify Student's Learning Problems	Identify Instructor's Design Problems
Secondary Purpose of Evaluation	Diagnose Instructor's Design	Identify Instructor's Design Problems	Identify Student's Learning Problems

which were *preached.* If anything, the students will have a greater tendency to pick up indirectly the affective objectives indicated by the instructor's observable emotional behaviors. As an old saying goes, *Learners not only learn what they were taught, they also learn how they were taught!*

In the learning of cognitive and sensory objectives, if students have negative attitudes and values towards the achievement of the objectives, they can control the situation and make the decision not to learn. Of course, in that case, the instructor would have to find some way to change their attitudes or values or to extrinsically motivate the students to want to learn the objectives. In either case, each student has control over whether or not he or she learns the cognitive and/or sensory objectives. However, in the learning of affective objectives, even if the students have negative attitudes and values towards the achievement of the objectives and actually do not want to learn them, it is possible for the instructional design to be so good that the students acquire some or all of the affective objectives in spite of themselves. Because affective objectives are taught indirectly, students don't have as much control over their own learning as they do with the learning of cognitive and sensory objectives.[3] For this reason, the teaching of affective objectives should be readily defensible in terms of how the acquisition of the

---

[3] Most people have had the experience of not wanting to like or fall in love with someone and in spite of your mental and sometimes physical efforts to avoid the development of a positive feeling, it happens!

107

attitudes and values will help the individual live a better life from the individual's point-of-view.

This is also why the teaching of affective objectives put the teacher in such a precarious position. If the teacher indirectly teaches students attitudes and values which are in conflict with their parents' and/or the community's, the teacher could be charged with *brain-washing*. Parents may not show much interest in whether or not their children are learning in the cognitive and sensory domain, or even in the affective domain as long as the att tudes and values being taught are similar to their own; but most parents will get very excited about situations in which teachers, books, and/or experiences develop conflicting attitudes and values in their children.

TABLE VII — LEARNING DOMAIN DIFFERENCES

	Cognitive	Sensory	Affective
The Effect of an Instructor's Conflicting Attitudes	Minor Effect	Minor Effect	Major Effect
Student's Control over Learning	High	High	Low

Many educators and psychologists have written about the need for a theory of instruction. In 1966, Jerome Bruner's *Toward a Theory of Instruction* was published. In line with much of his previous work, Bruner's emphasis concerned the development of a Cognitive Theory of Instruction. Because cognitive objectives are all general and non-measurable, it would be very difficult to develop designed instruction. This particular problem made it difficult to put into practice an instructional experience based on Bruner's ideas of a Cognitive Theory of Instruction. According to Bruner, a theory of instruction should have four major features:

1. It should specify the experiences which most effectively implant in the individual a predisposition toward learning.
2. It must specify the ways in which a body of knowledge should be structured so that it can be most readily grasped by the learner.
3. It should specify the most effective sequences in which to present the materials to be learned.
4. It should specify the nature and pacing of rewards and punishments in the process of learning and teaching.

The most flagrant assumption in the above four features is that all learners are assumed to learn the same way or that the goal of instruction is for only those involved in the group described by the word *most* to be able to learn and I don't know what happens to the rest of the learners. For this reason alone, Bruner's approach to instruction is destined for discussion, but not for successful application. Note also, that the first feature actually involves affective domain concepts rather than cognitive and Bruner states it in the form which indicates that affective objectives are best achieved indirectly (implanted).

In 1968, Richard Jones', *Fantasy and Feeling in Education* was published. Jones agreed with Bruner in a number of points, but claimed that a theory of Instruction should go beyond cognitive learning to an affective theory of Instruction. Many other writers have picked up this same concept and because their emphasis is on developing attitudes, values, feelings, emotions, etc., these writers (and Jones) like to look on their approach as *humanistic*. Anyone that is against their approach is thought of in the same context as one who is against motherhood, God, flowers, or anything else that is *good*. The major problem with an affective theory of Instruction is that it too concerns general non-measurable concepts and as such is not very practical. Also, since affective objectives are taught indirectly and the learners have limited control over their own learning of these objectives, the problem of brainwashing or menticide becomes a critical factor. Although, I will agree and have said so on numerous occasions (see Chapter II) that one of our most critical problems concerns *how to get along with our fellow man*. But emphasizing emotions alone will not necessarily help people to get along better. In fact, an emphasis on emotions at the sacrifice of necessary cognitive learning may very well *dehumanize* society by not helping learners to use cognitive or intellectual reasoning in their control of their emotions in various inter-personal situations. Some writers recognize the need for cognitive learning *and* affective learning, but they resist the concept of dealing with measurable objectives; consequently, their suggestions lack practicality.

In order to have a theory of instruction that is practical, it has to deal with all three types of learning domains and the objectives involved in the actual design of the instructional event have to be observable and measurable. Therefore, the most appropriate approach would be a Behavioral[4] Theory of Instruction which would be concerned with the measurable behaviors in all three domains of learning. But this assumes that the instructional approach is the same for the three domains of learning which Tables VI, V, VI, and VII indicate is not the case. Therefore, there is a need for two theories of instruction: *A Behavioral*

---

[4] Behavior — anything that an organism does that involves action especially an observable activity when measurable in terms of quantifiable effects on the environment whether arising from internal or external stimulus.

Theory of Instruction: Cognitive and Sensory Domains and A Behavioral
Theory of Instruction: Affective Domain.

TABLE VIII.

	A Behavioral Theory of Instruction: Cognitive and Sensory Domains		A Behavioral Theory of Instruction: Affective Domain
	Cognitive	Sensory	Affective
Types of Learning	Intellectual Skills	Sensoria Skills and Tendencies	Emotional Tendencies
Types of Objectives	General Only	General and Specific	General Only
How Measured	Indirect	Direct and Indirect	Indirect
What Behaviors Measured	Psychomotor Behaviors	Sensomotor Behaviors	Emotive Behaviors
Purpose of Behaviors	To Communicate Mental Thought	To Communicate the Degree of Sensoria Skills	To Communicate the Intensity and Direction of an Emotion
Objectives Given to Learners at the Beginning of Instruction	Yes	Yes	No
Learners Identified in Evaluation	Yes	Yes	No
Quality Control	100% Achievement	100% Achievement	Best Possible Achievement
How Taught and Learned	Directly	Directly	Indirectly
Instructional Emphasis	Individual	Individual	Group
Primary Purpose of Evaluation	Identify Student's Learning Problems	Identify Student's Learning Problems	Identify Instructor's Design Problems
Secondary Purpose of Evaluation	Identify Instructor's Design Problems	Identify Instructor's Design Problems	Identify Student's Learning Problems
The Effect of an Instructor's Conflicting Attitudes & Values	Minor Effect	Minor Effect	Possible Major Effect
Student's Control over Learning	High	High	Low

110

In presenting the two theories of instruction, I have divided each of them into four parts:
- — a statement describing what the use of the theory in an instructional event will do,
- — A description of the five elements in the instructional event,
- — a series of tenents related by number to one of the elements, and
- — a series of strategies to be used in helping learners to achieve the desired objectives.

The two theories are not complete in themselves, but when used as guidelines for the instructor in the instructional event combined with the other five factors to be described in subsequent chapters, it is possible to obtain the results described in the theory statement.

1. BEHAVIORAL THEORY OF INSTRUCTION: COGNITIVE AND SENSORY DOMAINS

Ninety percent or more of the learners in an instructional unit or course can achieve 100 percent of the specified learning objectives of that instructional unit or course if the instructor puts into practice, while managing the five elements in the instructional event, the tenents and instructional strategies upon which this theory is based.

Elements in the Instructional Event
1. Learners who will be learning in the instructional event.
2. An Instructor who manages the instructional event directly (live) and/or indirectly (via some other medium).
3. Specific measurable learning objectives which describe what it is that the learners are to learn and the instructor is to instruct.
4. An evaluation instrument in which each part or item measures the achievement of a corresponding objective and the achievement of each objective is measured by one or more corresponding parts or items in the evaluation instrument.
5. The learning environment which may include a particular method or technique, instructional materials and equipment, and a motivational set which has been built into the learning event and/or the consequences of the learning event.

Tenents Concerning the Elements
1-a. That learners are individually different in a multitude of ways with respect of the process of learning.

1-b. That differences in abilities of learners to learn primarily affect HOW a learner learns not what a learner can learn.

1-c. Although differences in abilities to learn *may* be a result of

111

nature, significant changes in these abilities can be brought about via *nurture* (instruction).

1-d. That whatever is to be learned (objectives) can be learned successfully different ways.

1-e. That learning is an individual event, so the learner's role in the instructional event is to learn.

1-f. That theories and principles of learning concerning covert and non-measurable events or processes are of little value in a theory of instruction concerned with overt measurable behavior.

1-g. That theories and principles of learning which ignore individual differences in learning and assume that all learners are the same are of little value in a theory of instruction which assumes that learners are individually different in many ways with respect to the learning process.

2-a. That instructors are individually different in a multitude of ways with respect to the process of instructing.

2-b. That differences in abilities of instructors to instruct successfully primarily affect HOW an instructor instructs not what an instructor can instruct.

2-c. Although differences in abilities to instruct *may* be a result of *nature*, significant changes in these abilities can be brought about via *nurture* (instruction).

2-d. That whatever is to be instructed (objectives) can be instructed successfully different ways.

2-e. That the instructor's role in the instructional event is to set up the learning environment and in the event of non-learning to manipulate the various aspects of the learning environment until the learners achieve the objectives, keeping in consideration the other tenets and strategies of this theory.

2-f. That non-learning is considered a result of a learning problem which can be solved by the manipulation of the learning environment rather than a result of genetic limitations, home environment, or other non-controllable (by the instructor) factors.

2-g. That theories of learning which are concerned with manipulation of the learning environment and are only indirectly concerned with the learner, are actually theories of instructional environment design and could be of value in the strategies of this theory.

2-h. That theories of teaching which are primarily concerned with the behaviors of the teacher (checklists of teacher behaviors) and are not evaluated in terms of whether or not learners are learning should not be considered as theories of instruction and

112

are of little value in this theory because they ignore the existence of individual differences in teachers and learners.

3-a. That whatever is to be learned (objectives) by the learner and instructed (objectives) by the instructor during the learning event is directly measurable and concerns the learning of intellectual skills and sensoria skills and tendencies.

3-b. That whatever is to be learned (objectives) by the learner *does not* concern changes in attitudes, value, emotions, etc. which are objectives in the affective domain. (See Behavioral Theory of Instruction — Affective Domain).

3-c. That a list of the specific objectives to be learned are given to the learners at the beginning of the instructional event so the learners know exactly what is to be learned.

3-d. That whatever is to be learned (objectives) is defensible in terms of its utility at sometime in the life of the learner.

3-e. That if whatever is to be learned (objectives) is only useful after a long period of time such that the learned objectives are forgotten before the learner can use them, then the specific objectives will be changed to the following two types of specific objectives:

(1) the learner should be able to identify when he or she needs to know the original specific objectives.

(2) the learner should be able to re-learn at that time on an independent study basis the original objectives.

4-a. That the evaluation instrument has a one-to-one behavioral correlation with the specific measurable objectives.

4-b. That the evaluation instrument *does not* include in any part a standardized normed test because traditional standardized tests have little if any behavioral correlation with important instructional objectives.

4-c. That the evaluation instrument *does not* include any so-called *objective type* test items (multiple-choice, true-false, or matching) because these items have little, if any behavioral correlation with important instructional objectives and have little, if any utility in the world environment outside of schools.

4-d. That the evaluation instrument is divided into two parts; first, rote memory performance in which no notes, books, or aids of any sort are available to the learner and second, thinking performance in which among other things the learner applies what has been rote memorized and utilizes whatever materials which might be normally available in a similar situation in the world environment outside of schools.

4-e. That since many learners will probably not indicate 100 percent achievement of the specified objectives on the first test,

113

the learners will have to be able to take the same test as many times as necessary in order to indicate an achievement of 100 percent of the objectives. The tests used for the first part or rote memory part will be exact duplicates. The tests for the second part or thinking part will be the same in reference to the behavioral objectives being tested but different in reference to the vehicle used to test for the achievement of the specific behavior.

5-a. That since learners and instructors are individually different, it will be rare, if ever, that the same learning environment will facilitate 100 percent achievement of the objectives by 90 percent or more of the learners.

5-b. That any learning environment or part of the learning environment which *does not* allow for individual learning differences in the learner should not be used as a basis for learning under this theory.

5-c. That since learning is the emphasis, changes in the learning environment should be made primarily, if not only, because of its affect on increasing the learners' learning speed and/or achievement.

5-d. Although the evaluation of the achievement of the specified objectives in an instructional event primarily evaluate the achievement of the individual learner, in looking at all of the learners collectively, the evaluation of these objectives secondarily evaluates the effectiveness of the design of the instructional event.

Strategies for Effectiveness and Efficiency in the Instructional Event

A. If non-learning is identified as a result of the lack of necessary prerequisite learning (cumulative ignorance), then the necessary prerequisite learning becomes that which is to be learned by the learner and instructed by the instructor.

B. Any learning objectives which are critical for success in learning subsequent objectives, units, or courses should be learned to the 100 percent level before the learner continues to other objectives.

C. Since what is relevant and interesting to one learner may not be relevant and interesting to another learner, it will be more effective and efficient to use vehicles for learning that are appropriate for each learner even though the learners are learning the same objective. The same or similarly appropriate vehicles should then also be used for evaluating the achievement of that objective.

D. Rather than spend a lot of time developing all new instructional materials for multiple pathways through an instructional unit or course, use materials which are already available and develop or buy

114

new ones only when necessary to solve an identified learning problem.

E. Minimize the amount of time that learners have to rely on getting the course content from the live teacher and maximize the amount of time that learners can get the course content from individualized sources (books, learning packages, films, audio and video tapes, etc.). This will maximize the degree of individualized learning and also the time that the teacher has available to solve individual learning problems. This will also help the student become an independent learner which is a necessary learned behavior for later adult life.

F. If the most effective and efficient learning style of the learner is not known, or even if it is known but the appropriate instructional materials to fit the learner's learning style are not readily available, start with that learning environment that the largest group of learners have learned successfully from. If the learner doesn't learn, use that learning environment that the next largest group of learners have learned from successfully. In the event of continued non-learning, use the next most successful learning environment. Repeat this process until learning occurs. If after the first try learning doesn't occur and alternate learning environments are not readily available and the decision is to develop the alternate learning environments, it is better to develop these alternate learning environments as solutions to specific learning problems of specific students rather than developing the alternate learning environments as solutions to general or imagined learning problems for imaginary learners.[5]

2. BEHAVIORAL THEORY OF INSTRUCTION: AFFECTIVE DOMAIN

More learners will learn the specified learning objectives in the affective domain if the instructor puts into practice, while managing the five elements in the instructional event, the tenets and instructional

---

[5] There is a growing movement to have a *learning resource center* or a *media center* in schools. At the present time, given that the course objectives are not specific and learning problems are generally considered to be genetic or related to external outside-of-school factors and as such are not capable of being solved in the schools, the instructional materials or resources put on the shelves of the learning resources are selected on the basis of the buyer's likes and dislikes and the imagined likes and dislikes of learners. As a result, the materials are often not related by design to desired important learning objectives and are rarely identified as solving specific learning problems. Under the approach suggested in this book, learning resource centers will open up with empty shelves and as teachers identify specific learning problems of specific learners, the shelves will become filled up with solutions which have been developed or purchased specifically to solve these problems.

strategies upon which this theory is based.

Elements in the Instructional Event
(The same five elements as in the main theory p. 111).

Tenets Concerning the Elements
(In addition to the tenets listed on p. 111-2 for elements 1 and 2)

1-h. Attitudes, values, feelings, etc., can not be learned directly, they can only be learned or acquired indirectly.

1-i. Attitudes, values, feelings, etc., are constantly changing as a result of the varied experiences of the learner.

1-j. Differences in abilities to learn rarely affect how learners acquire certain attitudes, values, etc.; but the learning environment in which learners with different abilities are placed will affect certain attitudes, values, etc.

2-i. Attitudes, values, feelings, etc. can not be taught or instructed directly, they can only be created or changed indirectly in the learner.

2-j. Instructors whose own attitudes, values, interests, etc. are in conflict with the desired affective domain objectives which they are trying to develop in the learners will not be as successful as Instructors whose attitudes, values, interests, etc., are similar or at least not in conflict with the desired affective domain objectives.

3-a. Whereas objectives concerning sensory and intellectual skills are learned or not learned depending upon the effectiveness and efficiency of the instructional event, the achievement of objectives in the affective domain are created or changed positively or negatively because of the total experiences of the learner in and out of school.

3-b. That whatever is to be learned (objectives) by the learner and designed into instructional events by the instructor is indirectly measurable and concerns the learning of affective domain objectives and does not concern intellectual and manual skills.

3-c. That the list of specific objectives in the affective domain are *NOT* given to the learners at the beginning of the instructional event.

3-d. That whatever is to be learned or changed (objectives) in the affective domain is defensible in terms of what the individual learner wants or needs in improving the quality of the learner's life from the point-of-view of the learner's wants or needs, and of improving the quality of the social relationships of the society within which the learner plans to live.

NOTE: Given that most learners have to live with or at least interact with their families and communities, to purposely teach attitudes, values, or beliefs which are in conflict with those held by the learners' families and communities is to purposely decrease the quality of the learners' social relationships and as such is not acceptable and should be considered a professional malpractice.

4-a. That the evaluation instrument has a one-to-one behavioral correlation with the specific measurable objectives.

4-b. That the evaluation instrument should be used on a pretest-posttest basis because some learners may already have the desired attitude or value and it is important to identify the direction of learning within the instructional event, i.e., did the learners go more positive or more negative with respect to the desired attitude or value.

4-c. That the learners are *not* graded or in anyway negatively evaluated as a result of the use of the evaluation instrument.

4-d. That the learners respond to the evaluation instrument (affective domain) under anonymous conditions unless the instructor is convinced that the students will be honest in their responses *and* the students are convinced that they will not be negatively affected by the teacher as a result of responding honestly — even if their attitude or values which they reveal are in direct conflict with the desired attitudes and values.

4-e. That the evaluation instrument is so designed that a range of attitudes or values can be identified rather than just a yes or no type item because affective domain objectives are generally measured in terms of a degree or number on a continuous scale.

4-f. In contrast to the evaluation of the achievement of intellectual and sensory skills where 100 percent achievement of the objectives is the goal, learners who are learning affective domain objectives are not expected to achieve 100 percent of the objectives, but the goal would be to have 100 percent of the learners to develop or change their attitudes or values in the *direction* of the desired attitude or value expressed by the objectives.

(In addition to tenets 5-a, 5-b, and 5-c listed on p. 114 for element no. 5).

5-d. Although the data resulting from the use of the evaluation instrument in the affective domain comes directly from the learners, the data primarily evaluates the effectiveness of the design of the instructional event and only secondarily evaluates the achievement of the learner.

Strategies for Effectiveness and Efficiency in the Instructional Event

A. Major key to remember with reference to the achievement of affective domain objectives is that these objectives can not be taught directly as is the case of intellectual and sensory skills. Affective domain objectives can only be created or changed indirectly.

B. Given an instructional event in which there are both intellectual and/or sensory skills (objectives) to be learned and also affective domain objectives to be acquired, it is better to first concentrate directly on the learners learning 100 percent of the intellectual and/or sensory skills (objectives) because the successful achievement of these objectives will have a positive affect on the attitudes, values, etc., of the learners while non-achievement and particularly failure to achieve the cognitive and/or sensory objectives will have a negative effect on the attitudes, values, etc. of the learners.

C. Because the achievement of intellectual and/or sensory skills frequently affect the creation or change in affective domain objectives, cumulative ignorance in the necessary intellectual and/or sensory skills can still be a problem to be solved prior to dealing with the affective domain objectives.

D. In the *creation* or extension of a desired objective in the affective domain, it will be facilitated if the instructor can identify to the learners a similar attitude, value, etc., which they have already.

E. In the changing *(reversing)* of an attitude, value, etc., it will be facilitated if the instructor can identify to the learners a stronger attitude, value, etc., which they have already and which is in conflict with the existing attitude, value, etc. which is to be changed.

F. Although it is possible to demand, urge, or require learners to learn intellectual and sensory skills (objectives) and this pressure actually may help in the achievement of these objectives (assuming an appropriate learning environment which is learner-oriented), to directly demand, urge, or require learners to acquire certain attitudes or values actually often interferes with the development or change in the desired attitudes or values.

G. Because attitudes and values are subject to constant change, once desirable attitudes and values have been acquired, plans should be established concerning the maintenance of these desired attitudes and values until such time as they become habitual.

118

H. Although learners can control whether or not they learn intellectual and sensory skills and whether or not they exhibit behavioral responses which indicate the acquisition of intellectual and sensory skills, it is very difficult for learners to control the internal development or change in attitudes and values. For those who have developed self-control, they can control the observable behavioral responses which indicate certain attitudes and values, but this does not mean that they can also control the development or change in internal attitudes and values.

I. Extreme care should be taken in the development of instructional environments or events concerning the affective domain, because developing, changing, or ·extinguishing someone's attitudes and values is tantamount to brainwashing or menticide. Therefore, instructors developing or using affective domain instructional environments should be ready to defend the use of these environments based on how the new attitudes and values will help the individual, his or her social group, and/or society.

Interrelationships Between the Philosophy and the Theories of Instruction

This first factor has actually been divided into two parts: the philosophy of instruction and the Behavioral Theories of Instruction. They best way to achieve excellence in the instructional event is to accept both of these concepts before going on. If an instructor accepts the philosophy that all students can learn, but doesn't accept the Behavioral Theories of Instruction, then the instructor will most likely find it difficult to achieve the goals of the philosophy. As a result of not reaching the goals of the philosophy over a period of time, the philosophy will slowly deteriorate until it is extinguished. If an instructor accepts one or both of the Behavioral Theories of Instruction, but doesn't accept the philosophy, then in trying to solve learning problems, the instructor will give up sooner by saying, *this or these student(s) probably can't learn anyway, why keep trying.* As a result, not as many students will learn as many of the desired objectives. If an instructor is unable to accept either the philosophy or the Behavioral Theories of Instruction, the value of the rest of this book will be much more limited than if the instructor could have accepted either one or both the philosophy and the Theories. However, many of the suggestions for improving the instructional event can still be put into practice without accepting this first factor.

NOTE: Whereas the Behavioral Theories of Instruction are in themselves Cognitive concepts and most of the tenets and strategies refer

119

to psychomotor behaviors (indirect measures of cognitive learning. the philosophy is a belief and is in the affective domain. If you did not have this belief when you started this book, hopefully you have developed it by this point. If not, maybe the following chapters (in this and subsequent volumes) will help develop it. Accepting the Philosophy is very important because as a belief, it helps instructors solve student learning problems which I may not have covered in these three volumes.

CHAPTER V

THE CHANGING ROLE OF THE TEACHER
FROM EDUCATOR TO INSTRUCTIONEER

General and Specific Objectives

GO — To recognize that the role of the teacher as an Instructioneer is more effective and efficient and yet more humanizing from the point-of-view of student learning than the traditional role of the teacher.

SO — Given the five elements in the instructional event, describe one or more characteristics of each element as found in traditional education and in the Behavioral Learning Systems Approach to Instruction.

SO — List at least ten out of the 16 disadvantages of the traditional teacher's role and give at least one example from past experience (as a teacher and/or as a student) which supports the view that each disadvantage is really a disadvantage.

SO — Given the three characteristics of a profession, describe how these characteristics support the statement that the teacher's role as an Instructioneer can be considered as professional, whereas the traditional role cannot be considered as professional.

SO — List the six statements which define the Instructioneer.

GO — To understand the importance of solving learning problems in making the instructional process more effective, efficient, and humanizing.

SO — Define a *learning problem* as defined in the chapter and give at least three examples of learning problems you have had which you think could have been solved.

SO — Given the five elements of an instructional event, describe at least one or more potential learning problems which could be caused by problems traditionally found in each element.

SO — Identify the student's greatest learning problem as stated in the chapter and describe at least two or more situations in which this was your problem.

SO — If you have an opportunity to work with students as a teacher, conduct the experiment described on page 151.

121

and prepare a brief paper describing the experiment and the results of the experiment.

SO — List the six steps in decision-making as described in the chapter and describe your actions in each of the steps for at least two decisions you have made recently.

SO — Describe how a low correlation between learning objectives and the evaluation for achievement of these objectives creates learning problems and describe at least two or more situations in which you have experienced such a low correlation.

SO — Describe at least two of the learning problems which affect success in reading and describe a personal experience you have had with each problem.

SO — Describe how *objective* type tests are really subjectively written or constructed and how the traditionally subjective essay tests can be objectively evaluated as presented in this chapter.

GO — To understand that recognition of individual differences involve action, not just words.

SO — Describe how the traditional role of the teacher forces the teacher to ignore individual differences of students, whereas the role as an Instructioneer is designed to recognize individual differences.

GO — To understand that the apparent intelligence revealed by contemporary tests and the rate of learning in educational activities could be considerably below a student's real intelligence.

SO — Given the traditional educational event where the time allowed for learning and the path for learning are set, describe how this could affect students' apparent rate of learning. Describe how learning time and learning pathways as variables help to increase the correlation between the students' apparent rate of learning and the students' real rate of learning.

GO — To realize that the changeover from the traditional role to the role as an Instructioneer can be accomplished without necessarily putting in more time.

SO — Using the equation for the humanization factor and the answers to the questions on pages 128-9, describe how the degree of individualized instruction can be increased without the teacher putting in more time than is being put in already.

SO — Describe why the development of the independent learner is critical to the teachers' role as an Instructioneer and to living successfully in our society.

122

GO — To know that making the instructional process more effective, efficient, and humanizing is best accomplished in a supportive environment.

SO — Describe how five or more of the 14 supporting roles actually assist the Instructioneer and the learner.

Because of the length of this chapter and also to help introduce the concepts and their sequence to the reader, a sub-table of contents for this chapter follows:

SUBTABLE OF CONTENTS

THE CHANGING ROLE OF THE TEACHER
FROM EDUCATOR TO INSTRUCTIONEER

INTRODUCTION

Recently, writers from both inside and outside of the field of education have written books and articles on the topic of *Do Teachers Make a Difference*. A significant amount of the research tends to indicate that other factors in the life of the learner have more affect on student learning than the teacher does. The topic itself assumes or at least implies that *Teachers SHOULD Make a Difference*. Since learning can take place anytime and at any place by chance, it would be reasonable to assume that taxpayers and others who financially support education, build school buildings, and pay teachers to meet with students in these buildings are assuming that the teachers do in fact make a difference. In order to increase the teachers' contribution to the teaching-learning event, teachers in elementary and secondary education are required to have had professional training (education courses) in a variety of teaching skills. Teachers in institutions of higher education, although not required to have had any professional training in *how to teach*, are usually required to have advanced degrees in the subject matter area they are teaching. B. F. Skinner states in his book *The Technology of Teaching* that

Teaching is the arrangement of contingencies of reinforcement under which students learn. They learn without teaching in their natural environments, but teachers expedite learning, hastening the appearance of behaviors which would otherwise be acquired slowly or making sure of the appearance of behaviors which might otherwise never occur.

In order to prove that *teachers do make a difference*, the achievement levels of students with teachers would have to be significantly greater than *chance* which would be the achievement levels of students without any teachers, schools, or learning guidelines prepared by teachers. In order to make a difference, teachers would have to start out with a philosophy that they can make a difference; a theory of instruction which will facilitate the achievement of a difference; be trained in the necessary role and accompanying behaviors which will help them implement the philosophy and theory of instruction such that a difference occurs by design not by chance or caprice; have specified measurable objectives which represent the purposes of the instructional event; and evaluation instruments which measure directly the achievement levels of the specified objectives and enable the identification of a difference.

The traditional philosophy of most educators is that the achievement levels of students are primarily controlled by nature (genetics)

and other out-of-school factors such that schools and teachers can't be held accountable for making much of a change. There hasn't been a theory of instruction available and the traditional teachers' role in practice is that of a presenter of course content and the achievement levels of the students are left up to the abilities of the students to learn in the given situation. A traditional teacher's spoken or implied comment to students at the beginning of a course might be, *My job is to present the course content to you. If you learn, good. If you don't learn, too bad.* The traditional training of teachers is so innocuous that whether or not the teachers have had the traditional professional education courses doesn't appear to change their behaviors or role in the classroom. Having advanced degrees in a particular subject matter area doesn't seem to affect the teachers' behavior or role in the classroom either. The traditional objectives used for decades in education are vague, ambiguous, non-measurable, and of the motherhood, flag, country, and God type. The traditional approach to measuring achievement involves the use of standardized tests and teacher made tests which are considered valid on the basis that the results of the tests approximate a normal probability curve which can be generated by flipping coins or throwing dice enough times. In other words, the evaluation instruments are designed to give results which are not much different than chance. Therefore, if the traditional philosophy says that teachers and schools can't affect nature via nurture and the teachers role in the classroom and the evaluation instruments emphasize *chance*, it isn't really any wonder that a variety of research comes up with the conclusions that teachers and schools don't make any difference. As stated by Alexander Mood in a U.S. Office of Education publication *Do Teachers Make a Difference,*

> at the present moment we cannot make any sort of meaningful quantitative estimate of the effect of teachers on student achievement.

Although many people may think of the teacher as having only one role, as one observes a teacher performing the many activities teachers are asked to perform during their school day, there are a number of different *roles* which the teacher performs. At one time, the teacher may be a teacher. At another time, the teacher may be a substitute mother or a *child sitter*. At some other time, the teacher may be a clerk filling out papers and forms. At other times, the teacher may perform a substitute policing role by standing in the hallway or attending dances as a chaperone. The teacher may also perform an advising role, in which the teacher meets with a student but the discussion concerns things other than academic problems. In fact, there are numerous other roles that the teacher may perform during the course of any one school day. However, the major concern of this book, is the role or roles of the

127

teacher in the teaching-learning situation. In order to emphasize the advantages and values of the teachers' role as it is practiced under a Behavioral Learning Systems Approach to Instruction, I want to first involve you, the reader, in identifying the contemporary role of the teacher as you practice it or view it, then I'll discuss the traditional role of the teacher and why it is ineffective, if not harmful, in the instructional event, and then I'll go into detail about the humanizing role for the teacher as an *Instructioneer*. At the end of the Chapter, I'll make some comments about some supporting roles as they relate to the *Instructioneer*. The reason for this, is that these roles are important and in some school situations it may be necessary for the teacher to perform one or more of the supporting roles in addition to being an *Instructioneer*.

A. CONTEMPORARY ROLE OF THE TEACHER: READERS POINT-OF-VIEW

To better understand the need for changing the role of the teacher and to identify whether or not a given teacher should change and how much of a change should be made, fill in the numbers for the following four questions on this page or on a separate piece of paper:

NOTE: If you are a teacher at the present moment, use numbers that reflect your present role. If you are an administrator, or in a non-teaching position, use numbers that reflect an average of the teachers with whom you work. If you are a student, use numbers which you feel would reflect a composite average of your teachers.

1. In an average week, how many hours are spent collectively in presenting course content to the total class? _____ hours.
   (It could be five minutes in one class, ten minutes in another class, 20 minutes in another class, etc. If you have laboratory or shop class and you spend ten to fifteen minutes explaining to the total class the experiment, project, or work for the period, this ten or fifteen minutes belongs in this category. If you are having a total class discussion, but you interject comments and information for the whole class at various intervals during the discussion, collectively, the time spent during those intervals belongs in this category.)

2. In an average week, how many hours are spent collectively in meeting with small groups and individuals? _____ hours.
   (This could include those minutes before and after classes and before and after school, if this time is actually spent talking with small groups or individual students. In laboratory or shop courses, if you spend time walking around and working with individual students, this time fits into this category. However, if you sit at your desk doing something on your own or go out of the room, the laboratory or shop time doesn't fit into this category. Office hours

128

for faculty in higher education or preparation periods for elementary and secondary faculty which are spent meeting with students fits into this category. If students don't meet with you during these hours, do not count them in this category. If you divide up your class into small groups or the students are working individually in class and you spend your time working with each of the groups or the individual students, this time fits into this category. If, however, the students are working in small groups or individually, and you do something else besides working with the students, this time doesn't belong in this category.)

3. In an average week, how many hours are spent collectively in preparation for your classes? _____ hours.

(This would include preparation periods for elementary and secondary faculty if these periods are actually used for preparation. This category would include for most teachers not only the time spent in preparation while in the school building, but also time spent in preparation for classes during evenings and weekends at home or any place else.

4. In an average week, how many hours are spent collectively directing or participating in classroom activities which are not associated with specific learning objectives and you don't expect them to result in measurable increases in learning? _____ hours.

(This would include any activities which are primarily carried on to keep the students busy, activities which are carried on because of some tradition, or any activities such as films, field trips, etc. which are used to fill up a course's time requirements.)

> NOTE: These four categories are not meant to include all of the teacher's time during an average week. There are many other categories of activities which could be listed, i.e., time spent filling out forms, time spent cleaning up a room, time spent in faculty meetings, etc. I selected these four categories because they are the major ones which involve the teacher in an instructional role. If you didn't actually write down any numbers for the four questions, go back and do it now as I will be referring to these numbers several times and the concepts being discussed will be easier to understand if you actually have some numbers to refer to.

B. TRADITIONAL ROLE OF THE TEACHER: A PRESENTER OF COURSE CONTENT

In order to examine the traditional and the systems roles for the teacher in an instructional situation, it is useful to look at each role from the point of view of the five elements listed in the two theories of instruction: the learners, the instructor, the general and specific objectives, the evaluation instrument, and the learning environment which includes instructional technology. Technology is included because during the past several decades, the increasing numbers of learners, increasing needs of these learners in order to participate more fully in our society and in life, and society's demands that the professional educators become more effective and more efficient in the teaching-learning process, have established a place in our educational institutions and in the teaching-learning process for technology.

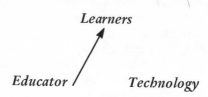

Learners

Educator   *Technology*

Figure 13 — The Educator as a *Presenter* of Course Content

The first and most common role is that of the traditional educator presenting course content to the learners as illustrated in the teaching-learning paradigm (Figure 13). This is the role performed by a vast majority of educators at all levels of education and to varying degrees of effectiveness. I claim varying degrees of effectiveness because the very fact that most teachers end up with students getting A's, B's, C's, D's, and F's indicates varying degrees of effectiveness. In examining the traditional instructional situation where the teacher is presenting course content, with reference to the five elements in instruction,

1. The learners are passive receivers of the teacher's message and have to guess what is important. Because it is a group or class event, individual differences among the students are ignored and the educator presents to the mythical average student who may not even exist.

2. The instructor will be referred to as an educator because in this role learning is occurring almost by chance. The whole situation is teacher-oriented.

3. Traditionally, the objectives in this role are general objectives and quite often are worded in such a manner as to emphasize what teachers should be covering in the course instead of what students are supposed to learn.

4. Since the course objectives are general and consequently non-measurable, the tests can be designed to give any desired results and there is no need to worry about any correlation between objectives and test items. Based on the assumption that the normal probability curve represents the expected distribution of achievement in most classes, tests are designed such that the students' scores resulting

130

from the tests approximate a normal curve.

5. The learning environment is designed for the convenience of the teacher's presenting role such as the teacher's desk at the head of the classroom, lecture halls, etc. The technology emphasizes the teachers role, i.e., a blackboard, overhead projectors, large slide and film projectors, etc., and the classes are scheduled at the teacher's convenience.

The evaluation of the educator is essentially based on, *Does the presentation of the course content look and/or sound professional in nature (professional* usually referring to how the person doing the evaluating would have made the presentations) and *Was the educator able to cover the content of the course by the end of the given period of time* (six weeks, quarter, semester, year, etc.) It should be noted that in the past and even at the present time, almost all educators and students who are or have been involved in a practice teaching experience were and are being evaluated on the basis of their ability to present course content, i.e., did the practice teacher have good eye contact with the students, was he or she dressed neatly, did he or she use convergent questions or divergent questions, did he or she use positive or negative reinforcement, etc. Rarely are student teachers ever evaluated on the basis of whether or not the students they were teaching were able to learn what they were supposed to learn (objectives, if any, on the student teacher's teaching plan). During the past few years, many teacher training institutions in their attempts to at least appear modern and up-to-date have jumped on the *microteaching* bandwagon. Microteaching is a concept which typically involves the use of a television camera and a video tape recorder in a situation in which the student teacher or teacher makes a four to twenty minute presentation to a small class (usually from three to ten students). This presentation is recorded by the television equipment for later examination by the teacher or student as an individual, or in cooperation with a supervising professor, teacher, etc. Some variations of the microteaching concept may also include a television recording of the reactions of the students to the presentation of the teacher. The emphasis in *microteaching* as in student practice teaching is on the presentation of course content regardless of learning and the evaluation of the student or teacher in microteaching is generally the same as just described for the traditional practice teaching event. The only difference between regular practice teaching and the microteaching concept is that the student teacher or teacher's presentation is recorded. The recorded presentation may be very useful in helping the student or teacher *improve* their presentation, but if student learning was not measured, how is it possible to know whether or not the presentation was

131

improved. (I'm assuming that *improved* presentations should have direct or indirect effects on the learning of the students being taught.)

Although the originators of the concept, Dwight Allen and James Cooper, give evidence in their articles of their concern for giving the teacher or student teacher immediate *feedback on the teacher's effectiveness, teacher's effectiveness* in most microteaching projects is based on whether or not the student or teacher's manner of presentation was effective according to a list of criteria (regardless of learning). In fact, in a paper prepared by Allen and Cooper in February, 1970, they listed some areas of needed research and made these comments:

> We know we can train teachers to acquire certain teaching behaviors, but *we presently have very little information regarding how these behaviors affect students*. Perhaps the most fruitful approach (in microteaching) is training (the teacher) *to achieve a prespecified criterion level* (in the students being taught) rather than a set number of teaching (presenting) experiences.

It should be obvious from these comments that the emphasis in microteaching is on the *training of students or teachers in the role of the traditional teacher* who presents course content to classes of students on the assumption that all of the students are at the same place intellectually rather than an emphasis on the development of instructors who will be trying to maximize learning for each and every student. In a system which emphasizes individualized instruction, the concept of a *class* is obsolete because there has never been and never will be a *class* of students who are all the same intellectually and therefore the concept of microteaching (as presently practiced) is also obsolete. As pointed out at the beginning of Chapter IV the second basic function of schools is scholarship and this function concerns the teacher as a producer or presenter. In this role, microteaching might be of value, but it should not be confused with instruction (learning by design). From this point of view, it might be better to call it like it is *micro-presentations.*

The emphasis on this role is so ingrained, that if a teacher has developed a series of videotape recordings which present the major content of a course, when that teacher leaves the school, the new teacher that comes in to teach the course may utilize the videotapes for possibly one semester or at most a year and then, on the basis of remarks such as *The material is obsolete, It is presented from the wrong point of view*, etc., the videotaped materials will be discontinued. The major problem here is not the obsolescence of the material; the problem is that it is not the new teacher's face on the videotape or his or her voice on the audiotape. As a presenter of information, educators are unable to individualize instruction mainly because it is almost impossible to do it on a mass basis and the educators are so busy presenting

there isn't much time left over to individualize. In addition to the problems already mentioned, the following list point out other disadvantages which accompany the presenting role:
— lock-steps the learners' pace of learning to the teacher's pace of presenting which ignores individual differences among students;
— discourages cooperation among teachers;
— discourages the use of books or other media which could also present the course content;
— necessitates preparation time;
— discourages the building of learning spaces and encourages the building of teaching spaces (classrooms);
— limits course offerings because of the necessity of having at least some minimum number of students to present to;
— educators' teaching load usually determined by number of presentations regardless of the number of students;
— tends to motivate the older and maybe better educators to want to teach higher level and *odd* courses because the student enrollment is smaller with the same teaching load (hours of presentation);
— distracts teacher training institutions from training teachers for the more important role;
— emphasis on treatments (presenting course content) rather than on learning encourages the researcher role and discourages the practitioner role;
— creates negative attitudes towards school because the slower students become lost and the faster students get bored;
— encourages the padding of the course with irrelevant material or the deleting of important material in order to fit time schedules;
— as a result of the necessary repetition because not all students will learn the first time through a concept or course, the students who did learn the first time are bored;
— because of the necessary repetition of presenting for multiple classes or in even one class year after year, the role promotes boredom in the teacher;
— because of the last problem, a lot of time, energy, and educational dollars go into developing *new* courses, i.e., the new math, new biology, new chemistry, new linguistics, etc., so that the presenting role will be less boring for the teacher — not because the new courses will help more learners learn more; and
— in trying to make a presentation which is designed to both cover the course content and to motivate students to learn, the cumulative effect of all the aforementioned disadvantages on the students while listening to the course content part of the presentation may significantly affect that portion of the presentation which is supposed to motivate students.

This last disadvantage refers to the overlapping of the learning function of schools with the scholarship function. If these two functions are separated, such that the presenting role is used only in the scholarship function and while in the learning function the teacher performs the systems role to be described, almost all of these disadvantages associated with the presenting role disappear. Probably the most serious problem with a teacher performing the presenting role during the learning function is that the teacher is forced to ignore individual differences among the students. When a teacher is presenting course content: the student's rate of learning has to match the teacher's rate of presenting; the amount the students' learn is limited to the amount that the teacher presents; the mode the teacher decides to use in presenting the course content may be the only mode within which the students are supposed to learn; those factors in an interpersonal relationship which might affect learning are limited to the one teacher doing the presenting and although different students are motivated in different ways, the teacher is limited in the number of ways which can be used during a presentation.

Whenever schools have to close for one or more days and the days can't be made up, the most common comments heard from faculty concern the fact that they didn't have time to *cover* the course or certain parts of the course. Most students have had the experience of a teacher who discovered that he or she was about four or five chapters behind and only a few weeks left in the term. By the end of the term, the teacher had made it to the end of the course, but most of the students are struggling two or three chapters behind still trying to catch up to the teacher.

In an urban school during the early sixties, a 16-year old student in seventh grade stabbed his seventh grade mathematics teacher during class. During the hearing which followed the incident, the teacher was asked to describe the situation. In describing the class, the teacher pointed out that the whole class was on the lowest track in seventh grade mathematics and in his opinion the students didn't even belong in school and particularly in his class. When asked why, the teacher stated that most of the students didn't even know basic arithmetic because almost all of them failed his first test in September and had failed every single test up until mid-April when the stabbing took place. The teacher was then asked, *If you knew that the students didn't even know basic arithmetic, what did you teach?* He replied, *Why I taught seventh grade mathematics of course, I'm a seventh grade mathematics teacher!* Can you imagine sitting in a classroom listening to teachers presenting content six and seven hours a day, five days a week, 36 weeks a year, year after year and without a ghost of a chance to learn anything. It is surprising that the stabbing didn't take place sooner!

134

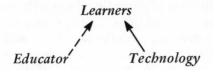

Learners

Educator   *Technology*

Figure 14 — Technology as a Substitute Presenter
of Course Content

With reference to the presenting role of the teacher, Figure 14 points out an almost obvious fact. Technology can also present course content. A wide variety of audiovisual equipment has been used to present course content, i.e., television, film, slides and audiotape, and audiotape by itself. Given that a teacher believes his or her role is to present course content, anything else that can also perform that role becomes competition. From this teacher's point-of-view, increasing the amount of technology in a school for the purpose of presenting course content is tantamount to a warning that the teacher will be replaced (fired) because there isn't any other role to perform.

A very important media for presenting course content which is often overlooked as being a part of technology are books. Many students and most faculty are familiar with teachers who resist the use of technology to present their courses. But not many students or teachers are aware of the fact that many teachers resist using books. These teachers are not resisting the physical format of the books. What they are resisting is the fact that the books might *teach* (present the course content). Stop and think back, did you ever have a teacher that presented in class what was already available in a book? Every student has had this experience. A teacher that presents what is available in a book is *resisting the book.* In my seminars, I have met a number of teachers who are so afraid of books that they don't even have texts for their courses, they claim that there aren't any books written that cover their subjects!

NOTE: A very interesting learner behavior is revealed when students are exposed to a teacher who presents course content which is duplicated in their textbooks. They either listen to the teacher and don't read the textbook or they read the textbook and don't listen to the teacher. Rarely will a student pay attention to both presentations — the teacher and the book. This is because in many ways, the human being is a model of conservation of energy. Why waste the energy to pay attention to the teacher *and* the book. Given this situation, an obvious way for teachers to get more time to individualize instruction is to let the students get the presentation from the book. The teacher is then free to work with those students who couldn't learn from the book.

135

A very common form of educational research concerns the comparison of a particular mode of presentation versus the live teacher doing the presenting. Television, audiotapes, slides and audiotapes, films, programmed instruction, computers, and books have been placed in competition with teachers. A vast majority of this type of comparative research has ended up with no significant differences. Because the concern is with the presenting role, this type of research can also be looked on as comparing two situations; on in which the teacher is important and earning money and the other in which the teacher isn't involved and probably out of work. If there is no significant difference in most of the research between the use of technology in the presenting role or the teacher in the presenting role, why not let the technology do it and replace (change the role of) the teacher.

NOTE: A teacher has given a test on Friday and as usual only a few of the students made 100 percent. During the following week, instead of the teacher presenting the course content for the week, this teacher uses technology to take over the presenting role and uses the release time to work with individual students who didn't make 100 percent on last week's test. Given this situation, it would be impossible not to increase learning and make a difference.

C. THE HUMANIZING ROLE FOR THE TEACHER: AN INSTRUCTIONEER

In order for teachers to *make a difference*, the teacher has to do something in the instructional event that shows results which are different than what would happen by chance. Under the traditional role, when the teacher is presenting course content and lets learning take place according to the varying capacities (supposed limits) of the students, the achievement profile (grades) for a class of 30 students might look like Figure 15.

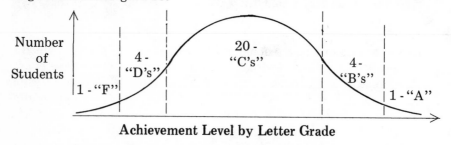

Achievement Level by Letter Grade

Figure 15 — Letter Grades Assigned on the Basis of
the Normal Probability Curve

Given the philosophy that all students can learn, and that the

136

varying capacities are actually varying abilities rather than limits, then an obvious way to make a difference would be to help the students who are not achieving an "A" to increase their achievement level. To do this, it would be necessary to identify why the student isn't able to learn and then try to solve it. By letting technology present the course content (since it doesn't make any difference), the teacher can use the release time to perform this role of identifying and solving learning problems. Since the lower the achievement level of the student, the greater the cumulative ignorance and more learning problems the student will have later on, the order of priority would be:

— to eliminate the "F" student(s) by identifying and solving enough learning problems to raise the student(s) to at least the "D" level;
— to eliminate the "D" students by identifying and solving enough learning problems to raise the students to at least the "C" level;
— to eliminate the "C" students by identifying and solving enough learning problems to raise the students to at least the "B" level; and if enough time
— to eliminate the "B" students by identifying and solving the balance of the learning problems so that all of the students are "A" students.

As pointed out in my book *Educational Malpractices,* if the grades given to a class of students approximate a normal curve of achievement, this means that the teacher is primarily a presenter of course content and is allowing learning to take place by chance and/or has purposely designed the tests to result in a normal curve distribution regardless of what the students have learned. If the grades in a class are all "A's" or all "A'S" and "B's" and the teachers can prove that the students were able to achieve all or almost all of the objectives of the course, this means that the teacher is primarily identifying and solving learning problems,[1] and is able to make a difference.

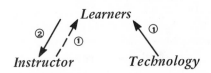

Figure 16 — The Instructor in the Role (2) of Identifying
and Solving Learning Problems and Technology
is Presenting the Course Content (1)

---

[1] Some teachers may give all "A's" and "B's" because they want to be a *good person.* These teachers usually do not have specific objectives for their courses and can't prove that the students have learned all or almost all of the course objectives.

Given a comparative research project in which television by itself would be compared to television plus tthe teacher, where the teacher's role is to help those students solve their learning problems and learn all of the objectives in the presentation made via the television, significant differences in favor of the teacher and television working in concert would result in every case. Of interest, is that a teacher who thinks his or her role is to present course content and a teacher who wants the technology to present the course content in order to be released to help identify and solve students learning problems on an individual basis can look at the same research which results in no significant differences between the teacher and technology and claim that it justifies his or her role.

The Presenting Role: If there is no difference in student learning, why buy all that expensive technology? Let me do the presenting.

The Identifying and Solving of Learning Problems Role: If there is no difference in student learning, let the technology do the presenting and let me work with the individual students.[2]

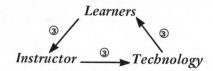

Figure 17 — The Instructor in the Role of Diagnosing Learning Problems and Prescribing Instructional Modules Via Technology

Another very important aspect of this role can be described as a teacher who is *diagnosing learning problems and prescribing instructional modules that will solve these problems* (see Figure 17). After teachers have solved enough learning problems, they will find that many learning problems are quite similar and that it will be useful and beneficial for both the learner and the teacher to develop *instructional modules* which are designed to solve particular learning problems. In that way, after a teacher has diagnosed the learner's problem it would be much more efficient to let the student go off on his own and learn on an independent basis from an *instructional module.* These *instructional modules* could be just a few pages or a chapter in a textbook, or it

---

[2] In a recent monograph of The Association for Supervision and Curriculum Development (ASCD), it was estimated that 85 percent of elementary and secondary teachers teach from textbooks. Just think of all the potential release time available to teachers so that they could help individualize instruction by identifying and solving students' learning problems instead of repeating what is in the book.

could be a special mimeographed handout, it could include audio tapes, or it could include slides or film strips or three-dimensional materials — whatever is necessary to solve the learning problem. For example, in tenth grade, all educators know that students have varying reading levels which range from fourth or fifth grade up to college level. If the teacher diagnoses the learner's problem as a reading problem and the learner is trying to learn from a textbook written at the tenth-grade level or higher, then the *instructional module* could be a textbook written at a lower reading level and possibly, if appropriate, the material might be written in a book from a different point of view, still covering the same learning objectives, but possibly in a more pictorial fashion or a more practical fashion. The *instructional module* could also be an audio or video tape recording which has been designed purposely for students with low level reading abilities.

If our instructional systems across the country were able to come to some kind of a common agreement as to the MINIMUM content of courses, then any *instructional module* that was successful in one school could be made available so that all learners throughout the country would learn at least the minimum core content of each course and release the teacher to be concerned about those students who may not be able to learn the mimimum content from available materials, and also for developing additional curricula to reflect local interests and desires. There is no logical reason why each teacher in each school has to independently identify and solve the same learning problems over and over.

As teachers begin to perform this humanizing role of diagnosing, prescribing and solving learning problems, it will change the teaching role from one that is labor-intensive and can be likened to primitive *cottage-type industry* into a much more professional role. In the definition of a *profession*, (see p. 7) there are three primary characteristics that identify a field as a profession:

1. has to have a specialized knowledge;
2. has to have high standards of achievement and conduct; and
3. has to have for its prime purpose the rendering of a public service.

Under the traditional role, millions of students annually are failed and graded down (the "C" and "D" students) and many of these students drop out and become a burden on society through unemployment, welfare, rehabilitation institutions, or simply as agitators in that they haven't learned how to get along with their fellow man. Obviously, this role doesn't represent *a public service* or *high standards of achievement and conduct.* As pointed out before, whether or not a teacher has had any of the traditional education courses doesn't appear to change their behavior in the classroom or the results of what happens in the classroom, so what is being taught in these courses must not represent *a*

139

specialized knowledge.

Under the systems role, where the goal is to help each individual student maximize his or her success by solving their learning problems, it is obvious that the *prime purpose (of the role) is the rendering of a public service with high standards of achievement and conduct* for both teacher and student. In order that the teachers can perform this role and *make a difference*, it is also necessary that they develop *a specialized knowledge.*

Because these two roles are so completely different, it would be convenient and almost necessary in order to avoid misunderstanding, to have a title for the humanizing role which differentiates it from the traditional role while at the same time communicates some of the characteristics of the teacher's role in the behavioral learning systems concept. In Chapters I and II of this book, I emphasized the differences between education and instruction and as a result, there is a great temptation to use the titles educator and instructor to identify the two different roles. I can accept the title *educator* for the traditional role because it has been used for decades and it does describe what occurs under the traditional role (see definition of education, educate, and educated on p. 6). The problem with the title instructor is that it has been used interchangeably with educator and for a long time has been used in higher education as a title for a low academic rank. During World War II when the man-machine systems concept really started, another field also started as a part of the systems concept. Since engineers generally were concerned with the *machine* part of the systems concept, there was a need for a field to concentrate on the other half or the human side of the systems concept. As this field developed, it eventually was referred to as *human engineering.* Since the emphasis of this book is on a *learning system*, it seemed logical to refer to the systems role as a *learning engineer.* Although they didn't use this title, Carpenter and Haddan in their book *Systematic Application of Psychology to Education* stated that the aim in schools should be to give control of the learning event to the teachers and learners such that:

> Emphasis is on *deliberate control* rather than on caprice, chance, or accident. The assumption is that human learning can be *engineered* in the sense that conditions can be realized that will produce maximum efficiency when compared with the less controlled means.

The problems with using the title *learning engineer* is that it tends to communicate the concept of the manipulation of learning. Since learning is the natural event and only the learner can learn, what is actually happening is the design and manipulation of the instructional event *to bring about* the desired learning. Therefore, the most appropriate and descriptive title is *instructional engineer.* A slight problem still

140

exists in that since *educator, teacher,* and *instructor* are only one-word titles and the human being is a model of conservation of energy, chances are that a two-word title would not catch on and be used to any great extent. In combining the two words into the one word, *INSTRUCTIONEER*, nothing seems to be lost and so I will use this title to refer to the humanizing role as described in this book. Under the early systems concept, the *human engineer* helped design machines keeping in mind the limitations, abilities, and comfort of the human being and then developed training programs for people so that they would be able to operate the machines when the machines were completed. The pervasive emphasis was on the development of an efficient and effective machine. In contrast, under the behavioral learning systems concept, the Instructioneer will help design learning environments keeping in mind the limitations and abilities of various forms of technology, methods, and vehicles in facilitating learning. The pervasive emphasis is on the development of a humane, effective, and efficient instructional situation. To support the use of the engineering concept in the title, examine the following statements found in Webster's Dictionary to describe an *engineer:*

1. a person who designs, invents, or contrives;
2. a person who carries through an enterprise or bings about a result, expecially by skillful or artful contrivance;
3. a person who is trained or skilled in the technicalities (not usually in the scope of engineering) who is engaged in using such training or skill in the solution of technical problems.
4. to act as an engineer in the laying out, construction, or management; and
5. to design or produce by the methods of engineering.

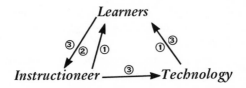

Figure 18 — The Instructioneer in the role of identifying and solving learning problems (2), and managing the instructional event through diagnosis and prescription (3). Technology is used to present the content of courses (1) and prescribed instructional modules (3).

The definitions of an *Instructioneer* are: (see Figure 18)
1. a person who identifies, diagnoses, and/or solves learning problems;

141

2. A person who designs and produces instructional modules which solve identified learning problems;
3. a person who manages instructional modules for identified or diagnosed learning problems;
4. a person who as a humanist brings about maximum achievement for each student in all prescribed and desired (by the student) instructional situations; and believes that all students can learn;
5. a person who develops in each student the ability to be an independent learner for continued self-instruction and self-learning; and
6. a person who is trained or skilled in the techniques and methods necessary to achieve one or more of the above five functions.

If this role makes as much sense to the reader as it has to me and the tens of thousands of teachers who have attended my seminars on the *Changing Role of the Teacher*, the question in your mind would be, *How come this role hasn't been identified before?* Part of the role has been identified before. In fact, the concept of the teacher's role as being one that diagnoses and prescribes has been around for decades. Conferences and conventions have been devoted to this aspect of the role. During the past decade, the concept of the Instructional Materials Center (IMC), the Learning Resource Center (LRC), and other similar centers have been incorporated into many schools at all levels of education on the basis that teachers would utilize the wide variety of materials for prescriptive purposes. At various times in one or more of the traditional education courses, the teachers *lectured* about the role of the teacher as one that diagnoses and prescribes.

If all this has occurred, why don't teachers actually perform this role? Consider the following situation:

You have just completed studying to be a medical doctor and in your pervious life and all through your medical training you have never heard of the word *measles*, have never seen or heard about anyone having measles, have never heard about the symptoms of measles, and have never heard about how to treat or prescribe for measles. During your first week as a doctor a patient comes into your office with measles. Would you be able to diagnose the problem as *measles?* Would you be able to prescribe appropriately for it?

Of course, the answer to both questions is *No* because one cannot diagnose a problem until *someone has identified the problem as a problem* and one cannot prescribe an appropriate solution for a problem until *someone has successfully solved the problem.* In other words, the function of identification and solving the learning problems is a necessary prerequisite to the function of diagnosis and prescription. Until such time as learning problems have been identified and solved, the role of the teacher as a diagnostician and prescriber of meaningful learning experiences will have to remain as it is — a role that is talked about but rarely performed.

A side effect of the inability of teachers to perform the diagnosis and prescriptive role, is that many of the instructional materials and learning resource centers become an expensive, frustrating and wasteful drain of educational dollars and energy. Since accrediting agencies and professional organizations which deal with these centers have not identified and/or solved learning problems either, the emphasis in accrediting and in guidelines for setting up the centers is on quantities of materials, i.e., so many books per student, so many film strips per 100 students, etc. As a result, these centers are typically filled with *solutions* to problems no one has identified and if used, the *solutions* are picked more by caprice than by design. Tragically, if some teacher in a school with one of these centers identifies an actual learning problem, there usually isn't any money left to develop a solution to the *real* problem because it has all been spent on solutions to imaginary problems. I have recommended for years that if a school wants to have one of these centers, open it up with almost empty shelves and the money in a special account. Then, as teachers identify real learning problems, there is money available to develop and mass produce (if appropriate) the solutions. In this way, the shelves of the center would be stocked with solutions to identified learning problems — which would be needed and used by teachers and students!

At the present time, there are not enough diagnostic tests or instructional modules available which are related to real learning problems which could be prescribed to make the performance of this function a viable one. This does not mean that this function of the instructioneer's role cannot be performed to varying degrees. As teachers identify specifically what it is they want students to learn in their courses, and as they develop test items to test, *Did the students achieve the behavior that they were supposed to learn?*, and these objectives and tests are shared with other teachers, then these objectives and test items can be used in the performance of the diagnostic function concerned with identifying learning problems (non-achievement). Because these objectives and test items have been shared, common learning problems will be identified and as these problems are solved[3],

---

[3] As a rule of thumb, any learning problem that takes over five minutes of the teachers time in working with the student in order to solve it and the same problem is encountered by over five students in any one class, the teacher should take time and develop the solution in a package, tape, or whatever so that other students can solve the problem independently once the teacher has diagnosed that the student has the problem.

common solutions will be identified, not only in a single classroom, but in school buildings, in school districts, in states, regions, and even nationally, so that rather quickly, a large number of *instructional modules* can be developed and utilized effectively to help learners learn.

Given that the function of identifying and solving learning problems is a necessary prerequisite to perform the function of diagnosing and prescribing, why haven't learning problems been identified and solved before and why isn't this function being performed now?

A critical prerequisite in the instructional event, in order for the instructor to perform this role, is to know specifically what it is that a student or students are supposed to be learning. Without specific objectives, it would be extremely difficult, if not impossible, to identify a learning problem and without identified learning problems, it would be extremely difficult, if not impossible, to develop solutions. As a result of these critical relationships between specific objectives, learning problems, and solutions, very few teachers are able to perform this role to any great extent because not very many teachers work with lists of specific measurable course and/or unit objectives. In addition to this limiting factor, at the present time very few educators know a learning problem when they see one. We have become accustomed by tradition to assume that certain students cannot learn and that to get a variation in learning achievement is to be expected, and in fact variation in learning achievement is often designed into the learning situation.

In order to have a better understanding of what a learning problem is and how they are solved, I will discuss the following aspects of this function of the instructioneer:

1. What is a Learning Problem?
2. Examples of Learning Problems.
3. Ignoring Individual Differences as a Learning Problem.
4. Humanizing Instruction through the Solving of Learning Problems.
5. The Changeover from Educator to Instructioneer.

1. WHAT IS A LEARNING PROBLEM

A learning problem exists whenever a student is unable to learn one or more of the instructional objectives of an instructional unit or course. In my experience of helping thousands of teachers identify and solve learning problems, about 50 percent of the problems can be solved when the educator defines specifically what behavior he or she wants the students to learn and communicates this to the students. Another 25 percent of the learning problems can be solved by developing tests which are appropriate for the specific objectives in the instructional situation. And the final 25 percent can be solved by changes in the instructional materials that are used in the instructional situation.

Because the symptoms of a learning problem have been considered normal under the traditional approach to education, most learning problems have been with us for a long time. For example, the following situations are considered normal but in fact these situations indicate learning problems which may be solved such that the desired learning objectives can be achieved by at least 90% or more of the students:

— students who are achieving only "C", "D", or "F" worth of a course (specifically when even the normally "A" and "B" students are only able to achieve "C", "D", or "F" worth of a course or of a particular unit of a course);
— test items in which one or more students are unable to produce the appropriate response (particularly when all of the students are unable to answer one or more of the test items in a given test);
— students whose existing behaviors are in conflict with the learning objectives of a course or a unit of a course;
— student comments such as *I don't understand the course (book, assignment, problem, principle, theory, etc.), What am I supposed to study for the test?, I don't think this course has anything to do with the real world*, etc.; and
— teacher comments such as *These students belong in a lower or remedial class, Some students just don't have the innate ability to learn, I can't understand why my students are unable to learn this content (unit, experiment, objective, text, etc), Some of my students are just not motivated to learn*, etc.

Once the symptoms of a learning problem are identified, the instructioneer should remember that the actual problem could be in any one of the five elements in the instructional event and the solution of the problem may involve one or more of these elements.

a. POTENTIAL PROBLEMS WITH OBJECTIVES:

The instructional objectives are not specific and measurable and/or may not be viewed as relevant by the learner. They may also be teacher or activity objectives instead of learning objectives and/ or possible inadequate analysis of instructional unit or course.

b. POTENTIAL PROBLEMS WITH EVALUATION:

The evaluation instruments may not correlate with the course or unit learning objectives. There may be a lack of appropriate tests to discover whether or not a students' cumulative ignorance will affect success in the course or unit — entry behaviors. Tests may not be given often enough to identify the development of cumulative ignorance before it interferes with learning.

c. POTENTIAL PROBLEMS IN THE LEARNING ENVIRONMENT

Lack of building in forward and backward branching in the method to accommodate individual differences in students entry behaviors — some already know part of the unit or course and should be skipped ahead and some are not ready for the course and need prerequisite learning and should be branched back to pick up the necessary learning. Lack of alternate modes of learning to accommodate individual differences. Lack of trying out materials on a sample of learners before using them for large groups. Lack of differentiating between learning objectives, learning vehicles, and learning methods and the lack of identification or awareness of attitudes and values being developed or diminished by the vehicles and methods used in the Learning Environment.

d. POTENTIAL PROBLEMS CAUSED BY THE INSTRUCTOR:

Not committed to or hasn't accepted the philosophy that all students can learn and/or that individual differences in learning exist and as such, the instructor doesn't try hard enough to solve identified learning problems. The instructor finds it too difficult to give up the traditional role in instructional activities completely and as such lock-steps learning and uses up time which could have been used to identify and solve learning problems. The instructor finds it difficult to allow students to learn on their own and as such, limits the progress of students and the number of students the instructor can work with. The instructor is not willing to accept diagnostic tools, prescriptive instructional modules, and/or course presentations (by technology) which have been prepared by other instructors, curriculum specialists, or publishing companies and as such wants to make all his or her own materials which limits the time available for identifying and solving learning problems. Lack of honesty with students in the evaluation of affective domain objectives as indicated by instructor blaming students for not having right attitudes and values instead of recognizing that the teacher's design of the learning environment is at fault.

e. POTENTIAL PROBLEMS CAUSED BY THE LEARNER:

Lack of communicating special interest areas such that the instructioneer can prescribe a more interesting vehicle, if available, for learning the course or unit objectives. Lack of honesty in reacting to affective domain evaluation instruments so the instructioneer can make changes in the design of the learning environment. Lack of communicating true basis of learning problems so that the instructioneer can perform his or her role. Even though the instructioneer can solve all of the learning and motivational problems, the student still has to put forth effort. [4]

2. EXAMPLES OF LEARNING PROBLEMS

During the past decade, I have worked with thousands of teachers in the identification and solving of learning problems in all subject matter areas and at all levels of education from preschool to graduate level. Sometimes, the problems are very difficult to identify and also difficult to solve. Sometimes, identifying the problem is difficult but the solution is easy and at other times, identifying the problem is easy but the solution is difficult and complex. Then there are the learning problems which are easy to identify and also easy to solve. These are typically learning problems which have been created by various traditions within the traditional approach to education. The following examples of learning problems are problems which can be found at almost all levels in education and in most subject matter areas. I will describe some learning problems in specific areas at several points in the rest of this chapter to demonstrate a point and in Chapter VII, I will describe more learning problems in specific areas as I identify the implications of the behavioral learning systems approach to instruction when applied to a number of different subject matter areas.

a. WHAT AM I SUPPOSED TO LEARN?

From the students point-of-view, the greatest learning problem at the present time is, *What am I supposed to learn?* Although most or maybe even all teachers will communicate to their students what the assignments are for studying, only a relatively few teachers actually specify for the students what they are supposed to learn in the assignment. Most people as students have been in a classroom in which they have said to themselves or to fellow students, *If the teacher would only tell me what I am supposed to learn, I would learn it!* or if you haven't said that, I'm sure that you like every other student has at one time raised your hand and asked your teacher, *What should we study for the test?* The answer given by most teachers is, *Everything we've studied so far!* or some other similar ambiguous, vague answer. In fact, under the traditional approach to education, it is considered dishonest if students find out what they are supposed to learn for a test. At most schools, if a student is caught with a copy of the test (without answers) before it is

---

[4] If a teacher has only tried one or two methods of learning, one or two vehicles for learning, and used limited, if any, diagnostic tools to identify if cumulative ignorance is interferring with learning and the teacher claims the fault is with the student because he or she hasn't put forth enough effort, this is not a problem of the learner. It is a teacher problem. If an instructioneer has tried at least three or four methods of learning, five or six different vehicles for learning, and sufficient diagnostic tests to insure that the learning event starts where the learner actually is intellectually, then it may be the learners' fault for not putting forth enough effort.

given out to the whole class, the student would be disciplined in some way. After all, the student might learn everything on the test! Isn't it sad that under the traditional approach to education it is considered wrong to have a chance at being successful! The best solution to this problem is to hand out to the students at the beginning of the course or unit a list of all of the specific objectives to be learned in that course or unit. If the teachers don't have the specific objectives for their courses, but they do give unit and/or course final examinations, then start the course or unit out by handing out copies of the final examination to the students. Most traditional teachers would reject this suggestion for one or more of the following four reasons:

(1) *If the students have the test ahead of time, the student will study only those things that are on the test.*

If this is true, then anything else a teacher thinks the students might overlook or choose not to study should be added to the test. The real problem is that rarely are tests actually designed to completely test what should have been learned during the course or unit. Most tests are designed to fit a time period, i.e., ten minute quiz, one or two hour examinations, etc.

(2) *It isn't possible to test everything that should be learned in a unit or course, so I just sample the test items.*

This reason sounds scientific, but teachers are not scientifically *sampling* because:

(a) In order to scientifically *sample*, it is necessary to have identified the total population of test items from which the teacher is sampling and it is relatively rare that a teacher has actually identified the total population of test items.

(b) In order to scientifically *sample*, the teacher has to assume that all of the test items are of equal importance and it is impossible to have a total population of test items for a unit or course in which all of the test items are equal.

(c) In order to scientifically *sample*, the teacher would use a table of random numbers in selecting the test items from the total population of test items and it would be rare to find a teacher who actually selects his or her test items in this manner.

Instead of scientifically sampling, teachers typically in reviewing their notes, materials, and textbook(s), select (by guessing) which items to include in the test. Under traditional guidelines, the teacher will try to pick some easy ones to encourage the students, some difficult ones that will separate the *men from the boys*, and the rest of the items of varying degrees of difficulty between the two extremes. This traditional technique will guarantee test results which fit a curve even though the test items may or may not represent what is important in the unit or course.

148

NOTE: While the teacher is in his or her office or home guessing which test items to pick for the test, the students are home trying to guess which test items the teacher will pick. Almost every student has had the experience of studying very hard for a test and when the student took the test, the student discovered that he or she had studied the wrong things. As a result of this guessing game, instead of grades indicating students' achievement levels, the grades tend to indicate the correlation between the teacher's guess as to which items should be on the test and the student's guess as to which items would be on the test!

(3) *How could I give the students a copy of the final test at the beginning of the unit or course, I don't even know what is on the final test myself until shortly before the end of the unit or course.*

This reason is not often stated as a reason for not giving the students a copy of the final examination at the beginning of a unit or course, but in actuality, unless a teacher uses a commercially prepared examination, this reason describes the situation for a majority of teachers. Teachers who might want to give this reason, are often afraid of the implications accompanying the statement. First, the statement tends to indicate that the teacher doesn't know what it is the students are supposed to be learning. Second, it is much easier to select test items towards the end of the course which will help the students' scores on the final test approximate a normal curve than if the test items are selected at the beginning of the course. Third, if traditional teachers had copies of their final examinations at the beginning of their courses, they would be afraid that they might be accused of *teaching to the test.* Psychologists, psychometrists, and standardized test companies have convinced several generations of teachers that it is wrong to teach to the test because if all or most of the students learn what is on the test, the results of the test won't approximate a normal curve and hence the tests would be considered invalid. Assuming that what is being tested in a test is important, there is nothing wrong with teaching students what is important (the test). If what is on a test is important, but the teachers are not supposed to teach the important things that are on the tests and yet the test is going to be used to evaluate the achievement of the students, then obviously, any achievement indicated by the tests must be a result of self-learning away from teachers. As mentioned before, during the past several years, several research studies have indicated that neither teachers nor schools seem to have made any difference in the achievements of their students. These results shouldn't be surprising, after all, the teachers weren't supposed to teach what was on the tests used in the research!!!

(4) *I use objective type test items (multiple-choice, true-false, and if I gave these tests to the students at the beginning of the unit or course, the students would memorize the patterns of the answers rather than the concepts involved.*

This is the only reason that is acceptable for not giving the tests to the students at the beginning of the unit or course. In turn, however, this raises the question of why do educators use objective type test items in the first place? I am going to ask you to turn to another page in the book and have you briefly took at the phrases within the two triangles and then turn back to this page — only look at the other page for two or three seconds — no more. Turn to page 154.

Now that you are back to this page again, read the footnote at the bottom of this page.[5] A very critical part in the development of objective type test items is the use of distractors which are words or phrases which distract the students from getting the right answer or from selecting a wrong answer and are based on the concept again, of *selective perception.* Although the objective type test item is called objective from the point-of-view of scoring (Given choice "c" is the right answer, did the student pick choice "c"?), *the writing of the objective type test items is extremely subjective.* A professional test item writer can take almost any so-called objective type test item and by holding the stem of the question and the correct choice constant and varying the distractors in the wrong choices (putting in more or taking out some in order to increase or decrease the distraction), the writer can get almost any percentage of students he or she wants to get the item right or to make a mistake — regardless of whether or not the students know the concept involved. This is why most psychologists, psychometrists, standardized test makers, and teachers like objective type test items, besides the fact that they are easy to score, it is relatively easy to design test items such that the results of using the tests will approximate a normal curve (or any other desired learning curve). Therefore, any teacher who uses the so-called objective type tests is involved in deceiving and tricking their students either consciously or unconsciously (see Chapter VI,

---

[5] Did you see *Once In a Lifetime* in one of the triangles and *Paris in the Spring* in the other triangle? If you did, you are like almost everyone else who sees these triangles for the first time. Turn back to page 154 again and check. In one triangle you should see, *Once in a a lifetime,* and in the other triangle, *Paris in the the spring.* There are 2 *a's* and 2 *the's.* This very common psychological phenomenon represents a principle referred to as *selective perception.* What this means is that people see what they want to see and hear what they want to hear. They do not always see and hear what is actually there.

Volume II for a more detailed discussion of the faults in using objective type tests).

For those readers who are teaching (even practice teaching) and would like to prove to themselves that letting students know what they are supposed to learn at the beginning of a learning event will significantly increase the achievement levels over a situation in which the students don't know what they are supposed to learn, here is a simple experiment you can conduct. Hundreds of teachers have tried it and it works everytime. The next time you plan on showing a film, preview the film and decide what it is you want the students to learn from it. Then in class, split the class randomly into two groups and just before you show the film pass out to one of the groups a list of objectives of what they should learn from the film and at the top of the list put a statement telling the students that at the end of the movie they will be tested on their achievement of the following objectives. Pass out to the other group a similar page with information about some other activity. Give them a few minutes to study the handout and then show the film. After the film, give a test that tests for the achievement of the objectives. You will find that those students who know what they are supposed to learn will learn more than those students who didn't know what they were supposed to learn! The fact that they will have a test will also motivate the one group to learn more than in the usual situation where tests are not given right after showing a film.

b. DECISION-MAKING AS A LEARNING PROBLEM

A number of teachers in trying to defend the use of multiple-choice questions stress their similarity to a critical learning problem found in all subject and occupational areas, decision-making. Multiple-choice questions and decision-making do have in common the concept of making a choice from among alternate choices; but that is where similarity stops.

— The choices in the multiple-choice question are selected by the teacher. In decision-making, the person making the decision has to identify the alternate choices.

— In a multiple-choice test, almost all of the questions have the same number of alternatives. In decision-making, rarely will two or more decisions have the same number of alternate choices.

— In the multiple-choice test, the teacher puts in distractors in the alternate choices to make the choice more difficult. In decision making, the decision-maker tries to clarify each alternative to make the decision easier.

— In most multiple-choice tests, there is a correct answer. In decision-making, the defense of the choice in a given set of circumstances, makes the choice correct.

— One of the best ways to study for a multiple-choice test is to *psych-out* the teacher or maker of the test and have a good memory. The best way to study for decision-making is to bring together all pertinent materials and practice going through each step of the decision-making process.

— In multiple-choice tests, there is only the one step — make the choice. In decision-making, there are six steps and the making of a choice is the least important step of the six.

Of the six steps in decision-making, some claim that the most important step is the first step.

(1) *To be able to identify that there is a problem to be solved which has two or more possible solutions.*

If one can assume that the problem has been identified for the student, then the second step may become the most important step.

(2) *To be able to identify and specify the parameters involved in the solutions to the problem and the limits within which a solution might be called reasonable.*

If one can assume that the first two steps have been given to the student, then steps three and four become the next important steps.

(3) *To be able to identify and specify all of the possible and reasonable alternative solutions.*

(4) *To be able to identify and specify the consequences of each of the possible and reasonable alternative solutions.*

The fifth step is the least important step because if given the same decision to be made but with one or more different parameters in the solution and/or different limits within which a solution might be called reasonable, almost any of the alternative solutions could be considered the best solution.

(5) *Select a solution.*

In multiple-choice tests, when the selection of a choice is made, the simulated decision-making is completed. In learning the actual process of decision making, after the choice is made based on an examination of the information derived in the second, third, and fourth steps, the student has yet another step.

(6) *To verify or defend the choice based on the parameter limits and the consequences of all the alternative solutions. In other words, describe in writing the mental processes that the student went through which led the student to make the choice he or she made.*

If a teacher wanted to use multiple-choice questions as a first step in teaching decision-making, it would be acceptable under the following conditions:

— that the choices included all reasonable choices whether it be two, three, four, five, six, or more;

— that unreasonable choices are not included to distract the stu-

dent;
- that after each question, there is a space within which the student has to defend his choice (step six in decision-making);
- that if a student selects the *correct* choice but is unable to defend the choice, then and answer is considered incomplete;
- that if a student selects a choice other than the *correct* choice and is able to defend that choice, then the answer should be accepted as correct;
- that the answers are not scored by a paper key, or machine which is only able to identify the letter or number used to indicate the choice selected by the student; and
- that part of the designed learning sequence in the course involves the student in all six steps of the decision-making process in related problems.

Decision-making as a behavior is a very critical behavior in contemporary society and as the rate of change in our society continues to increase and as more and more decisions have to be made in our daily lives, it becomes more and more important that students learn all of the steps in decision-making. In the so-called *good old days* when people were raised, they worked, and they died all within about ten miles of where they were born, there were very few new people to meet, very few changes occurring, and very few decisions to make. In that kind of environment, it was not so critical to learn decision-making by design and the crippling effect resulting from the use of multiple-choice questions in which the learner only learns one of the steps (and the least important one at that) in decision making was not so serious. But our contemporary society today is *not* the *good old days* where decisions to be made are few and far between. As Alvin Toffler in *Future Shock* describes our society, he points out that many of our young people and people who represent the far right and the far left are retreating from the avalanche of decisions which have to be made as a result of the many changes occurring in our society and the numerous options available at almost every decision point.

As the rate of change increases, as more and more options become available, and as more and more information is produced, the need for critical thinking and the learned ability to make decisions becomes more urgent. In the not too distant future, the very existence of some of the elements of our society and possibly even our total society may depend on the members being able to make intelligent defensible decisions. This does not mean selecting one or more choices from amongst four, five, or more rigged choices in a multiple-choice test in which the emphasis from the learner's point-of-view is to *out-psych* the teacher or the author of the test (select the best answer — according to the teacher or author of the test); but it does mean to be able to go

153

through each step in the decision-making process in many different aspects of our social, vocational, and private lives. The inability of an individual to make decisions in our society is tantamount to being a prisoner in the midst of freedom wherein each unmade decision or undefensible decision becomes another barrier in the cell of limited freedoms. This inability to make decisions is even more dangerous when it concerns professional occupations (doctors, dentists, nurses, etc.) because the decisions or lack of decisions affect other people and their physical and mental health. For this reason, it is even more imperative that the use of multiple-choice, true-false, and matching test items in the professional fields be discontinued and replaced with *real world* decision-making. As an example, in order to obtain a pilot's license, pilots have to pass a FAA (Federal Aviation Administration) multiple-choice examination. Since in the *real world*, no pilot, in facing a flying problem in the air, ever found a multiple-choice problem on the windshield helping him to *out-psych* the plane, FAA Examiners in the simulator cockpits set up a problem and the pilot has to make complete decisions and defend them. Sad to admit, even though most of the people involved in the professional testing programs (students and teachers) will agree that the so-called objective tests are very irrelevant, the tests continue to be used because until such time as the professional groups decide what is really important to learn in their field (not known at present), almost anything is better than nothing.

Figure 19

c. CHEATING AS A SYMPTOM OF A LEARNING PROBLEM

Under the traditional approach to education where the tests and what is on the tests are kept hidden from students until the *moment of truth* when the students take the tests, cheating is looked on as a form of dishonesty perpetrated by the student and deserving of a variety of punishments from a simple reprimand, to a "F" on the test, to a humiliating verbal chastisement in front of the class, to being suspended from school for a brief period of time, or to the extremes of the U.S. military academies where students caught cheating are dropped permanently from the school and their names given out to be published in national newspapers in order to bring about maximum degradation.

If a student has to cheat in order to find out what he or she is supposed to learn, it is the fault of the teacher who is hiding the

154

objectives and/or tests from the student. Under the behavioral learning systems approach to instruction, there is no need to cheat, the students know what it is they have to learn. They also know that if they miss out on the first test, they will have other chances to retake the test. The first test is not a do or die situation. In fact, many teachers that I have worked with in secondary and higher education, knowing that by the time many of the students get to them they have already developed a tendency to cheat, take advantage of this behavior. They tell their students that they can bring an 8½" by 11" sheet of paper to the final or unit examinations with anything and everything that they can squeeze on to the one page. By the time the students condense the whole course or even a unit to one page, they have probably studied harder than ever before because they thought they were getting away with something. There is nothing wrong with letting students have crib notes or even textbooks, charts, graphs, etc., during an examination as long as the test is composed of *thinking questions.* It is very difficult to obtain answers to thinking questions from any source except the mind of the individual students. On the other hand, if the test contains some rote memory test items, then these should be handled separately and should be called rote memory items. Almost every course and even many units contain some critical objectives which are pure rote memory. The mistake of the teacher is in hiding these items from the students and trying to ignore the fact that they are rote memory. If handled separately, the rote memory part of the test would be given to the student first. If there are, for example, 20 rote memory items on the test and a student only gets 18 right, tell the student to go out in the hall or wherever he or she learns best and practice memorizing some more. The student shouldn't be allowed to go on to the second part of the test, the thinking or application part, until he or she has learned 100 percent of the necessary rote memory items. There is nothing wrong with rote memory learning as long as the student does something with whatever has been memorized. If the teacher can't think of an application for the rote memory material, then maybe the student shouldn't have been asked to learn it in the first place. The tragedy of rote memory is in the packing of the mind with rote memorized information which has no utility or application. With reference to the use of various reference sources during the *thinking* portion of an examination, remember, that in the real world, few people rely on their memory when making important decisions.

d. CUMULATIVE IGNORANCE AS A LEARNING PROBLEM

In most courses and in most units of courses, successful learning of the course or unit objectives is dependent upon the students having learned certain prerequisite objectives in previous units or courses. If the student hasn't learned these necessary prerequisite objectives, he or she will have cumulative ignorance (see page 36-39) which will interfere with subsequent learning. The very fact that students are presently allowed to leave units and courses with "B's", "C's", "D's", and even "F's" gives evidence that the students will have varying degrees of cumulative ignorance as they go on to subsequent units or courses. To make the matter more complicated, a particular grade is not usually associated with specific learning achievement or non-achievement. Most letter grades tend to indicate a percentage of achievement. For example, if a "C" grade indicates 70 percent achievement and 20 out of 30 students in a class recieved the "C" grade, the 30 percent which each of the 20 students missed could represent very different degrees of cumulative ignorance because they missed different items on the tests. For one student, the 30 percent he or she didn't learn may be made up of critical concepts which are necessary for success in subsequent units or courses and consequently develops serious cumulative ignorance. For another student, the 30 percent he or she didn't learn may not contain any of the critical concepts which may be necessary for success in subsequent units or courses and consequently goes on without any cumulative ignorance.

The most serious aspect of cumulative ignorance as a learning problem is that it is cumulative. Under the traditional approach to education, where tests are typically given at the end of units or courses, the cumulative ignorance a student brings with him to a unit or course is not identified until a later test indicates that the student didn't learn something in this unit or course. In trying to solve the problem, the teacher doesn't know whether the problem concerns the objectives of the present course or cumulative ignorance from one or more prerequisite courses.

In order to minimize cumulative ignorance as a problem from prerequisite units or courses, develop preentry tests which are given at the beginning of a unit or course and are designed to test if the students starting a unit or course have all the critical behaviors for success in that unit or course which they should have learned in prerequisite units or courses. If the students know 100 percent of the preentry behaviors, then let them start the unit or course. If the students get less than 100 percent, then give the students a prescription for each of the items missed such that the students can learn the critical behaviors before the lack of having them causes more cumulative ignorance to develop. Because of the large amount of cumulative ignorance carried by many students, this extra task of diagnosing and prescribing becomes a task which may be avoided by busy teachers. Actually, there is a simplified way to handle this task. Give the preentry test in duplicate (use NCR paper or carbon paper). When the students complete the test, they hand in a copy to the teacher who in turn hands out to the students a special

156

answer sheet. Next to each answer on the sheet is a prescription citing sources, readings, and problems which will help the student learn the behavior of the test item if the student missed that item. Within a matter of minutes, each student has corrected his or her own paper and each student also has an individualized prescription for each of the items missed on the test. Any student who believes he or she got 100 percent of the items brings his paper to the teacher who now checks the duplicate copy of the test which was turned in before the answers were given out.

In order to minimize the development of cumulative ignorance in units or courses which the student is presently taking, don't allow any student to leave a unit or course until the student has achieved 100 percent of the objective or at least 100 percent of those objectives in the present course which if not learned will affect learning in subsequent courses. For example, in a given test of 100 items, there may be only 40 which represent critical objectives and would contribute to cumulative ignorance if not learned and interfere with successful learning in subsequent units or courses. The students would have to learn 100 percent of the specific 40 items and then learn any percentage of the remaining items that the teacher feels necessary.

e. LOW CORRELATION BETWEEN OBJECTIVES AND TESTS
    AS A LEARNING PROBLEM

This is such a serious problem, that a significant part of Chapter VI, Volume II, will be devoted to a discussion of it. But being such a critical problem, I felt I should at least briefly describe it here among other learning problems.

It should seem so obvious as to be assumed, that if your travel objective is to get to Denver, Colorado, you would evaluate the achievement of that objective by whether or not you got to Denver, Colorado. You wouldn't test the achievement of that objective by checking to see if you had arrived in Miami, Florida or even in Denver, Indiana. In the same way, whatever tests that are used to measure student achievement should have a one-to-one correlation with the objectives of the instructional event. During the past decade, and particularly during the past few years, it has not been unusual to find teachers who have worked very hard in developing specific measurable objectives and then they end up using the same tests they were using before writing the objectives. The problem is that the relationship between objectives and tests is so obvious that no one has ever made an issue out of it.

Not quite so obvious a problem would be in a situation where the travel objective is vague and you are told to just take a trip someplace. Later on, you were asked if you got to Seattle, Washington. Under the traditional approach to education, one of the long standing traditions has been the use of vague general objectives. Yet, at the end of the unit

157

or course, the students are given a test which is supposed to measure whether or not the students achieved what they were supposed to learn. Given this type of situation and particularly when the tests are made up at the end of the unit or course, if you wanted to prove that the students were very smart, you would ask questions you were sure they would all know or you could use the so-called objective type test items (multiple-choice, true-false, and matching) and put in distractors to distract the students from getting wrong answers such that the students would all get high scores. If you wanted to prove that the students were stupid, you would ask questions you were sure they didn't know or you could use objective type test items and put in distractors to distract the students from getting the right answers. If you wanted to prove you had a normal distribution of students, you would put in a few items all the students could answer, a few items that would separate the *men from the boys*, and the rest of the items of varying degrees of difficulty. It is possible to get any results desired as long as the objectives are vague and/or it isn't necessary for the test items to reflect the objectives.

NOTE: The variations in results are more dependent upon manipulating the test items than they are upon what students have learned.

If it seems fair, honest, and obvious that the test items should match the objectives of an instructional unit, wouldn't it also be fair, honest, and obvious that the teacher should teach the objectives which will be tested? But wait a minute — wouldn't that be the same as *teaching the test?* Sad as it may seem, one of the strong traditions in education today is that it is wrong to teach what is being tested. By not teaching what is tested (students will fail) and by teaching what is not tested (they'll learn a lot), it is possible to end up with a lot of smart people flunking out of school.

NOTE: News item— *Based on the results of standardized achievement tests, schools and teachers don't seem to make any difference in student achievement in school or after they graduate.*

f. DIRECTION OF LEARNING AS A LEARNING PROBLEM

This learning problem is just a small one but I find it in many courses. The most common source of the problem concerns vocabulary tests. Whether or not the specific objective is written down, the objective is typically, *Given the following list of words, the student will be able to define them.*

WORDS   DEFINITION

The direction of learning is from the words to the definitions. When it comes time to test, because it takes to much time to correct the definitions in essay form, many teachers will list the definitions and ask the students to identify the word. The direction of learning has now been reversed.

WORDS  DEFINITION

and represents a different behavior. Given one direction of learning, you cannot assume that the students have learned the reverse direction.

Since learning vocabulary is generally a rote memory task, many teachers will ask the learners to cite examples or applications of the word. In this case, although the teacher may actually test in the same

WORDS  DEFINITION APPLICATION

way as the objective, when asked why students should learn these words, most teachers state that when the students see the application in the real world they should be able to identify and name it. If a teacher

WORDS DEFINITION APPLICATION
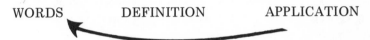

wants the students to learn both directions, the objective should be worded that way or an easier way would be to write two separate objectives.

Another very similar problem concerns the solving of problems in a situation where the answers are available, i.e., in the back of the book, on the next page, etc. This is a normal situation in mathematics, business, accounting, science, chemistry, physics, etc. It is not uncommon to hear teachers of these courses state that they have students who are having someone else do their homework. I ask them how they know this. They tell me that the homework is handed in and all the problems are correct, yet in the test, the student can't do them. Conclusion — someone else is doing the student's homework. This could be a valid conclusion, but look at the situation again. When the answers are available for homework problems, it is the rare student that hasn't worked backwards through a problem — from the answer to the prob-

PROBLEMS  ANSWERS

lem and in very difficult problems, almost all students have worked a problem from both ends until it matches in the middle. In the home-

159

work assignment, the objective is to get the problems done right and turned in. The direction of learning isn't important until the students

PROBLEMS  ANSWERS

take a test in which they now have to go from the problem to the answer and they haven't learned this behavior. The easiest way to solve this

PROBLEMS ➡ ANSWERS

problem is to tell your students about the direction of learning and remind them that if they solve their homework problems by going from the answer to the problem or from both ends to the middle, that they still haven't learned the behavior you are going to test — going from the problem to the answer. Tell them also, that there is nothing wrong with going backwards through a problem or working both ends to the middle as learning aids, but after they have achieved one or both of these steps, they should turn their paper over and try solving the problem using the direction you are going to test — from the problem to the answer.

g. READING AS A LEARNING PROBLEM

Probably the most critical learning problem in our schools is reading. It affects practically every subject and almost every level of education. More and more materials to teach reading are appearing weekly. The shame of it is that the majority of the material is invalid because of the dependency on the use of multiple-choice tests to evaluate the materials. Initially, the behavior of discrimination (which multiple-choice items *may* test) is important, but very shortly after learning the alphabet, the discrimination behavior is only important for certain look-a-like words and even the multiple-choice concept is irrelevant. In all of the reading I have ever done, I have never come across a multiple-choice item on the margin of a page or in a footnote to help me identify what I am reading. If a student is supposed to identify the theme of an essay, short story, or a novel, the desired behavior is not *given four choices of the theme for the story select one*, the desired behavior is *after reading the selection, write a statement identifying the theme of the selection and defend your decision by quoting excerpts from the selection which support your decision.* On top of this, most schools ignore individual differences among their students and use only one vehicle (set of materials) for all students. In Los Angeles where there are critical reading problems, (like most large urban areas), the school district changed reading programs several years in a row without raising the reading levels very much except in certain schools. It was

160

discovered that in these schools the teachers had saved the previous reading program materials and if the students didn't learn from the current reading program, the teachers tried one or more of the previous programs until they found a program that worked. Under the traditional approach to education and in the newspapers, the teachers who solved the learning problems and helped more students increase their reading levels by using multiple programs, were considered as playing *dirty pool* because they used more than one program. Educational research has had a preoccupation for decades on trying to find one method, one program, one type of teacher, one form of technology, etc., that will do the best job. As long as there are individual differences among students, there will never be one method or one vehicle that will work for every student.

(1) LACK OF SPECIFIED OBJECTIVES

The biggest problem in teaching reading is that not only in the teaching of reading but most of the time where reading is the vehicle for learning something else, the students don't know why they are reading or what they should be learning. Of course, most teachers give reading assignments; but this just tells the student *what to read*, it does not communicate what it is the student *should be learning* from what he or she is reading. This situation is bad enough for the students whose reading level ability equals the materials they are reading, but the poor students who read two or more grade levels below the materials they are supposed to be reading, are really lost. Typically, there are so many words that these latter students don't know, because they don't know which of the unknown words they will be tested on many of them give up without hardly trying. Everyone who reads runs into words they don't understand, but out of school it is a different situation. At the time you or any of us pick up or select something to read, we already have an idea (general or specific objective) of what it is we are looking for. When we come across an unknown word, we ask ourselves the following question, *Will not having a meaning for this word affect what I want to get out of this article?* If the answer is *No*, then we just skip over the word and forget about it. If the answer is *Yes*, then we typically study the word more closely, then look at the surrounding words and the context of the message, if we still can't develop a meaning for the unknown word, we may then go to a dictionary. When a student is given an assignment, *Read pp. 81—95*, with no general or specific objectives listed, the student can't make the decision of whether or not an unknown word is important. If the student wants success on subsequent tests, then he or she will look up all of the unknown words in the dictionary. In general, the greater the difference between the student's reading ability level and the reading level of the materials, book, etc., the more words the student will have to look up in the dictionary and also, the more apt the student is to get discouraged and give up. Consider the following situation:

The teacher has given the assignment to read pages 81-95 and then do problems 1-3 (see Figure 20).

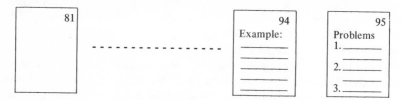

Figure 20 — Assignment: read pp. 81-95, do problems 1-3.

It would be the rare student that would actually start reading at page 81 and continue reading through to the example on page 94 and then do the problems on page 95. Almost every one else would start first by looking at the problems to see if they could do them and to estimate what they need to know to do them, then they would go through the example. If they could now do one or two of the problems, they would. When stuck, they would *scan read backwards* through the reading assignment until they learned what was necessary to complete the three problems. The emphasis (objectives) is to complete the problems — not read pages 81—95. If have seen many students who normally read two, three, or more years below the reading level of the textbook successfully complete the problems in an assignment. Depending on the problems assigned, the clarity of the example, and the student's need for additional information, a student might actually read from 10—75 percent of the assignment. That is why in courses where doing problems is what is important, students with lower than *normal* reading levels can have more success than in courses where the objectives are other than doing problems.

In many social studies and language arts courses, there is a similar situation in which at the end of a chapter are a series of questions students can answer. If the students know or believe that answering these questions is what is important, most students — but not as many as in the above situation — will use the same technique described with Figure 20 except that they will probably read a greater percentage of the material. Because this situation involves more detailed reading, reading ability level becomes more important. But even at that, since the questions (objectives) are available, many more students will have success than in a situation where there are no questions or the students find out that although there are questions at the end of the chapter, these are not the questions the teacher asks on the tests. In the latter situation, now knowing that the questions at the end of the chapter are not what they are supposed to learn, students will start at the beginning of the reading assignment and hope they can *out-psych* the teacher!

A very similar problem affects the results of standardized reading tests. Since the questions are always placed *after* the passage to be read, the students don't know what they are reading for and consequently can't adjust the amount of the passage they have to read in order to answer the questions correctly. By using a scissors and scotch tape and placing the questions *before* the passage to be read, reading scores can be increased from one to two grade levels. Because of the distraction of the wrong choices, an even better approach would be to place brief phrases or statements before the passage indicating to the students what they should be looking for as they read the passage in order to answer the questions correctly. This would allow the students to adjust the amount they have to read and would result in faster apparent reading and higher comprehension scores.

NOTE: Either of these techniques could be considered *dirty pool* by the traditional educators and especially the test makers and the testing companies because it is being honest with the students instead of the usual designed trickery of the multiple-choice test items.

Since reading is a service course like most English and Mathematics courses, the real value of the courses is realized only after the student successfully uses the behaviors learned in the service courses in his or her other courses. A common problem is that all too often, the testing for achievement in the service courses emphasizes what was taught and learned in the service course rather than testing for the transfer of the learned behaviors to other courses. This is particularly true in reading. In a school situation where students are recommended to a reading specialist, the reading specialist should see the teacher who thought the student needed special help in reading and ask the teacher to describe the situation(s) in which the symptoms or results indicated that the student needed help in reading. Be sure to check on whether or not the student was given any specific objectives *before* starting the reading assignments. As high as half of the students with reading problems can be eliminated if the teachers would specify what it is the students are supposed to learn from their reading assignments.

If the student isn't given the objectives before reading the assignment, have the teacher try that technique before putting the student in a special reading program. Without the objectives, a student may complete all of the special reading programs successfully and go back into the classroom and have the same old problems. In other words, it is a teacher problem not necessarily a student problem.

If the student is given the objectives but has very low comprehension, then put the student through whatever programs you think will help. Before the student goes back to the classroom, the student should be tested for transfer. For every course the reading course serves, the reading specialist should have sample reading assignments with accompanying objectives and tests. When the student completes the reading programs, the reading specialist should give the student a sample reading assignment from each of the students courses in which success depends on the students reading ability. If the student has success in these assignments, whatever reading programs the reading specialist used they must have been good. If the student doesn't have success in transferring the learned reading behaviors to the assignments in his or her other courses, then no matter what the reading specialist used, something was wrong and the student still needs help.

(2) PROBLEMS IN SPEED READING

It should be apparent from the foregoing, that if students are given the specific learning objectives (problems, questions, etc.) before they start a reading assignment, they will adjust the amount they read to the amount needed to achieve the objectives. In other words, given the same objectives (do problems 1—3), most students will read about the same amount of material.[6] Depending upon the objectives, the actual amount of the reading assignment that has to be read for successful achievement of the objectives will vary considerably. Since reading speed is calculated on the number of total words in the assignment (whether or not they are all necessary for the achievement of the objectives) divided by the number of minutes it takes to achieve the objectives, it is possible to have students with apparently high reading speeds but in actuality their reading speed isn't very high. For example, if there are 5000 words in a selection and a student completes the reading in five minutes and then answers the questions correctly, it would appear as if the student is reading 1000 words per minute. But what if the student only needed to read 20 percent of the selection in order to answer the questions correctly! Since the student only read 1000 of the 5000 words during the five minutes, the student's actual reading speed is only 200 words per minute. Although there are many speed reading techniques that are valuable and are taught in speed reading courses, the real secret in speed reading is to know what you are reading for — objectives — and then to adjust your speed and *the amount you actually read* to the needs of the objectives. Probably the greatest recruiters for speed reading courses are the elementary teachers

---

[6] Students with cumulative ignorance with reference to the problems may have to read more by referring to information in previous reading assignments in order to complete the problems.

that condition their students to sub-vocalize each word as they read so that their spoken reading speed is about the same as their silent reading speed. This is done by having a total class read together with each student reading aloud one or more sentences. I was so conditioned to sub-vocalize each word, it wasn't until about five years ago that I finally broke the habit and forced myself to learn to read faster by scanning through the reading materials.

Hopefully, as the classroom concept is accepted as obsolete and more elementary teachers let students learn reading on an individual basis, fewer students will be trained to sub-vocalize while reading and they can concentrate on the two major factors in speed reading.

— to be able to adjust the amount to read in an assignment in order to achieve the objectives for reading (apparent reading speed) and

— to be able to increase their speed in reading the amount that has to be read in order to achieve the objectives for reading (actual reading speed).

A critical factor which affects the apparent reading speed and the apparent comprehension is caused by the fact that most comprehension test items are multiple-choice items. By putting in distractors such that the choices are overlapping and confused, the students can be forced to go back and re-read some parts of the reading assignment. In re-reading, it is possible that a student may read 2000 words in a 1500 word essay — 500 words were re-read. If this student took ten minutes to read the selection, his or her apparent reading speed would be 150 words per minute, but the students actual reading speed would be 200 words per minute. By putting in distractors which make the wrong choices obviously wrong, so that students can't help but get the right answers, it is possible to obtain high comprehension scores with high apparent reading speed. For example, out of a 1500 word selection, a student may only have to read 150 words to enable him or her to select the right choices. If this student did this in two minutes, he or she would have an apparent reading speed of 750 words per minute but an actual reading speed of 75 words per minute.

NOTE: Some speed reading courses offered by both public and private agencies take advantage of the effect the test has on the apparent speed of reading and use a tough test as a pretest to prove you read slow and an easy test as a post-test to prove how great the new techniques are.

Of interest, in the National Assessment of reading rate and comprehension, they had each age level read two passages and then answer five multiple-choice comprehension questions about each passage. In their November, 1972 report, they claimed that super-readers were a myth because they didn't find any. Remember, if students can adjust their speed of reading at all, they will adjust it according to the objectives for reading. The more difficult the test items are to answer, the slower the students will read. Obviously, the questions used in the National Assessment tests were difficult enough that if there were any students who were capable of adjusting their apparent or actual rate of reading to super speeds, they decided to slow down to match the difficulty level of the questions. The use of multiple-choice test items in reading tests is not only irrelevant under almost every condition, but they also provide unreal crutches if the distractors used make the items easy and they provide unreal pitfalls if the distractors used make the items difficult.

(3) PHONICS AND OTHER WORD ATTACK SKILLS AS LEARNING PROBLEMS

The idea of using the phonics approach to reading was developed upon a very good basis. The belief was that since students start school with anywhere from 3000—5000 word speaking and listening vocabulary (or even more), why not take advantage of this. By showing the students the words in print that they already have meanings for and helping them to learn how to pronounce these words, the students would discover that they already know the word. Then if these words which they recognize and have meanings for are put into short simple phrases and sentences which are also similar to the short simple phrases and sentences that beginning students use already, the teachers would have an almost automatic 3000—5000 word reading vocabulary. This built-in reading vocabulary could then be parlayed into a 3000—5000 word writing vocabulary. As long as teachers adhered to the basic concept, it worked for many teachers and students. But as soon as the concept became even seim-popular, commercial publishers and even school districts and teachers started to develop materials to be used in the teaching of phonics using words that they assumed were a part of the spoken and listening vocabulary of the students. As a result, a series of problems developed. Since the mass produced materials are designed for the mythical *average* student, students who are more advanced than the materials get bored because they already know the material and students who are behind at the beginning are lost from the start. The teachers don't take the time to find out whether or not the words are in the spoken and listening vocabulary of each student. Once the students start the reading program, they are generally lock-stepped through the program regardless of what they know or don't know. When word lists start being used, rarely does a teacher check to see if the words in the list are a part of the students' spoken and listening vocabulary. Given that the student has learned to pronounce the beginning, middle, and ending consonants and the vowels, if the student uses these skills on a word he or she doesn't have any meaning for, there is no discovery and without meaning there will be no usage and the word will be forgotten quickly. Given that you as a reader have learned all of the phonics skills usually taught in school, use them to pronounce the following word: *holectypina.* Isn't it wonderful that you can pronounce it? Do you feel elated? Unless you have a meaning for the word, pronouncing it correctly probably isn't any more exciting than learning to pronounce any of the nonsense words often used in research projects. Because so many words are used that the students don't have meanings for, the students' learning load is doubled. Not only do they have to learn how to pronounce the words but they also have to learn meanings for the words. This brings up one of the more serious traditional tragedies in education, the *bass-ackwards* approach to meanings for words. Do you believe that words have meanings? If you do, look at the word in the footnote[7] and see if you can tell me what *the word means!* Some readers may think that it is not a word. It is a word and if you happen to read this language, you would have a meaning for the word. Notice, I said that *you would have meaning.* People have meanings. Words don't have meanings. It is a very easy trap to fall into. I still catch myself saying, *This word means —.* Among adults, this problem isn't too serious, but it does cause some communication problems when two people have different meanings for the same word. However, among children learning to read, this problem can retard reading progress because the teacher keeps telling them that the word attack skills they are learning will *unlock the meaning in the word.* Since there isn't any meaning in the word, the frustrated students are opening up empty closets. The real behavior involved is to *develop a meaning in the student for the word.* Student and teacher behaviors are very different in the two situations: *finding meaning in the word* and *developing meaning in the student.* In the former, the emphasis is *on the word* while in the latter, the emphasis is on *developing meaning* in the student. In reference to learning new words, the use of phonics is useless until the student has developed a meaning for the word. In using other word attack skills in developing meanings for new words it is important to differentiate between those words that can be analyzed in isolation and those they have to be analyzed in context in order to develop meanings in the student. It is acceptable to present lists of words to students as long as the words in the lists are the words which can be analyzed in isolation from other words. To present lists of words to students in a situation where the development of meanings for the words depends upon the context within which the words are used is not

---

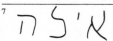

acceptable. Words that depend upon the context for word clues in the development of meanings in the students should always be presented in context (being careful that the other words in the context are not also unknown). A related problem concerns the use of a dictionary in helping students develop multiple meanings for certain words. Again, it is the context which determines which meaning the students should develop or have. Therefore, words for which people have multiple meanings should always be presented in context with sufficient word clues that the students can discriminate as to which meaning the writer intended for them to develop or have. With reference to the use of a dictionary, in the lower elementary levels, the students' reading ability may prohibit the use of a regular dictionary. Because of this, an aural dictionary becomes a very useful learning device. This type of dictionary makes use of a large number of audio cards on which the meaning(s) held by most people for the new vocabulary words are recorded (one word per audio card) for the students use as needed. Once the student has developed a meaning for the new word via the aural dictionary and it has become a part of the student's spoken and listening vocabulary, the phonics concept can be used to help the student discover the new word in reading and then the student can add this new word to his or her writing vocabulary.

In the use of the various word attack skills other than phonics which are primarily used to help develop a meaning in the student for new words, the emphasis is on the students' reading and writing vocabulary. In order to help the students add these new words to their spoken and listening vocabulary, phonics concepts again become useful in helping the students learn to pronounce the new words. The use of phonics will not necessarily help students learn to listen to the sounds of the new words unless they are working with other students. A very useful device in helping students increase their listening vocabulary and also their speaking vocabulary on an independent study basis is a special two track audio playback/recorder which uses cards of various sizes instead of reels, cartridges, or cassettes (see Photograph 1). On the top

PHOTOGRAPH 1 — LANGUAGE MASTER AND CARDS

of the card is the new word, a written definition, and anything else that will help the student develop a meaning for the word, i.e., photograph, chart, diagram, three-dimension article attached to the card, etc. On the bottom of the card there is attached a strip of audio tape. On the top or master track is recorded the correct pronounciation of the word[8] and the bottom track is open for the student to practice speaking the word. In using this approach, the Language Master (or other similar devices) could be located in a classroom, laboratory, learning resource center, or library and a rack could contain the new words associated with lessons in different courses or different lessons in the same course. The major advantages of this type of playback/recorder over the other types (reel-to-reel, cartridge, or cassette) are that the students are able to compare their responses to the master track within such a short time that any differences in pronouniciation are easier to discern; since each card represents a different word, it is easier to individualize instruction because each student can use only those cards which he or she needs; and the device is easier to use than most other types of playback/ recorder.

NOTE: In learning new vocabulary, be aware of the purposes for learning the new vocabulary, particularly as the purposes affect the *direction of learning* (see page 158-160).

In summary, concerning the use of phonics, it is important to first identify the purpose. If the purpose is to increase the students' reading and writing vocabulary based on their spoken and listening vocabulary, then the concepts of phonics can be used with previously *unknown written words* in order to discover that the students already have

$$\text{spoken and listening vocabulary} \longrightarrow \text{reading and writing vocabulary}$$

meanings for these words once they are able to pronounce the words. If the purpose is to increase the students' spoken and listening vocabulary based on their reading and writing vocabulary, then the concepts of phonics can be used to learn the pronounciation of *known written words.* In minimizing the traditional problems associated with the use of phonics in early elementary levels, it is critical to identify the words,

---

[8] If the cards are not commercially prepared, the teacher can record the master track. However, if the teacher has an accent which my interfere with the teacher's pronounciation setting an example of how the word should be pronounced, then the teacher should still record his or her pronounciation of the word to aid the students listening vocabulary for that teacher and then have another person record the correct pronounciation on the same master track to aid the student's speaking vocabulary and their listening vocabulary with other people.

169

phase and sentence patterns which are a part of each student's spoken and listening vocabulary.

spoken and listening
vocabulary
————————————→
reading and writing
vocabulary

The easiest way to approach this task is to formulate or take a list of all words used in the materials of a particular level and have parents identify, in working with their children, which words on the list are a part of the student's spoken and listening vocabulary and that the student's have meanings for. Any student whose spoken and listening vocabulary does not include the words used in the materials for learning, should be given different materials — even if necessary to custom make them for that student. In order to minimize the need to custom make materials for students whose spoken and listening vocabulary doesn't include all of those words used in the available materials, the lists of words can be given to parents in June with instructions on how to identify which words their child does not have any meaning for (ask the child directly, *What does this word mean?*). The parents could then be asked to try to use the unknown words as much as possible in their conversations with the child during the summer in order that the child will develop meanings for the unknown words and by fall will be able to use available materials.

Another critical point concerns the delay between learning and useful application. I have been in a number of kindergarten and first grade classrooms in which the students spend a lot of time learning the concepts of phonics, but the useful application of the concepts may occur anytime up to over a year later. In these very same classrooms, the teachers indicate a concern about the students short attention span and their short retention. If the students are learning something they won't actually use for a long time (months later), their retention is predestined to be short and it is difficult to maintain an interest or attention in the learning of something which probably won't be used for a long time. The rationale of the teachers in defending the long delay goes something like this: since most words are made up of more than one or two letters and they may involve any of the twenty six letters, in order for the student to apply phonics, the student has to first learn the sounds of all twenty six letters in all positions (beginning, middle, and ending). In order to shorten the time between learning and application, it helps to combine sight reading (oral/aural memory associated with visual rote memory) with phonics. As with the initial use of phonics, sight reading should be limited to those words that are already in the students spoken and listening vocabulary and for which the students already have meaning. The major difference between the two

170

approaches besides the obvious techniques involved in teaching them concerns the transfer of learned behaviors to new situations. Under sight reading, the known pronounciation of each word is associated with the visual stimulus of the word itself. An increase in reading vocabulary is accomplished by associating more known pronounciations with the corresponding written words. Under phonics, the pronounciation of each letter (consonants and vowels) are memorized in different positions and combinations. An increase in reading vocabulary is accomplished by applying these memorized pronounciation concepts to new words (new in reference to reading) and the students discover they already have meanings for the new written words. Under sight reading, a student with a 3000 word reading vocabulary has had to memorize 3000 visual word-pronounciation associations. Under phonics, a student with a 3000 word reading vocabulary has had to memorize about 100 visual letter (position and combination) — pronounciation associations. Sight reading develops an initial reading vocabulary rapidly for most beginning readers (if using known words in the students spoken and listening vocabulary) while phonics involves a considerable delay in the development of an initial reading vocabulary because of the time needed to memorize all the sounds. Once the students get out of the beginning reading level, the application of phonics concepts increases the reading vocabulary so much faster than sight reading, the continued increase in reading vocabulary via sight reading becomes tedious in comparison (remember, this is still concerned with words that are already in the students spoken and listening vocabulary). Therefore, a combination of the two approaches will keep the advantages of both and eliminate the learning problems of both. As the students learn a phonics concept, they apply it to a part of one or more words in which the pronounciation of the rest of the word is based on rote memorized sight reading. As the students learn more and more phonics concepts, less and less of the pronounciation of the word is based on rote memorized sight reading. In this way, by the time the students complete the learning of all the phonics concepts, they have also built up a reading vocabulary of 200—300 words. Because the students applied the learned phonics concepts almost immediately, the retention and attention is increased. Because of the combination approach, it will be easier to handle those phonics problems in which the same word used in different contexts is pronounced differently, i.e., I *read* the book — Did you *read* the book?, I see a *tear* on your cheek — Did you *tear* up the paper?, etc.

Because of the emphasis and publicity given to reading problems, many publishers have produced special materials concerning important reading concepts. Although the concepts are important in learning to read, all to frequently the programmed texts or other instructional units do not actually facilitate the learning of the important concepts.

In fact, some of these materials leave the learner more frustrated than he or she was before starting the materials. For example, the concept of *identifying word clues* and using these word clues to *develop a meaning (in the reader) for an unknown word* is a very important concept. A programmed instructional unit on word clues published by a well known publisher of reading materials gives these examples (the unknown words are italicized):

When an atom undergoes *fission,* or splitting, a tremendous amount of energy is released.

When a liquid or solid changes into a gas or vapor, we say it *evaporates.*

Not all mammals live on land. There are many *aquatic* mammals, such as the otter, polar bear, and whale.

In each of these three examples there are word clues in the context which will help the reader develop a meaning for the unknown words. The behavioral objective for the entire programmed text is (not actually stated by the publisher):

Given the following sentences and paragraphs with unknown words (italicized) and word clues in the context of the sentences and paragraphs, the student will be able to identify the word clues and using the word clues to develop a meaning and/or synonym for the unknown words.

In teaching this behavior, the publisher (author) used a psychological concept, commonly used in programmed texts, *successive approximation,* which refers to the use of repeated steps in which each step is closer and closer to the desired behavior. This instructional text used the following three step sequence:

first — the student is given a sentence or paragraph with an unknown word and asked to write out a synonym or definition for the unknown word based on any word clues;

second — the student is given an expanded paragraph containing more word clues and the choices for a synonym or definition are narrowed down to four choices; and

third — the student is given the definitions and synonyms listed in a dictionary plus a multiple-choice form of reinforcement.

In looking at the sequence, it appears to fit the concept of *successive approximation* at least in theory. Let me show you some actual examples and see what happens in practice. Remember, in looking at these examples, pretend you do not know the unknown word (italicized).

First — My *recovery* was rapid.

What are the word clues in this first step? Are there any? As you may have suspected, there aren't any word clues. Most of the first steps

172

throughout the text do not contain any word clues. In asking students, who have used this particular program, what they do in this first step, most of them reply, *Since there aren't often any word clues, I usually skip the first step.*

Second — In less than a week, my *recovery* was complete. I had had only a mild case of pneumonia.

Recovery means:

a — ability to breathe
b — sense of balance
c — return to health
d — loss of fever

At first glance, it would appear that there are some word clues in this expanded paragraph. However, give a second consideration, it may be possible to raise the question that if the student didn't know the word *recovery,* he or she might also not know the word *pneumonia.* Aside from that, examine the four possible choices. If the student really didn't have a meaning for the word *recovery,* any one of the four choices could be picked by the student as being the correct choice based on the given word clues. Yet, when the student turns the page, one of the four choices will be identified as the correct answer. No reasons will be given as to why the other choices are not acceptable. In asking students who have used this particular program what they do in this second step, most of them reply, *Since I usually guess wrong anyway, I just turn the page and see what the text says is the right answer.*

Third — (Dictionary definitions and synonyms for the unknown word *recovery)*

Which of the following words mean about the same as *recovery?*

a — refusal   d — rejection
b — regaining   e — cure
c — return

(The correct choices are listed on the next page as b, c, and e.) In this third step, the student is being asked to achieve the following objective:

Given the dictionary definitions and synonyms for an unknown word and a list of words or phrases, the student will be able to select one or more of the words or phrases for which his or her meaning is similar to the definitions or synonyms listed in the dictionary.

In examining the choices presented to the student, a question chould be raised as to the possibility that a student who doesn't have a meaning for *recovery* might also not have meanings for the words *regaining* and *rejection.* But more important, the above objective which is being achieved in this third step has very little to do with the main objective

173

of the whole instructional unit (see page 172).

The most critical step is to examine how the students are tested to see whether or not they have achieved the main objective of the unit. As expected, the test is a multiple-choice vocabulary test. The test item for the so-called unknown word in the above exercise is:

(The students meaning for recovery is most similar to)
a — replacing a covering
b — return to health
c — state of health
d — course of an illness

Assuming that the students select *b* as the correct choice, what does this indicate? Based on the behaviors the students were actually involved in the third step and in the above test item (the first and second steps are skipped by most students), all the achievement of this test item indicates is that:

if given the dictionary definitions and synonyms for a word and practice in selecting from a list of words or phrases these words or phrases which are similar in meanings to the dictionary definitions and synonyms for a word, the student will be able to select a word or phrase out of a choice of four words or phrases for which his or her meaning is closest to his or her meaning for the so-called unknown word.

In evaluating the whole instructional unit, consider these comments. First of all, it could have been a wrong assumption that the so-called unknown words are actually unknown to the student. Second, the first and second steps which are related to the main objective of the unit are usually skipped by students going through the program. Third, the sub-objectives associated with the third step and tested by the final test item are not related to the main objective of the unit. Fourth, the multiple choice format is unreal and hence irrelevant because in the students' reading, they will never come across lists of multiple choices in the margin, footnotes, or body of the text concerning what they should be learning from their reading. Fifth, the final test is not even testing so-called unknown words because the same words have been used in the programmed text. Sixth, assuming that the importance of having an instructional unit on the behavior of identifying and using word clues in forming meanings for unknown words is dependent upon the students being able to transfer this behavior to new unknown words not in the instructional program, then since the students going through this particular program didn't even learn the critical behavior in going through the program, obviously they can't transfer a behavior which hasn't been learned and as a result, the program is a waste of money and students' time *as it is used presently.*

In order to solve this type of learning problem, it is necessary to

174

keep in mind the main objective of the instructional unit while synthesizing the instructional materials. Actually, it is possible to use a part of
the instructional program just described and end up with an effective
instructional unit. Although the first step in the programmed unit
doesn't have any word clues for most of the so-called unknown words
and as such is useless in the development of the main objective, the
second step does usually contain sufficient word clues to help students
learn the main objective. By taking two of these programmed units, a
scissors, and scotch tape, the following programmed unit could be
developed:

First step — Give the students a list of all the words used in the
program as a pretest and ask the students to define them or give
synonyms for the words. In this way, you can identify which
words are really unknown.[9]

Second step — The student is given the paragraphs containing the
word clues for the unknown words identified in the first step.
These paragraphs are the same ones which were in the second
step of the regular programmed unit minus the multiple-choice
clues (or distractors). The student is asked to underline the
word clues in the paragraph.

Third step — The student turns a page and there is the same
paragraph (taken from a second copy of the programmed unit)
but the word clues are already underlined. The directions for
the student is to compare the word clues he or she identified
with those identified by the teacher. If the student can't understand any differences (word clues the student picked but the
teacher didn't or word clues the teacher picked that the student
didn't), he or she should check with the teacher.

Fourth step — In looking at the identified word clues, the student
should write a synonym and/or definition for the unknown
word and defend whatever is written by relating the synonym
and/or definition to the word clues (this means for the student
to describe in writing his or her thinking processes used to arrive
at the synonym and/or definition).

Fifth step — The student then turns the page and there is the
dictionary definition and synonyms (also a part of the regular
programmed unit) which will serve as reinforcement for the
student if the word clues were used correctly.

In order to verify that the student has learned the right behavior and it

---

[9] The word clue programmed units are available with different difficulty levels of
vocabulary words. If a student already know must of the words, select the next
higher programmed unit for the student to work on. It would be difficult for a
student to learn the desired behavior of the objective if the student is working
with known words.

is transferable to other situations, the reading teacher should have a file folder on every subject and for each grade level. In each of these file folders are paragraphs taken from the regular materials used in each course. Each paragraph contains one or more unknown words that students usually have trouble with in the subject and also some word clues which can be used to infer a definition or synonym for the unknown word.

Evaluation — the student is given one or more sample paragraphs (described above) from the course materials in each of the subjects the student is taking and is then asked to identify the word clues in the paragraphs and then based on these word clues to state a synonym or definition for the unknown word in each of the paragraphs.

If the student gets these correct, he or she has learned the critical behavior of identifying and using word clues and is able to transfer it from the instructional unit to other subject matter areas.

(4) INTEREST AS IT AFFECTS READING SKILLS AND SCORES

In 1965, I was consulting with a *store front* school[10] and one night after leaving the school, I stopped in a drug store about a block away from the school. Standing and sitting among the magazines in the drug store were some of the *students* from the store front school. I noticed that these students were looking at *Modern Mechanics* and other similar magazines, auto and motorcycle racing magazines, and sports magazines. The peculiar part is that the magazines were written for an eighth grade reading level or higher and yet these students had been tested on regular reading tests and scored at the third and fourth grade reading levels and a few of them were rated at being not much above functional illiterates. I asked the *students* if I could look at the magazines they were reading. I then asked them some questions about what they were reading. To my surprise, the students were able to answer some general and also some specific questions about the content of the magazines which they had already read. Since that time, similar instances have happened many times. If students who are reading below their grade level are really interested enough, they will be able to dig out the critical information from their reading assignments, even if the material is usually considered to difficult for the students. This indicates that there must be for each student a range of reading levels depending upon how interested the student is in the materials he or she is reading. In order to identify this range, reading tests should be made up using a variety of subject matter areas. When students are ready to be tested,

---

[10] A *store front* school is a school which is operated very informally, often at odd hours, and with students who have more than likely dropped out of school or have been suspended from school.

176

they are presented with a list of all the subject matter areas available in the reading test, i.e., twenty topics. Each student is asked to identify the topic he or she likes the most and the topic he or she likes the least and then the student takes a reading test in each topic. For example, if a student had a reading range of from 6th grade level to 10th grade level and the student was having trouble comprehending 9th grade reading level materials, the learning problem to be solved is not a reading problem, it is an interest problem. If the same student is having trouble comprehending 12th grade reading level materials, the learning problem is primarily a reading problem although it could also be secondarily an interest problem.

This solution to a learning problem suggests that if the desired specific objectives are process-oriented rather than content oriented, that it would probably be more effective and efficient to use vehicles for learning which are matched to the students major areas of interest and conversely, it would tend to be ineffective and inefficient to use vehicles for learning which concerned topics of least interest to the students.

(5) EDUCATIONAL MALPRACTICES IN READING

Of the 41 traditional malpractices identified in my book, *Educational Malpractices,* there are six which are directly related to learning problems in reading. The most serious and wide-spread is the first malpractice EM1.

EM1 — When a teacher requires a student to learn from certain materials, particularly textbooks, knowing that the student is not able to learn from these materials because the student reads at a level which is below the actual reading level of the textbook, i.e., students in tenth grade who read at fifth or sixth-grade level are given materials to learn from which are written at the tenth grade or higher reading level; college freshmen who read at eighth or ninth-grade level are given college textbooks to learn from which are written at the professorial level, etc. When the student shows that he or she can't learn from the materials in these situations, the student is failed or graded down.

This malpractice is found at all grade levels in elementary and secondary education and up to at least the junior level in colleges and universities. The only reason it isn't found at higher levels is that students who would have this problem are failed out before they reach their junior year. However, in some minority group programs, this malpractice can be found even in graduate school. The obvious solution to the malpractice is to find reading materials at a lower level but which still allow the student to learn all of the course objectives. In a situation where a teacher has not specified the course objectives, it is difficult for the teacher to change textbooks because he or she doesn't know

177

whether or not the new textbook facilitates the same objectives as the other textbook. Another solution is to remember a generalization which I have observed in solving learning problems with teachers and students. *Although a student may read one or more years below grade level, most students are able to talk and listen at grade level.* This suggests that a solution for this malpractice could be a tape recording of the reading assignments. In making the tape recording, the teacher is not necessarily the best one to do it. I have found that the most effective audio tapes are made by an "A" student who has just finished the course and the teacher believes that this student has learned everything he or she should have learned in the course. This student is taped while reading the course materials to another student who is having lots of problems in comprehension. The recording would include all of the questions and answers about the content which naturally occur during the tape recording. Once the recording is made, the next time a teacher identifies a student as having problems in comprehension because the student reads below grade-level, the teacher could prescribe the tape. As a note of caution, don't let the student sit and passively listen to the tape recording. Have the student who is recording the reading involve the listener by asking the student to look at certain statements, titles, names, dates, graphs, flow charts, etc.

EM6 — When a teacher purposely misleads the student as to what he or she is to study, or is vague and ambiguous about the learning requirements of the course, while the tests for the course are made up of test items requiring achievement of specific learning objectives.

This malpractice is also very common and refers to situations in which the teacher gives reading assignments but doesn't let the student know what they should be learning while reading the assignment. There has to be (or at least-should be) a reason for having a student spend his time and energy reading. The best solution for this problem is to give the students the general and specific objectives associated with each reading assignment before they start reading or a copy of the test used to evaluate whether or not the students learned what they were supposed to learn in the reading assignment.

EM9 — When a teacher starts a course at the beginning of a textbook, knowing that some of the students already know part of the course, and other students are lacking the necessary prerequisites to even start the course.

If students are bored because they already know a part or all of what the teacher wants them to know, yet the teacher wants them to start at Chapter 1 — page 1 with all of the other students, the students are going to develop negative attitudes towards the teacher *and the textbook.* By the time these students get to a place in the textbook

178

where they could be learning and should be learning, the negative attitudes may very well interfere with comprehension and learning. If students are lost righ from the start of the course because they haven't learned prerequisite skills and behaviors in previous courses which are necessary for successful achievement in this course, they will also develop negative attitudes towards the teacher *and the textbook.* If the cumulative ignorance is not elminated, these students may give evidence of their frustrations by becoming disciplinary problems. The solution to this problem is to individualize the instruction such that the students who are already part way through the course can start wherever they are in the course. For the students who are behind, it is necessary to test the students to find out where they are and start them there. In starting students where they are intellectually, students will be in all different parts of the course at the same time and as such, there won't be a traditional class for the teacher to present to. The only role for the teacher to perform in this situation is the humanizing role of identifying and solving learning problems — to diagnose (students at different intellectual levels) and to prescribe (start the students where they are).

EM10 — When teachers teach students certain facts, how to deal with facts, how to interpolate certain facts, how to diagnose situations based on certain facts, etc.; then they test the students' knowledge with multiple-choice test items, which test the students' ability to discriminate between answers, which may or may not be an important behavior, and it may not test the behaviors of dealing with facts, interpolating facts, diagnosing situations, etc. In other words, when teachers teach students certain things during the course, but test the students' achievement of something else which was not taught or learned during the course. A similar situation is when teachers use charts, graphs, visuals, films, slides, tape recordings, phonograph records, demonstrations, etc., in their teaching, and then turn around test with words only.

I have already discussed the learning problem in which the students are told to learn one thing and then they are tested on something else. The particular aspect of this malpractice which is important from the point-of-view of a reading problem is that in using written verbal tests, not only is the teacher testing for the achievement of the course objectives, the teacher is also testing the students ability to read the test items. It should be rather obvious that if the student can't read the test items, it will appear as if the student doesn't know what was being primarily tested by the test item. If it doesn't make any difference in the achievement of the objective, the test could be made available on a cassette tape such that the student can be looking at the test and hearing the teacher give the test orally. Sometimes, it appears as if the

179

student can't read the test items and yet the test items are not as difficult as the regular reading materials which the student appeared to comprehend. This could indicate that the student has developed a mental block against the testing situation itself. This is a common problem under the traditional approach to education and is developed by students as a result of a series of negative experiences either in the testing situations or in reference to the results of the testing situations. Initially, students with this problem may have to be tested informally.[11] After students have been involved in the Behavioral Learning Systems Approach to Instruction for a period of time, the open honesty of the approach and the continued positive successful experiences tend to alleviate or eliminate the high anxiety usually associated with testing situations.

EM16 — When teachers, school districts, colleges, universities, and even state departments of education use the same textbooks and/or other learning experiences for all students in a given course, knowing that because of individual differences among students in how they learn will result in differences in achievement. In order to have equal opportunity for achievement, unequal students need unequal materials, textbooks, etc.

The results of this malpractice are really a combination of EM1 and EM9 and is typical of the traditional approach to education which blatantly ignores individual differences among students. To use the same textbook in any one grade level where the teacher, administrators, students, and even parents know that there is a range of at least four or more years differences in reading abilities, is to facilitate a design for non-learning.

EM28 — When a teacher, department, school, school district, college, or university requires students to take standardized tests which are camouflaged as achievement tests but in fact are not based on the achievement of specific measurable objectives and their primary purpose is to spread students out over some type of curve(s). This is a particularly serious malpractice when the results of these disguised tests are used to place students in certain courses or levels of instruction.

This malpractice refers directly to the use of standardized reading tests — particularly those which depend upon the use of multiple-choice test items. Reading is such an important skill to learn that the testing should reflect the achievement of real reading behaviors. There is no room for, and no reason for, designing the test items to force the results

---

[11] Over the years, I have orally tested many students who have had problems with mental blocks during testing situations. I usually have the student come to my office and while we are talking, (a copy of the test is lying visible in an open drawer) I slip in a question here and there.

to fit a curve regardless of what students know or to even use test items which don't even relate to critical reading behaviors (the so-called objective type test items).

Although the next two items are not listed as malpractices, the effects of the two practices are negative with respect to student learning. The first negative practice is in reference to a common limitation in using textbooks as a presentation device. Once a book is printed, it is for all practical purposes frozen in time. Given the individual differences among teachers as to what each one thinks is important in a course and an ever-changing world, every book has to create teaching-learning problems. Every teacher that I have asked, *Are you happy with every chapter in the textbook you are using?* has answered me with a *No.* Under the traditional approach to education, the solution is usually to change the book as soon as possible. Not only is this procedure expensive (if the taxpayers pay for the books), but the teacher now has to make up a lot of new presentations based on the new book. The sad part is that no matter what new book the teacher selects, he or she will find one or more chapters that isn't right. Even if a teacher writes the whole book, a year later the teacher will probably be unhappy with the whole book. In a learner-oriented environment, it is important to remember that while a teacher is waiting to replace the present text-book with its one or more bad chapters, the students in that class have to try to learn from the bad chapters. Instead of putting off doing anything until the whole book can be changed, solve the problem as soon as possible after identifying it. Of course, in order to identify a learning problem, it is necessary to have the specific learning objectives which the students are supposed to be learning. Without specific objectives it is difficult to clarify the learning problem much behond a *gut feeling* and without specific objectives, it is impossible to tell for sure if the problem was solved.

One might be tempted to solve a learning problem in printing with a solution in printing. The problem with this is that not that many teachers are good writers and if the solution is prepared very quickly, the students might find out that their teachers can't write, spell, punctuate, etc. Therefore, whenever a teacher prepares a solution in print, a lot of time is spent in editing, proofreading, and rewriting. Because of the amount of time involved, most teachers prefer to live with the problems rather than solve them (doesn't hurt the teacher, but it might hurt the students). The easiest way to solve these problems is with a cassette tape recorder. The teacher essentially talks the student through the bad chapters. For example, the teacher could tell the students that when they get to chapter 7, be sure to check out cassette tape 7A. On the tape the teacher could say, *From the beginning of chapter 7 on page 102 until page 109, the book is all right. Turn off the tape player now and turn it back on when you get to page 109.* When the student turns the tape player back on, the teacher could say, *In the middle paragraph on page 109, where the author says —, well, that concept has been proven wrong (is obsolete, from the wrong point-of-view, etc.) —.* I have come across some teachers who go so far as to say to students via the tape, *I don't even know what the author is saying in chapter 7, but the following is what I think you need to know instead of what is in chapter 7.*

The second negative practice is almost the same as the first in that it refers to parts of the book which are causing learning problems. In many books, where complex visuals are used, i.e., photographs, graphs, diagrams, flow charts, etc., the narration explaining the complex visual is often two or three pages away from the visual. The problem is that it is impossible to have your eyes on the visual and reading the narration at the same time. For simple visuals, most students can learn whatever is necessary from the simple visual just by flipping back and forth between the visual and the narration. For complex visuals, only a few students learn all of what they are supposed to learn. In situations like this, it is very easy to develop a solution. Just record the narration on a cassette. Now, as the students are looking at the complex visual with their eyes, their ears are hearing the narration. For some visuals, particularly complex flow charts, it may be necessary to separate the visual into several parts and discuss (on tape) one part at a time.

h. ESSAY WRITING AS A LEARNING PROBLEM

Based on your previous experience as a student and as a teacher (if you are one or have ever been one) and your observations of other students and teachers, answer the following multiple-choice item.[12]

If a student's essay was given to a group of teachers and each of them was to grade the essay independently, the grades would be:

a — all the same   c — mostly different
b — mostly the same   d — all different

I have asked over 200,000 teachers this question. If your choice agrees with the vast majority (over 90%) of these teachers, then you picked either choice (c) or choice (d). Try to imagine the significance of this response. What you [if you picked choice (c) or (d)] and the vast majority of teachers are really saying is that the letter grade a student gets on an essay reflects more the teacher who graded the essay than the student who wrote it!!! Can you even conceive of the number of

---

[12] There are three types of multiple-choice items which are acceptable for evaluation pruposes under the Behavioral Learning Systems Approach to Instruction. This is one of them. Notice, I am asking for an opinion. There is no such thing as a *right answer* to an opinion question. Every answer is a right answer. As such, there would be no point in scoring or grading the answer in this kind of item as to its correctness.

students whose present and future lives are being affected negatively by this extremely subjective process. Although some of the students' essays would obviously be graded higher than they maybe should have been, this is not as positive a situation as one might think at first, because the higher grades build up the students' self-image on a foundation of make-believe quality. Sooner or later the students whose grades were inflated will identify the truth and the fall from the greater heights will be more destructive of the self-image than those students whose grades were correct or deflated.

As a result of this extreme subjectivity, there is a strong tendency among teachers to minimize essay type test items and to use objective type test items. As pointed out earlier in several places, objective type test items (multiple-choice, true-false, and matching) are objective only in scoring. The writing of these test items is extremely subjective. Given a multiple-choice test item, a professional test item writer can hold the stem and the correct choice constant and by varying the distractors in the wrong choices can get almost any percentage of students to get the item right or wrong (regardless of what the students know). What makes the situation even worse, is that the extreme subjectivity of the so-called *objective type* test items is hidden under the very title *objective type*. Given that you can accept that essay grading is subjective and that the writing of the *objective type* test items is also very subjective, the obvious question becomes, *What kind of test items can I use?*

The best type of test item is one that tests directly on a one-to-one basis the achievement of a specific objective. If the specific objective asks the students to solve problems, then the best test item for that objective are problems to be solved. If the specific objective asks for a number, a name, a date, or a phrase, then the best test items for that objective are ones that ask for a number, a name, a date, or a phrase. As pointed out previously, one of the important reasons why objective type test items are not the right forms to use for evaluation is that rarely, if ever, is a specific objective worded in such a manner that it could have a one-to-one behavioral relationship with an objective type test item. Of the thousands and thousands of specific objectives which I have read and critiqued, the majority of the objectives and corresponding test items asked the student to communicate to the teacher in either an oral essay form or a written essay form. As such, these test items are also testing the students ability to communicate orally or in writing in addition to the content of the oral or written essay. This also indicates that the skills involved in writing become even more important and critical under a behavioral learning systems approach towards instruction because most test items are of the essay type.

Even under the present traditional approach, one of the most critical courses at the college and university level is Freshman Composition. This course has many different titles, but the most important objective and activity in the course is the writing of essays. What makes this course so critical is that it is considered one of the biggest problem courses at most schools, it generally has the most students enrolled in it, it generally has the most teachers teaching it, more students are failed or dropped out of school for not achieving passing grades in it, and the writing behaviors to be learned in the course are basic to almost every other course in higher education. In addition, as pointed out in the previous paragraphs, the evaluation of the achievement in this critical course is extremely subjective. To top it all, the course and its critical objectives shouldn't even have to be taught at the college or university level. After all, most of the same objectives have been part of English courses every year since the students were in third or fourth grade.

If the skills involved in written communication are so critical and yet the course is such a problem course, how can these problems be solved such that students can have success in achieving these critical basic skills? In order to analyze this problem, it is necessary to break the problem into two major parts: the evaluation of the essays (the key role for the teacher) and the learning of the actual writing skills (the key role for the learner). For decades in each grade from the third or fourth grade up to and including Freshman Composition, the emphasis has been on the teaching of what the student was supposed to learn. This would seem to be the obvious way to go; but remember, although the teachers may be in agreement on what writing skills the students should be learning, they are not in agreement on how to evaluate the product produced by the students. Given this conflict between what is being taught and what is being evaluated, the results should not be very surprising.

Students don't really know what to learn in order to be evaluated positively because what is important changes from teacher to teacher. As a result, in order to improve the present situation with respect to ineffective writing skills, it is necessary to solve the evaluation problem first then worry about the writing skills later.

(1) EVALUATION OF ESSAYS . . .

In addition to the major problem of disagreement in the evaluation of essays pointed out in the beginning of this section, a second major problem in evaluation is that very few teachers who are evaluating students' written communications actually communicate to the students what they did wrong. A third problem that is closely related to the second problem, is that seldom do teachers who are evaluating students' essays ever take advantage of the evaluation as the beginning of a significant individualized learning event.

Educational Testing Service conducted an experiment in which they

184

had 300 essays graded by 60 teachers.[13] The teachers were asked to sort the essays into nine piles representing different levels of quality, i.e., A+, A, B+, B, C+, C, D+, D, and F. No instructions were given to the teachers as to the criteria to be used in grading the essays, since ETS wanted to find out what the teachers looked for. Of the 300 papers, 101 received all nine grades, 111 received eight grades, 70 received seven grades, and no essay received less than five grades. The average agreement (correlation) among all of the teachers was .31, and among the college English teachers it was .41 (perfect correlation would be 1.0). ETS then asked each of the 60 teachers to identify their criteria for grading. In analyzing these criteria, ETS identified eight categories of criteria which could be used to grade essays.

(a) Ideas

The student has given some thought to the topic and has written what he really thinks. He discusses each main point long enough to show clearly what he means. He supports each main point with arguments, examples, or details; he gives the reader some reason for believing it. His points are clearly related to the topic and to the main idea or impression he is trying to get across. No necessary points are overlooked and there is no padding.

(b) Organization

The paper starts at a good point, has a sense of movement, gets somewhere, and then stops. The paper has a plan that the reader can follow; he is never in doubt as to where he is or where he is going. Sometimes there is a little twist near the end that makes the paper come out in a way that the reader does not expect, but seems quite logical. Main points are treated at greatest length or with greatest emphasis, others in proportion to their importance.

(c) Wording

The writer uses a sprinkling of uncommon words or of familiar words in an uncommon setting. He shows an interest in words and in putting them together in slightly unusual ways. Some of his experiments with words may not quite come off, but this is such a promising trait in a young writer that a few mistakes may be forgiven. For the most part he uses words correctly, but he also uses them with imagination.

(d) Flavor

The writing sounds like a person, not a committee. The writer seems quite sincere and candid, and he writes about something he

---

[13] Diederich, Paul B., John W. French and Sydell T. Carlton, *Factors in Judgements of Writing Ability*. Research Bulletin 61-15 (out of print). Princeton, N.J.: Educational Testing Service, 1961. (Permission received to reprint these 8 categories from Paul B. Diederich, author of the article entitled: *Factors in Judgements of Writing Ability*.

knows — often from personal experience. You could not mistake this writing for the writing of anyone else. Although the writer may play different roles in different papers, he does not put on airs. He is brave enough to reveal himself just as he is.

(e) Usage, Sentence Structure

There are no vulgar or *illiterate* errors in usage by present standards of informal written English. The sentence structure is correct, even in varied and complicated sentence patterns.

(f) Punctuation, Capitals, Abbreviations, Numbers

There are no serious violations of rules that have been taught. Note, however, that modern editors do not require commas after short introductory clauses, around nonrestrictive clauses, or between short coordinate clauses unless their omission leads to ambiguity or makes the sentence hard to read. Contractions are acceptable — often desirable.

(g) Spelling

(ETS) — In a testing situation: The paper usually has not more than five misspellings, and these occur in words that are hard to spell. The spelling is consistent; words are not spelled correctly in one sentence and misspelled in another — unless the misspelling appears to be a slip of the pen.

(Stewart) — In a learning situation: There should be no spelling errors in the essay after the last revision.

(h) Handwriting, Neatness

The handwriting is clear, attractive, and well spaced, and the rules of manuscript form have been observed.

In workshops which I have conducted during the past ten years, I have replicated the first part of the ETS experiment many times by asking the teachers to grade an essay. If there are over 20 teachers in the group, I will always get at least one or more teachers that will assign each of the five letter grades to the same essay. By picking one or more of the eight categories for grading essays and telling the teachers that they can only grade the essay on those criteria, it was a rare event for any essay to receive more than two adjacent letter grades. In other words, as teachers identify and agree on common criteria for grading essays, subjectivity is minimized and objectivity is maximized.

In the experiment, the teachers were told to use a certain set of criteria; but in real classrooms, teachers resist having someone else tell them what criteria to use. Therefore, in order to bring objectivity into essay grading in the classroom teachers have to get together and agree on common criteria. Although most curriculum committee meetings try to accomplish this goal, most curriculum meetings develop much more heat than light and not much ligh at all. Because of individual differ-

186

ences in teachers and personality conflicts between teachers, curriculum committee meetings can be held for weeks, months, and even years with little success. However, there is a process in which these common criteria (objectives) can be identified relatively quickly. (See Chapter VI, Volume II).

The second most cirtical problem in evaluating essays is that teachers generally don't communicate to the students what is wrong with their essays. Almost every student has had the experience of getting back an essay with a grade of less than "A". but no indication whatsoever as to what was wrong. There are three reasons for this problem.

1. Most writing course objectives concern the quantity of essays turned in not the quality of the essays. A student would be more often failed for not turning in the right number of essays than for turning in the right number of low quality essays.

2. If the teacher is really going to communicate to the student, then the grading process would take up a lot more time.

3. Even if the teacher did communicate what was wrong (a diagnosis), the students don't actually rewrite their essays or do anything with the diagnostic information.

With reference to the first reason, given that few teachers have actually written out their criteria for grading essays, it is difficult to communicate something to students if the teachers don't even know specifically what it is they want. By using the procedure described in Chapter VI, Volume II, all of the teachers involved in the procedure would end up with a minimum list of specific criteria. It would then be much easier to become concerned about quality rather than quantity.

With reference to the second reason, teachers are right in that communicating to students in complete sentences would take longer. In addition, in the rush of writing the evaluation, many teachers might make mistakes in their own grammar and spelling. In order to solve this problem, I have found the cassette recorder to be very useful. By using a cassette, teachers just talk to students as they evaluate the essays. Because of the redundancy of errors in student essays, another time saver could be to develop special cassette units dealing with common problems. For example, during the process of evaluating a number of essays, instead of the teacher giving many brief lectures on agreement between the noun and the verb in a sentence, the teacher could refer the student to this special unit each time he or she encounters the lack-of-agreement problem. In using the cassette, I have found it easiest to use numbers which I write on the essay and explain on the cassette tape. (This process will be explained in more detail under the next unit.)

With reference to the third reason, most educators have the problem I call the *Backwards Ostrich Philosophy*. In almost every area of society, it is the custom to diagnose first and design the treatment second. Only in traditional education do teachers reverse these such that the students are given the treatment first and then the diagnosis. Then most educators record the grade indicated by the diagnosis, ignore the diagnosis, and go on to the next treatment. If as teachers, we really want to change students' writing behaviors, then we are going to have to look on tests and essays as diagnostic in nature and design subsequent treatments which reflect each student's individual diagnosis. In the usual approach, after the first essays are evaluated, the typical teacher spends class time talking about the average mistakes committed by the average students then assigns a second essay and the repeats the process. The present result is that few students actually change their writing behavior. Even if a student does go back over his essay and corrects his or her mistakes, rarely will teachers change the student's grade to an "A". If we want students to change their writing behavior, then teachers will have to not only diagnose first and design the treatment second, but they will have to motivate the student to make the changes by allowing students to improve their writing skills and *their grades.*

(2) THE TEACHING AND LEARNING OF WRITING SKILLS

Assuming that a group of teachers (or even one teacher) has improved their own behaviors in evaluating essays as previously indicated, then it is now possible to set up procedures for the teaching and learning of the various writing skills (these skills should represent the minimum common criteria used to evaluate the essays). One of the most common mistakes in the traditional approach of teaching is that educators talk about individual differences among their students and then by their actions assume that all of their students are alike, i.e., all or almost all students use the same materials for the same length of time. How a teacher teaches or what materials a teacher uses is not a concern here. What is important is whether or not the students have learned.

In the teaching-learning process, a very critical component is that of *quality control* or *zero defect.* At the present time students from lower elementary levels up through high school are allowed to get out of their writing assignments with B's, C's, D's, and even F's and still pass on to the next course. The fact that the students didn't achieve A's indicates that they missed achieving some of the necessary writing skills. Since what each student didn't learn collectively includes almost all of the necessary writing skills, the next teacher has to almost repeat the same course. Because the tradition is to give the treatment first and the diagnosis second, teachers typically don't know which students need which treatment, so all of the students have to sit through the repeated presentations regardless of whether or not they need it. As a result, the teaching of writing skills is essentially the same thing repeated each year from third or fourth grade up to and including freshman composition at the college or university level. Another obvious result of the traditional approach is how boring this part of English courses become for students and teachers.

By recognizing not only vocally but by our actions that there are individual differences among students (using different materials, techniques, and allowing different lengths of time for learning) and by building in quality control such that a student doesn't leave an essay assignment until he or she achieves 100 percent of the writing skills involved in the evaluation of that essay, it is possible for the vast majority of students to learn to write correctly before they even get into high school. The first thought that comes to the mind of the traditional educator is that in order to achieve 100 percent, some students would be in the class for years. In actuality, this is not the problem; but even if it was, it would still be better to spend several years in order to learn 100 percent of the necessary writing skills and have subsequent success not only in English but in those parts of most other courses which involve writing than to continue the present practice in which a minority of students graduating from high school can write correctly. (In the National Assessment of Writing, 29 percent of the young adults tested refused to even attempt the writing exercises.)

Although every teacher who teaches writing would like their students to achieve 100 percent of the writing skills (assuming the teacher had identified the necessary skills and could evaluate measurably — not subjectively — whether or not the student had the skills), a common problem plagues most teachers who are trying to teach writing skills (especially in high schools and at the college and university level). This problem concerns the belief that the non-measurable criteria or difficult to measure criteria such as creativeness, *freshness of thought*, and other criteria without even a name are more important than the criteria which are measurable. It is convenient to believe this way because if students don't learn how to achieve the measurable criteria, the teachers can always defend the results by saying they concentrated on the more important things — the non-measurable criteria. Of course, since these more *important* criteria are not measurable, no teacher can prove that the students actually did learn them or that they are actually more *important*. To compound this aspect of the problem, many teachers think of these non-measurable criteria as the humanistic part of writing skills in contrast to the measurable criteria which are considered mechanical. In the belief that the non-measurable criteria are humanizing, many teachers spend time trying to teach these criteria at the sacrifice of the time that could have been spent teaching the measurable mechanics of writing. As a result of not learning the mechanics of writing, millions of students receive failing grades on their essays every year and hundreds of thousands of students have failed out of high school and college because they can't write well enough. Consequently, many teachers of writing in trying to be humanistic actually end up being indirectly very inhumane by ignoring the serious results of their misplacement of priorities. It has been my consistent experience that in trying to achieve general (non-measurable) objectives and specific (measurable) objectives, more success can be found in teaching the specific objectives first to the 100 percent level and then if any extra time is available, try to teach the general objectives. In fact, quite often the specific objectives concern the achievement of tools which are the necessary prerequisites in order to learn the general objectives.

In learning the mechanics of writing, some students are able to learn multiple skills simultaneously to the 100 percent level, but many students may have difficulty in achieving more than one skill at a time. Therefore, it may be more successful to concentrate on one skill until it is achieved to the 100 percent level, then learn a second skill to the 100 percent level and then combine them together, then learn a third skill to the 100 percent level and then combine the three together, etc. This procedure will help learners to build up a repertoire of writing skills one at a time. In this process, it is critical to communicate to the student *in writing* the actual criteria being learned and evaluated. To illustrate the value of this rule, ask any group of students to answer four short answer essay questions, but preface the first two questions with the phrase, *Using correct spelling,* — . I have had hundreds of teachers who have tried this experiment. The usual results will be that there will be very few, if any, spelling errors in the first two answers, while in the last two answers there will be the usual number of spelling errors. The results of this brief experiment substantiate that if the students know exactly what the criteria are that are going to be used to evaluate their writing, they will try to perform accordingly (if the skills are a part of their repertoire of writing skills).

One of the most successful ways to help students achieve the skills necessary to write a *good* essay, particularly if they are in a remedial writing course (which is the case of most writing courses after about sixth grade), is the use of an individualized writing workshop which utilizes cassette recorders. One of these can be set up for a class of 30 students for about $1000 and includes 30 playback only recorders, one playback-record recorder, and a number of cassette tapes. For this price, five, six, or even more classes of 30 students each can use the workshop each day. In this way, the cost is about $6.00 per student using the equipment.

In this individualized writing workshop, the teacher would start out by assigning the first essay and giving to the students a list of the specific measurable criteria which will be used to evaluate the essay. In grading the essay, the teacher talks to each student on a cassette (separate cassette for each essay) using numbers to indicate locations in the essay being discussed. Instead of writing on the essay the usual word *unclear* which is unclear by itself, the teacher can now repeat the *unclear* statement in several ways to demonstrate its lack of clarity. By using supplementary learning materials (commercially available and/or teacher-made), the teacher can direct the student (on the cassette tape) to a specific prescription for diagnosed problems. One very important guideline in critiquing the students' essays, teachers should be careful not to do the correcting of the writing. Let the student do the correcting. The teacher's function is to identify a problem and provide the student with the necessary learning experiences so the student can make the correction. For example, most teacher's when seeing a misspelled word indicate that the word is misspelled by crossing out the word and/or by writing the letters *sp* by the word. Many teachers will even write in the word correctly spelled. These teacher behaviors do not help students learn to spell. The critical spelling behavior in writing is not so much in knowing the spelling of a word as it is in knowing that a word is misspelled or as most people describe the situation, *the word just doesn't look right.* Everyone in their writing misspells words. The difference is that some people recognize that the misspelled words *don't look right,* and correct the spelling. I'll bet that you have misspelled one or more words during the past week in your writing. If the writing was not for a class where a teacher would correct it, how did you know that it was misspelled? Probably because the word just *didn't look right.* In order to teach the behavior of *it doesn't look right,* teachers should indicate the line in which there is a misspelled word and ask the student to identify the word and then to correct it. Since the human being is generally a model of conservation of energy, a student will not look up every word in the line. Instead, the student will look at the words in the line and try to identify which word *doesn't look right the most* and then check upon the spelling of that word. That is how you teach the behavior *it doesn't look right.*

The same situation occurs with punctuation. In most cases, teachers put in the commas, periods, etc., which are missing in student essays or cross out excess punctuation. If there is a problem with missing, incorrect, or excess punctuation, teachers should indicate the line or lines involved and if appropriate, ask the student questions concerning the message he or she was trying to communicate. The teacher could also suggest a technique that many of us use. Unless you are an English teacher, chances are that when you are in doubt about the punctuation of a sentence or a paragraph, you read the sentence or paragraph out loud to yourself and when your voice wants to take a pause, this is considered a clue that maybe some mark of punctuation belongs there. If the student tries this procedure and seems to locate the right places for marks of punctuation but doesn't know which ones to use, the teacher could suggest or require the student to review supplementary materials or punctuation in order to learn the necessary behaviors to correct his or her own essay. The guideline to remember is that ultimately, the student has to identify the errors and correct them.

After the teacher has orally corrected the students' essays on the cassette tapes, she hands back the essays and cassettes to the students. Since each desk has a cassette playback unit, each student can work on correcting his or her own essay right there in class by listening (via earphones) to the teacher's recorded comments. In this way, instead of the teacher spending class time talking about the average errors made by the average student in the average essay, the teacher is free to individualize instruction. If a student doesn't quite understand what the teacher's remarks were on the cassette, the student can ask the teacher for clarification in the classroom. To reduce or minimize the problem of the student introducing new errors by rewriting the whole essay, students should be allowed to cut out the bad lines or parts of their essays and to paste or tape in their corrections. When the students have completed the corrections indicated by the teacher on the cassette, they hand in the corrected essay and the cassette. If the essay is still not completely correct according to the specified criteria used for evaluation, the teacher should critique the essay again on the cassette and the process is repeated as many times as necessary until the student achieves an "A" or at least a "B" (a minimum of 100 percent of the measurable criteria). As soon as a student completely corrects his or her first essay ("A" or "B" worth), then the student goes on to the second essay assignment. Although this procedure invariably takes longer per essay than the traditional approach the first time it is used, over a period of time, the time needed by the teacher to correct essays is greatly reduced because the students are writing better essays. Most important, however, is the fact that the students' writing behavior has been changed and in a positive direction. Instead of concentrating on the quantity of essays in which the quality doesn't change significantly and students doing "C" work or less develop negative attitudes towards English and writing, it is possible to concentrate on improving the quality of the students essays with an accompanying increase in positive attitudes towards English and writing.

This same procedure is not only useful in courses specifically concerned with writing, but can be used beneficially in any course where teachers evaluate students' achievement via essays or term papers.

As a special note, it is common after a student has gone through several cassette critiques of an essay and corrected all the mistakes in his or her essay by cutting out the errors and taping in the corrections, that the student will ask the teacher if he or she can rewrite the whole essay and have the "A" or "B" letter grade (gained by correcting the essay) written on the completely rewritten essay. This can be very rewarding for the student as it may be the first time he or she has ever written an "A" or "B" essay.

Another procedure which can be used successfully with students who have had a series of negative experiences in writing essays particularly if their writing problems concern making outlines, writing paragraph sentences, editing, and rewriting essays. This procedure is referred to as *Backward Chaining*. Generally, in most writing courses, students are taught how to write essays by following more or less the pattern of (1) selecting a topic, (2) collecting notes, (3) making an outline, (4) writing paragraph sentences, (5) writing the first draft, (6) editing the first draft, and (7) the final rewrite. Many students have learned to write by following these steps, but some students have trouble achieving steps 2—6 and as a result, the errors in these substeps are compounded and the students rarely, if ever, have success in writing an "A" or "B" essay in the last step. Having never written a good essay, these students just aren't aware of how much each step in writing an essay depends on an adequate achievement of the previous step. In *Backward* Chaining, (see Figure 21) the students are given prepared materials in which the first six steps have already been completed correctly and the students are only asked to achieve the last step. Once this is done successfully (maybe using the cassette critique approach), then the students are given prepared materials in which the first five steps have already been completed correctly and the students are asked to achieve the last two steps. When each of these last two steps have been completed correctly, then the students are given prepared materials in which the first four steps have already been completed correctly and the students are asked to achieve the last three steps. This process of *Backward Chaining* is continued until the student is asked to achieve all seven steps.

For students who have a lot of problems (skills and motivation) to overcome in learning to write, the *Backward Chaining* process can be repeated several times starting out with simple essays the first time through the process and increasing the complexity of the essays each time the process is repeated.

This process of backward chaining can be applied to any complex behavior in a wide variety of fields in which success in the total process is dependent upon the successful achievement of each step in the process. Students who have a history of negative experiences in educa-

193

tion generally lack motivation to finish projects because they haven't experienced the rewards of successful completion very often.

SEVEN STEPS IN WRITING AN ESSAY

	Selecting a Topic	Collecting Notes	Making an Outline	Writing Paragraph Sentences	First Draft	Editing	Rewrite	Quality Control Level
1st Essay —	Given	Given	Given	Given	Given	Given	student does	A or B
2nd Essay —	Given	Given	Given	Given	Given	student does	student does	A or B
3rd Essay —	Given	Given	Given	Given	student does	student does	student does	A or B
4th Essay —	Given	Given	Given	student does	student does	student does	student does	A or B
5th Essay —	Given	Given	student does	student does	student does	student does	student does	A or B
6th Essay —	Given	student does	student does	student does	student does	student does	student does	A or B
7th Essay —	student does	student does	student does	student does	student does	student does	student does	A or B

Figure 21 — Backward Chaining applied to writing an essay.

In backward chaining, the students experience success each time they go through the process even though the amount of work necessary to complete the project successfully varies from only one step (the last step) backwards to finally include every step in the process.

i.   INCREASED EFFECTIVENESS AS A POTENTIAL LEARNING PROBLEM

As teachers, in accepting this new role, began identifying and solving more and more learning problems, a unique learning problem will be encountered. Under the traditional approach, students, teachers, and parents have become so accustomed to the ineffectiveness in the instructional situation where the majority of students learn only 50—75 percent of the desired objectives of each course, that as more and more students start achieving "A" and "B" worth of their courses, teachers and even students may start to resist the efforts to continue increasing the effectiveness of the instructional event. It seems strange that our society, particularly students and teachers, have been conditioned by the traditions of education to view success for everyone as wrong. Among the students, the first ones to complain will probably be the so-called "A" students. Under the Behavioral Learning Systems Approach to Instruction, all of the students will eventually end up with an "A", so becoming an "A" student is not so unique anymore. In order

194

to solve this problem, the traditional "A" student has to perceive some advantage. The easiest way to solve this problem is to let the students progress at their own pace through the course. As soon as the traditional "A" student completes the course (and every other student too), be sure that the student knows he or she is through with the course. Chances are in most courses that the traditional "A" student will be one of the first ones completing the course. The advantage for this student is that he or she is through earlier and has more free time to do what he or she wants to do. This does not necessarily mean that all traditional "A" students will complete courses and school early. Whenever a student completes a course or sometimes even a unit (particularly if the student is learning faster than the average students), the student should be given a choice of five things to do:

— continue studying vertically by going on to the next unit or course;

— continue studying horizontally by going back and studying some interesting aspects of the course in greater depth;

— to go off into an independent study unit of his or her own choosing for the sake of learning or to prepare for a presentation to other students and teachers under the scholarship function of schools;

— to study other courses where the student feels he or she needs to spend more time; and

— to stop studying for awhile and relax.

For the teachers who feel guilty or feel like they are cheating someone when too many students have success,[14] they have to learn that all students can have success and that having all or most of the students having success is not a bad situation. For students who are not accustomed to success and may not even believe that they can make it, they have to learn that they can learn and the teachers, schools, and the community wants them to have success. To accomplish both of these problems simultaneously, instead of having teachers jump from their traditional approach with a normal curve's worth of achievement into the systems concept where all students eventually get "A's", start out the first quarter or semester with A's, B's, C's, D's, and I's (incompletes). When the teachers and students discover that everyone can make "D" or better, then the next quarter or semester have the teachers try giving only A's, B's, C's, and I's. When the teachers and

---

[14] It is still very common, particularly in higher education, for presidents, chancellors, provosts, deans, and other administrators to send out memos to faculty concerning the fact that too many A's are being given out. Can you imagine a hospital administrator calling in his staff and saying, *We have a serious problem, too many patients are getting well. You are going to have to do something to keep them sick longer and to kill a few more!*

students discover that all of the students can make "C" or better, then the next quarter or semester have the teachers try giving only A's, B's, and I's. When the teachers and students discover that all or almost all of the students can make "B" or better, then the next quarter or semester have the teachers try giving only 100 percent and I's where the 100 percent could be an "A" or a "B" depending on your grading pattern (see Chapter VIII, Volume III).

For some students, drop-outs, and push-outs, who have hardly ever had a successful experience in school and have been convinced by teachers, fellow students, parents, relatives, and even neighborhood friends that they are *dumb* and can't learn, it is a difficult task to convince these students they they can learn even if their teachers believe they can. I have found with these students or young adults that it is necessary to use very short instructional units, ten to fifteen minutes long. Start out with a pretest to see if the students have the necessary skills to even start the instructional unit and also find out if they possibly already know a part of the instructional unit. Knowing what they don't know, the students start on the brief unit. When they finish the unit, they should be given a posttest. Any item that the students miss on the posttest should be taught such that within about 30 minutes or so after starting the unit, every student has learned 100 percent of the unit objectives. For many of these students, it may be the first 100 percent score they have ever received. After receiving 100 percent on several of the brief units, it is possible to increase the instructional unit time to 45 minutes or an hour in length (for the average student). Remember, it took from five to ten years to completely break down the self-image as they may see themselves in a formal learning situation, so don't expect these students to recover in a matter of days or weeks. It may take some of these students six to eight weeks before an instructional unit can be spread over several days before receiving evidence of success. In the process of increasing the length of the instructional units, if a student becomes discouraged about his or her ability to achieve success, decrease the length of the units.

A very common objection voiced by some faculty is that if the students keep having success all of the time, it is not adequately and honestly preparing them for the real world because out in the real world most people experience some forms of failure. When I ask these teachers what it is about failing that they think is important most of them will honestly answer by saying that they feel it is important to learn how to *cope with failure.* In other words they actually want the students to be able to have success in coping with failure. I can agree with this viewpoint. Therefore, it may be necessary to develop an instructional unit in which part of the design is to be sure that the student experiences failure. But since the unit is concerned with teaching the student how to cope with failure, the evaluation of the students concerns their coping behavior and each student should stay in the unit until he or she achieves an "A" or "B" in the unit, *How to cope with failure*.

There are a few teachers that enjoy giving F's to students as it makes them feel *God-like* to have such power over the future of students. In addition, giving F's to students helps this type of insecure teacher to feel more intelligent and special in our society. From time to time in my seminars and workshops, one of these teachers will be identified by their extreme vocal resistance to the giving up of the "F" grade much to the shock and amazement of their colleagues. For example, in meeting with a social science faculty group (college level) following up two days of general sessions we were discussing grading practices. (As pointed out earlier in this chapter, my belief is that any student that gets less than an "A" or a "B" in a course or unit of a course has learning problems which should be solved such that the desired learning takes place.) One teacher in the group, an educational psychologist, became very vocal about wanting to retain the right to fail students. I kept pushing the teacher to state what it was that he didn't want some of his students to learn in order that he could fail them for not learning. Finally in desperation, the teacher proclaimed that the failing grade had nothing to do with learning or not learning! At that point, his colleagues in the room were really bewildered by his incredible statement. I insisted that the teacher reveal his criteria for failing students since it had nothing to do with learning. I also wanted to know if the students had any idea as to what the criteria were. In a highly agitated and emotional response, the teacher said, *Dammit! Of course the students know, if I like them, they get an "A". If I don't like them, they get an "F"!* (This particular teacher happened to be teaching at that time a course titled *Educational Measurement.*) Hopefully, as our instructional system becomes more and more success-oriented, these teachers will eventually like helping students become successful, will realize that they need psychiatric help, or will become sufficiently unhappy because they can't fail students and will quit their jobs.

NOTE: In concluding this section on Examples of Learning Problems, I would like to recommend for further study, if desired, Robert Mager's and Peter Pipe's booklet *Analyzing Performance Problems or You Really Oughta Wanna* published in 1970 by Fearon Publishers, Belmont, California.

3. *RECOGNITION OF INDIVIDUAL DIFFERENCES IN ACTION INSTEAD OF WORDS*

For about three-fourths of a century, we have been talking about individual differences among students but we have very rarely done anything about individual differences in the teaching-learning situation. In 1926, the following statement appeared in the Yearbook of the National Society for the Study of Education:

It has become palpably absurd to expect to achieve uniform results from uniform assignments made to a class of widely differing individuals. Throughout the educational world there has therefore awakened a desire to find some way of adopting schools to the differing individuals who attend them.

By the mid 1960's, when the information was gathered for the Coleman report, *Equality of Educational Opportunity,* evidence indicated that not much had been done in adapting our schools to the individual differences of our students.

— most of the variation in (student) achievement could not possibly be accounted for by school differences, since most of it (differences in achievement) lies within the school. This result indicates that despite the wide range of diversity of school facilities, curriculum, and teachers, and despite the wide differences among student bodies in different schools, over 70 percent of the variation in achievement for each group (student body) is (a result of) variation within the same student body.

In the charter or constitution of almost every single educational institution in our country, there is a statement which essentially says *to develop each student to the maximum of his or her ability.* This statement actually commits the teachers and schools to the concept of individualized instruction. Luckily for the teachers and schools, no student and/or parent has really pushed the issue during the past decades. Under the concept of *educational malpractices* however, their luck may be about to run out. To many, it is a very perplexing problem because every teacher believes in individual differences among students, many teachers have attended conferences dealing with the concept, most elementary and secondary teachers as students in the teacher-training institutions have had one or more courses dealing with the concept, and yet, very few teachers actually perform in their classrooms with *deeds* as if they really believe in individual differences. In fact, by observing the way teachers act in their classrooms and by examining the structure of the traditional educational patterns, the irrefutable evidence is that the concept of individual differences is *not recognized* in *actions* in the vast majority of schools and classrooms.

How can this apparent hypocrisy exist so widespread among our country's (and the world's) intellectual aristocracy (teachers) and how has it been able to exist for so long? There is one major *foundation* for this hypocrisy existing in education, and two *supporting walls* which have helped maintain this hypocrisy. The major cause concerns the role of the teacher. As long as the three functions of the school: learning,

198

scholarship, and record keeping are confused and overlapping such that the record keeping function structures the time intervals and calendar limits for learning, i.e., six week sessions, periods, quarters, semesters, years, etc. and the teachers' function is to present the course content and students are forced to go in lockstep through a course for the interval of time and between the calendar limits set by the record keepers, learning will be negatively affected by the other two functions. In the role as presenters of course content, it is practically impossible for teachers to individualize instruction from the point of view of allowing for individual differences among students. As presenters of course content, teachers have to assume that all students are at the same place when they start presenting the course and yet, when asked point blank, almost all teachers will admit that students aren't all at the same place at the beginning of a course. Although all teachers will agree that students learn at different rates, when teachers are the presenters of course content, the students have to learn as fast or faster than the teacher presents or they'll fall behind and incur cumulative ignorance.

Even though all teachers will readily admit that some students will learn best using one particular pathway or mode of learning while other students will learn better using other pathways or modes of learning; yet, as long as teachers are presenters of course content, the modes for student learning are restricted to the mode or modes used by the teacher in presenting the course. Each of us as human beings have different attitudes, values, and beliefs and these differences affect our learning patterns in such a way that what motivates one person to learn may not motivate another person to learn and the interpersonal relationship between one teacher and a student facilitates learning while the interpersonal relationship between another student and the same teacher may interfere with learning. However, the differences among students in their attitudes, values, and beliefs as they affect motivation and interpersonal relationships have to be ignored most of the time by teachers who are in the presenting role. The function of the role has to assume that students are motivated to learn by the same things, if not, it is assumed that the students can't be motivated to learn anyway. In addition, under the traditional approach, all of the students in a given class are expected to learn from the same teacher and the same textbook regardless of interpersonal conflicts either live or indirect via print.

A very strong *supporting wall* which helps maintain the non-recognition of individual differences is that *teachers tend to teach the way they were taught, not the way they were taught to teach.* I know that I have mentioned this before, but it is such a true statement and has such an impact on every new generation of teachers, that it has to be

199

emphasized again and again.[15] To illustrate, in most teacher training institutions, the teachers who are teaching the courses concerning *individual differences among students* actually ignore the individual differences among the students who are taking the courses! This factor is so strong that it actually overcomes what is taught in education courses to the degree that after five years or sooner, it is very difficult to differentiate by their *actions* with students in their classrooms, between those teachers in elementary and secondary, and higher education who have had education courses and the majority of teachers in higher education who haven't had any so-called professional education courses. A very integral part of this supporting wall is the loyalty to traditions and the security in tradition which is a part of the personality makeup of many educators. *After all, we've been doing it this way so long, surely, if there was something really wrong with what we were doing, changes would have been made before this!*

The other *supporting wall* concerns the concept of intelligence which has been developed over a period of years in the minds of most educators and non-educators. Intelligence has been defined by many psychologists and educators as the level of achievement on a standardized test within a set period of time. Since the traditional point-of-view is that the distribution of intelligence in a random group of students approximates the normal curve distribution (the *bell* curve), any test that can be designed to give results that approximates the normal curve distribution is looked on as a measure of intelligence. Therefore, the emphasis in making tests is to get a good distribution of scores, and when the scores do actually vary such that the distribution approximates a normal or *bell* curve, this in turn reinforces the teacher's belief that the scores indicate each students ability to learn (or intelligence). Since psychologists and biologists have also convinced most educators and non-educators that intelligence or *ability to learn* is based on genetics or *nature*, then teachers can't see any value for changing their role because they are already achieving *maximum* learning under the present traditional approach (a normal or *bell* curve of results). In support of this belief, is the evidence from sporadic efforts to individualize instruction which lacks the dramatic results one would expect to find. For example, Gage and Unruh of Stanford University, stated in *Current Research on Instruction* (1969),

Why are not the mean scores on achievement measures of pupils taught with due respect for their individual needs and abilities substantially higher, in unmistakable ways, than those of students

---

[15] This is why it is so critical that all teachers who are teaching *teachers-to-be* should be practicing the humanizing role of identifying and solving learning problems, not just the teachers of the professional *instruction* courses.

taught in the conventional classroom, where everyone reads the same book, listens to the same lecture, participates in the same classroom discussion, moves at the same pace, and works at the same problems? For the fact is that, despite several decades of concern with individualization, few if any striking results have been reported.

Supposedly in changing the role of the teacher from a presenter of course content to the solver of learning problems and prescriber of solutions, it will be possible to truly individualize instruction by not only allowing for a variety of individual differences but by actually taking advantage of individual differences to increase the effectiveness and efficiency of the instructional environments. But then, if what Gage and Unruh say is true, why should anyone go to all the trouble to make the change? First of all, remember in comparing an experimental group (individualized instruction) with a control group (traditional lecture group) in order to identify any differences in instruction, it is necessary to use the same test for both groups. I am assuming that the *achievement measures* are standardized tests. If this is true, then the research is invalid to begin with (see Chapter VI, Volume II). Assuming the test is valid and standardized, the important things to remember about standardized tests is that the validity of the test is dependent upon whether or not the results of using the test fit or approximate the desired curve. A good test item, according to tradition is one that 50 percent will miss — a good discriminator. A good discriminating test item is not usually an important item (as too many teachers would teach it and too many students would learn it — a non-discriminating item) nor is it a trivial item (as too many teachers would not teach it and too many students wouldn't learn it — also a non-discriminating item). According to tradition, it is considered wrong if the teachers or students in the comparative research project see a copy of the standardized test before it is given. If they have seen the test or even have an idea as to what is on the test, it is considered *dirty pool* to teach to the test. Therefore, the evaluation instrument used to compare the two methods, traditional vs. individualized instruction, have the following invalidating characteristics:

— the results of the test are built into the test items when it is written;

— if the test contained any multiple-choice type test items, the use of distractors in the items are more apt to control the students selection than what the student knows;

— the majority of the test items are designed to be concerned with mediocre or inconsequential aspects of possibly more important concepts (good discriminators); and

— neither the control nor the experimental groups could have

201

learned too much of what was on the test — teachers aren't supposed to teach what is on the test.

In addition to the tests being invalid, consider the problems in comparing *traditional vs. individualized instruction*. First of all *individualized instruction* can be defined in many ways:

(Traditional view of *individualized or independent instruction*)

— students learning on their own from the same book the traditional teacher lectured from (shouldn't expect any differences):
— students receiving the same lectures via same audio visual media on an individualized basis (shouldn't expect any differences);
— students learning from independent study materials developed around the same general objectives which were used to develop the lectures (shouldn't expect any differences);

(A Behavioral Learning Systems point-of-view of *individualized instruction*)

— students learning from independent study materials developed from a list of specific measurable objectives, starting from where each student is intellectually (based on pretest data) to eliminate learning problems from cumulative ignorance or boredom from already knowing part of the instructional unit and ending only when each student learns 100 percent of the specific measurable objectives (any mistake or problem in learning should be treated as a learning problem and solved in whatever way necessary to bring about the necessary learning (SHOULD EXPECT CONSIDERABLE DIFFERENCES IF THE EVALUATION TESTS EXACTLY THE SPECIFIC OBJECTIVES OF THE INSTRUCTIONAL UNIT — A CRITERION TEST).

As typical educators and especially traditional educational researchers look at the above, they will object to the comparison of Individualized Instruction *ala systems* versus traditional instruction on one or more of the following grounds:

— by the time all of the students learn all of the objectives, it could take two, three, or more times as long as the lecture method, to compare these two methods in research, have to use the same time! (If time cannot be left as a variable, then you don't have true Individualized Instruction);
— can't use the criterion test, because the students were taught what was on the test. Have to use a standardized test for both groups! (Already answered this one — standardized tests invalid);
— students used different types of materials, some used books, some used films, some used slides, some even went out of the schools in order to learn all of the objectives — NOT FAIR — have to stick to one method of individualized materials! (If

202

can't use whatever materials and methods necessary to bring about learning, then you don't have true Individualized Instruction);

— students were motivated to learn with a variety of techniques, some were motivated to learn by using relevant materials, some were rewarded for learning with money, — NOT FAIR — have to stick to only one method of motivation if any — after all listening to lectures is not very motivating for most students! (If can't use whatever motivation and interpersonal relationships necessary to help learners to learn all of the objectives, then you don't have true Individualized Instruction);

All right then, the traditional educators and researcher will say, *if you won't be fair and change your approach to Individualized Instruction, then how about one of the following;*

— since the students in the Individualized Instruction had a list of specific objectives, how about letting the students in the lecture group have the same list of specific objectives (sounds like a good idea, but if the students know exactly what they are supposed to learn, that is no longer traditional instruction);

— since the teacher in Individualized Instruction who is diagnosing and prescribing instructional units based on the use and results of the criterion test, how about letting the teacher who is the lecturer have the criterion test in order to teach to the test too (sounds like a good idea, but traditional teachers don't often have tests ready ahead of time in order to teach to the test — anyway under the traditional concept, it is bad to teach to the test);

— since the students in Individualized Instruction actually take the criterion test several times in order to find out what they haven't learned so they'll know what to study in order to ultimately learn 100 percent of the test, how about letting the students in the traditional group take the test several times with additional lecture time in between tests. (Sounds like a good idea, but under the traditional approach students don't usually have a second chance to take a test over again let alone getting a third, fourth, or more chances);

— since many of the students in Individualized Instruction are getting their course content via books, television, films, etc., the teacher in Individualized Instruction isn't really teaching (presenting course content), he or she is working with small groups and individuals, helping them learn. How about letting the Traditional class have an extra person to work with small groups and individuals too because the teacher in the traditional class is too busy teaching (presenting course content) — (again, sounds like a good idea, but under the traditional approach it wouldn't generally be done).

In that case, the traditional educators and researchers will say, *if you won't reduce the flexibility of the structure in the Individualized Instruction class in order to make it possible to compare it to the traditional class or you won't let us add some flexibility to the structure of the traditional class in order to make it possible to compare it to the Individualized Instruction class, then the two classes can't really be compared because they represent two entirely different situations — like trying to compare oranges and apples. — and they would be right,* the two situations are entirely different. They each are conducted under different philosophies, orientation, emphases, and with the teachers performing very different roles. If these two classes were to be compared properly, one would have to identify the practical and measurable benefits which should occur from a given class or course, i.e., third grade social studies, seventh grade earth science, first year algebra, second year cooking, twelfth grade English, first year accounting (college level), philosophy, etc., according to the parents, students, and taxpayers in consultation with the teachers. Then, make up a test that would test for the achievement of these practical and measurable benefits and test several classes of students which have been educated in the traditional manner and several classes of students which have been instructed under the Individualized Instruction manner. Obviously the Individualized Instruction group would be significantly better because the philosophy is that all students learn all or 100 percent of the course whereas the philosophy in the traditional group is that the average or most students in the group learn only 70—75 percent of the course (depending where "C" is — in some courses "C" is only 50—60 percent).

a. INTELLIGENCE AND INDIVIDUAL DIFFERENCES

Chances are that at this point, there are some readers who just can't quite believe that all or almost all students could learn 100% of an instructional unit even if the objectives were specified and individual differences were recognized and allowed for by the teacher's actions. In order to help convince these readers and to help those readers who are already convinced but need help in convincing others who don't believe it, I am going to use the concept of intelligence, defined as the *rate of learning*, and illustrate how the observance of individual differences affects *rate of learning* and hence intelligence.[16]

---

[16] Intelligence is frequently defined in terms of being able to do certain things, i.e., capacity to know, to transfer old knowledge to new things, to use symbols and relationships, etc. Given whatever skills you want to list, a person who can learn them faster than other people is usually considered to have more intelligence than the other people.

$$\text{Intelligence} = \frac{\text{Rate of}}{\text{Learning}} = \frac{\text{Amount Learned}}{\text{Time for Learning}} = \frac{L_t - L_e}{T_t - T_e}$$

Equation I — Rate of Learning

Rate of Learning is equal to the amount a student learns divided by the time necessary for learning (see equation I). The amount learned is equal to the amount the student knows (L_t) at the termination of the instructional unit at time (T_t) minus what the student knew (L_e) as he or she entered the instructional unit at time (T_e).[17]

b. RATE OF LEARNING — TRADITIONAL SITUATION

The problem under the traditional approach to education is that specific objectives which are necessary for measurement are not used, so it would be difficult, if not impossible, to measure amount learned by students ($L_t - L_e$). Since the primary emphasis is on the teacher, the amount *to be learned* was essentially the course and the amount learned by students was evaluated by giving tests, writing papers, giving reports, doing projects, etc.

$$\frac{\text{Rate of}}{\text{Learning}} = \frac{\text{Sum of all the evaluations}}{T_t - t_e} = \text{"B" for the semester} \quad \text{or} \quad \text{"C" for the 6 weeks}$$

Equation II — Traditional Rate of Learning

c. RATE OF LEARNING AS AFFECTED BY THE AMOUNT TO BE LEARNED

Because of the emphasis on the teacher as a presenter of course content, the course is determined by what teachers present. The beginning of the course (C_e) is where the teachers start on the first day and the end of the course (C_t) is where the teacher terminates the course on the last day. Therefore, the amount to be learned is ($C_t - C_e$) and is equated to ($L_t - L_e$). Although it might be possible for the end of the course (C_t) to be essentially equal to the terminal sum of objectives

$$\frac{\text{Amount to be learned}}{\text{Amount of time to learn it in}} = \frac{L_t - L_e}{T_t - T_e} \neq \frac{C_t - C_e}{T_t - T_e}$$

Equation III — Amount to be Learned

---

[17] Any reader who has trouble understanding equation I, may find it easier to think of the concept rate of learning, as being similar to the rate of driving (in miles per hour) which is equal to the distance between two points divided by the time it took to travel between the two points

$$\text{rate} = \frac{\text{Distance}}{\text{Time}} = \frac{100 \text{ miles}}{2 \text{ hours}} = 50 \text{ miles per hours}$$

(L_t) which a student should learn in that course, it is rare that where the course starts (C_e) is equal to where the student actually is (L_e). In other words, the amount each student has to learn ($L_t - L_e$) is *not usually equal* ($\neq$) to the content of the course ($C_t - C_e$).

Teachers at every level of instruction are very much aware of the fact that students in their classes vary considerably in what they may know of prerequisite information and also what they may know about the course itself. For example, there has been a considerable amount of research which indicates that children from disadvantaged backgrounds start school anywhere from one to three years behind the more advantaged students. This indicates immediately that students from the disadvantaged environment have more to learn than their more advantaged classmates. If this extra learning does not take place, the disadvantaged students become further and further behind their more advantaged classmates.

In a classroom, when a teacher is a *presenter of course content* then all of the students have to start where the teacher starts, and stop where the teacher stops, which may not be appropriate for the student's needs in the teaching-learning situation. The very fact that students with "C's," and "D's" (in elementary schools even "F's") are allowed to proceed to the next course should automatically indicate to the teacher that the students are not all at the same intellectual level, and consequently should not all be expected to start on page one of the textbook. When the teacher starts on page one of the textbook he is very likely to lose the students who are not properly prepared and bore the students who already know that part of the course. If teachers do not give any type of pretest at the beginning of the school term in order to determine where the student is (intellectually) and if the teachers have never specified objectives of their courses so they know where the students are supposed to go (intellectually) by the end of their courses, then the learning variable *amount to be learned* is really quite meaningless. Traditionally, in most schools, all students start on page one of the textbook for that course, regardless of whether or not they are properly prepared to start on page one, or whether they may already know enough about the content of the course that they are on page fifty or one hundred of the textbook. Consider for a moment the students in Figure 22.

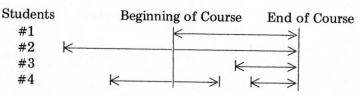

Figure 22 — Amount to be Learned

206

Student #1 doesn't know any part of the course, but does know all of the prerequisite material. Student #2 needs some developmental work (not remedial)[18] before he can start the course. Whether or not Student #2 takes his developmental work prior to the course or concurrently with the course depends upon the subject matter, the student, and the dependency of the course on the student's knowledge of prerequisite materials. Student #3 knows most of the course and in most instances would probably be wasting his time and the teacher's if he were to go back through the material in the course which he already knows. Student #4 is more likely to be typical of most of the students today. He needs a certain amount of developmental study, and in addition, he already knows a considerable part of the course.

In order to put into practice the belief that there are individual differences among students, a teacher should start out with some kind of test to find out whether or not each student has the proper amount of prerequisite information necessary to start the course and how much, if any, does each student already know about the course which will be taught. Then, depending on where each student is, the teacher should allow the students to start as close as possible to that point, such that the students do not have any gaps nor any unnecessary overlapping in the instructional process. In order to take this variable into account, the concept of the teacher as a presenter of course content has to be dropped because every student is different with respect to the *amount to be learned* and very few students would be ready to start on page one with the teacher.

As a possible compromise during the changeover from the traditional approach to the Behavioral Learning Systems approach and a common request from students who attend my seminars, at least use this approach in developmental units, courses, or when students are repeating courses (being held back). It should be obvious that most of the students may not need the whole course. After all, the students must have learned something in going through it the first time. By the

---

[18] When students are not up to the expected level of their grade, there is a temptation to suggest that the students take *remedial* work. Generally, *remedial* work is taken to mean that the student is going to go back over material that he once learned, but has since forgotten and needs only to refresh his memory. But this is based on the assumption if the teacher has presented the information to the learner, he should have learned it. This is a false assumption. Just because a student has been exposed to certain material, certainly does not guarantee that the student has learned the material. Generally, students develop a negative attitude towards the designation of being a student in a so-called *remedial* class because it is traditional to blame the student for the problem. The placement of a student in a *remedial* class is actually more apt to be a result of the student being exposed to ineffective and inefficient educational practices than the fault of the learners. Therefore, most *remedial* courses are really remedying the teaching-learning situation the students were exposed to and not necessarily remedying the students. For this reason, I prefer to refer to the so-called remedial classes as developmental classes.

use of pretests, it is possible to find out if the student has any critical cumulative ignorance from previous courses which may have caused the student to have trouble in the course the student is repeating. In addition, the pretests should identify how much of the course the student is repeating that he or she needs to learn for success in subsequent courses.

In recognizing that students have different amounts to be learned, it should also be recognized that the differences affect both the student's *apparent rate of learning* and his or her *actual rate of learning*. Before recognizing these differences, the distance or amount learned was only identified at the end of the entire course when the tests were given, then the apparent amount learned and the apparent rate of learning was supposedly represented by the grade received: an "A" is 95—100 percent of the course per semester, a "B" is 85—94 percent of the course per semester, a "C" is 70—84 percent of the course per semester, a "D" is 60—69 percent of the course per semester, and "F" anything less than that. With reference to Figure 22, student #3 might very easily get an "A" because the student already knows almost half of the course, student #3's apparent rate of learning, before identifying amount to be learned, would be an "A" or 95—100 percent of the course per semester. After identifying that student #3 already knew one-half of the course, if it really took the student a full semester to learn only half of the course, student #3's actual rate of learning is 50 percent of the course per semester which is equivalent to the apparent rate of learning for the "F" student (less than 60 percent of the course per semester). Student #2 needs some prerequisite skills and knowledge in order to be successful in this course. If the teacher is traditional and starts at the beginning of the course rather than where each student is, student #2 will probably get an "F". If the student repeats the course a second time, still starting from the beginning of the course rather than where the student is, the student may finally achieve a "D" with an apparent learning rate of say 65 percent of the course per two semesters. By identifying where the student is intellectually and starting from there, the student might very easily become a "C" student by the end of the semester with an actual rate of learning of 125 percent (50 percent of the previous course and 75 percent of this course) per semester which is better than the rate of learning for the "A" student and over twice as fast as student #3 if it took student #3 a full semester to learn one-half of the course. Given that almost every student has a different amount to be learned, a teacher cannot assume that all students are at the same place to start any course which makes the presenting role or any role which lock-steps students through a course very inhumane because it ignores individual differences in amounts to be learned.

208

Once all the cumulative ignorance is eliminated and students aren't allowed to leave a course without learning 100 percent of the course, the ending point of course four (L_{t_4}) will be essentially equal to the beginning point of the next course, course five (L_{e_5}). Under the traditional approach, not only are there gaps and overlaps in reference to comparing the amounts to be learned by the students and the content of a given course, but there are also gaps and overlaps between courses. If the average student coming to a teacher of a second course in a sequence has learned "C" worth of the first course, then this means that approximately 25 percent of the first course was not learned. Compounding the problem is that rarely will the 25 percent which wasn't learned be the same 25 percent for two or more students. Realizing this, the conscientious teacher of the second course may very well include at least a summary of the first course in the first part of the second course, an overlapping condition. Another teacher may start on page one of the second course which would leave a gap between the first and second course for most students. Because the concept of *academic freedom* is interpreted by many teachers as the *freedom to do anything they want to*, two or more teachers teaching the same course will not start and stop at the same place in the course content and will not even have the same amount of content. This lack of continuity and agreement accentuates the gaps and overlaps between courses under the traditional patterns. Figure 23 compares the patterns of course sequences between the traditional and the Behavioral Learning Systems approaches.

(1) IDEAL COMPOSITION OF AMOUNT TO BE LEARNED

Under the traditional approach, as pointed out previously, the *amount to be learned* was and is generally determined by whatever the teacher wanted to present and any incursion into this content has been and is considered a violation of the teacher's academic freedom. But since the teacher's freedom may very well ignore the needs of the students and the needs and desires of the society which supports the schools and teachers, then this view of academic freedom is one-sided, biased, limits the freedoms of others, and as such, cannot be considered real academic freedom.

Under a *mod* approach used by some misguided teachers and by other teachers trying to evade accountability, the *amount to be learned* is generally determined by whatever the students want to do and any incursion into this is considered by these teachers and students as a violation of the students' academic freedom. This approach leaves the teacher without a role to perform, but the teacher still wants the society to support them in sort of an elite welfare arrangement. If the students decide *not to learn* what they need to know to earn a living and to get along with their fellow members in our society, the society

209

suffers by having to support them via unemployment, welfare, and to endure their interpersonal conflicts and infringements on the freedom of other members of our society. Again, because the students complete academic freedom limits the freedom of others, this view of academic freedom for the students cannot be considered real academic freedom.

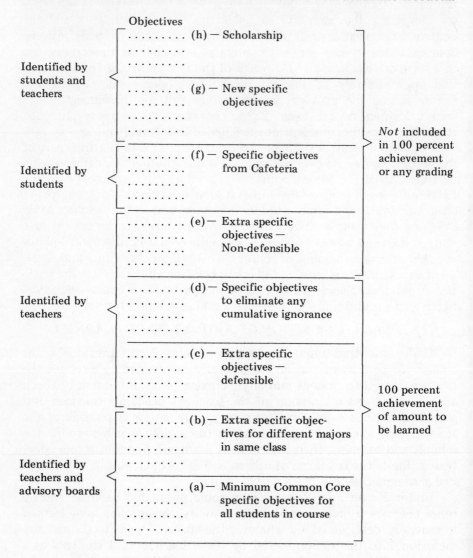

Figure 23 — Composition of *Amount to be Learned*

Under the Behavioral Learning Systems approach to instruction, the amount to be learned would be made up of specific objectives which

210

represent necessary and desired intellectual and sensory skills. In order that the amount to be learned can allow for the involvement of all concerned, there are actually eight categories of specific objectives (see Figure 23).

Category (a) — These are the specific objectives which the teachers and any advisory board have agreed upon. The advisory board would usually consist of other teachers who are teaching the same course and might include persons from the community or other nearby institutions if appropriate. It could be reasonable to include students who have already completed the course in the discussion of any changes and updating of the minimum common core content objectives. Students who haven't had the course yet would not know enough about the course to be involved in the setting of specific objectives, but they could be involved in the identification of the general objectives from which the specific objectives are developed. The process used to arrive at an agreement will be discussed in the next chapter (see Chapter VI, Volume II). It should be considered a students right to challenge the need to require the learning of any objective in this category. If the necessity for the objective cannot be defended, then the objective may be taken out of this category and put into the *cafeteria* of objectives (pool of specific objectives).

Category (b) — Depending on the course, there may or may not be a need for this category. Given a course that is a basic course for two or more majors, it is possible that certain specific objectives, available in the basic course, might be considered critical in preparing for one major area but not necessarily critical for other major areas. In this way, if a student has already had the basic course and the extra objectives associated with one major, and the student changes major goals, the student only has to learn the extra specific objectives associated with the new major to gain full credit for the basic course as preparation in the new major. If a student hadn't decided on a major area of study at the time he or she started this course, it would be possible to take this course as a non-major which would then eliminate the learning of any specific objectives from this category. In recording the completion of this course on the students' transcripts, the course number should identify the basic course content (category 1 — specific objectives) and the extra major area content (category 2 — specific objectives), i.e., General Biology 100 for students who are not planning to take any more courses which might be dependent upon biology as a basic course, Biology 100 CH — for students majoring in chemistry, Biology 100 BI — for students majoring in biology, Biology 100 HE — for students majoring in home economics, Biology 100 SC — for students majoring in other service areas, etc.

Category (c) — These are extra specific objectives which the other

211

teachers and the advisory board didn't think were critical, but the individual teacher believes these to be important and is prepared to defend them to the students as being necessary.

Category (d) — In testing the students at the beginning of the course, if the teacher indentifies critical skills which the student doesn't have and which should have been learned in previous courses, these have to be included in the course in order to start from where the student is intellectually. If the student doesn't have any cumulative ignorance, then there would be no specific objectives from this category in the amount to be learned.

Category (e) — These are extra specific objectives from the pool or cafeteria of objectives which the teacher thinks are important, but are not defensible in terms of being useful in future courses or in life.

Category (f) — These are extra specific objectives from the pool or cafeteria of objectives which the individual student feels he or she would like to learn.

Category (g) — These are extra specific objectives which have been developed by the student independently or with a teacher because of a special interest of the student.

Category (h) — These objectives may or may not be specific and are primarily associated with a student's decision to prepare for a presentation under the scholarship function of the schools.

(2) COMPROMISE COMPOSITION OF AMOUNT
   TO BE LEARNED

Recognizing that very few teachers have specific objectives available for their courses, there are several other definitions of *amount to be learned* which can be used by teachers while in the transition stage from the traditional approach to the Behavioral Learning Systems approach. Also, there are teachers who evaluate students by assigning grades or by giving tests and then assigning grades who at the time disclaim having any objectives.

(a) For those teachers who don't have any objectives, don't give any tests,[19] but do assign different grades to students which indicate that the students have different levels of achievement — In grading the student down from an "A", (100 percent, "S", or any other mark indicating highest achievement) the teacher is indicating to the student that *something?* wasn't achieved (learned). The further down the achievement scale the student is graded, the greater the *amount to be learned* that wasn't learned. If the teacher can't identify what it (?) was

---

[19] The word test is used throughout this book refers to any form of evaluation: objective type tests, problem-solving tests, short or long answer essay tests, evaluation by observation of the students' performance, evaluation by observation of the students' products or work, etc.

that the student didn't learn, then the teacher has no right to grade a student down for not learning it (?). In grading the student down for not achieving something, the teacher is placing importance on what was not learned. Anything in a course that is important enough to grade a student down for not learning it, must be important enough to be considered one of the goals or *objectives* of the course. To grade a student down for not learning something (?) that the teacher is unable to specifically identify is to be inhumane and unjust. It may be acceptable under the traditional approach to grade students down and let it go at that; but under the systems concept, the acceptable role is for the teacher to identify what wasn't learned and that becomes what should be taught or *amount to be learned.*

(b) For those teachers who don't have any objectives, but do give tests[19] and grades and assuming that the course grades are related to the tests such that if items are missed on a test, this is reflected in the grade — If you as a reader are a teacher in this category, ask yourself the following question? *Is there any test item on my tests that I don't want my students to learn?* I would expect most or all teachers in this category to answer *No.* This means that if you want students to learn what is on your tests, then your test items actually are your course objectives and collectively, the test items represent the *amount to be learned* in the course.

(c) For those teachers that have some general objectives, some specific objectives, and give tests[19] and grades and assuming that the course grades are related to the tests such if items are missed on a test, this is reflected in the grade and assuming also that the tests relate to the general and specific objectives such that if items are missed on a test, the general or specific objectives associated with the students' errors can be identified.[20]—If each specific objective has one or more test items associated with it and there aren't any test items left over that are not

---

[20] An easy way to relate test items to general and specific objectives is to get a scissors and scotch tape and cut up a copy of each test such that each test item is by itself. Do the same with the lists of specific and general objectives such that each specific and each general objective is by itself. Now, put each general objective at the top of a sheet of paper. Then, sort out the specific objectives by putting each specific objective with its associated general objective. Any specific objective that is not related to any of your general objectives should be put on a separate sheet of paper. This indicates that you should either write general objectives to cover the odd specific objectives, or delete them from the course. Any general objective that doesn't have any specific objectives associated with it means that you should try to write some specific objectives to fit the general objective. Then, sort out the test items by putting each test item with its associated specific and/or general objectives. Any test item that is not related to either a specific or general objective should be placed on a separate sheet of paper (keeping duplicate or related items together). Any test items which are not associated with the specific and/or general objectives of the course indicates either a need to write specific objectives to fit the test items, or that they should be deleted from the course.

associated with any specific objective, then either the specific objective or the test items can represent the *amount to be learned* in the course. If there are test items left over that are not associated with any specific objective, then ask yourself, *Is there any of these test items that I don't want my students to learn?* If the answer is no, then the *amount to be learned* in the course is the total of the specific objectives or the associated test items *plus* the extra test items (which is the same as saying all of the test items). If there are some test items which you don't want your students to learn, delete them.

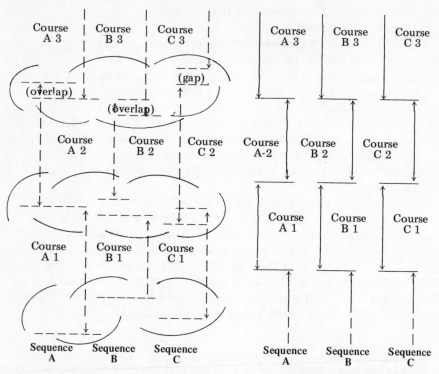

Traditional Patterns	**Learning System Patterns**
Typified by obscure entry and terminal course behaviors permitting gaps and overlaps in a sequence of course.	Typified by defined entry and terminal course behaviors such that the terminal behaviors of one course are the same as the entry behaviors of the next course.

Figure 24 — Patterns of Course Sequences

(3) CONTEMPORARY EFFORTS TO RECOGNIZE DIFFERENCES IN AMOUNTS TO BE LEARNED

The concept of *multiple tracking* or *ability grouping* is at least a partial recognition of different amounts to be learned, but sort of arrived at through a back door and with negative consequences.

Some schools may actually use the term *multiple-tracking*, or they may also use the term, *ability-grouping*. Also, in many schools, although they do not actually use either of these terms, they are in actual practice carrying on some form of multiple tracking. This is supported by the fact that, in addition to the regular classes, they also have special classes for the gifted students or honor classes, and then they have special classes for the slow learners. Regardless of the name involved, the concept of multiple tracking typically consists of identifying students who have similar apparent rates of learning which means they should be able to learn about the same amount in a given period of time. These students are then grouped in as many levels as the schools' program permits. In theory, the idea is that students who are more homogeneous can learn more effectively, because the teaching-learning situation will be geared to their rate of learning. Practically, if the teacher is going to be presenting course content, it is a lot easier to present course content to a group of students whose rates of learning are more homogeneous than to students in a typical classroom with extreme differences in rates of learning. As such, when the content of these different levels is being identified, it is rather apparent that the gifted students should be able to learn the content faster than the average students, so more content is added to the course for the gifted students (see Figure 25), in order that they will end up spending the required amount of time in the course. For the group that is not quite as fast as the average students, teachers realize that this group cannot cover the same amount of content as the regular students, so some of the content is left out. Similarly, the slow learning group, which is at the lowest level, has even more of the content removed from the course. Notice, the major emphasis here is that given a standard period of time, i.e., a semester, quarter, etc., to have all of the students in each group complete (not necessarily learn) the amount of content presented to each group.

A very serious problem develops in multiple-tracking because those students who are in either of the two tracks below the regular track (see Figure 25) are going to suffer from cumulative ignorance by the design of the system. For example, if a student has been in the third or fourth group in mathematics from kindergarten through eighth grade and this student decides he wants to go on into ninth-grade mathematics, but they don't have enough students to have ability grouping in ninth grade, then the student will be placed in the same class with the rest of the students from the other tracks. It should be rather obvious that where the amount of learning for the students in the lower tracks has been compromised or reduced for eight years, the student can't possibly have an equal opportunity for learning. This result is particularly true when many of the learning experiences which were left out over the

215

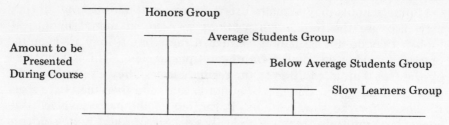

Figure 25 — Compromising on Learning

period of the eight years might have been necessary in order to have success in ninth-grade algebra and their absence assures the student of eventual failure. This is why the concept of multiple tracking has been ruled unconstitutional in Washington, D.C. (Hobson vs. Hansen). Once a student is in one of these lower tracks where learning is compromised in order to keep time constant then the student ultimately suffers from the experience.

A second and almost as serious an objection to the multiple track concept as it is actually practiced in the schools is the use of curve grading within each of the tracks (see Figure 26). From this particular approach to grading in the multiple track concept, the "A" students of the lower tracks very commonly have learned less than the "C" students of the regular track and maybe even less than the "F" students of the top track. This practice tends to mislead the students by discouraging the top-track students who get low grades and falsely encouraging the bottom-track students who get high grades.

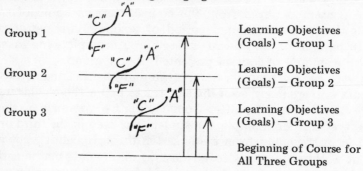

Figure 26 — Learning Objectives (Goals) and Grading Curves in Multiple tracking or Ability Grouping

This practice also causes many problems for schools and colleges who try to interpret the meaning for these grades particularly from the point-of-view of grades being equated to different rates of learning. It is difficult to understand how an honor student can get a "C", "D", or

216

"F" when in fact he has learned more than what the average students are required to learn in the course, and on the other hand, it seems difficult to understand how the below average learner can get an "A" for only learning a portion of what they were supposed to have learned in a course.

In identifying the different amounts to be learned by students and realizing that every student also has a different rate of learning, a very critical decision has to be made. Given the three functions of schools, is student learning the most important of the three or is scholarship defined in terms of the teachers' role as a presenter of course content (lock-stepping student learning with teacher presenting) the most important? If learning is really our most important product in our instructional institutions, then we have to let students start from *where they are* not from where the teacher starts a course. In order to avoid further development of cumulative ignorance, students will have to learn all of each course. To do this, because of different rates of learning, we will have to recognize this variable in *action* also, not just in words.

d. RATE OF LEARNING AS AFFECTED BY TIME AS A VARIABLE

Traditionally in education and even in training, the record keepers are the ones that set up the time interval for learning and often even the beginning and end of learning situations, i.e., fall semester starts August 25th and ends December 14th, fall quarter starts September 24th and ends December 17, summer session is eight weeks from June 11th to August 3rd, six weeks course, 1600 hours, 950 hours, etc. Once the period of time has been set, then the educators or training instructors start to fill it in. If there is more for the average student to learn than time available to learn it in, the teachers start cutting out important parts of the course in order to make the course fit the preset period of time. If there isn't enough to learn in the course to keep even the good student busy for the preset period of time, then the teachers have to start padding the course. It is unreal and beyond the possibilities of chance that the important concepts of all the courses in a school fit a semester or quarter time period!

In looking at the equation for rate of learning (Equation IV), of the three variables: amount to be learned, rate of learning, and time needed to learn, the time period was the easiest to identify.

$$\frac{\text{rate of}}{\text{learning}} = \frac{\text{amount to be learned}}{\text{time needed to learn}} = \frac{C_t - C_e}{\text{time period}}$$

Equation IV — Rate of Learning

Without any specific objectives to identify the amount that should have been learned, the course content as presented by the teacher was substituted for student learning. Since psychologists and educators claimed that the rates of learning of a random class of students should approximate a normal or bell curve, it was easy to design tests of the teacher's presentation that would result in such a curve. It was assumed that whatever was missed the students couldn't learn. Everything fit together so nicely, no wonder the traditions and malpractices were so well entrenched. Finally, it was observed that students who weren't supposed to be able to learn were learning in remedial courses and it became obvious that if given more time, these students might have been successful the first time they were in the course. Throughout the 1960's programmed instruction research and other individualized instruction projects indicated that when time was made a variable instead of a constant, more students were successful. Even though all teachers realize that students need different amounts of time in order to learn, we still force students to learn whatever they can in one week, one semester, one year, etc. When you take students who need different amounts of time for learning, and force them to fit a time schedule, it is predetermined, before you even check the results, that you are going to have varying amounts of learning taking place. Even parents who know that their children need different amounts of time for learning the same thing, are apt to insist that their child who happens to need more time for learning in some subjects than in other subjects, be passed along with his classmates, regardless of the learning that didn't take place, because they are afraid of the stigma of having a so-called *slow learning* or *mentally retarded* child. In many cases, students who are classified as slow learners or mentally retarded are nothing more than instructionally retarded. They are being forced to fit into situations in which they are not prepared properly to learn what they are expected to learn, and when they are not able to learn, then they are labeled as slow learners or mentally retarded. If as teachers and parents we really believe that students need different amounts of time for learning, then it is absolutely a must that the teaching-learning situation be designed to allow for variations in amount of time for learning. In this way, all students can learn everything that they are supposed to learn, rather than cutting them off too early in order to fit a time pattern convenient for the registrar or the records keeper, but not convenient for the learner. When discussing the concept of varying rates of learning, many parents and also many teachers are worried that if you allow for varying rates of learning that some students will hardly learn at all and will take many years to go through a given course or grade level. This could be the case, particularly in a situation where the teachers and the schools are not able to specify what it is a student is supposed to learn. Accordingly, the student may spend many years trying to identify what it is he is supposed to learn through his own efforts. Given a situation in which the teacher doesn't know specifically what it is that the students should be learning and the students have to guess, the students' apparent rates of learning will be less than their actual rates of learning in the same situation but where the students know what it is they are supposed to learn. For example, the faculty of a two-year nursing school I had consulted with several times, had worked and were working very hard to identify all of the necessary specific objectives for their courses. The last time I was there, one of the faculty members appeared very anxious and made several negative comments about specifying objectives. I asked the teacher what the problem was. She replied, *These — students, just as soon as we specify the objectives, they go out and learn them. All of them are going to finish this two-year course in less than one year!!!*

NOTE: Before specifying the course objective, all of the students needed the full two years to guess what they were supposed to learn. In the process, almost 50 percent were failed out of the program because they could not make it (guess it!) and the rest ended up with the usual curve of grades (a common situation in many nursing schools).

If a school or even just one teacher in a school decides to let time be a variable such that the students can have as much time as needed to *learn the course*, be sure that *learn the course* refers to specific measurable objectives. Without knowing specifically what the content of the course is, neither the students nor the teacher will be able to tell when the students have *learned the course.*

(1) LEARNING TIME AS A VARIABLE: THE OPEN ENTRY—OPEN EXIT PLAN

Given that the objectives for the courses have been identified and recognizing that students learn at different rates, the ideal situation would be one where the functions of schools are completely separated from one another. Under this approach, students would truly learn at their own pace and as a consequence, some students would be starting courses and some students would be finishing courses almost every day of the year (see Figure 27). The major difference teachers would notice when both *time for learning* and *amount to be learned* are made variables to be recognized in action and students would have to learn 100 percent of one course before going on to the next course, is that under the traditional approach the teachers would know the date that students would come to them and start their courses and they would know the date the students would stop the course and leave them. As far as learning is concerned, they wouldn't know what students knew at

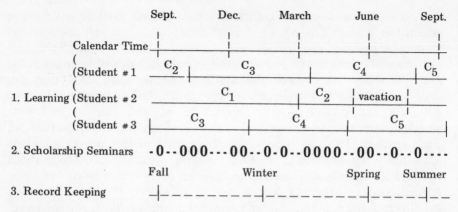

Figure 27 — Ideal — Time as a variable, Scholarship and Record Keeping as separate activities.

the beginning of the course and because of the faulty tests used by so many faculty, the teachers weren't really sure of what was learned during the course. Under the Behavioral Learning Systems Approach, the teachers would never know when the students were going to start or complete their courses, but they would know as a *minimum* what the students would know before starting the course and they would know *as a minimum* what the students would know when they complete the course. If students are truly learning at their own pace, there will be no classes as they are known and used under the traditional approach. Under the learning function, groups may meet to accomplish group learning objectives, but a majority of the learning time will be spent in individualized instruction. Since learning will be the emphasis rather than time, there will be no need to pad courses to fit a time period or to delete important concepts from a course to fit a time period. It will become very common for the average completion time of courses to vary considerably instead of all being the same length i.e., 10 weeks, 15 weeks, 18 weeks, etc. By allowing students to progress at their own pace, doesn't necessarily mean that the first students through courses and school will be the better students. Although the students who learn fast may get through the minimum common core of each course before other students, they may also decide to add a lot of extra objectives to their *amount to be learned* and actually complete some courses after the *slower* learners. By observing in action the fact that the students have different *amounts to be learned* and that because of different rates of learning they need different amounts of time in order to learn 100 percent of the amount to be learned, almost all students will learn *as much or more than* the minimum common core content of their courses whereas under the traditional approach, almost all students

220

learn less than 100 percent of the desired achievement of their courses ("A" worth).

Under the Scholarship function, groups of varying sizes (depending upon interest) will be meeting at whatever time of day or night is convenient for the presenter and the audience. The groups will also meet on any day of the week or at any time during the year. These scholarship seminars could last from one hour to several days if the interest holds up. There would be no required attendance on the part of teachers or students. There would be no objectives or tests. The persons doing the presenting could be the teachers, students, or people from the community. There would be plenty of time for informal group interaction. Every teacher who has been teaching very long has had the experience of a class discussion just getting exciting when the bell rang and stopped the class. Under the Behavioral Learning Systems approach, since there are no classes, there are no bells to interrupt great moments of scholarship.

As far as the record keeping function is concerned, it is possible to count student bodies at any time, it isn't necessary to start and stop courses at body counting times. When courses have all become specified, it will be possible to change the basis for state and federal support from physical attendance on certain days of the year regardless of whether or not learning is taking place, to the amount of learning being accomplished by students in their courses regardless of where they are physically located. Under this approach, a school which has been built for 1000 students (and might have had 1200 students in it under the traditional approach) might only have 500 or more students in it at any one time. The rest of the students could be learning at home, at a library, out in the world community, at a local learning resource center, etc. As long as the learning can be specified and measured, it doesn't matter where the students learn as long as it happens. Whereas under the traditional approach, fees, tuition, and other support funds are based on the concept of a student taking a certain number of courses for a certain period of time (regardless of learning); under the systems concept, tuition, fees, and support funds can be based on the rental of faculty and physical facilities for a certain period of time. The student who can learn more in the same amount of time or less time than other students will get through their formal instruction faster and at less cost than other students.

(2) COMPROMISES IN USING TIME AS A VARIABLE DURING THE TRANSITION TO THE IDEAL

Although it is possible to make the jump from a traditional situation where *time to learn* and *amount to be learned* are preset regardless of student needs to the systems concept where these two factors are

221

treated as variables, most schools will find it easier for students, faculty, administrators, and parents to use one or more of the following transition stages between the two extremes. New schools and even lower elementary schools may find it just as easy to make the complete jump from the traditional approach to the Behavioral Learning Systems Approach.

(a) Using the summer session as a time variable.

This compromise is the easiest one to use as it involves a minimum of changes during the regular nine months school year. The major change would be the identification of the specific objectives and associated test items for each course and then through testing to identify the amount to be learned for each student. The teachers' role would hardly be affected during the nine months of the regular school year. At the beginning of each year (September), one or two weeks would be used to do the testing of the students so they and the teachers will know the students' *amount to be learned*. The students (and parents in elementary and secondary schools) should be told that at the end of the school year they would be given a comprehensive test covering everything they should have learned during the year. These tests would be scheduled during the last one or two weeks of the regular school year. These tests would be designed to cover the entire course regardless of the time it takes students to go through the test except in the achievement of certain objectives where rate of performance is an integral and important part of the objective, i.e., typing; shortland; commercial preparation of income tax reports; repair of cars, appliances, etc.; the construction or making of a garment; the preparation of a meal, etc. To reduce the amount of time the teacher would spend correcting the tests in order to identify what the students still needed to learn and to reduce the time used to prescribe for each student's needs, the teachers might have the students make duplicate copies of their paper and pencil portion of the tests using carbon paper or NCR paper (as mentioned earlier). When the students complete the paper and pencil part of the tests, a copy is handed in to the teacher and then the teacher hands back an answer sheet and on this sheet, next to each answer, is a prescription describing how the student would go about learning that item. The prescription could include the use of one or more books, tape recordings of the teacher's presentations during the school year, films, three dimensional materials, experiments, etc. By using this type of answer sheet, each student could correct his or her own paper and pencil test and at the same time would be identifying what each student had left to learn and would also have an individualized prescription for learning what was left to learn. When first trying this compromise, it might be best to have it on a voluntary basis involving

222

only those students who want to change their grades to an "A" (learn 100 percent of the course objectives) and then after a year or two make the extra time mandatory. The summer session would be an abridgement of the ideal. Although the teachers would be there for a set length of time, i.e., 12 weeks, the students would only attend the session for as long as necessary to learn what they needed to learn as identified by the comprehensive tests. Some "D" students may become "A" within a few weeks then they realize they are missing out on their summer vacation (see student #3, Figure 28.) Some "C" students may need almost the entire summer session to become "A" students (see student #2, Figure 28). Some students, of course, will have achieved 100 percent of the course objectives by the end of the regular spring semester and they would have the summer off as usual (see Student #1,

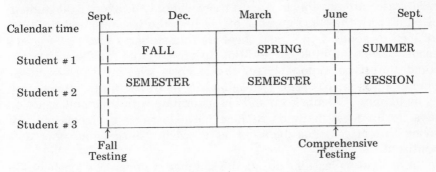

Figure 28 — Summer Session Compromise

Figure 28). It is important to point out that the teachers who are going to teach during such a summer session would not know what they are going to teach until they examine the results of this final comprehensive examination. Their purpose throughout the summer is to help the student learn those things he or she doesn't know, not to present the content of a given course regardless of student needs. In other words, during this summer session the teachers will be performing the role of the teacher as an instructioneer.

Some parents of students may object to the additional summer program because of the potential interference with summer vacation plans. This would not be the case in this instance because each student is only learning what he or she needs to learn, and if the students leave for two or three weeks for family vacations, upon their return they would just continue on where they left off. The major benefit of this approach would be that by the end of summer a much higher percentage of students are going to be essentially A or B students as far as prior levels are concerned, and by erasing potential cumulative ignorance it is very possible that some of those students who have now achieved A or

223

B levels may be able to perform at an A or B level during the following school year without the additional help of the summer period.

This approach would also facilitate year-round teacher employment and use of the school buildings. During the summer session, the approach would reduce the teacher-pupil ratio for those students who need it. For example, in a school of 1,000 students suppose that 30 percent were able to reach the required achievement level. This would mean that about 70 percent of the students would be attending summer school. Assuming that approximately 70 percent of the teachers would also like to work throughout the summer, the teacher-pupil ratio at the beginning of the summer would be the same as during the normal course of the year, possibly 30 to 1. As the students achieve the required levels and drop out of the summer program, the teacher-pupil ratio will begin to decrease until possibly in August there will only be about 100 students left, and with the same number of teachers the teacher-pupil ratio has dropped to about 4 to 1, and these are four students who really need a teacher across the table. In addition to the benefits for the learners, it would almost be impossible for the teachers who are working in the summer program to spend two-and-a-half or three months concentrating on helping students learn and brainstorming with their colleagues on ways, techniques, methods to help solve learning problems without having this affect their behavior as a teacher during the other nine months of the year.[21]

In facilitating learning during the summer program, the teachers will have to develop various instructional modules to solve the learning problems with certain objectives in order to enable some students to reach the required achievement levels. The summer materials and techniques can then be made available and used during the regular school year. Consequently, as this summer program is continued, year after year, there will probably be a smaller and smaller group that has to spend the summer time in order to reach the required achievement levels. A bonus benefit of this approach would be that many teachers will be forced to re-evaluate some of the test items they are using because they will have to teach it successfully to all students. As they identify test items that aren't really testing what is important, the teachers will tend to develop new and more complex objectives and test items to test these objectives.

(b) Summer Session and Winter interim as time variables.

Because cumulative ignorance is a very serious problem in many courses, waiting until the summer session to learn those things which the

---

[21] Although most educators will tend to be very traditional from September to June, almost all teachers will attempt to be innovative, creative, imaginative and/or attempt a variety of instructional techniques from June through September.

students didn't have time to learn completely during the regular school year may very well cause more objectives not to be learned and thus create greater amounts to be learned during the summer session. By having a winter interim period after the fall semester and using that time to eliminate as much of the cumulative ignorance from the fall semester as possible before the students start the spring semester, fewer students will have learning problems during the spring semester and fewer students will have to attend the summer session.

Actually a number of colleges have already identified the time after Christmas vacation as sort of a *lame duck* period in which nothing much happens. As a result, these colleges have come up with a schedule referred to as the *4-1-4* program. There is a four month fall semester from about August 20th to about December 20th, a one month interim period during January, and a four month spring semester from February 1st until about June 1st. During the one month interim period, students take a concentrated three credit course. These short concentrated courses can be taken at any one of a group of cooperating colleges. In this way, students can take advantage of special courses, equipment, and/or teachers that are not available at their regular school.

In using the winter interim period as a time variable, a comprehensive test covering the fall semester would be given at the end of the fall semester. Any student who learned 100 percent of the objectives in all his or her fall courses, could use the interim period for a new course, could use it as vacation time, or could work on his or her own projects. Students getting less than the 100 percent would attend the winter interim period until he or she achieved the 100 percent or at least learned as much as possible during the extra learning time. The summer session would be used in the same manner as described in the previous compromise (a) except that the comprehensive test at the end of the spring semester would only test the spring semester instead of both semesters. In other words, the winter interim period and the summer session would act as buffer learning zones between the semesters (see Figure 29). Student #1

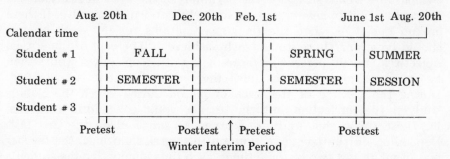

Figure 29 — Winter and Summer Buffer Learning Zones

225

was able to achieve 100 percent by the end of each semester, so this student could use the winter and summer buffer learning zones for taking courses, vacation, etc. Student #2 was able to achieve 100 percent of the course objectives at some point during the buffer learning zone. Student #3 may have been able to just make the 100 percent by the end of the extra time or if not, at least the student will have a greater chance for success than under the traditional approach.

A slightly different version of this same compromise would use a 3½—1—3½—1 program. In this version of the compromise, there would be a winter and spring interim periods and no summer session. In which the fall semester would start at the more traditional time (about September 1st) and end just before Christmas (3½ months). Again, January would act as a buffer zone. The spring semester would start February 1st and end about May 15th (3½ months) and the spring interim period would be from May 15th until about June 15th.

For those colleges and universities on the quarter schedule and for elementary and secondary schools that want to reduce even further the opportunities for cumulative ignorance to develop and create more learning problems, they could use a 2—1—2—1—2—1 in which there would be a three or four week buffer learning zone at the end of each of three quarters lasting from six to eight weeks.

(c) Changing the teacher's role and using time as a variable week.

If a teacher is willing to change his or her role so as to be more in tune with the role of the instructioneer, it is possible to apply the same concepts on a unit by unit or a week by week basis. If during a given week or curriculum unit the teacher knows specifically what the students are supposed to learn (objectives) as a result of their studies during this period, then the teacher could make the learning of the specific objectives as a homework assignment and then arrange a class session at the beginning of the week or study on the curriculum unit to answer any questions the students may have. If there are no questions, then the final examinations for the week or unit should be given. Those students who achieve 100 percent of the critical objectives and 90 percent or more of the other objectives would then be excused from the class until the next assignment is scheduled. During the balance of the week or period during which the class is studying the curriculum unit, the teacher would concentrate on teaching those things that were not learned as indicated on the first test. Depending on the length of time on this curriculum unit, the teacher may want to test two or three times, each time eliminating the students who have already achieved and concentrating more and more time on

226

the students that are left.[22]

A recent innovation tried in a few schools is the four-day school week. The students only go to school four days and the fifth day is used for administrative tasks, preparation time, and inservice training time. Outside of maybe temporarily motivating students and teachers (Hawthorne effect[23]) because both groups have more time off than before, it would be difficult to prove that this innovation actually results in increased learning. However, if the teachers tested the students on Thursday of each week and any students who were able to achieve an "A" worth of the week's work by Thursday would have Friday off. Then on Friday the teachers would work specifically with those students who didn't achieve "A" worth of the week's work and try to solve their learning problems such that the students can go on to the next weeks work with a minimum or no cumulative ignorance. I think it would be relatively easy to prove that a four-day school week of this type would increase learning. Under the present approach where the fifth day is spent away from students, it is most likely another way for those teachers who don't really like teaching to reduce their student contact hours and hence productivity.

(3) CONTEMPORARY EFFORTS TO ALLOW AMOUNT TO BE LEARNED AND TIME FOR LEARNING TO BE VARIABLES

In realizing that people need different amounts of *time for learning* and that some people just can't take time to attend a formal school, correspondence instruction has been popular for many years. As of the writing of this book, approximately five million students are learning away from schools and at their own learning pace. I am not suggesting that correspondence instruction is an ideal, because it is not the ideal *as it is presently practiced* by most correspondence schools. They have many of the same problems as regular schools, i.e., few, if any, specific objectives; the tests are not correlated very highly with objectives; use of objective type tests; etc. The fact that they allow their students to take as much time as necessary in order to learn the course materials is a big plus in their favor.

A new trend that combines the pluses of correspondence instruction with formal schooling is the use of challenge or proficiency

---

[22] Ideally, as the students complete a week's or unit's work, the student should be able to go on to the next unit, but if this is not possible, at least the faster students will have some release time at the end of each week or unit and the teacher will have smaller classes to work with because students were allowed to learn on their own.

---

[23] The Hawthorne effect is the name given to the gains in learning right after a change is made. As the learners become accustomed to the change, the gains in learning disappear. Another term used for essentially the same thing is the *novelty effect*.

examinations where a student can learn the content of a course in any way (correspondence, independent study, formal classes, etc.) and as long as the student can pass the examination, he or she is given the grade and credit. The Empire University of New York will allow a student to earn a degree in this manner. Again these are steps in the right direction, but having *time for learning* and the *place for learning* as the only variables are not enough, particularly when the new trend still carries with it the same old problems of few specific objectives; the use of objective type tests; the use of standardized tests in courses where there is no such thing as standardized objectives (the achievement of which the standardized tests are supposed to be testing), etc.

In elementary and secondary schools, the two most well known efforts to allow time as a variable are in *modular scheduling* and in the so-called *nongraded schools.*

(a) Modular Scheduling

In the majority of our elementary and secondary schools throughout the country, students have five, six, or seven class periods per day. Modular scheduling is an effort to provide a little more opportunity for the individual needs of the student but not quite to the degree of a continuous progress or nongraded situation in which the students are at so many different levels that the holding of classes is rather difficult. The compromise is to break up the school day into fifteen, twenty, or thirty-minute modules and then the student could spend as many modules in a particular subject as is necessary in order to learn what the student needs to learn. An integral part of this modular scheduling concept is the fact that the students' needs may vary daily or weekly as to how many modules the student might need in a particular subject. Instead of the subject maintaining a specific class schedule for an entire semester or year, the students' class schedule may be changed daily or weekly depending on the particular philosophy of the school, and in part on the availability of a computer to help in the scheduling process. If this modular scheduling is done by hand, then the rescheduling of the students' study and class time is rather infrequent. But where the school is able to utilize its own computer or rent time on someone else's computer, then the scheduling and rescheduling can be done much more frequently. In either case, whether the scheduling is done by hand or by computer, the concept of modular scheduling is relatively expensive in contrast to the traditional approach. Although modular scheduling represents certain concessions toward the concept of independent study, it still hangs on to the traditional concepts that students can only learn in a school and mainly in a classroom with a teacher.

One of the major problems with modular scheduling is the same problem with the nongraded school or the traditional schools. If the

228

educators haven't specified exactly what it is the students are supposed to learn, then how is it possible to diagnose the fact that some students need more time (modules) to learn something which we can't identify or haven't specified. As an example of this, I visited a school that had just completed their first year of using the modular scheduling approach to instruction. Although numerous educators from across the country had visited the school to observe the program, the teachers in the school were not very happy with the results of their experiences during the first year of modular scheduling. The opinion of the teachers seemed to indicate that they were particularly disappointed because the students did not take advantage of the extra modules of independent study time to improve their learning. In asking the teachers if they had lists of specific measurable objectives that the students were supposed to learn in their courses of study, it was quickly apparent that none of the teachers had these lists. This raises an interesting question. If the teachers did not know exactly what they wanted the students to learn, how are the students supposed to take advantage of their independent study modules and study what they were supposed to learn? The students are not magicians, so if they do not know what they are supposed to learn, it should be rather obvious that the student is going to use the time for whatever he thinks is the best use of the time, which may be for nonacademic purposes, if the academic purposes are not made clear.

Modular scheduling, like nongraded schools and other *modern* concepts that are being applied in our schools, are all too often put into practice to improve public relations, rather than actually to solve the problems of the learner. As pointed out, to make either of these very effective, it is necessary to have specified measurable objectives for each of the curriculum units. If these objectives are available, then there really isn't any need to have modular scheduling as it is a very expensive in-between step, and the school might just as well go directly to a continuous progress or nongraded approach.

(b) Nongraded Schools

In an effort to treat learning as a continuous process, the concept of the non-graded school has spread rather rapidly through our country in recent years. Although at the present time, the number of nongraded schools is still rather small, there is probably a nongraded school within driving distance of almost any locality. Just because a school is called *nongraded* does not necessarily mean that the teachers in the school consider the learning process as a continuum. All it means is that the school has been designated by the school district as *nongraded*. If the teachers in these schools have not been involved in sufficient and appropriate in-service training to help them change their

229

traditional point of view of looking at learning, then regardless of whether the school is called *nongraded*, what goes on in the classrooms is still rather traditional. As a result, in some schools that are called *nongraded*, the only difference between that school and any other *graded* school is that they do not have classes which are referred to as first grade, second grade, third grade, fourth grade, etc. But the students in this so-called *nongraded* school still stay in their common age group for one year and progress accordingly year by year through the school just like any other *graded* school. In some other schools, the first two years of elementary school have been grouped together, and they call this early elementary. The middle two years of elementary education have been put together and they refer to this as intermediate elementary, and then the last two years are referred to as advanced elementary. There is also a school that refers to its classes as alpha, beta, delta, gamma, etc., rather than first, second, third, fourth. In most of these schools, the same old traditions are there, but under different names.

If you are familiar with the nongraded concept, or sometimes referred to as *continuous progress*, you may know that the most common statement made in regard to the advantages of the nongraded system is that *the student progresses at his or her own pace.* If a student progresses at his or her own pace through the curriculum of the various gardes, then we should be able to tell exactly where the student is at any time and be able to measure his or her progress. For example, see Figure 30, illustrating the nongrading or continuous progress concept.

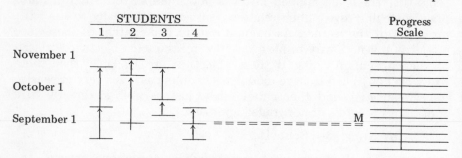

Figure 30 — Nongraded or Continuous Progress Concept

Students 1, 2, 3, and 4 were tested on September 1, and the lowest of the three lines underneath each one of the four students #1, #2, #3, and #4 indicate where the students were on September 1. The next line above that bottom line indicates where the students were on October 1, and the top line indicates where the students were on November 1. In order to measure exactly where the student is at any one time and to allow the student to progress at his own rate, it would be a necessary

230

prerequisite that we not only know where the student is going specifically, but specifically each of the steps between where he is and where he's going, so that we can actually measure his progress (as indicated by the progress scale at the right-hand side of Figure 30). Since we do not know in our elementary and secondary schools and in higher education exactly what it is the student is supposed to learn in our courses, then it is extremely difficult to have a nongraded school. If you visit a nongraded school, ask one of the administrators or teachers what determines whether a student is ready to progress to the next unit. If he says to you that the teacher or team of teachers get together with a vice principal or possibly the parent and discuss the student, then this is not a nongraded system. Theoretically, if Student #4 (see Figure 30) has tested out to be a Point M on the progress scale, then he is ready for the next step, regardless of whether the team of teachers thinks so or the principal thinks so, or the parents think so. If continuous progress is based on a measurable scale, *Where the student is* becomes the important factor, not where the teachers *think* the student is.

If a *nongraded school* is truly operating along the concepts of continuous learning, then those students who complete the equivalent of sixth grade should all score at the sixth-grade level on any kind of achievement tests. But what has typically happened so far is that the results on achievement tests in nongraded schools are not too much different than the results in many of the graded schools. One of the reasons for this is that the students in both situations are essentially learning the same things with the same materials and in the same amount of time. The *nongraded* concept is in name only.

In visiting a nongraded school, along with asking the question, *What actually determines the students' progress through the school?*, there are several other questions which should be asked?

If students progress at their own pace, then because of individual differences, you should have students completing the required curriculum at different times throughout the year. In the instance of a nongraded elementary school, what happens to the student who finishes the sixth-grade curriculum in October, December, March or April?

So far, in all of the nongraded schools that I have visited, they admit that this is one of the problems. Usually, the students are kept busy until June, rather than to let them go ahead on to seventh grade work. In most nongraded schools which are supposedly operating on a continuous progress basis, most students seem to end up completing their work in June, rather than at a wide variety of times throughout the year, which would be the expected result of allowing for individual

231

differences between students in their rate of learning. Another question to ask:

May I look at a test that is given to the student to determine whether or not he is ready to progress to the next unit?

If the test is a multiple-choice, and/or true-false test, chances are that the test is not truly testing the objectives of the specific unit the student is supposed to be learning. Then ask:

Could this test have been made harder, or could you have made it easier?

If in answer to this question the teacher says yes, he or she could have made it harder or easier, then this also indicates that the test was made up without a high correlation between test items and objectives. If the test was actually testing the specified objectives of the curriculum, the teacher should not be able to change the test and make it harder or easier without also changing the objectives of the curriculum the test items are testing. When teachers tell me that they can make a test easier or harder, I am always tempted to ask the following question:

If you could have made the test harder or easier, by what magic did you arrive at the actual items which you did use and how do you know that they are hard enough or easy enough to verify that the student has actually LEARNED the objectives of the curriculum unit?

No one has this magic ability to identify how hard test items should be or how easy they should be, because it is the specifying of the objectives for the course that determines the difficulty level of the test item.

The concept of the nongraded school is ideally what we should have in our schools; but the term *nongraded* should be based on what actually happens in the schools, not based on a title given to a school without affecting what actually happens in the school. If the school is truly nongraded, then there should be a wide variation in time and materials used by students in order to learn the same minimum levels of achievement. The important part of the concept is that ALL students learn ALL of the objectives of their courses. In other words, ALL students can be "A" and "B" students.

e. RATE OF LEARNING: TRADITIONAL vs. SYSTEMS
    (2 VARIABLES)

$$\text{Intelligence} = \frac{\text{Rate of}}{\text{Learning}} = \frac{\text{L (amount to be learned)}}{\text{T (time for learning}}$$

232

Traditional	Systems
(1) Rate of learning (intelligence) is designed into the tests such that the results fit a curve almost regardless of what students actually learn.	(1) Rate of learning (intelligence) is the apparent rate when the actual learning (L) is divided by the actual time (T) taken in order to learn 100 percent of L.
(2) Time is a constant in a given situation.	(2) Amount to be learned is a constant in a given situation.
(3) Amount to be learned is the dependent variable and varies according to time available.	(3) Time for learning is the dependent variable and varies according to the amount to be learned.
(4) Tests used to evaluate learning reflect to varying degrees the amount to be learned and are terminal in nature.	(4) Tests used to evaluate learning reflect exactly the amount to be learned and are diagnostic in nature.

In recognizing both *amount to be learned* and *time for learning* as variables in individualizing instruction, there are definite advantages gained for the learner, teacher, and taxpayer.

— By allowing *amount to be learned* to be identified for each student, gaps and overlaps in the learning are eliminated along with the boredom and hostility which accompanies learning gaps and overlaps.

— By allowing *time for learning* to be a variable dependent upon the *amount to be learned*, the critical problem of cumulative ignorance is minimized or eliminated.

— By using tests which actually test what was supposed to be learned the students encounter a much more honest situation which in turn facilitates the development of positive attitudes.

— By using test results as diagnosis of students' learning problems which should be solved rather than to record the scores as terminal learning or achievement, students can be helped to learn more and thereby increase their self-image.

— By recognizing that the traditional *rates of learning* represent pre-designed rates of learning rather than the students' actual rates of learning, helps to dispel or at least to weaken the entrenched myths about some students that supposedly *can't learn*.

Even with these benefits, it is important to point out that learning situations which recognize *amount to be learned* and *time for learning*

233

as variables still assume that students all learn the same way and for the same reasons. Even though almost every teacher would agree that students learn best in different ways and learn best for different reasons, these two variables are not often recognized in action. The instructioneer, in recognizing these two areas as variables which affect learning, will solve learning problems in these two areas in order to increase the effectiveness and efficiency of the learning environment and to identify more accurately the students actual rate of learning.

f. RATE OF LEARNING AS AFFECTED BY THE STUDENTS' INTELLECTUAL AND SENSORY LEARNING SKILLS

Although intellectual skills in the cognitive domain and sensory skills in the sensory domain are conceptually different, they overlap in behavioral identification and frequently work cooperatively in learning.

NOTE: The intellectual and sensory skills referred to in this section are the existing skills which a learner brings to the learning environment and utilizes in learning all types of objectives in the cognitive, sensory, and affective domains.

There are three sub-variables to be discussed in attempts to solve learning problems which fall into this section. They are related in such a manner that any one, two, or all three of them can be varied in efforts to solve a learning problem. The three sub-variables are: the degree of simulation used in the instruction, the method of instruction, and the language used for instruction (see Figure 31).

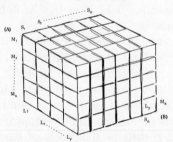

Figure 31 — nxy combinations of ways to learn: (n degrees of simulation) times (x number of methods) times (y number of languages)

In attempting to solve a students learning problem in this area, there are almost an infinite number of potential combinations which could be tried. Some student may learn best (see point "A" in Figure 31) using the smallest degree of simulation (S_1) combined with the first method (M_1) and the first language (L_1). Some other student might learn best using the fifteenth degree of simulation (S_{15}) combined with the ninth method (M_9) and the eleventh language (L_{11}). And yet, another

234

student might learn best (see point "B" in Figure 31) using the nth degree of simulation (S_n) combined with the xth method (M_x) and the yth language (L_y).

Any one of these combinations can be thought of as pathway for learning. Most educators make certain assumptions about how students learn, which may in fact reflect more about how the educators teach than how their students learn. Although almost all educators talk about individual differences, in almost every classroom, all students are expected to learn from the same pathway such as a textbook and a set combination of other instructional materials. In many cases, all students in a particular subject throughout a school district or even a state, may be expected to learn from the same pathway. At the college level, once the teacher has selected the pathway that he wishes to use, all students are expected to learn equally well from that same textbook or set of instructional materials, whether it is 20 students or 6,000 students. If all students do learn the same way, then one would expect to find a national, regional, or local program directed towards teaching young children before they start school in *how to learn?* As we all know, there is no such national, regional, or local program directed towards teaching children on *how to learn.* As a consequence, children *learn how to learn randomly.* In fact, there are children in some homes who are probably learning *not to learn.*[24]

Since children from the time they are born until they start school learn how to learn *randomly,* then when the student starts school, the individual child's progress really is an indication of the correlation between the pathway that the teacher has selected to use in teaching and the pathway in which the student learns best. If in the teaching-learning situation a particular student does not seem able to learn from a particular teacher, this does not necessarily mean that the student can't learn. What it may indicate is that this student cannot learn with that teacher, and if the student is changed to another teacher, the student may learn very well. Just because a student can't learn from a given teacher, but can learn from a different teacher, does not mean that the first teacher is not able to teach. What it may mean is that the pathway in which the teacher teaches successfully is not the same

---

[24] Children may learn not to show evidences of learning, particularly when the non-performance of the preferred behavior results in greater rewards than the performance of the preferred behavior. For example, when a parent or parents are trying to toilet train their child, the child is faced with the following two alternatives:

Performance of preferred behavior — sitting on cold, hard seat of a potty chair, or

Nonperformance of preferred behavior —washed, powdered, cuddled, and loved.

If it was your choice, would you indicate learning or nonlearning?

pathway in which the student learns successfully. This should be expected to be typical in a situation in which students learn how to learn randomly and teachers learn how to teach randomly, which is the case when teaching is considered an art, and few, if any, teacher-training institutions practice what they preach.

(1) THE DEGREE OF SIMULATION AS A FACTOR IN A LEARNING OR INSTRUCTIONAL PATHWAY

In setting up the teaching-learning situation, which in a sense is a synthetic situation in reference to the real-life environment for which we are trying to prepare the student, there are a variety of instructional media and many different ways of utilizing these media, and they can become integrated into the curriculum to varying degrees, allowing the teacher great flexibility in the development or design of the teaching-learning situation. Almost every teacher has said at one time or another that they have some students who can learn very adequately at the verbal level (lectures and textbooks) and that they have some other students who only seem to be able to learn adequately when still or motion pictures are used (films, television, slides, etc.). Many teachers, and also many parents, have made statements along the lines of *the only way that this student (child) will learn is to take him or her right into the real-life situation, or in a simulated real-life situation, so that the student can be actively involved in pushing the button or talking to people or performing the appropriate tasks, or at least able to observe at first hand these things occurring.*

For the purposes of this section, where the same set of one or more related objectives can be learned from various pathways of presentation in a synthetic situation in addition to being able to be learned by chance in *real life*, then the various modes of presentation will be considered a *simulation* of the real life situation.

A better understanding of the concept of simulation as presented in this section will be assured by beginning with a statement of the assumptions upon which this concept is based.

(a) There is such a thing as a *life environment.*
(b) There is such a thing as an *academic environment.*
(c) The purpose of the academic environment is to prepare the learner for the life environment.
(d) The value of exposure to the academic environment is measured by the Learner's performance in the life environment as a consequence of behaviors that have been transferred and adapted from the academic environment.

In the real life situation, the learner's performance usually consists of perceiving certain stimuli and responding to them in some appropriate way. It is important to note that the learner's response generally is

236

not made to one stimulus, but to patterns of stimuli. An objective of the academic environment is to present to the learners certain stimulus patterns that represent the appropriate specific experiences from which it is hoped they will be able to generalize to other experiences they need in life. Transfer of learned responses from the stimulus pattern presented in the academic environment to the stimulus pattern the learners meet in life is referred to as *stimulus generalization.* These stimulus patterns are similar in some respects yet dissimilar in other respects (see Figure 32).

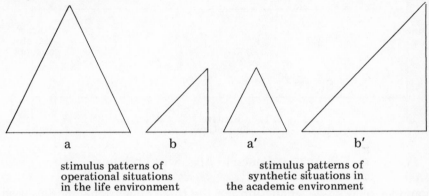

a	b	a′	b′

stimulus patterns of operational situations in the life environment

stimulus patterns of synthetic situations in the academic environment

Figure 32 — Stimuli Patterns

Because the evaluation of the academic environment is measured by the learner's performance in life as a result of *stimulus generalization* from the stimulus patterns presented in the academic environment, it is important that the stimulus patterns in the synthetic situations of the academic environment be such that:

  (a) they establish in the learner certain responses,
  (b) that these responses transfer positively to the real life or operational situation, and
  (c) that these responses constitute the desired and appropriate reaction to the real-life stimulus patterns.

When there is a demand for transfer of learning to superficially different situations, some pathways of learning which emphasize responses to *patterns of cues* will be more effective than others which emphasize specific responses to *specific cues.* Learning which directs responses towards the commonalities in a variety of different situations in the real-life environment will therefore enable the student to cope with wider varieties of real-life situations, including transfer from synthetic to actual real-life environments.

The process of simulation is the setting up of a synthetic situation which enables the learner to learn responses which through stimulus

237

generalization are desired and appropriate when used in the operational or real-life situation.

As a process, simulation can be positive or negative. In the concrete-abstract continuum (Figure 33) *positive simulation* refers to the condition wherein the synthetic situation (S_2) is more concrete than the real-life situation (S_1).

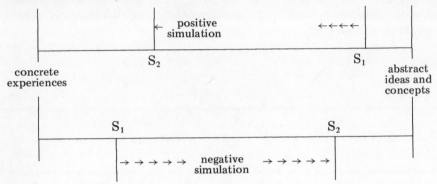

Figure 33 — Concrete-Abstract Continuum

Examples of positive simulation are the three dimensional models used in chemistry and mathematics as concrete demonstrations of abstract ideas or concepts; paper and pencil models of theoretical concepts, i.e., communication models, learning models, flowcharts, etc.; role playing or performing in such a manner that it demonstrates an attitude, value, or belief. *Negative simulation* refers to the condition where the synthetic situation (S_2) is less concrete than the real-life situation (S_1). Examples of negative simulation are the simulated cars used in driver training; the simulated planes used in air crew training; the scenery in theatrical plays; audio-visual aids used in vocational training; and verbal descriptions of real things or actions with real things. In some situations, the only difference between positive and negative simulation is a point-of-view. For example, if you were trying to teach someone the concept of *kindness* and found that verbal descriptions weren't successful in communicating the concept, you might role play various acts of *kindness* or go out into the streets and stores and point out acts of *kindness*. This would be considered positive simulation because the direction is from the abstract concept to concrete acts. If you were observing acts of *kindness* and you wanted to talk to someone about it, the words would be an example of negative simulation because the direction is from the concrete act to a more abstract verbal concept.

The problem in simulation with reference to the setting up of a synthetic situation is not only concerned with the copying of equipment and other physical items found in the real-life situation, but it is also a matter of copying the psychological environment of the real-life situation. Therefore, simulation is made up of two components: physical simulation — the copying of that part of the real-life situation which is physically involved in the desired responses or behaviors of the learner; and psychological simulation — the copying of that part of the real-life situation which is psychologically necessary to obtain the desired responses or behaviors of the learner. Psychological simulation can be divided into three distinct types:

(a) The copying of that part of the physical environment of the real-life situation that is *not* physically involved in the desired responses of the learner but nevertheless does affect the learning of the desired responses. Examples of this are the use of films with the driver training simulators and the airplane cabins in the air crew simulators.

(b) The substitution of symbolic stimuli for physical realism based on stimulus generalization. Examples of this are the use of stubby wings on the flight simulators and the use of a small hood on the driver training simulator to symbolize the real thing.

(c) The use of symbolic stimuli words and/or visuals) to retrieve from the learners memory information concerning past experiences that will help in the setting up of a synthetic situation. An example of this is the use of directions given prior to role-playing (a form of simulation), i.e., *You are the owner of a toy manufacturing business doing three million dollars worth of business a year. You have 100 employees, etc.*

Failure to recognize the significance of psychological simulation may be very costly. Given the task of simulating a real-life situation, one may be tempted to produce a physical replica of the real-life situation, limited only by available budget and the state of the engineering art. It is true that there are kinds of behaviors and degrees of learning which may profit from a high degree of physical fidelity in the simulated environment, but other behaviors may be learned and may transfer quite adequately from synthetic situations having relatively little physical or functional realism.

Once it is recognized that there are degrees of both physical simulation and degrees of psychological simulation, it can be realized that practical decisions about the specifications for a synthetic environment must rest on economic and learning objective compromises. And from the standpoint of economy, the development of synthetic situations should rest on psychological simulation rather than on physical simulation because as the degree of physical simulation increases, the physical environment (models, films, equipment, etc.) becomes more

239

expensive to build and maintain.

With low degrees of physical simulation the student will be making verbal responses and will be transferring to the real-life situation little more than identification of specifics and perhaps certain ways and means of dealing with these specifics.[25]

At least up to a point, there are increased increments of transfer of learned behaviors with increased degrees of physical simulation ("A" section of transfer curve, Figure 23), but human receptor channels, like other receivers, have limitations in sensitivity. That is, for any stimulus input, there will be ranges through which physical differences in the synthetic situation will not be matched with behavioral differences ("B" and "C" sections of transfer curve, Figure 34).

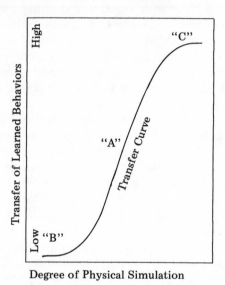

Degree of Physical Simulation

Figure 34 — Relationship between Degree of Physical Simulation and Transfer of Learned Behaviors

In setting up a synthetic situation, various instructional media and varied methods of utilizing them can be integrated to varying degrees, giving a flexibility in the means of the desired simulation. It is important to remember that a particular synthetic situation (simulation) which involves a variety of instructional media should be designed in accordance with the predetermined learning objectives and not accord-

---

[25] Of course, if the above is all that the learning situation needs to teach, then transfer of learned behaviors can be high for these specifics, with a low degree of physical simulation.

ing to the characteristics of the instructional media. In other words, fit the media to the objectives, not the objectives to the media.

Figure 35, which shows a variety of instructional media placed on an abstract-concrete continuum in the form of a pyramid, can be used as an aid in the selection of media to fit certain objectives.[26] The

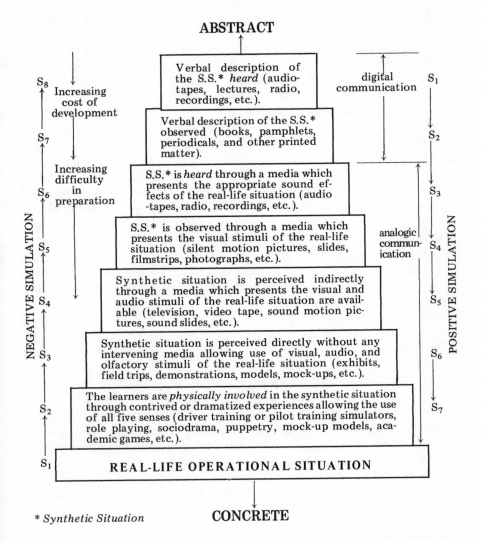

ABSTRACT

S_8 — Increasing cost of development

S_7

Increasing difficulty in preparation

S_6

S_5

S_4

S_3

S_2

S_1

NEGATIVE SIMULATION

Verbal description of the S.S.* *heard* (audio-tapes, lectures, radio, recordings, etc.).

Verbal description of the S.S.* observed (books, pamphlets, periodicals, and other printed matter).

S.S.* is *heard* through a media which presents the appropriate sound effects of the real-life situation (audio-tapes, radio, recordings, etc.).

S.S.* is observed through a media which presents the visual stimuli of the real-life situation (silent motion pictures, slides, filmstrips, photographs, etc.).

Synthetic situation is perceived indirectly through a media which presents the visual and audio stimuli of the real-life situation are available (television, video tape, sound motion pictures, sound slides, etc.).

Synthetic situation is perceived directly without any intervening media allowing use of visual, audio, and olfactory stimuli of the real-life situation (exhibits, field trips, demonstrations, models, mock-ups, etc.).

The learners are *physically involved* in the synthetic situation through contrived or dramatized experiences allowing the use of all five senses (driver training or pilot training simulators, role playing, sociodrama, puppetry, mock-up models, academic games, etc.).

REAL-LIFE OPERATIONAL SITUATION

digital communication S_1

S_2

S_3

analogic communication S_4

S_5

S_6

S_7

POSITIVE SIMULATION

* *Synthetic Situation*   **CONCRETE**

Figure 35 — Simulation Through Use of Instructional Media

---

[26] Based in part on Edgar Dale's *Cone of Experience* as presented in his book, *Audio-Visual Methods in Teaching.*

placement of a specific medium in a specific tier is based on the general use of the medium; the number of senses involved; whether the synthetic situation is preceived directly or indirectly (through media); whether the synthetic situation is observed, heard, or both; and whether the perception involved is the synthetic situation or a verbal description of the synthetic situation. It is relatively easy to affect the placement of a specific medium by incorporating into it some new features or characteristic that would relate to the criteria used for deciding placement on the diagram, e.g., adding sound to filmstrips would move the combined media to the next tier below.

Simulation in a specific synthetic situation can be evaluated for its effectiveness. *Perfect simulation* is a relative concept and results in the performance of specified terminal behaviors in the real-life operational situation as a consequence of the transfer of learned behaviors from the synthetic situation. If some behaviors are missing or are not being performed adequately, it is an indication of a need for a greater degree of simulation. For example, if in the testing of learners who have taken a course or unit utilizing a specific media group or tier, it is revealed that only 50% of the terminal behaviors are transferred to the operational situation[27] (thus indicating 50% successful simulation, then the course materials should be restructured utilizing the media represented in the next lower tier or group — increasing the degree of simulation (see Figure 35). The testing of learners who have taken the restructured course should indicate an increased transfer of learned behaviors as a result of a greater degree of simulation which has been set up in the synthetic situation. In a similar way, if in the testing for retention of learned behaviors over a period of time a decrease or loss is noted, increased simulation should be built into the course materials to increase retention.

The teacher in the traditional role as a presenter of course content would select a certain pathway through a course and any students that didn't learn from that one pathway would be considered as being incapable of learning the subject matter of the course. The instructioneer would recognize non-learning as a learning problem which should and could be solved. The problem-solving and decision-making behaviors of the instructioneer would involve:

— identifying exactly which objectives the student is having trouble learning,

---

[27] It might be possible in a given course developed in accordance with the systems approach to have 90% of the learners learn 100% of the content as measured by achievement of the *terminal behaviors of the synthetic situation*, but when presented with the *terminal behaviors in the operational situation*, the achievement is only 50%. This result indicates a need for a greater degree of simulation in the synthetic situation.

242

- verifying whether or not the learning problem is really a problem of the degree of simulation,
- locating the present ineffective pathway on the pyramid (Figure 35),
- deciding which direction (positive or negative) the increased degree of simulation should go (based on the objectives to be learned), and
- deciding whether to increase the physical or psychological simulation, or both.

In using the abstract-concrete pyramid (Figure 35) for problem solving, notice that starting with the real-life operational situation at the bottom of the pyramid and going up the pyramid, each step represents increasing degrees of negative simulation. Starting at the top of the pyramid with a verbal concept and going down the pyramid, each step represents increasing degrees of positive simulation. Starting in the middle of the pyramid with a visual concept, each step up the pyramid would be increasing negative simulation, while each step down the pyramid would be increasing positive simulation. Another important aspect to remember is that with each step down the pyramid, the costs for development of the pathway will be increased and the difficulty in the preparation of the pathway will also be increased (see arrow on left side of Figure 35).

The first two levels of the pyramid dealing with verbal descriptions heard and verbal descriptions seen can be referred to as *digital communication*. The next five levels below the top two levels can be referred to as *analogic communication*. Digital communication can be effectively and efficiently used when the receiver has similar meanings for the symbolic use of the words involved. This is why educators in common subject-matter areas can carry on conversations using digital communication very effectively, but the learner does not have this common background of prior experiences and so it is necessary from time to time to build in analogic communication to help the learner to develop the necessary meanings in order that the student will be able to carry on conversations with his colleagues and teachers using digital communication in the given subject-matter area and to learn the unit and course objectives and to indicate this learning in appropriate evaluation instruments. A teacher shouldn't even assume that students all have common meanings for the symbolic use of visuals, sounds, etc. in analogic communication.

Throughout the research literature on instructional media, the reader is confronted with conflicting comments, i.e., students were bored — students were captivated; students learned faster through programmed instruction — students learned faster through television; students learned more — students learned less; students learned better by branching programmed instruction — students learned better by linear programmed

243

instruction; etc. Because of their varied abilities, interests, and prior experiences, some students will learn better and faster in certain subject areas through one pathway while other students will learn better and faster in the same subject areas through a different pathway. The teacher should be willing to manipulate the learning environment for each student in order to facilitate learning rather than spend his time presenting the course content which obviously limits the students to one mode of learning. The learning systems approach towards the development of instructional materials necessitates the efficient utilization of a variety of media and materials (programmed instructional materials, films, slides, demonstrations, face-to-face lectures, etc.) for presenting course content when and where necessary for learning. It is not an efficient use of learning time to have a student go through an hour of the stereotyped textbook form of programmed material when the same learning objectives could be accomplished by having him read a regular textbook for ten minutes or view a five-minute demonstration. Conversely, it is not efficient use of learning time to have teachers and students in a lecture situation for an hour when the same learning objectives could be accomplished through independent study by the students of a programmed text for fifteen minutes. It is not an economical use of the taxpayers' investment in education to develop hundreds and perhaps thousands of hours of instructional materials that need expensive television, dial access or computer equipment to present to the learner when the same amount of learning could be achieved by a textbook. Conversely, it is not an economical use of the taxpayers' investment in education to use textbooks, lectures, or other materials which do not produce the learning that the student needs.

One of the reasons programmed instruction has been so successful is that it combines active involvement along with the verbal content. When programmed materials utilize records, films, or kits of materials, the resultant is even greater because the experiences are more concrete.

Ideally, since learners learn best in different ways, there should be a wide variety of multiple pathways through any given course, in order that every student could find a pathway which is successful to his particular way of learning. Most teachers will accept this concept, but the problem becomes one of, do teachers have to have all of these multiple pathways through their courses before they can start teaching and which pathway should be tried first? This approach to instruction could be extremely costly and very time-consuming on the part of the teachers who are developing the instructional materials if these materials and pathways are developed without knowing exactly what the students are supposed to learn (specific objectives), without knowing whether or not any students actually need any alternate paths, and without knowing whether or not each teacher in each school district, college, or university has to develop their own materials (re-inventing the curriculum wheel). Therefore, the first step is to specify what students are supposed to learn and then to identify how this specific learning is going to be tested for achievement. Since the most common and readily available sources for learning are textbooks and teachers' lectures, these would normally be the first sources to use in the teaching-learning situation. If according to the tests, one or more students didn't learn what they were supposed to, this does not mean that the objectives should be changed or that the students can't learn at all, but it does mean that the students can't learn certain objectives successfully from the textbooks and lectures the students were given to learn from and that the teacher should now try different approaches or materials. The immediate value of the pyramid is that it provides guidelines as to what to do when learning does not take place utilizing a particular existing form of instructional media or methods. As common learning problems are identified and solved, this information should be shared with other teachers in order that more students can learn more.

Marshall McLuhan has been quoted as saying, *The medium is the message.* If this is true, and there are many who believe it is, instead of letting the medium determine the message, why not let the message and the learners determine the medium?

(2) THE METHOD OF DESIGNING INSTRUCTION AS A FACTOR IN A LEARNING OR INSTRUCTIONAL PATHWAY

Given a set of objectives to be learned and a degree of simulation that is going to be used, there are a variety of methods that can be used. These methods can and do represent a variety of learning theories and learning principles. Again, the important point to remember is that some students will learn best using one method and some other students will learn best using some other method. Because of individual differences among students, there is no one method that will work successfully for all students. As pointed out previously, since children before they even start school, are not taught by design *how to learn best by any one method*, children end up learning by chance and at the same time they are learning the message, they are also learning the method of the medium of instruction.

One of the reasons why we have so many different theories and principles whose founders are convinced their concept is the *one and only* way is that under the traditional approach, it is expected and considered desirable to get a curve of results. Under the curve concept, only a few students out of a class achieve 100 percent of the tests (objectives). Almost any theory or principle will give the curve results, but the 100 percent students under different methods are not always

245

the same. By using whatever method works best for a student, almost all of the students can be 100 percent students.

NOTE: Although a student may not know enough about a course to specify the course objectives,[28] most students have a much better idea as to the method they learn best with than any teacher. After all, they have observed themselves learning for more years than most teachers they might have. The longer a student is involved in learning situations, particularly if they are successful learning situations, the better the student will be able to identify the method by which he or she learns best.

The following are examples of the different methods which can be used. The total list of different methods would be rather extensive — maybe even as high as a hundred or more.
- From the simple to the complex,
- From facts to generalizations,
- From generalizations to facts,
- From a part of a concept to the whole concept (inductive),
- From the whole concept to a part of the concept (deductive),
- From the concrete to the abstract,
- From the abstract to the concrete,
- From the practical to the theoretical,
- From the theoretical to the practical,
- From the known to the unknown,
- From the past to the present,
- From the present back to the past,
- From the present to the future,
- From the future back to the present,
- From learning by inquiry to learning by discovery,
- From learning by discovery to learning by inquiry,
- Linear programmed instruction,
- branching programmed instruction,
- cause and effect,
- case studies
- analogies,
- parables,
- From the ridiculous to the sublime,
- From the sublime to the ridiculous,
- From the normal to the abnormal,
- From the abnormal to the normal,

---

[28] If the student did know enough about a unit or course to specify the objectives, the student should be given credit for the course and passed on to the next unit or course.

- From the common to the rare event,
- From rare events to the common,
- From the individual to the universe,
- From the universe to the individual,
- From the center to the perimeter,
- From the perimeter to the center,
- From the problems to the solutions,
- From the solutions to the problems,
- Overstatements,
- From the functional to the frivalous,
- From the frivalous to the functional, etc.

In an effort to recognize that students do learn best from different methods, Oakland Community College in Michigan is utilizing a concept they call *Cognitive Style Mapping*. When students first come to their school, the student takes a variety of diagnostic tests which they feel are designed to reveal the student's cognitive learning style. The student is then assigned to a teacher and pathway for learning which best fits his or her cognitive style map. Although different *amounts to be learned* and different *rates of learning* aren't necessarily recognized or allowed in Oakland's approach (similar to most other educational institutions), they have put into action a belief held by practically every educator, but practiced by very few, *that students learn best in different ways.* As of 1972, only a third of Oakland's students are involved in their Cognitive Sytle Mapping program and among these students the *not passed* rate was reduced from 45 percent to about 30 percent. Further recognition of other learning variables would allow reduction of this *not passed* rate to less than 10 percent or maybe even zero.

(3) THE LANGUAGE USED FOR INSTRUCTION AS A FACTOR IN A LEARNING OR INSTRUCTIONAL PATHWAY

The language for instruction refers back to digital or verbal communication and analogic or sensate (senses) communication. When a teacher decides on a certain pathway through a unit or course, the teacher often assumes that all students can learn from the same verbal level and/or the same sensate levels. In almost every situation where a teacher has made these assumptions, there is one or more students for which the verbal and/or sensate level is very inappropriate.

In addition to the other learning variables, the appropriateness of the learning experiences relative to the students' abilities is becoming increasingly more critical in the teaching-learning situation. Actually, this particular variable should be so obvious that it shouldn't be necessary to consider it a learning variable. Examples of the need to identify *appropriateness of the learning experiences* can be found at all levels of instruction. Consider the typical tenth-grade class in any high school in the country. Teachers and administrators in the high school will admit that the reading levels of the students in the tenth grade class will range from fifth grade (second or third-grade level in some schools) to college level. The reading tests given in ninth grade in most school districts will support the existence of these variations in reading levels. Yet, in most tenth-grade classes, students are given textbooks which are written at the tenth-grade level or higher. Obviously, the textbooks are not *appropriate* for some of the students because it is already known by the teachers that the students who have low reading levels can't learn from them. Under the present approach to education which generally ignores differences in learning except for grading purposes, students who can't learn from inappropriate learning experiences are failed or graded down accordingly. *Appropriateness* as a variable affecting learning can be found not only in textbooks, but also in total courses, units of courses, lectures, films, television, laboratory experiences, field trips, etc.

Given that different reading levels exist in almost all classrooms, another more subtle assumption being made in most classrooms is that English is the only language for instruction. As an extreme example, a foreign student who is studying here in the United States may read English at the third grade level, but is able to read Spanish at the ninth grade level, German at eleventh grade level, and his own native Norwegian at college level. If the teacher insists on ignoring the student's obvious learning problem and uses a college level English textbook and professional level English lectures as the language for instruction, the foreign student will fail the course and the teacher will have doubts as to the mental ability of the student. A little less extreme, but just as serious are students who are United States citizens, but their families speak a language other than English at the home. For decades, the *Ugly American Syndrome* has evidenced itself in the situation where almost anyone who speaks with an accent and makes grammatical mistakes in speaking and writing is considered to have below average mental abilities — after all, the intelligence test in *English* proves that the people who don't read or speak English very well are only *trainable* or worse! In a country so scientifically advanced that we have successfully sent space ships to the moon and brought them back, our traditional education system just discovered a fantastic revelation in the late 1960's. If a teacher uses bilingual materials such that a Spanish speaking student is given Spanish materials to learn from, that these students who often were placed in remedial, special education, slow learners, or even mentally retarded classes *can now learn!* Fantastic!! Remember though, among traditional educators, this concept isn't an accepted fact and bilingual materials are generally only being used in experimental situations. It is very difficult to give up the old beliefs and accept that people who don't speak, write, and read English correctly are capable of learning.

An even more subtle problem, but actually the same thing, concerns students who do speak English but with a different dialect, jargon or vernacular than that of the English used in the language for instruction. These students may not have a serious enough language problem to fail in their courses like the students whose primary language is a foreign language, but the language problem is serious enough to interfere with the instruction such that the best these students can achieve is a "C" or a "D" in their course. The more damaging result concerns the students self-image because the language problem may very well affect their achievement on any intelligence tests and standardized tests which in turn reinforces their teachers' belief that they can't learn because they don't speak, read, or write classroom English.

In some experimental projects where the teachers have custom prepared reading materials which reflect the dialect, jargon, or vernacular of the students, they have found that the students can learn to read faster. In January, 1972, the Massachusetts legislature passed a bill which required the schools in the state to provide bilingual materials for students in whose home the primary language was other than English. This bill is reported to have affected about 40,000 students in Boston alone. Although Massachusetts was the first State to recognize via legislation that students who speak languages other than English will have problems learning via English, a dozen or more other States are actively trying to do something about it and finally in 1974, the Lou vs. Nichols case brought the problem to the Supreme Court. The result of the Supreme Court's action was to make it a violation of the Civil Rights Act to not provide special language assistance to students who are deficient in English-speaking ability.

In thinking of *the language of instruction*, it is easy to assume that this factor only consists of verbal language problems. That is not true. In thinking of language in a more general sense, anything that can be manipulated for the express purpose of conveying a message to someone uses various forms of a language. Each of our senses is involved in a sensate language of their own. As with verbal language, there are different dialects which are often caused by cultural patterns and also by sensory adaptation. For example, in tasting and smelling, what may smell and taste good in one cultural group may not smell and taste good in another cultural group. If a student who is from a cultural group that eats highly spiced food is in a chemistry, biology, home economics, or any other class where the students might taste something or the description of the taste of something is talked about and the teacher is from a cultural group that eats rather bland food, these two will have difficulty communicating to one another about their taste reactions and sensations. Some people will like certain perfume odors and other people will prefer other perfume odors.[29] Sensory adaptation refers to the adaptation of one or more senses to a condition which at first is noticeably different but after adaptation the condition is almost unnoticeable. For anyone who has lived through cold winters, it is a common occurance that in the fall a temperature of 40—45 degrees F. necessitates the wearing of a sweater or coat. After a cold winter, a temperature of 40—45 degrees F. is almost shirt-sleeve weather. This type of sensory adaptation usually affects everyone in a community area alike and would probably not contribute to a communication or learning problem. However, because of the differences from one home environment to another, there can be individual differences within a community with respect to sensory adaptation and as such, these differences could cause communication and learning problems.

Although it would be difficult to prove, it has been suggested that as high as 80 percent or more of what anyone learns has been learned via their eyes and ears. Therefore, individual differences in seeing and hearing are much more critical in a learning environment than the other senses. Learning problems involving the senses and particularly seeing and hearing are usually referred to as *perceptual* learning problems. One of the first steps in solving such a perceptual learning problem is to help the learner perceive that a problem exists. Consider for a moment Figure 36. For many people this figure is very disturbing. The amount of disturbance appears to be in relation to a person's prior exposure to art, mechanical drawing, etc. Young children are not as bothered by Figure 36 as adults are. In fact, some young children see nothing wrong with the picture. It is of interest to note that if you cover up one side, Figure 36 looks all right and if you cover up the other side, Figure 36

---

[29] Taste is one of the senses that can be proven to be part nurture (culturally affected) and part nature. Researchers for years have used P.T.C. paper to illustrate how the reactions to this particular paper are a matter of heredity. In any group of over 10-15, the differences in taste can be easily demonstrated. Give each person a piece of P.T.C. paper and warn them that when they put the paper in their mouth that they should keep a *poker face* and keep their face and voice without expression. Then have everyone put the strip of P.T.C. paper in their mouth and chew it. Wait about 15 seconds, then ask everyone who tastes just plain paper to raise their hand. Have them keep their hands up and then ask the others what they taste if anything. Those that taste something will give a variety of reactions, but a few — then more later — will claim the paper is very bitter and will stare in disbelief at the ones that didn't taste anything — CAUTION — DO NOT ask first these people who taste something bitter. Because not only will those who really get a bitter taste say so, but the others who don't taste anything will think they should have tasted something bitter and may say so in order to not be different. It is difficult for many people to accept that other people might have different taste reactions. Remember the situation where your friend has said, *You'll love my wife's spaghetti (or some other dish), it's the best.* Then when you taste it, you can hardly eat it and hold it down!

still looks all right. It is the middle of Figure 36 that is distracting. Notice that your mind does not want you to look at the middle part of Figure 36 because for most adults your prior experiences preclude a rationalization of how the two extensions, A and B, all of a sudden become the three extensions C, D and E.

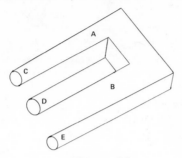

Figure 36

Depending on the strength of your prior conditioning, forcing your eyes to focus on the middle of Figure 36 may cause certain symptoms of nausea. Most people who look at Figure 36 will find that their eyes will vacillate from one side to the other side. They are in effect trying not to see the problem. Some learners may be this way also. If they are unable to rationalize or perceive a possible solution to a problem, it is possible that they may refuse to acknowledge that a problem exists.

There are two types of *perceptual* learning problems:
1. Problems which are actually based on the utilization of the five senses.
2. Learning problems which are figuratively based on the five senses.

Quite often in education we may actually ask a student to *see* something in an actual sense by looking through a microscope or at a photograph, a three-dimensional object, a picture, a test tube, etc. Perceptual learning problems that are actually based on the five senses can generally be solved by the development of instructional materials which will facilitate the learning of finer discriminations and more complex recognitions. Almost as often, we may ask the student to *see* something figuratively, such as, *Do you see the author's point in the story, Do you see the strength of the formula, Do you see the relevance of this conclusion to the problem, Do you see what I'm driving at,* etc. Learning problems which are figuratively based on the five senses are more difficult to solve. These learning problems are found in almost all subject matter areas. In solving these problems, the first step is to specifically identify what it is you are figuratively speaking about. Once this is done, then it is possible to develop instructional materials that will help the learner to *perceive* what you, the teacher, want the student to *perceive* (figuratively). Consider Figure 37, are you able to see the face of Christ as he is popularly portrayed to have looked? If

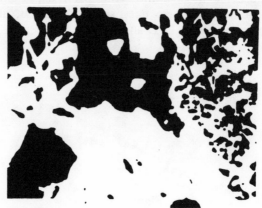

Figure 37 — Christ in the Snow

you do, you are one of the few who are able to see the face right away. Some people are able to see Christ's face in Figure 37 only after hours of looking at it. Some people have never been able to see Christ's face in Figure 37 and probably never would if someone didn't help the person solve the perceptual problem. Consider how often in education and in instructional activities we expect the learner to *see* something that we *see* in a visual, a concept, or in a situation! Generally, when the learner does not *see* what the teacher *sees*, it is assumed that the learner is dumb, stupid, and incapable of learning. Under the teacher's role as an instructioneer, when a learner is unable to *see* what the teacher *sees*, the teacher solves the learning problem. Therefore, if you did not see Christ's face in Figure 37, look at Figure 38. If you can see Christ's face in Figure 37, skip

Figure 38 — Christ in the Snow

252

to the paragraph after Figure 42. Figure 38 is the same as Figure 37 except for the letters which have been added. At the top and middle of Figure 38, letters a-b indicate that the top edge of the drawing cuts through the middle of Christ's forehead. Line c-d is the right eyebrow. Line d-e goes from the bridge of the nose down to the end of the nose. Line e-f outlines the left nostril of Chirst's nose. At point f the line goes down part way into the upper lip and then cuts across the cheek to g. Right above the shadow h is the shadow under the left eyebrow. The white space i is the right cheek. The tiny white dot above the white space i is the corner of the right eye next to the nose. The white space k is Christ's chin. The imaginary line m-n on the left side of Figure 38 represents Christ's right shoulder. The imaginary line o-p opposite m-n represents Christ's left shoulder. Now look back at Figure 37. Can you now see Christ's face. If you can, skip over to the paragraph after Figure 42. If you still can't see Christ's face, look at Figure 39. If you can see Christ's face in Figure 39, look back at Figure 37, if you can still see Christ's face, skip over to the paragraph after Figure 42. If you

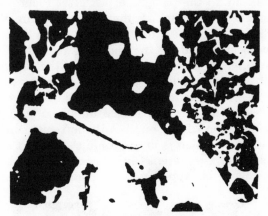

Figure 39 — Christ in the Snow

can't see Christ's face in Figure 39, look at Figure 40. It is the same as Figure 37 except for a few extra lines and shadows and some letters I can use to identify the added lines and shadows. In the upper middle of Figure 40, curved line q-r outlines the left eye socket. Just below the r is an s which is next to the left nostril. Just in from the left side in the middle is a t and then a line curving down to a u. This last curved line is the draping of Christ's cloak coming over the right shoulder at t and curving down to u in the middle of Chirst's chest. Now look at Figure 39. If you can see Christ's face, look back at Figure 37, if you can still see Christ's face, skip ahead to the paragraph after Figure 42. If you still can't see Christ's face, look at Figure 41. If you can see Christ's

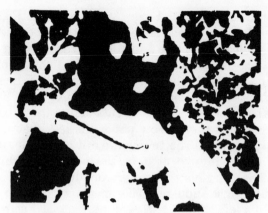

Figure 40 — Christ in the Snow

face in Figure 41, then look at Figure 39. If you can see Christ's face in Figure 39, then look at Figure 37. If you can see Christ's face in Figure 37, then skip ahead to the paragraph just after Figure 42. If you still can't see Christ's face in Figure 41, then look at Figure 42. Figure 42 is the same as Figure 37 and Figure 39 except more lines, black spaces, and letters have been added. In the middle lower half of Figure 42, the shoulder to shoulder semi-circular hood covers the top part of Christ's mantle or cloak. In the middle of the upper half, the letter v is on the nose which has been outlined. To the right of the letter v is the letter w. Directly above the letter w and in the middle of the shadow is the semi-curcular suggestion of the pupil of the left eye. Directly above the letter v is the letter x which is in the middle of Christ's forehead. The lines around the letter x represent Christ's worried look because you are not that familiar with his appearance (as commonly thought of). Now

Figure 41 — Christ in the Snow

254

Figure 42 — Christ in the Snow

look back at Figure 41. If you can see a face and top half of a body dressed in a cloak and hood, then look at Figure 39, and then look at Figure 37. If you see a face in Figure 41, but can't see Christ's face in Figure 39 or if you see Christ's face in Figure 39 but can't see it in Figure 37, then try looking back and forth at the Figures very quickly. If you still haven't been able to see Christ's face in Figure 37 after all this, it doesn't mean that you can't see what I and most others will see, it just means you need more help and more time.[30]

In every subject area where there are things to see and learning is affected by whether or not the students see them as the professional in the subject area sees them, visual language becomes very important particularly in solving learning problems. Although most of us take for granted the visual language in films and television, people who haven't seen films and television have to learn the symbolism or language of film conventions, i.e., the fading to black from one scene and then fading into another scene usually is meant to convey the passing of time, crossfading directly from one scene into another usually is meant to convey simultaneous events, the close up view is usually meant to convey something emotional, etc. Rarely are these conventions taught and if a learner hasn't learned them, learning problems may very well be a result. These same problems occur frequently in art. If the artist is only developing a particular form of art to communicate to himself or herself or is using the art medium as an emotional release and is not

---

[30] Several years ago, I was conducting a three day seminar with 80 members of the training department of a large appliance manufacturer. When I showed the three visuals of Christ (Figure 37, 39, and 41), the only one out of the 80 participants that didn't finally see Christ's face in Figure 37 was the Vice President in charge of Training. Finally, on the last day, after two days of looking at the visuals from all directions, even he was able to see Christ's face.

concerned with communicating anything to anyone, then the use of conventions in the particular medium is not necessary and the artist can really *do his or her own thing.* On the other hand, if the artist is trying to communicate something to someone other than himself or herself, it is necessary to utilize some of the conventions of the art form and to be sure that the people being communicated to are knowledgeable about the conventions being used. Learning problems in art are common because many art teachers resist teaching the conventions in the various art forms. They usually feel that in teaching the conventions or craft of an art form, the students' creativity is inhibited. Creativity in an art form in which the artist is the only one that understands it, may be recognized as being creative but it will not be appreciated because it doesn't communicate to the perceiver. Creativity in which the artist used one or more conventions in creative ways such that it still communicates via the conventions, will not only be more easily recognized as being creative but it will also be appreciated. In addition, if a student doesn't learn the conventions, his or her ignorance may very well limit creativity.

As an example of learning to see with the eyes of the professional or subject matter specialist, if you or an acquaintance have recently purchased a different make, model, or color of a car than you have previously driven, did you or your friend notice how many more cars of the same make, model, or color there seemed to be after the purchase was made? If you answer is yes, then you or your friend have experienced a common phenomenon.

With reference to hearing, it is also very much affected by language and selective perception. It should be obvious that if a student is listening to a teacher who is speaking a completely different language, the students learning will be essentially at a stand still. If the student has to sit and listen even if there is no hope of learning, the student may develop sufficient negative attitudes towards the learning environment that other previous and future learned behaviors in similar environments are also negatively affected. It should also be apparent that as the teacher's spoken language gets closer and closer to the language that each student listens and learns from best, that the degree of learning should also increase.

Because of the seriousness of this learning variable, the first objectives to be written in every instructional unit should concern the new words, symbols, or visuals which will be used in the instructional unit to facilitate learning and/or to convey the message to be learned to the learner. If the instructional unit and objectives are only concerned with symbols and words as they may be read or written, a printed or written glossary of terms may be sufficient. However, if the student is going to be expected to use the symbols and words orally and/or to listen to a

256

teacher using the words or symbols in lectures or discussions, then it will be necessary to utilize some other media. The Language Master, Photograph 2, (or any similar device) could very easily be used to facilitate the behaviors of reading, speaking, and listening to the new words and symbols. The word or symbol can be printed on the card along with a definition, diagram, chart, photograph, or even a three-dimensional article can be attached to the card[31] to help the learner develop a meaning for the new word or symbol. The strip at the bottom of the card is a piece of audio tape and the recording mechanism is designed for two tracks. One track is for the teacher to record his or her pronounciation of the new word or symbol and the other track is used by the student to practice pronouncing the new word or symbol.

NOTE: In case the teacher has an accent such that the teacher's pronounciation of a new word is different than how it would be pronounced by most other teachers, it would be best to have someone else pronounce the word or symbol correctly at the beginning of the master track as a model for the students to copy in practicing the pronounciation of the new words or symbols and to have the student's regular teacher also record his or her pronounciation of the word or symbol at the end of the master track in order to facilitate the students' ability to listen to and identify the word or symbol when used by the teacher in class.

Photograph 2 — The Language Master

---

[31] A home economics teacher who had attended one of my seminars and wanted her students in a clothing class to not only know the names of the various synthetic fabrics reading, writing, speaking, and listening, but also to recognize the fabrics by feel, observation, and simple tests with the fabric itself. To do this, she stapled swatches of the fabric to the Language Master Cards.

g. APPARENT vs. REAL INTELLIGENCE AS AFFECTED BY STUDENTS' INTELLECTUAL AND SENSORY LEARNING SKILLS

At the present time our instruments for identifying intelligence are very limited and so it is necessary to differentiate between a person's apparent intelligence and a person's real intelligence. Since no one, at this time, has been able to identify the full 100 percent capacity of the human mind or what THE ideal learning environment is for any one learner, the concept of *real intelligence* remains an unknown quantity. A person's apparent intelligence is a variable and depends on the situation in which it is evaluated. At this point in time, all measures of intelligence are measures of apparent intelligence. As pointed out already, by ignoring individual differences in *amount to be learned*, the apparent intelligence can become very misleading. Combined with the problem of the *self-fulfilling prophecy*, apparent intelligence often becomes the imaginary *limit* of intelligence.

Given that almost every educator will agree that learners learn best in different ways, from different methods, and in languages (auditory, written, and visual) most nearly like their own, it should be obvious that the further the ways, methods, and languages are away from how the learner learns best, the greater the disparity between the apparent intelligence resulting from observations or tests of the learner trying to learn from these ways, methods, and languages and the learner's real intelligence. Conversely, the closer the ways, methods, and languages are to how the learner learns best, the closer the apparent intelligence comes to the learner's real intelligence. Therefore, in looking at rate of learning as a measure of intelligence, it is necessary to include as factors the correlations between the ways, methods, and languages used in instruction and the ways, methods, and languages in which the learner will learn best.

$$\frac{\text{Rate of}}{\text{learning}} = \frac{\text{Amount to be learned}}{\text{Time for learning}} \; X \; \frac{1}{r_{cog_s}} \; X \; \frac{1}{r_{cog_m}} \; X \; \frac{1}{r_{cog_l}}$$

where:

r_{cog_s} = the correlation between the way (degree of simulation) the instructional event was set up and the way the learner learns best.

r_{cog_m} = the correlation between the method used in the instructional event and the method within which the learner learns best.

r_{cog_l} = the correlation between the languages used in the instructional event and the languages from which the learner learns best.

cog = refers to the intellectual and sensory learning skills that each learner brings to the instructional event to facilitate learning.

The reason for using the reciprocal form ($1/r_{cog_s}$) is that if the correlation between the way the instructional event is set up and the way a learner learns best is 1.0 (both the same), the factor becomes $1/1.0$ or 1 and as such has no affect on the apparent intelligence (Rate of learning). However, as the correlation decreases so also will the apparent intelligence. Therefore, by using the reciprocal form, as the correlation decreases, the reciprocal form is closer to the real intelligence of the learner. For example, given two students who are supposed to learn the same 100 objectives in an instructional unit, one student learns all of the objectives in two months and the other student learns all of the objectives in four months. The correlations for the first student are r_{cog_s} = .95, r_{cog_m} = .90, and r_{cog_l} = .95. The correlations for the second student are r_{cog_s} = .75, r_{cog_m} = .60, and r_{cog_l} = .70.

(1) Using the traditional approach, it would seem obvious that the student who learned the objectives in two months was twice as fast a learner as the student who took four months. Also, in using the traditional approach, time would have been held constant at say three months. As a result, the first student who learned the objectives in two months waited around for an extra month and became bored. The second student was only able to learn 3/4ths of the objectives (three months learning time given while the student needed four months). From this evidence, the apparent rate of learning for the first student would be

$\frac{100 \text{ objectives}}{3 \text{ months}}$ or 33.3 objectives/month. The second student's

apparent rate of learning would be $\frac{75 \text{ objectives}}{3 \text{ months}}$ or 25 objectives/month.

(2) In recognizing individual differences in *amounts to be learned*, tests revealed that the first student already knew 15 of the objectives in the instructional unit so he only had to learn 85 objectives. The second student had cumulative ignorance of 20 objectives from prerequisite courses which he had to learn before he could successfully learn the 100 objectives in the instructional unit. Now the apparent rate of learning of the first

259

student is $\dfrac{85 \text{ objectives}}{3 \text{ months}}$ or 28.3 objectives/month. Since the second student had a total of 120 objectives to learn and because of the time limitation was only able to learn ¾ths of them or 90 objectives. The second student's apparent rate of learning was then $\dfrac{90 \text{ objectives}}{3 \text{ months}}$ or 30 objectives/month.

(3) In recognizing individual differences in time for learning, it was discovered that the first student was actually able to learn the 85 objectives in two months, so his apparent rate of learning is now $\dfrac{85 \text{ objectives}}{2 \text{ months}}$ or 42.5 objectives/month. The second student needed four months to learn his 120 objectives so his apparent rate of learning was $\dfrac{120 \text{ objectives}}{4 \text{ months}}$ or 30 objectives/month.

(4) In recognizing the effects of the correlations between the ways, methods, and languages used in the instructional unit and the ways, methods, and languages the learners learn best from, the apparent rates of learning change accordingly.

For the first student:

$$\begin{array}{ll} \text{Rate of} \\ \text{learning} \end{array} = \frac{42.5 \text{ objectives}}{\text{month}} \times \frac{1}{.95} \times \frac{1}{.90} \times \frac{1}{.95}$$

$$= \frac{42.5 \text{ objectives}}{\text{month}} \times 1.05 \times 1.11 \times 1.05$$

$$= \frac{52.0 \text{ objectives}}{\text{month}} [32]$$

For the second student:

$$\begin{array}{ll} \text{Rate of} \\ \text{learning} \end{array} = \frac{30 \text{ objectives}}{\text{month}} \times \frac{1}{.75} \times \frac{1}{.60} \times \frac{1}{.70}$$

$$= \frac{30 \text{ objectives}}{\text{month}} \times 1.33 \times 1.67 \times 1.43$$

$$= \frac{95.3 \text{ objectives}}{\text{month}} [32]$$

---

[32] It is important to remember that the rate of learning expressed in terms of *objectives/month* is only useful for purposes of comparison between students who are learning essentially the same objectives. The difficulty level of objectives will vary considerably from one course to another and even between objectives in the same course. The comparison of rates of learning expressed in terms of objectives/month between two or more students who are in different courses is a meaningless concept.

As a result of recognizing that different students learn best differently, the second student's rate of learning turns out to be almost twice as fast as the first student. If as educators and instructioneers, we really believe that students learn best in different ways, using different methods and different languages, than we have to recognize how these differences have significant effects on the learners' apparent rates of learning and consequently, cannot assume that an apparent rate of learning in a traditional educational event is indicative of the learners' real rates of learning.

h. RATE OF LEARNING AS AFFECTED BY THE STUDENT'S EMOTIONAL TENDENCIES

The concern of this section is on how the emotional tendencies which the learner brings with him to the instructional event affects the learner's rate of learning in learning objectives in the cognitive, sensory, and affective domains. There are two categories of emotional tendencies which affect learning: those emotional tendencies which are concerned with motivation and those emotional tendencies which are concerned with interpersonal relationships.

(1) MOTIVATION AS IT AFFECTS RATE OF LEARNING

This learning variable has been the topic of many conferences in education during the past several decades. Although this is a learning variable that all teachers and most parents are familiar with, it is very common for parents and teachers to make comments about the slow or nonlearning student, such as *What can you do if the student doesn't want to learn?* or *How can you teach the apathetic student?* Somehow, it is assumed that no matter what the instructional materials are that are developed and no matter in what way they are used in the teaching-learning situation that they will automatically have the proper motivation built into them, and when the student does not learn, then it must be the fault of the student. The only statement that can actually be made in a situation where the student is an apathetic learner, a slow learner or a nonlearner, is that the student is reacting this way to the kinds of instructional materials and learning experiences that he is being exposed to, which does not mean that if the student was exposed to something more interesting, that the student might not want to learn and will learn. The term *more interesting* does not mean the course objectives are changed. What it does mean is that the course objectives are presented to the student in such a manner or in such a situation that the student will want to learn them. The concept of motivation is like the concept of individual differences; almost all educators will agree that what will motivate one child will not

261

necessarily motivate another, yet in the classroom, we continue to assume that all children are motivated in the same manner and that there are not any individual differences. Quite often, teachers and parents when faced with a nonlearning student will retreat to the old cliché about how *You can lead a horse to water, but you can't make the horse drink.* My answer to this excuse for not recognizing the problem as a learning problem and trying to solve it, is *but you can run the horse around the pasture until it gets thirsty!*

There are two types of motivation; the first type of motivation could be called *intrinsic* (internal) motivation. This is the type of motivation that is evidenced when the student says, *I want to learn this because I like it.*

For example, if students make the remark that a particular subject or textbook is dull and uninteresting, this does not mean that the subject or textbook is naturally dull and uninteresting or that the students are incapable of becoming interested in the subject; it means that using that particular textbook makes the subject dull and uninteresting to those students. If it is possible to separate the *vehicle for learning* from *what is to be learned*, it is possible to find other vehicles which might facilitate the learning of the same objectives. These other vehicles could be other textbooks written from a different point-of-view or more practical. All too often, because teachers haven't specified exactly what it is they want their students to learn, the vehicles for learning (books, tapes, etc.) become the objectives. This in turn limits the flexibility in solving students' learning problems. For example, in many literature courses, a particular piece of literature which serves as a vehicle for learning also becomes the objective. If the objective of a literature course is to learn to do a literary analysis or to recognize a particular author's style or to learn certain things about a particular form of literature, the teacher should use an appropriate piece of literature as a learning vehicle during the course and a different piece of literature (with the same characteristics as the vehicle) in the testing situation. If the student can't transfer the learned behaviors from one vehicle to another, what he or she has learned has very limited use and will be forgotten quickly. Ideally, it would be best if a student could be motivated to learn because the student wanted to learn. Students who have had continuous success in learning and consequently have a positive self-image, may very well learn for the sake of learning even if what is being learned is not immediately relevant and useful or even if it may never be useful. Students who have had mediocre success in learning (the "C" and "D" students) and especially those that have experienced failure in trying to learn, quite typically have a negative self-image as far as *academic learning* is concerned and may very well seek out other areas in which they can have success in order to build up

262

positive aspects in their self-image. Too often these *other areas* involve behaviors which are considered illegal, anti-social, vandalism, etc. To these students, it is very critical that the objectives to be learned, the vehicle for learning, and the evaluation instruments are viewed as relevant at least until such time as the students self-image in *academic learning* is positively rebuilt.

One of the best examples of the need for relevancy as it affects intrinsic motivation is Stephen Corey's, *The Poor Scholar's Soliloquy.*

No, I'm not very good in school. This is my second year in the seventh grade, and I'm bigger and taller than the other kids. They like me all right, though, even if I don't say much in the classroom, because outside I can tell them how to do a lot of things. They tag around me and tag around me and that sort makes up for what goes on in school.

I don't know why the teachers don't like me. They never have very much. Seems like they don't think you know anything unless they can name the book it comes out of. I've got a lot of books in my room at home — books like *Popular Science, Mechanical Encyclopedia,* and the Sears' and Ward's catalogues — but I don't very often just sit down and read through them like they make us do in school. I use my books when I want to find something out, like whenever Mom buys anything secondhand I look up in Sears' or Ward's first and tell her if she's getting stung or not. I can use the index in a hurry.

In school though, we've got to learn whatever is in the book and I just can't memorize the stuff. Last year I stayed after school every night for two weeks trying to learn the names of the Presidents. Of course I knew some of them, like Washington and Jefferson and Lincoln, but there must have been thirty altogether, and I never did get them straight.

I'm not too sorry though, because the kids who learned the Presidents had to turn right around and learn all the Vice Presidents. I am taking the seventh grade over, but our teacher this year isn't so interested in the names of the Presidents. She has us trying to learn the names of all the great American inventors.

I guess I just can't remember names in history. Anyway this year I've been trying to learn about trucks because my uncle owns three and he says that I can drive one when I'm sixteen. I already know the horsepower and number of forward and backward speeds of twenty-six American trucks, some of them Diesels, and I can spot each a long way off. It's funny how that Diesel works. I started to tell my teacher about it last Wednesday in science class when the pump we were using to make a vacuum in a bell jar got hot, but she said that she didn't see what a Diesel engine had to do with our experiment on air pressure so I just kept still The kids seemed interested though. I took four of them to my uncle's garage after school and we saw the mechanic, Gus, tear a big Diesel truck down. Boy, does he know his stuff.

I'm not very good in geography either. They call it economic geography this year. We've been studying the imports and exports of Chile all week, but I couldn't tell you what they are. Maybe the reason is I had to miss school yesterday because my uncle took me in his big trailer truck down state about 200 miles, and we brought almost 10 tons of stock to the Chicago market.

He had told me where we were going, and I had to figure out the highways to take and also the mileage. He didn't do anything but drive and turn where I told him to. Was that fun. I sat with a map in my lap and told him to turn south, or southwest, or some other direction. He made seven stops, and drove over 500 miles round trip. I'm figuring now what his oil cost and also the wear and tear on the truck — he calls it depreciation — so we'll know how much we made.

I even write all the bills and send letters to the farmers about what their pigs and beef cattle brought at the stockyards. I only made three mistakes in my letters last time, my aunt said, all commas. She has been through high school and read them over. I wish I could write school themes that way. The last one I had to write was on *What a Daffodil Thinks of Spring*, and I just couldn't get going.

I don't do very well in school in arithmetic, either. Seems I just can't keep my mind on the problems. We had one the other day like this: *If a 57-foot telephone pole fell across a cement highway so the 17-3/6 feet extend from one side and 14-9/17 feet from the other, how wide is the highway?*

That seemed to me like an awful silly way to get the width of a highway. I didn't even try to answer it because it didn't say whether the pole had fallen straight across or not.

Even in the shop I don't get very good grades. All of us kids made a broom holder and a bookend this term and mine were sloppy. I just couldn't get interested. Mom doesn't use a broom any more with her new vacuum cleaner, and all our books are in a bookcase with glass doors in the parlor. Anyway, I wanted to make an end gate for my uncle's trailer, but the shop teacher said that meant using metal and wood both, and I'd have to learn how to work with wood first. I did not see why, but I kept still and made a tie rack at school and the tail gate after school at my uncle's garage. He said I saved him ten dollars.

Civics is hard for me too. I've been staying after school trying to learn the *Articles of Confederation* for almost a week, because the teacher said we couldn't be good citizens unless we did. I really tried, because I want to be a good citizen. I did hate to stay after school, though, because a bunch of us boys from the south end of town have been cleaning up the old lot across from Taylor's Machine Shop to make a playground out of it for the little kids from the Methodist home. I made the jungle gym from old pipe, and the guys made me Grand Mogul to keep the playground going. We raised enough money collecting scrap this month to build a wire fence clear around the lot.

Dad says I can quit school when I am fifteen, and I am sort of anxious to because there are a lot of things I want to learn to do and as my uncle says, I am not getting any younger.

A second type of motivation is extrinsic motivation. Evidence of this type of motivation is when students say, *I don't like this, but I'll learn it because of what you (the teacher) are going to do.* What the teacher can *do*, consists of two very conflicting concepts: reward and punishment. A reward for learning is viewed as positive extrinsic motivation. Threats of punishment used to facilitate learning is viewed as negative extrinsic motivation. The most important fact to remember in dealing with both positive and negative extrinsic motivation is that reward and punishment is a very personal thing and as such is receiver-oriented. What is rewarding for one person may be nothing or even punishment to another person. A reward can only be called a reward if the person receiving it considers it a reward. A punishment can only be called a punishment if the person receiving it considers it a punishment.

If a teacher is unable to get a learner to learn for the sake of learning or for the sake of his or her interest in the learning experience itself, then by identifying the kinds of activities that are considered rewarding by the learner, these activities can then be used as rewards for learning something which the student considers not rewarding in itself. This latter type of motivation utilizes two concepts. The first concept has been developed by Westinghouse Learning Corporation in many of their projects carried out in Albuquerque, New Mexico, and is referred to as *contingency management.* Contingency management can be defined as a situation in which the learning is contingent upon a reward offered. The second concept is based on Premack's principle that preferred behaviors can be used as rewards for the performance of less preferred behaviors. For successful utilization of either of these concepts or the ideas of intrinsic or extrinsic motivation, the educator is going to have to become aware of what is rewarding to the learner.

At the present time in education, all too often what is considered rewarding by the educator is really punishment to the learner, and what is considered punishment to the educator is rewarding to the learner. For example, in most elementary and secondary schools throughout the country, if a student skips school enough, sooner or later he is expelled from school as a punishment, when in fact being expelled from school is exactly what the student wanted to achieve in the first place. In most elementary schools, it is also very common to find teachers punishing students by having them write extra sentences, paragraphs, essays, problems, etc. Teachers look on these extra activities as punishing because they have to correct them. When students first start these activities, they generally consider them positively or at least in a neutral state; but after a teacher uses these learning activities as punishment for a few times, students are very quickly convinced that writing and doing problems are forms of punishment. If students put off to the last moment to do their homework, this does not necessarily mean that they are lazy. It could mean that they look on homework as punishment and healthy minds do not look forward to punishing themselves on purpose (masochism).

In setting up an extrinsic motivational situation, be very careful how the student is oriented to it. A slight change in wording can change a statement which indicates a reward into a statement which indicates punishment. For example:

As soon as you finish these problems, you can go out to play. (Reward)

You can't go out to play until you finish these problems. (Punishment)

It is very common for parents to change their childrens' attitudes from positive to negative towards various household duties by falling into the same semantic trap. For example, too many parents say:

You can't go to the movie until you finish the dishes. (Punishment)

What they should be saying is:

As soon as you finish the dishes, you can go to the movie. (Reward)

At the present time, science courses for the nonscience majors and humanities courses for the nonhumanities majors are courses which are *specifically designed* to give the learner some minimal knowledge in nonmajor areas which will contribute to his general education. In actuality, very few of these courses are really designed specially for the student who may be starting out with an extremely low motivation and attitude towards courses out of his major interest area. Generally, most of these courses end up being a condensed version of the regular course for the students who are majoring in the subject matter area and cover

266

exactly the same concepts, principles, rules, theorems, etc. As a result, most condensed courses of this type usually convince the nonmajor students that they were right in deciding not to major in the subject of the course.

If these special courses for the nonmajors were designed from the point of view of *What can the nonmajor learn in this subject matter area that will be useful to the student throughout his life,* it is very possible that some students could become so motivated by finding out that the subject matter area is relevant to the real world and to his major interests that he might change his major interest and goals. This is another way of saying that nonscience-oriented students have not been exposed to science courses in which the learning objectives were relevant and useful from their point-of-view, and the science-oriented students may not have been exposed to learning objectives in the nonscience courses which pointed out how the nonscience courses could be relevant and useful in their lives.

In addition to being concerned about the use of motivation to encourage students to learn, it is critical to remember that students come to the instructional event with certain emotional tendencies which in themselves may significantly affect learning. For example, if a student comes to the instructional event with positive attitudes, a positive self-image, and confidence that he or she can learn the objectives, it may not even be necessary to build in a motivational set into the instructional event as the student may learn for the sake of learning. At the other extreme, if a student has had many negative experiences in schools and comes to the instructional event with negative attitudes, a negative self-image, and confidence that he or she will not be able to learn the objectives, it may be necessary not only to build in motivation into the instructional event, but to also rebuild the learners self-image. This can usually be done by using brief instructional units (less than 30 minutes) which are designed for maximum success. These units have the following characteristics:

(a) Starts where the learner is intellectually or below where the learner is such that a pretest of the unit would indicate that the student already knows part of the unit.

(b) The first part of the unit is a pretest of the unit so that the student is made aware of what he or she knows and doesn't know about the instructional unit.

(c) The second part of the unit lists the specific objectives to be learned as a result of going through the unit.

(d) The major part of the instructional unit is designed such that the learner is constantly reinforced that he or she can learn and is learning (probably some type of programmed instruction).

267

(e) The last part of the instructional unit should be a posttest to prove that learner did achieve all of the objectives.

(f) In addition to the unit, it is critical that the teacher using these materials be an instructioneer. No matter how good these instructional units are, not every student will achieve 100 percent of the objectives and that is when the instructioneer steps in and using whatever materials and techniques may be necessary helps the student finish learning 100 percent of the objectives of the instructional unit.

After a student has had repeated success in learning and his or her self-image has been made a little positive, it may be possible to use non-programmed materials and to extend the learning time depending upon how many years of negative experiences in schools a student has had, some students may take a proportionately longer time to rebuild their self-image as a successful learner.

It is very important for a teacher to remember that self-image is a learned concept. Children are not born hating themselves or feeling good about themselves. A person's self-image is developed as he or she encounters life and a sign ficant part of a person's self-image is a result of encounters in school with teachers and other students. Under the traditional approach to education, millions of students are treated negatively by what teachers do and say in the classroom (via tests, grades, and comments). Under the systems approach where the teacher is the instructioneer, the constant emphasis is on success and positive feedback to the learner.

The Scholarship function of schools can be very instrumental in providing motivation for learning. Because the Scholarship Seminars are put on by teachers or students who are excited enough about their topics that they want to share it with others, their excitement may very often generate motivation in the participants to learn more about the topics either formally or informally. (Remember, the Scholarship Seminars are scheduled whenever a teacher or student has something they want to share and discuss with others. There are no objectives listed, no tests or grades given, no one is required to attend and neither the teacher nor the student is paid to put on these Seminars. It is purely a voluntary function on the part of presenter and participants.)

In recognizing that motivation does have an affect on learning, Gordan Flammer of Utah State University, developed a model of motivation and achievement which indicates some practical ways to manipulate motivation and subsequently affect achievement (Figure 43). During any one instructional event, there are demotivating forces acting on the student which tend to lower the student's achievement level and there are also motivating forces acting on the student which tend to raise the student's achievement level. The resultant or difference

268

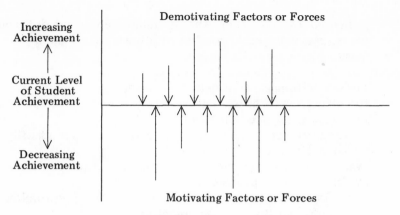

Figure 43 — Motivation and Achievement

between these two opposing forces is the positive or negative motivation which affects the student's achievement. Therefore, there are two ways to increase positive motivation in an instructional event. First, to decrease or eliminate one or more of the demotivating factors or forces, or second to increase or add new motivating factors or forces. Some of the demotivating factors or forces are:
— cumulative ignorance which inhibits subsequent learning;
— a self-image of failure or mediocrity caused by "C's", "D's", and/or "F's";
— not enough time to learn or too much time left over to waste after learning;
— lack of success in *out-psyching* the teachers as to what should be learned;
— the evaluation of achievement (test items) doesn't match the stated objectives;
— the unit or course *treatment* is given first regardless of need or appropriateness and any testing or diagnosis is done at the end of the treatment;
— evaluation or diagnosis is used to assign grades instead of being used to identify learning problems;
— irrelevant and uninteresting content;
— in a learning environment where the teacher will not solve the student's learning problems;
— presented in a way which is other than the best way for the student to learn;
— presented via a method which is other than the best method the student is able to learn from;
— presented in a visual and/or verbal language which is different from the visual and/or verbal language the learner can learn best in;

269

- presented by a teacher who is unmotivated and dull and/or whose personality is in conflict with the student; and a
- negative learning environment.

Some of the motivating factors or forces are:

- positive self-image, confident of success;
- the objectives to be learned are clearly stated and are defensible in terms of relevance and utility;
- opportunities are available to meet with teachers to identify any additional objectives desired by the student;
- evaluation of achievement is primarily used to identify a student's learning problems;
- students' learning problems are viewed as opportunities for teaching rather than as a genetic problem;
- the learning environment is such that a variety of learning pathways are available to learn any unit or course objectives;
- the students are tested or diagnosed first and the results determine the *treatment* or course content to be learned;
- the need for any remedial work is eliminated because no cumulative ignorance is allowed to develop;
- the instructioneers, in diagnosing and prescribing, either fit the learning materials (not the objectives) to the abilities of the student or nuture the abilities of the student such that the changed abilities enable the student to learn from available materials; and
- students and teachers are encouraged to conduct motivational seminars on topics of their own interest for other teachers and students (Scholarship Function).

In the hundreds of seminars which I have conducted concerning the topics in these three volumes and especially on the motivating and demotivating factors, it is common to have teachers and particularly parents comment that it seemed as if my goal was to make instruction easy and pleasurable for students. In schools where they have experimented with individualized instruction such that students are actually progressing at their own pace, it is also common to have other teachers, administrators, and parents make comments, while they are viewing a classroom in which students are involved in a variety of activities and seemingly enjoying it, that it appears as if the students are *playing*! For some reason, in our society, it has become accepted that work and learning are not supposed to be enjoyable. Just because students are playing and/or happy doesn't mean that the students are not learning. In a recent Tax Court case, the Treasury Department claimed that a taxpayer couldn't deduct the expenses from his business of chartering his 65 foot boat because the taxpayer derived pleasure from the *business* and as such this made the *business* a hobby and hence the expenses were not deductible. The Tax Court in ruling against the Treasury Department said:

> A business will not be turned into a hobby merely because the owner finds it pleasurable; suffering has never been made a prerequisite to deductibility. Success in business is largely obtained by pleasurable interest therein. (Thomas W. Jackson, 59 T.C. No. 31)

In a similar way, the same ruling could be interpreted in instruction as follows:

> Learning will not be turned into playing merely because the student finds it pleasurable; suffering has never been made a prerequisite for instruction. Success in learning is largely obtained by pleasurable interest therein!

(2) INTERPERSONAL RELATIONSHIP (STUDENT-TEACHER) AS IT AFFECTS RATE OF LEARNING.

It would perhaps be ideal if everyone loved everyone else, but in reality, this is not the situation and it is highly probable that there never has been such a situation and there never will be such a situation. As such, the interpersonal relationship between the teacher and student, the author and the reader, the film director and the viewer, etc. can have varying affects on the achievement of the student. There are at least three factors which affect interpersonal relationships and all three are primarily a variation of the same thing: first, is a person's personal philosophy which is the sum of all the person's attitudes, values, and beliefs; second, is a person's personality which is the observable expression of the person's attitudes, values, and beliefs; and third, is a person's style which is the manner in how a person consistently expresses his or her personality.

Many people have been aware of these factors for years, but little, if any, effort has been made to classify them as learning variables and to take them into account in the learning situation. These particular variables became especially noticeable in a programmed instruction project I was involved with in which it was noted that about 30 percent of the students didn't like a particular programmed text. In fact, in a number of research projects concerning programmed instruction, there always seemed to be 25—30 percent of the students who indicated negative attitudes towards learning from programmed instruction. In trying to solve this problem, it was discovered that by allowing the students a choice of three or four programmed texts covering approximately the same content and objectives, almost every student was able to choose a text that he or she liked and could learn from. Since then, I

271

have had teachers try the same thing with regular textbooks and they have found the same results.

A student may be able to learn from one book but not from another book even though both books concern the same content and objectives. If you ask a dozen people who like baseball, chances are that they will not all like the same writer who writes about baseball. For most people, depending upon where you live, there are two or more television stations from which to choose if you want to watch the evening news. Not everyone watches the same television news program. Even though the news, weather, and sports which are presented on each station are essentially the same, most viewers prefer one station over the others. This is because of individual preferences. All women do not wear the same dresses. All men do not wear the same suits. We don't all drive the same cars or live in the same kinds of houses. Why should we all have to learn from the same book or all learn from the same teacher? Many parents have had the experience of having one of their children in the classroom of a particular teacher and the child loved the teacher and learning took place. Later on a younger brother or sister was assigned to the same teacher; this child did not like the teacher and learning did not take place. What is so important about making children use the same text or staying with teachers they do not like and cannot learn from? Are we worried about the problems in paperwork or administration? *If our ultimate goal is learning,* then whatever will facilitate learning should be a part of the system. If a student is not learning and a change in the textbook or a change in the teacher does result in learning, then why not do it! I am not suggesting that we should have popularity polls in our schools to determine which students are assigned to which teacher, but I am saying that if nonlearning is associated with an interpersonal conflict between the teacher and the student, then the student should be changed. This change of the student from one teacher to another should never be regarded as a negative comment on the teacher's ability to teach unless there is a high percentage of students who are neither learning or able to like the teacher. It is entirely possible that you may take one or more students from one teacher and put them in another teacher's classroom and end up taking one or more students from the second teacher's classroom and bringing them back to the first teacher. Since teachers should be hired to facilitate learning, the fact that students may or may not like them isn't as important as whether or not the students are learning. If all the students in a particular class are learning and having success, the fact that some students don't like the teacher isn't a critical factor. In fact, as a student, I can remember about a dozen courses in which I was really aware of my learning. Among the teachers of these courses, there were several teachers which I disliked because of their particular

272

philosophy, personality, and/or teaching style (I didn't know which at the time). Over the years, my dislike for these teachers has mellowed and now I include them among the teachers who had a positive effect on my life through their efforts in helping me to learn. I can hardly remember the teachers in whose classes I learned very little and generally when learning did take place it was in spite of the teacher rather than because of the teacher regardless of whether I liked or disliked them.

Seldom do people identify why they like or dislike someone else except in terms of liking or disliking. Since students are not actually taught how to recognize differences in philosophy and personality in other people and how to cope with these differences, most people assume that everyone else should be like they are and when they discover that other people are different, these differences often result in feelings of distrust or dislike. This is why it is so important to teach humaneness by design if as a society we really want people to learn how to get along with one another.

Since a person's philosophy is the sum of all their attitudes, values, and beliefs, there is potential conflict whenever people meet who have different attitudes, values, and beliefs except in certain cases where like philosophies repel and unlike philosophies attract. For example, a person who is self-oriented or a *taker* will get along very well with people who are other-oriented or *givers* and may have trouble getting along with people who are also self-oriented or *takers*. The same situation holds true but in reverse for a person who is other-oriented or a *giver*. This person would probably get along very well with people who are self-oriented or *takers* and may have trouble getting along with people who are other-oriented or *givers*.

NOTE: The concept of *givers* and *takers* is not a dichotomy in which a person is either one or the other. It involves two continuums (see Figure 44).

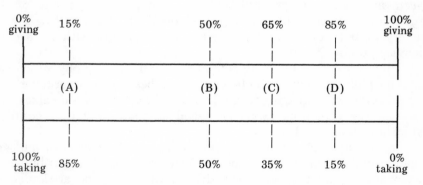

Figure 44 — *Giver* and *Taker* Continuums

A person who is philosophically at D in Figure 44 would be classified as a *giver* and so would a person who is at C in Figure 44, yet the person at D is more of a giver than the person at C. The person at D would probably get along very well with a person at A and not very well with a person at C or D. However, two people at B in Figure 44 might get along fine.

This philosophical concept can be easily observed in marriage. A person who is a 65 percent giver and a 35 percent taker marries someone who is an 85 percent taker and only a 15 percent giver. Sooner or later the one who is other-oriented gets tired of giving so much because during those times when the Giver would like to be a Taker (35 percent of the time), the marriage partner only wanted to give 15 percent of the time. Generally, many of the Giver's friends and relatives will sympathize with the Giver and support the Giver's belief that his or her spouse was taking advantage of the Giver. After the divorce, to the amazement of the Giver's friends and relatives, the Giver started going with other potential spouses who were also takers and who also take advantage of the Giver.

In schools, whereas the students of the early 1900's and before tended to be givers and other-oriented and the teachers tended to be self-oriented, takers, and authoritarian, the students starting schools today tend to be self-oriented and takers as a result of being raised in a permissive environment. Therefore, successful early elementary teachers tend to be givers and other-oriented. One of the common goals in early elementary education is to help children become socially and emotionally mature as measured by the students *playing well with others* (shares or *gives* toys to others). As many of the children become other-oriented in upper elementary grades and in junior and senior high school, there becomes a place and a need for the teacher who is self-oriented, a taker, and authoritarian. Because the development of *givers* and *takers* is primarily without design and a result of the experiences we encounter as we go through life, there will be a wide variety of both types in almost every group or class with the accompanying potential conflicts.

There are many other aspects of a person's philosophy which can portend philosophical conflicts with others besides the giver-taker concept. People with differing religious and political beliefs and values who meet in the classroom as teachers and students may have conflicts which interfere with learning.

Personality and philosophy overlap in a sort of *chicken and egg* relationship in which philosophical differences may be attributed to personality conflicts and personality conflicts may be attributed to philosophical differences. As with philosophy, there are personality differences which can affect learning. For example, students who tend to be *open-minded* (as defined by Rakeach's Dogmatism Scale) may feel confined and uncomfortable in a classroom with a teacher who tends to be *closed-minded* and authoritarian and students who tend to be *closed-minded* may feel lost, a need for structure, and uncomfortable in a classroom with a teacher who tends to be *open-minded.*

A person's style, although generally reflecting a person's personality, is the manner in which a person consistently expresses their personality. Because it is consistent, style in speaking, writing, and behaving becomes habitual and over a period of time, changes in personality may not be reflected in changes in style. As a consequence, a person's style or mannerisms in writing, speaking, and behaving may not reflect the person's personality. Although a person's personality is a very personal concept with wide variations in any one group, social, cultural, peer group, religious, political and occupational pressures bring about certain commonalities in any one group in their attitudes, values, and beliefs and these commonalities can be observed in the philosophies and styles or mannerisms of the individual members of the group. It is important to note that sometimes the attitudes, values, and beliefs result in certain habitual styles or mannerisms and at other times social, cultural, and peer group styles and mannerisms are copied and over a period of time these mannerisms may develop certain attitudes, values, and beliefs. As an example of style, some newscasters in reporting the news consistently use the present tense while most of the others use the past tense. Some authors write in a style that is so unique that their writing can be identified as easily as a fingerprint. Even more common are the various styles of art which may be associated with a particular artist or with a period or *movement.* Art, literature, and music of a particular period frequently represents or are affected by the general philosophy (attitudes, values, and beliefs) of that period. Again, a student who is comfortable learning from a teacher with a particular style or set of mannerisms, may not be so comfortable trying to learn from a teacher with a different style or set of mannerisms and may not learn.

In solving learning problems involving one or more of three variables in the last section concerning the student's intellectual and sensory learning skills and/or involving one or more of the three variables in this section concerning the student's emotional tendencies, the approaches are very similar. If a teacher identifies a student's learning problem as related to the student's intellectual and sensory learning skills, the teacher has two general methods of attack to follow in solving the problem: first, the teacher could prescribe an available alternate pathway or develop a new pathway either of which would be more in accord with the students intellectual and sensory learning skills;

275

and second, the teacher could teach the student the intellectual and sensory learning skills necessary to learn from the pathway within which the student encountered the learning problems. If a teacher identifies a student's learning problem as related to the student's emotional tendencies, then there are also two general methods of attack in solving the problem: first, change the student to another teacher or to a different instructional unit which might be more appropriate for the student's emotional tendencies and second, since affective domain objectives (emotional tendencies) cannot be taught directly, the student could be counseled concerning the basis for the conflict and either through changes in the student's emotional tendencies or in developing an understanding of the problem, the conflict might be resolved such that learning can take place.

Although we generally may want to believe that the ideal teaching situations would be one teacher with one student, if we are going to be realistic, we may find out that there are some students who will learn much better from inanimate objects such as a textbook, an instructional learning package, a teaching machine, or a computer, rather than from the live teacher. If our goal in instruction is that each student learn, then it shouldn't make any difference who or what teaches a student as long as the student learns what he is supposed to learn.

At the present time, there is a lot of controversy in various cities and school districts around the country concerning the right kind of teachers for students. In some cases, parents and/or students are objecting to a particular teacher being in the classroom because of a difference in the teacher's color, racial background, political beliefs, etc. In a teaching-learning situation in which the teachers are performing the first role, that of presenting course content, the objections of a particular teacher may be valid. This would be particularly true if the teacher looks on the teaching-learning situation as a dichotomy or the teacher was presenting information to students in such a random fashion that what the students were actually learning was not only against what the parents would like the students to learn, but against what even the teacher would like the students to learn. If the objections of the parents or students against a particular teacher or teachers concerns the teacher's environmental or language background, it is understandable, because attitudes or dialects (different from the learners) may very well affect the presentation of the content in such a way that students may not learn what they are supposed to be learning. In teaching-learning situations in which no one seems to know exactly and measurably what it is the students are supposed to be learning, common racial or experiential background is probably as good a measurement as any towards guessing the success of the teacher in a teaching-learning situation. On the other hand, in situations where the teacher is performing the second role (solving learning problems — diagnosing and prescribing), who the teacher is does not make that much difference. If the teacher has specified the learning objectives of a particular course and the students achieve them, that is what should be important, not particularly who the teacher is. If, in the diagnosis of a learning problem, the teacher realizes that the problem is caused by the cultural differences between himself or herself and the students, then the teacher should make the appropriate changes or get another teacher to teach the students, that is, if the other teacher really wants to perform the role of a solver of learning problems. If a black teacher can be more successful in teaching white students what they are supposed to learn than some other white teacher, I am sure that their parents would prefer a situation in which their children can learn the most. Similarly, if a white teacher can teach black students better than another black teacher, than I'm sure that their parents would want this also.

i. APPARENT vs. REAL INTELLIGENCE AS AFFECTED BY STUDENTS' EMOTIONAL TENDENCIES

As pointed out previously, a person's apparent intelligence depends on the situation in which it is evaluated. The further the learning environment is away from a learner's ideal learning environment, the greater the disparity between the learner's apparent intelligence and the learner's real intelligence. In view of the last section, in looking at the rate of learning as a measure of intelligence, not only is it necessary to include *amount to be learned* and the three correlation factors concerning the student's intellectual and sensory learning skills, but it is also necessary to include the four correlation factors concerning the students emotional tendencies.

$$\frac{\text{Rate of}}{\text{Learning}} = \frac{\text{Amount to be learned}}{\text{Time for learning}} \times \frac{1}{r_{cog_s}} \times \frac{1}{r_{cog_m}} \times \frac{1}{r_{cog_l}} \times \frac{1}{r_{aff_m}} \times \frac{1}{r_{aff_{ph}}} \times \frac{1}{r_{aff_{per}}} \times \frac{1}{r_{aff_s}}$$

where:

r_{aff_m} = the correlation between the type and level of motivation in the instructional event and type and level of motivation under which the learner learns be

$r_{aff_{ph}}$ = the correlation between the philosophy of the teacher or the designer of the materials in the instructional event and the philosophy under which the learner learns best.

$r_{aff_{per}}$ = the correlation between the personality of the teacher or the designer of the materials in the instructional event and the personality with which the learner learns best.

r_{aff_s} = the correlation between the style of the teacher or the designer

277

(author) of the materials in the instructional event and the style with which the learner learns best.

aff = refers to the emotional tendencies that each learner brings to the instructional event.

As pointed out on page 259, the reason for using the reciprocal form $(1/r_{cog_s})$ is that if the correlation between the way an instructional event is designed and the way a learner learns best is 1.0 (both the same), the reciprocal factor becomes $1/1.0$ or 1 and as such as no affect on the learner's apparent intelligence (rate of learning). However, as the correlation decreases (the learning environment is further away from the learner's ideal learning environment), so will the learner's apparent intelligence (rate of learning). Therefore, by using the reciprocal form, as the correlation decreases, the reciprocal form increases keeping the resulting apparent intelligence closer to the real intelligence.

j. THE ELUSIVE CONCEPT OF *REAL INTELLIGENCE*

In addition to the learning variables identified in the last four sections, J.P. Guilford in his book, *The Structure of Intellect*, claims to have identified almost 100 learning variables. If these are really learning variables which affect individual learners in different ways and to different degrees, then the chances are practically zero of any one learner finding himself or herself in an ideal learning environment where each learning variable is incorporated exactly at maximum learning for the learner. Given that there are that many variables, the obvious fact is that for the average learner very few of the variables in any instructional event would actually be best for that learner. In other words, the correlations for most of the variables would be less than 1.0. Assume for a moment that in a given instructional event, all of the variables had correlations of 90 percent. This would make the reciprocal form $1/.9$ equal to 1.11. Although a 0.9 correlation seems pretty good, by the time only nine variables are considered, the real intelligence is about twice the value for the apparent intelligence. By the time only thirteen variables are considered, the real intelligence is about three times the value for the apparent intelligence. By the time almost a hundred variables are considered, the real intelligence is thirty or more times the value for the apparent intelligence.

In developing standardized intelligence tests, the process emphasizes the use of test items which can be easily scored and that differentiate between the people who might take the test such that the results fit some predetermined curve. If the goal is to differentiate or discriminate, it is relatively easy to do this because of the individual differences already present in almost any group. To give the same test to any number of people and interpret the results as indicative of innate

278

intelligence assumes all people learn equally well from the same materials. To use objective type test items (multiple-choice, true-false, and matching) with the accompanying use of detractors such that the desired curve of results (which supposedly validates the test) can be obtained regardless of what the people know that are taking the test and to claim that the results in any way reflect innate intelligence is probably one of the greatest hoaxes perpetrated on the public in generations. As pointed out in the last paragraph, because of all the learning variables which should be taken into account, a person's real intelligence may be as much as thirty times the value identified as apparent intelligence. Now, on top of this, is the fact that our techniques and instruments for identifying apparent intelligence is so primitive and misleading, that to make any statements with reference to the limits of someone's innate intelligence has about as much chance of being accurate as someone predicting the name of an unknown being on a unknown planet in an unknown galaxy.

Given any so-called intelligence test, a person's score would have to be interpreted as follows:

This score indicates what this person was able to achieve on this test, in the time limits given at this particular time, and under the following limitations:

(1) The use of detractors may make the person miss items the person really knows and to get items right which the person actually doesn't know;

(2) no attempt was made to match the testing environment to the myriad different best learning environments of the people taking the tests;

(3) no attempt was made to eliminate cumulative ignorance which a person might have and which could affect the results of the test;

(4) although the test is standardized and used throughout a region, nationally, or even internationally, there is no matching effort of establishing standardized objectives concerning what has been specifically taught in any region, nationally, or internationally. As a result, any correlation between what is taught and what is tested by the standardized test is almost pure chance; and

(5) teachers are not supposed to teach what is on the standardized tests, so that the scores are more indicative of what was learned out of the classrooms and in spite of the teachers and doesn't indicate what was taught in the classrooms.

k. COMPARISON OF EDUCATION, INSTRUCTION, AND THE MEDICAL FIELD

(1) The *ability to learn* is similar to the *ability of a client to get well*

in that it is part nature and part nurture.
- (a) Education — abilities to learn are considered to be mostly nature and are viewed as limitations of *what* can be learned regardless of what is done.
- (b) Instruction — abilities to learn are considered to be mostly nuture and are viewed only as guidelines as to *how* a learner learns.
- (c) Medical — abilities to get well are considered to be mostly nurture and are viewed only as guidelines as to *how* a patient gets well.

(2) The philosophy of the professional with respect to his or her clients.
- (a) Education — to present the content of units and courses and let the levels of achievement be determined by the *innate* abilities of the learner. Emphasis is on the group or class.
- (b) Instruction — to help all of the learners learn all of the objectives in each unit or course by solving their learning problems. Emphasis is on the individual.
- (c) Medical — to help all patients get completely well from any sickness or accident by solving their health problems. Emphasis is on the individual.

(3) The design and selection of treatments.
- (a) Education — the design of the treatment is to cover unit or course content. The selection of a treatment is determined by what the teacher likes best and is interested in. Any changes in treatment is primarily motivated by the needs and interests of the teacher.
- (b) Instruction — The design of the treatment is to solve a learning problem and the selection of a treatment is either one that will most likely solve the learning problems for a specific learner or one that will solve the learning problems for the most learners. Changes in treatments occur when it is identified that a particular treatment isn't helping to solve the learning problem. The next treatment used is the next treatment in hierarchical order that solves the learning problem for the next highest number of learners.
- (c) Medical — The design of the treatment is to solve a particular health problem and the selection of a treatment is either one that will work for a particular patient or one that works for the most patients having a particular problem. Changes in treatments occur when it is identified that a particular treatment isn't working. The next treatment used is the next treatment in hieraichical order that works for the next largest group of patients with the same problem.

280

(4) Justifying or rationalizing non-success

    (a) Education — When students can't solve a learning problem and don't achieve, it is assumed to be a genetic problem or due to factors beyond the control of the teacher. To make sure that the students know they haven't achieved, the students are failed, put on academic probation, and often dropped from school. In elementary schools, students can fail and still be passed on even though the cumulative ignorance may eventually cause the student to be dropped (by that time, non-success can probably be blamed on genetics). The failures are recorded and are continually referred to by teachers and potential employers with the subsequent problems of the *self-fulfilling prophecy* and more failures.

    (b) Instruction — When an instructioneer is unable to help a student solve a learning problem, it is assumed that either with available materials, techniques, etc., the instructioneer was unable to solve the learning problem, or the student didn't want to learn and the instructioneer was unable to motivate the learner to want to learn. In either case, the student is given an incomplete (I) grade and anytime new materials or techniques are developed which can solve the learning problem or the student wants to learn (in the case of a motivation problem), the learner can complete the unit or course. The I's may stay on the school record, but they are not put on the transcript for future teachers and employers.

    (c) Medical — When a doctor is unable to help a patient get well, it is assumed that either with available drugs, surgery, etc. the doctor was unable to help the patient get well, or the patient doesn't want to get well and the doctor was unable to motivate the patient to want to get well. In either situation, the case is left open and if new drugs, techniques, etc. are identified that will work, they will be used and in the case of the motivation problem, anytime the patient decides he or she wants to get well, the doctor will try to help the patient.

4. HUMANIZING INSTRUCTION BY IDENTIFYING AND SOLVING LEARNING PROBLEMS

In meeting with tens of thousands of educators throughout the United States and Canada, it is common to have some teachers claim that they are already doing the things I have suggested and that further changes are not necessary. I would agree with any teacher if all of the students in that teacher's classes were doing "A" work and were getting 100 percent on all of the teacher's tests and if the "A" achievement can be defended in terms of a list of specific objectives which each student had to achieve in order to receive an "A". However, this is rarely the case. There are millions of students throughout the country who receive failing grades in one or more of their courses at every marking period and tens of millions of students throughout the country that are getting "B's", "C's", and "D's", or number grades which are below 100 percent and above failing. These letter or number grades indicate that there are students who are encountering learning problems and in not solving them, the teachers are letting the situation imply that some students are inferior to others.

Although students may grow in size and physical strength, their self-image, curiosity, and compulsion to learn are very sensitive to demotivating forces such as unsolved learning problems. As students progress through school these unsolved learning problems accumulate and cause more learning problems to develop which in turn tend to destroy the students' self-image, curiosity, and desire to learn. These latter concepts are in the affective domain and as such are non-measurable directly. However, the results of this cancerous affect on the student's emotional tendencies are measurable directly. Students start cheating. They try to stay away from classes, skip school, and may eventually become drop-outs or push-outs. In forcing the students to attend school and endure more mental cruelty — the accumulation of more unsolved learning problems — the students may resort to vandalism and petty crimes in order to strike back against the schools, teachers, and society which they see as the causes for their problems. If they are unsuccessful in their attempts at vandalism and petty crimes by getting caught and punished and continue to be unsuccessful in solving their learning problems or in getting help from teachers in solving their learning problems, they may just mentally give up and float through life accepting whatever handouts society may give in the form of unemployment and welfare, they may seek escape in drugs, or they may just sink to the bottom. If the students are successful in their attempts at vandalism and petty crimes and continue to be unsuccessful in solving their learning problems, the future pathway becomes almost predetermined. After all, success breeds success regardless of the pathway upon which success is found.

Admittedly, I am pointing out the extreme negative results if one considers the millions of students in our schools; but since the results of our present educational approach tend to fit a normal bell-shaped curve, this means that there are relatively only a few students at the extreme positive end and all the other millions of students are enduring varying degrees of the negative results just described. Given that this situation exists, any educator that doesn't want changes to occur certainly is not a humanist and the best way to bring about these changes is to change your role from that as an educator to the role as an instructioneer: from that as a presenter of course content and a teacher of subject matter to that of a solver of human learning problems and a teacher of students.

Just in case, as a reader, you are more affected by the economics of the problem, than you are by the humanitarian aspects of the problem and you may resist the changes in the role of the teacher because you think it will cost more, let me assure you that it is costing us more not to change. For example, when students have to repeat entire courses rather than just learn whatever objectives they didn't achieve, they take up space in classrooms and double the costs for each course repeated. Whenever students stay away from school because they don't like it or they become drop-outs (push-outs), this costs the school money because of reduced ADA (average daily attendance). When students are passed on with sufficient cumulative ignorance that they eventually end up needing remedial classes, these classes generally cost even more than the regular classes. The irony of the situation is that the students in elementary schools who are labeled by their teachers as being unable to learn, get into remedial classes in junior high school and have success. Students in high schools who are labeled by their teachers as being unable to learn, get into remedial classes in a community college and have success. The students who need remedial help and don't get it and those who get into remedial classes but don't have success end up out in society with a high probability of needing unemployment and welfare funds at some time in their lives.

NOTE: Remember, the word *remedial* refers to the remediating of an ineffective teaching-learning situation, not the remediation of the student.

In addition to the extra school related costs, there are other costs such as the cost of repairs as a result of vandalism, the costs of guards, fencing, and other protective devices or safeguards. At the extreme negative end, where these ex-students end up in any one of a variety of rehabilitation institutions, the costs really sky-rocket. Although the costs vary from state to state, to keep an ex-student in the Maryland Training School for Boys for one year (1972) cost the taxpayers $18,235 which is enough to send the student to Harvard for three years and throw in a summer trip to Europe.

NOTE: In several performance contract projects around the country that were concerned with students who normally would have failed in school with all the resulting costs to society as just described, it was found that these students could be motivated to learn through the use of extrinsic motivation, i.e., toys, games, movie tickets, money, etc. However, certain groups of *humanitarian* teachers decided that it would be better to let the students fail than to use external motivators particularly when it became known that the teachers who were responsible for the students' successes were also rewarded with money (merit pay).

It would seem to me that the traditional teachers resistance to changing their role is not only very costly for the student, but also to the taxpayer and even for the teacher. For several decades now, traditional educators have been claiming that there is nothing wrong with the schools that more money can't fix. But after several cycles of tax increases, bond issues, and special state and federal programs, the problems are still there. More money has not made the difference! A major reason for not being able to see a difference is that the problems in schools have been viewed as teaching problems rather than learning problems and these two points-of-view are very different. By identifying specific measurable learning problems and putting money into solving these problems, you can't help but see a difference. Typical of the traditional approach to problems, when the unemployment rate among minority teenagers (black, Puerto Rican, Mexican American, Indian, etc.) rose to almost 40 percent, efforts were made to give them jobs, money, training, etc. while at the same time the schools that contributed to their unemployable condition continued to *push out* and graduate thousands more that are unemployable. Treating the symptom instead of the cause does not cure the cause. The rationale behind this type of approach is not only typical of the traditional educator, but it would be typical of a majority of our society who because of their faith in the schools and in I.Q. tests (written in classroom English) believe that the minority children couldn't learn anyway even if something was done for their schools. Although most people believe that the prejudice and bigotry here in the United States has to do with the color of someone's skin. Notice that people with black and brown skin from other parts of the world are not put into the same class as the black, brown, and red skin people who are from our own country! Given that the traditional approach to education has been practiced in almost every school, almost everyone has observed black, brown, and red skinned students who are failing in school which of course reinforces their belief that there is a correlation between the color of a person's skin and intellectual abilities (limits). Prejudice and bigotry are not caused by the color of someone's skin — that also is just a symptom. The real cause for prejudice concerns mental abilities. When a segregationist says, *"Would you want your daughter to marry one?"*, the surface problem is that there may be children of mixed color. But why should that be a problem? There have been children of mixed color since the first white man saw a woman of a different race. The real problem is that the segregationist believes that the children of a mixed marriage of white and another race may not be as smart as the children from white parents. Although Shockley at Stanford and Jensen at Berkeley may be among the few who are honest enough to voice their beliefs (even if misguided), they have tens of millions of fellow travelers. Given that most of the students with other than white racial backgrounds start the white-oriented schools six months to two years behind in achievement from their average white classmates and in accord with the traditional educational philosophy these learning problems are never solved, the load of cumulative ignorance for these non-white students increases and their self-image decreases as they are socially promoted year after year until some of them drop-out, some are suspended from school, some graduate only with attendance certificates, and some manage to graduate in spite of the system. Once the majority of teachers become instructioneers who will solve the learning problems of all students, we will discover that the achievement levels of the non-white students is only limited by the ability of the instructioneers to solve their learning problems. The sad part is that although the non-white students' intellectual and sensory learning problems can be solved rather quickly, the effect of years, decades, and generations during which the self-image and pride of the non-white population has been destroyed or at least badly damaged, may not be resolved so quickly. It may help to be proud of being black, brown, or red, i.e., *Black is beautiful;* but the real key is when the instructioneers say *A or 100 percent is beautiful and you can all make it (regardless of color)"!*

5. *TRANSITION FROM EDUCATOR TO INSTRUCTIONEER*

a. THE HUMANIZATION FACTOR

Because of the individual differences among teachers, some teachers are closer in their teaching behaviors to the role of the instructioneer than other teachers. In order to help you as a reader (if you are a teacher)[33] to know where you should make some changes and how you compare to other teachers look back to page 128-9 where you filled in on the page or on a separate piece of paper the number of hours you spend during the average week doing the following:

---

[33] If you are not already a teacher, role play a composite of the teachers you have had. Be sure you have filled in some numbers in answer to the four questions on page 128-9 before you continue reading. These numbers should reflect your view of the composite teacher. Without these numbers, the concept of the Humanization Factor may not be very clear.

a — presenting course content or information to the total class;

b — working with small groups and individuals; and

c — preparing to teach; and

d — in non-measurable learning activities.

Substitute the numbers in the following equation:

$$\frac{\text{Humanization}}{\text{Factor}} = \frac{b}{a + c + d} =$$

If the resultant fraction is less than one, you have a lot of changes to make and the smaller the fraction the greater the number of changes you will have to make if you want to humanize instruction in your classes.

If the resultant fraction is close to one, you are at about the halfway mark in the transition between the educator and the instructioneer. You are on the right track, but you still have changes to make.

If the resultant fraction is much greater than one you are already performing most of the behaviors of the instructioneer and with just a few slight changes you'll be there. The larger the value of the fraction the fewer the changes that need to be made.

In view of the results of identifying the Humanization Factor for your classes, you may want to make some changes. A very common comment I hear from teachers is that they would be glad to change, but they don't have any extra time. In answer to this problem, I will give you four suggestions which won't cost you a minute more than you are already putting in teaching.

b. CHANGING THE NUMBER OF HOURS SPENT
   PRESENTING COURSE CONTENT

This is probably the easiest place to get extra time. Most of the hours that are spent in presenting course content represent potential release time in order to individualize instruction. I didn't say all of the hours, I said *most* of the hours, because there are some things which are best presented on a face to face basis. Since research has shown that in a majority of the studies there were no significant differences between whether the teacher presented the course content live or it was presented via some form of media, the quickest resource is to let the students get the content from a book or books. Whatever is not available in book form, try recording it on an audio tape recorder and if you need still visuals, use slides, filmstrips, or photographs. If you need motion visuals, use films or television.

I know very well that the technologists claim it takes many hours of preparation, recording, and editing to make one hour of audio or video tape. This is true if the objective is to make a technically almost perfect or perfect presentation. But then, if the research claims no significant difference between the one hour recorded presentation which took 40 hours to prepare and the one hour presentation by the live teacher which has been presented possibly many times before and may or may not need any additional preparation time, then record your regular presentations as they are being presented to a class.[34] Once you start using these recordings which were prepared *on the run*, you will have release time to solve your students learning problems. Then, in the solving of the students learning problems you will identify where any changes in the recordings should be made and you will also know what to change. The important difference is that the changes will be made for *the sake of improving learning* not for the sake of having a technically perfect recording. After all of your students' learning problems are solved and they are learning all of your unit or course objectives, then take time to dress up the recordings. Be careful, however, that in dressing up the audio or video (or other media), that these "changes" don't interfere with learning!

The worst problem with the presenting function is that it is always predetermined by time and the objective becomes to fill up a prescribed length of time. For example, consider a three (3) credit college course and a five (5) credit college course. What is the difference between the two courses besides the obvious two (2) credits? As I'm sure you know, the main difference is the two extra hours spent sitting in class in front of the teacher. Have you ever had a three (3) credit course which if measured by the work involved, should have been a ten (10) credit course? Have you ever had a five (5) credit course which, if measured by the work involved, should only have been a one (1) or two (2) credit course? Course credits in higher education have very little relationship to how much the students learn or how much work the students have to do. Course credits are determined by the number of presentations a teacher thinks have to be made to *cover* the course.[35] Therefore, a college degree based on so many credits doesn't represent any specific amount of learning. What it does represent is a specific number of hours

---

[34] If you audio tape record your usual presentations, have a student keep track of everything you write or draw on the blackboard on a separate sheet of paper. This is necessary because few teachers can remember all of the things they put on the blackboard to clarify or emphasize certain points. Then after the class is over, look at the student's notes. Those things that are important, prepare well and make up sort of a panel booklet to go along with the recording. Don't worry about recording all of the students questions and your answers which occur during the class. Students who will be listening to the recording at a later time may have the same questions.

---

[35] Notice, this is how most teachers' *teaching load* is determined — by how many presentations they make and regardless of how many students are involved or how much learning is supposed to take place.

spent in classrooms and that is really about all! An experience that every new teacher has or even an experienced teacher who is going to teach a new course has, is that odd feeling in the pit of the stomach (sometimes almost nausea) the day or two before starting the new class as the teacher is thinking, *What the hell am I going to do in this class for 180 days?* (Elementary and secondary) or *What the hell am I going to do in this class for 54 lecture hours?* (3 credit college course on a semester or 18 week basis). I can remember back when I was sitting in a high school faculty lunchroom and an English teacher came in all excited about a great film on Hamlet she had used that morning. A bookkeeping teacher asked her if he could use the film that afternoon as he didn't have anything prepared for one of his classes. Before that film left the school, it had been shown in six different courses and several students told me they had seen the film three times!!!! After teaching the same course three, four, or more times, the problem has been reversed. Now, the typical teacher finds that there isn't enough time in the course to cover everything he or she wants to include. In education, we teachers become very good at padding courses to fit the allotted time. But we are not very good at deleting some of the chaff. One of the values of specifying what it is that you want your students to learn is that it helps you to identify and separate the *kernels of wisdom* from the *chaff of triviality.*

The major advantage in recording your presentation is that students will be able to study them as they would a textbook. Although it might be nice to believe that the best learning occurs when the live teacher is talking to live students, this assumes that all students learn at the rate the teacher presents and that students only need to hear the presentation once to learn what's important. Obviously students don't all learn at the teacher's rate of presenting and some students need to hear a presentation two, three, or more times. Since few teachers are equipped with *rewind* buttons or are able to split themselves up into 30 pieces such that each student can take part of the teacher to the study hall or home with them to hear the presentations again and again, a recording of the teacher's presentation and a playback device can be very useful and can result in increased learning. It is tempting to say that the students should take notes, but if the students don't know specifically what it is they are supposed to learn, i.e., given a list of specific objectives at the beginning of the course, unit, or presentation, they won't know when to write and when not to write. A very common event is when teachers will say to students, *Don't write so much, I would rather that you listen.* Then when the next test is given and the students are tested on what they heard, the students all wish they had written down notes on the presentation rather than just listening to the presentation.

NOTE: A very useful concept to use with recorded or live presentations and even reading assignments is what I call an *Active Involvement Form* or a structured note-taking form. I use such a form in all of my presentations whether it's only a one hour presentation, a full day, a full week, or a total course. The *Active Involvement Form* for this series is available separately. There are three advantages and one *disadvantage* in using the Active Involvement Forms.

(1) The design of the form is such that it communicates to the listener or reader when they should write notes and when to just listen or to just read.

(2) If as a listener the student is distracted from the task of listening by something external (someone talking to the student) or something internal (thoughts about something else which at the elementary and secondary level is called *daydreaming* but among adults it is called *meditation*), the student can very easily find his or her place again and it is easy to identify what was missed so that he or she can ask someone else, the teacher, or play the recording again to pick up what was missed.

(3) If students are listening to a recorded presentation, particularly audio only, The Active Involvement Form will help the student concentrate on the presentation. People brought up with multi-sensory media like films and television find it a little more difficult to concentrate with a single-sense media.

(4) The main *disadvantage* is that although it is possible even after specifying the objectives for a unit or course to include a lot of *padding*, when the Active Involvement Form is used in addition to the specific objectives, it is very difficult to get by with a lot of padding which doesn't relate to the objectives to be learned nor is it mentioned in the structured notes. From a students point-of-view, this point is actually an advantage because it facilitates zeroing in on what is important. However, from the teacher's point-of-view, this may mean having to drop the teacher's favorite padding which might fit very well into a supplemental Scholarship type seminar but is irrelevant to a particular unit or course.

The two biggest problems with a teacher presenting the course content is that first, it locksteps the learning process such that students who could learn faster have to wait and could get bored and lose interest and students who can't keep up, fall by the wayside academically and also get bored, lost, and will lose interest. The second problem is that the teacher is so busy presenting course content that the teacher doesn't have time to help individual students solve their learning problems. As a teacher allows the students to get more and more of the course presentations from books and recordings, these two problems diminish except under one condition. If the teacher decides that certain presentations have to be given live and these presentations are spaced at intervals through the unit or course, then the teacher is still lockstepping the learning process even though the teacher has more time to solve learning problems because he or she doesn't have to give many of the presentations live anymore. To avoid this problem, try to condense all of the live presentations to the very beginning of a unit or course which will then allow the students to proceed at their own pace until they complete the unit or course. A slight compromise would be to repeat your critical live presentations at the appropriate place in the course to small groups of students as they achieve the prerequisite information so at least learning would be small group paced rather than class paced or teacher paced.

c. CHANGING THE NUMBER OF HOURS SPENT PREPARING TO TEACH

Most of the hours spent by teachers in preparing to teach is wasted time. If a teacher has ever taught the course or anyone else has ever taught the course before, why reinvent the *curriculum wheel*. It is the rare course that has never been taught previously by anyone anywhere. For example, there are almost 100,000 teachers teaching each of the grades from kindergarten to sixth grade, almost 50,000 teachers teaching each of the subjects usually offered in junior and senior high school, and about 10,000 teachers teaching many of the subjects offered in colleges and universities. When I hear of teachers requesting more release time in order to prepare to teach, I always wonder, *What are they reinventing?* Most of these very same teachers that want more time to reinvent *curriculum wheels* probably graded their students on a curve the last time they taught the course. Since, the variation in grades indicates a lot of students encountered learning problems when they took the course, I could understand the need for extra time if it was spent solving learning problems such that more students would have more success. But that isn't the situation in the vast majority of cases. The preparation time is either spent in reinventing *curriculum wheels* or it is spent in some other non-teaching function.

Why does it seem necessary for teachers to reinvent what most teachers have already taught before? Consider the following:

(1) When a new teacher starts teaching or even when an experienced teacher starts teaching a new course, rarely are they given a list of specific objectives of what the students should learn in the course or even a detailed list of what they should be presenting. If the teacher is given anything, it might be a list of general topics to be covered during the

course and/or a textbook. As a result, the new teacher feels that it is necessary to reinvent curriculum wheels as if no one had ever taught the course before and the tendency is to teach to the book (at least the first few times through a course).

(2) Because few teachers have really specified what it is they want students to learn and they tend to teach to the book, whenever the textbook is changed, the presentations have to be essentially reinvented to fit the new book.

(3) Traditionally, teachers are partially evaluated on their ability to present course content and rarely on whether or not students are learning anything of what is being presented.

(4) If teachers did present the course content the same way as other teachers or even the same way several times in a row, there is a possibility that they could be videotaped and replaced (out of a job).

(5) If the teacher's role is to present course content and one teacher copies another, this indicates very little input by the one that copies and is not very creative or mentally stimulating.

(6) To present course content the same way for several classes during the same quarter or semester and then repeat it again and again for several years, almost any teacher would have to become bored and want to make a change.

As a result of these pressures, teachers individually and in small and large groups try to reinvent *curriculum wheels.* In hundreds of schools and school districts throughout the United States, there are curriculum committees meeting to change the curriculum. These committees typically develop much more *heat* than *light* because of personality conflicts among faculty. When the reports are finally finished and turned in for administrative approval, they typically end up laying on some administrator's desk or shelf and are not usually implemented. National groups come up with the New Math, the New Chemistry, the New Biology, the New Linguistics, etc. Rarely are the new curriculums defended in terms of learners learning more (primarily because neither the old or the new are often developed with specific learning objectives of what learners should be learning). As of the writing of this book, there are rumors in several of the major subject matter areas of movements to develop the New New — — (whatever)!

One noticeable change however, whereas the motivation for the curriculum study groups prior to the last decade has been based on one or more of the six pressures mentioned previously plus some obvious changes in the field of study; during the past decade as more and more student activists claimed that the curriculum was irrelevant, there were

291

more and more curriculum study groups that meet primarily to change the curriculum in order to make it more relevant. Given the point-of-view that *teaching* is equated to *presenting course content*, if one changes what is presented and makes the presentations more relevant, then it is assumed that what is learned is more relevant. First of all, it cannot be assumed that what teachers present is automatically learned by the students. The very fact that students end up with "C's", "D's", and "F's" indicates that they didn't learn all of what the teacher presented. Second, if the learning objectives and test items didn't reflect the desired relevancy, then it is very doubtful that the students viewed the changed curriculum as being any more relevant. Since relatively few teachers had any specific objectives before or after the curriculum change, the only way to know what students are learning is to look at the tests they take. Most students when using the word *relevancy* are not just thinking of contemporary topics, they are concerned with, *How can I use or apply what I'm supposed to learn?* If the tests are not testing application and utility then even contemporary topics can be irrelevant. Since relatively few teachers are taught how to make up test items that test for application, then changing the topics of the presentations without changing objectives and the form of the test items may not really make the presentations more relevant. Based on my experience in working with teachers and students, *relevancy* can be more easily obtained by just changing the format of the test items and objectives to reflect potential application and utility then by changing the topics to be presented and continue to use the same test item format. Even more critical than the problem of *relevancy*, it should be recognized that when students complain that the curriculum is irrelevant that this is a symptom of learning problems. If the learning problems of the students are not identified and solved, changing the topics to be presented, the objectives to be learned, and/or even the format of the test items may still not affect the learning problems which were the cause of the symptom, irrelevancy!

Consider for a moment the tasks of other professional people, i.e., doctors, lawyers, dentists, engineers, etc. and especially consider the tasks of the professional who is a specialist. These specialists may work with 20 different types of problems during their entire professional life! Some professionals are so specialized that they may only work with less than 10 types of problems during their entire professional life! Why don't they get bored and try to invent new types of problems? Can you imagine the doctor who closes up his office early because he or she needs time to invent new types of diseases (at a time in which the doctor is probably already overloaded trying to solve his patients' problems with the types of diseases he or she already knows about — let alone invent some new ones)! Can you imagine a group of professional lawyers getting together and inventing new types of cases even if there aren't any clients with those types of problems!

The real professional whose prime responsibility is public service, works with people and their problems not with his or her own problems. Even though the real professional may only work with five (5) different types of problems for twenty or thirty years, what makes it different, interesting, and challenging is that each problem is associated with a separate unique human being. Whenever you find a real professional who has forgotten that he or she is working with people who are each different from one another, even though the type of problem may be the same, you will also find a professional who is bored with his or her work, is becoming sloppy and careless in his or her work, and is probably thinking about another field of work.

This problem of needing time to reinvent *curriculum wheels* actually is tied in with the difference between *education* and *instruction.* As mentioned in Chapter one, the emphases in education are on the teacher, what the teacher is supposed to teach, how the teacher has taught, teaching spaces, solving of teaching problems, etc. The emphases in instruction are on the learner, what the learner is supposed to learn, whether or not the learner has learned, learning spaces, solving of learning problems, etc. What makes educational research and education a *non-science* is that the concern is the researching and study of media, methods, etc. all devised by man. What makes instructional research and instruction a *science* is that the concern is the researching and study of whatever is necessary to facilitate the learning of specific objectives by learners where the concern is learning which is a natural phenomenon.

In instruction, the curriculum may be the same year after year, but since the emphasis is on solving the learning problems of each individual unique learner, the role of the instructioneer is interesting, different, challenging, and humanizing. Ignoring the problems of the learners and solving the problems of the teacher is dehumanizing.

For decades there has been a controversy between the large university and its large classes which is viewed as depersonalized and inhumane and the small college and its smaller classes which is viewed as personalized and humane. As long as the emphasis in both schools is on the teacher's role as a presenter of content, the claim of depersonalization vs. personalization *may be* partially correct; but they both give "C's", "D's", and "F's" and as such are about equally inhumane. If a teacher in a large college or university has a large class (hundreds of students) assigned to him or her and through the teacher's design of the course the learning problems of each student are solved to the extent that 90 percent or more of the students are learning 100 percent of the specific objectives of the course, then this teacher is much more humane and personalized than the teacher in the small college or university who only has about 20 students in a class but teaches and tests in such a manner that the majority of the students achieve 75 percent or less of the course objectives (curve grading).

We will continue to have teachers at all levels of education who need to reinvent *curriculum wheels* and who ignore individual learning differences and student learning problems as long as:

— teacher training institutions keep emphasizing the role of the teacher as a presenter of course content;

— there is little, if any, difference between the teaching behaviors of a teacher who has had professional *education* courses and a teacher who hasn't had any of these courses;

— colleges and universities ignore *instruction* as a profession and hire faculty because of their academic degrees and assume that the knowledge of subject matter content is equivalent to the knowledge of how to identify and solve learning problems;

— teachers at all levels are evaluated on the basis of their ability to present course content and other irrelevant criteria, regardless of whether or not the teachers' students are learning;

— grading students' achievement on a predetermined curve is the *god* of evaluation upon whose altar millions of students are sacrificed;

— it is fashionable to be an educational hypocrite who proclaims and extols the virtues of the individual and then ignores individual differences in the classroom; and

— there are educational bigots who as pseudo-humanists teach potentially humanizing courses, demand professional privileges, but refuse to accept professional responsibility and let their students do *their own thing* instead of helping all of them learn by design to be humane, and then bemoan a society which reacts in inhumane ways.

In order to have most of the time that is presently being spent reinventing *curriculum wheels* as potential release time to identify and solve individual learning problems, all teachers have to do is cooperate with one another. Sure it is a lot of work to specify all of the objectives of a course and then to identify and solve all of the students' learning problems, but if two teachers work together, it is only half as much work. If three teachers work together, it is only a third as much work. If ten teachers cooperate, it is only a tenth as much work. If a hundred teachers share the work, it is only a hundredth as much work. If a thousand teachers cooperate, it is only a thousandth as much work and if all the teachers in a given subject matter area cooperate, the amount of work involved in identifying the specific objectives will be negligible.

A cliche in education for decades has been the question asked of a teacher by another teacher.

First teacher: *What do you teach?*
Second teacher: *I teach — (some subject or grade level). What do you teach?*
First teacher: *I teach students!!!!*

d. CHANGING THE NUMBER OF HOURS SPENT IN ACTIVITIES NOT ASSOCIATED WITH MEASURABLE LEARNING

There are many activities which are carried on in school under the label of education which may or may not contribute to increased achievement. Sometimes teachers include these activities because they think the students like to do them, i.e., *rap sessions* in which the classroom is used as a forum for scholarship type functions (one or more students presenting to the rest of the class) or for just open discussions ala Glasser *(Schools Without Failure).* Sometimes teachers include these activities because they think that students should be exposed to an experience just for the sake of the experience even though there are no measurable objectives involved and if any tests are involved, they are primarily used to motivate the students to pay attention, i.e., some literature of varying forms which are often favorites of the teacher; some laboratory experiences, some arts and crafts, music, or physical education experiences, etc. Sometimes teachers include these activities because they are traditional or they feel the activities are part of their role, i.e., finger painting and story telling in early elementary grades, preparation of abstracts in graduate education, etc. Sometimes these activities are included to fill time (particularly for the new teacher or in new courses).

I am not trying to say there these activities are not valuable or that they should be eliminated completely. What I am suggesting is that if these activities are not associated with specific measurable objectives and/or measurable evaluation instruments, then the teachers don't know whether or not any learning is taking place nor if there is learning, how much in quantity and to what degree of quality. On the other hand, in most of these same teachers' classrooms, students are receiving "B's", "C's", "D's", and "F's" because they were not able to learn some things that are measurable. If any teacher is grading a student down for not learning something, then it had better be measurable. Because, any teacher that grades a student down for not learning something that even the teacher doesn't know what it is the student didn't learn, is in for a potential malpractice suit. When teachers grade students down, they are measuring something and whatever that something is, it must be important. The guideline to remember is:

Anything that is important enough to grade a student down for not learning must be important enough to teach. If it is not important enough to make sure that all students learn it, then it must not be important enough to grade a student down for not learning it!

It is really a matter of priority. Since grades and measurable learning have direct affects on the learners and we don't know whether or not the non-measurable learning (?) will affect them or not, our first obligation as a professional teacher is to teach *every student* 100 percent of the measurable things in our courses which are important enough that the students would be graded down if they didn't learn them. After all of the students have learned 100 percent of these things that are measurable, if there is time left over, then spend as much of it as desired on the nonmeasurable topics. Under this approach and because learners learn at different rates, some students might be exposed to a lot of the unmeasurable stuff and some students may not be exposed to very much if at all.

Consider the traditional teacher who as a pseudo-humanist at the end of the course feels very good because the students had some *good* discussions on race relations and other contemporary topics (not measurable objectives of the course and not tested). At the same time, however, the teacher assigned grades which were based on test results covering the content of the course and the majority of the students received "C's", "D's", and "F's" which affected the students self-image, their grade point average, pushed several students closer to the *drop out* point, and the students went on to the next courses with sufficient cumulative ignorance to affect their chances for success. When the teacher was asked why he or she didn't work with the students who didn't achieve whatever it was they were graded down for not learning and help them learn it, the teacher replied, *The class just didn't have time!* (after all, this teacher and following teachers can always blame the non-achievement on outside factors beyond their control, i.e., genetics, skin color, divorced parents, lack of breakfasts, etc.)

In the early elementary grades there are usually a large number of activities scheduled because in most professional elementary education textbooks and courses, the students are taught that children have a relatively short attention span, and depending upon the author of the textbook or the teacher in the elementary education course, this attention span may vary from 15 to 30 minutes. Yet in almost every home with children, on Saturday morning, the parents are very much aware that the attention span of children can last for hours in front of the television set. Even with children of three and four years old, it is not that uncommon to observe them playing with a toy, a box, etc., for two or more hours. As long as an event is interesting and presents a challenge, most children can maintain much longer spans of attention than we think. So what we should be saying in professional education courses is *not* that the children's attention span is 20 minutes and stop; we should be saying that the children's attention span for the learning experiences we are involving them in is about 20 minutes, which doesn't say that if we had more appropriate and challenging experiences, the students' attention span wouldn't be longer. When children first start school, they aren't quite so willing to be quiet and to sit still when they are bored because they already know what is being taught or they are lost because they are so far behind they can't understand what is being taught. As children get older, they become more accustomed to the traditional educational setting and can accept the boredom or being lost without upsetting the class. Students in traditional schools who have learned to accept the fact that their individual differences will be ignored are labeled *emotionally mature.* Students in traditional schools who cannot accept a classroom situation that ignores their individual needs and differences are labeled *emotionally immature.* If in their not accepting the situation they become hyper-active, then it is possible to put them on tranquilizers until they become more accustomed to the situation or maybe they become candidates for a drug abuse program!

During the elementary levels of instruction, it is very critical that all of the learners achieve the basic foundation which is necessary for success in subsequent instruction. This is in reference to their ability to read, write, use simple mathematical concepts, etc. But since in most elementary school situations teachers have not specified what it is the students are supposed to be learning, teachers end up essentially performing the social function of *babysitting* instead of teaching the children something they are supposed to learn. In observing teachers' behaviors in elementary classrooms, it is readily apparent that many teachers are so busy trying to keep the children involved in activities that they really don't have time to worry about whether or not the children are learning. If it is a necessary part of our society that children be away from their homes four, five, or six hours a day in some kind of organized activity, then school districts might just as well admit that this function is a necessary part of our social system and hire people who can be professional *babysitters.* I don't believe that these professional *babysitters* need to have four, five, or more years of college education to perform adequately. In looking at the teaching-learning situation, if our goals are to make it effective and efficient, then teachers who are supposed to be helping the learners learn should be involved in learning activities, and para-professionals who are hired to be *babysitters* should be involved in that kind of activity. It is a waste of a trained teacher's time and training to have them involved in activities, which, regardless of what you call them, are no different than

297

public babysitting.

As an example, in a so-called modern elementary school which I visited recently, the half-day kindergarten schedule alloted 45 minutes to measurable learning and two hours and fifteen minutes to activities in which there were no measurable learning objectives. At the end of the school year five children had to be held back to repeat kindergarten because they didn't learn enough to go on to first grade. During the year over 400 hours were spent in non-measurable learning activities while only about 135 hours were spent in measurable learning activities. By just taking away some of the time from the non-measurable activities, not all or even most of the time, those five students could have made it and gone on with their friends.

e. CHANGING THE NUMBER OF HOURS SPENT WITH SMALL GROUPS AND INDIVIDUALS

Obviously, if the hours which were previously spent presenting course content to the total class, the hours which were previously spent reinventing *curriculum wheels* and the hours which were spent in activities without measurable results in learning were changed over and spent working with small groups and individuals, there would be significant changes in the humanization factor. In order for the teacher to assume this new role as an Instructioneer and perform effectively and efficiently in the role, it is necessary that the other four elements in the instructional event are also operating effectively and efficiently.

(1) Objectives to be learned. — In order for the teacher to perform the role of an instructioneer and identify and solve learning problems, it is critical to know specifically what it is the learners should be learning. The more specific the objective, the easier it is to identify and solve a learning problem. The more ambiguous and vague the objective, the more difficult it is to identify and solve a learning problem.

(2) Evaluation of achievement. — In order to develop tests which can be used to diagnose learning problems, it is critical to know specifically and measurably what it is the learners should be learning. It is also necessary that the correlation between the objectives and the test items be 1.0 or as close as possible. Otherwise, if the test items do not match the specific objectives and they are used as a diagnostic instrument, it would be very difficult to identify which objective or part of an objective is being identified as a learning problem.

(3) The learning environment. — Unless a teacher knows what is to be learned, how it is going to be evaluated, and who are the students, it is very difficult to design a learning environ-

ment which will facilitate learning. Because of the myraid of individual differences, the key concept to keep in mind is flexibility to the extent that in any grouping of students, any grouping of media and materials, etc. can be accommodated to fit the needs of each learner.

(4) The learners — In order to perform the role as an instructioneer effectively and efficiently, the learners have to know specifically what it is they are supposed to learn and they have to be in a learning environment which will facilitate the learning of the specific objectives. However, the most critical factor is whether or not the learner knows how to study independently and to learn independently. If the students don't know how to study independently, the teacher will have to spend a great deal more time with each student or groups of students than would otherwise be necessary.

f. DEVELOPING THE INDEPENDENT LEARNER

There are actually two problems involved with the developing of the independent learner and they are in opposition to one another. The first problem is the reluctance of many teachers to cut the *umbilical cord* of learning and let the students go. There is little value in developing independent learners if their teachers won't let them learn independently. One of the most common questions I get from teachers during my seminars, institutes, and workshops with reference to individualizing instruction is, *If the students are at different places in a unit or course and I'm working with one student or small group of students, what will the others be doing?* This question is based on the assumption and belief that students can't study and learn on their own and that the teacher has to lead each student through the unit or course. Given the situation that exists in most classrooms in which the objectives to be learned have not been spelled out specifically enough such that they could act as the students' instructional map through a unit or course, most eachers have probably observed students trying to study and learn on their own and not be very successful at it. It is very difficult for a student to study on his or her own if they haven't been given the objectives they are supposed to learn. This is the major reason why innovations which involve independent study time without specific objectives are not very successful, i.e., modular scheduling. If a teacher does have specific learning objectives for whatever it is that the students are supposed to learn, students can study successfully on their own and enjoy doing it provided that they know how to do it and have had success studying on their own.

It constantly amazes me to hear of teachers willing to go on strike to reduce the size of their classes by three or four students when almost every class over twenty students could be reduced by five or more students just be letting them study on their own. For some reason when teachers first start trying the instructioneer role, if the students are successful in studying on their own, many teachers feel a little less of a teacher. But once the teachers start getting involved in identifying and solving students' learning problems, it becomes very apparent that the instructioneer role is a much more important and challenging role than that of just presenting the course content.

A model that I frequently refer to as an illustration of handling multi-level or multi-course classes is the one-room school where there were six or eight grades all in the same room. Teachers in one-room schools never present course content to the whole class (eight grades) at the same time. Their objective was to start with one row or grade level and get them started studying independently and then move on to the next row or grade level, etc. until the whole class is studying independently. Then the teacher would work with any student that needed help.[36]

The second problem is to help students learn how to learn on an independent study basis. Every educator that I have worked with has agreed that one of the primary goals of formal schooling is to develop the independent learner. Almost typical of traditional educators, even though the development of the independent learner is a professed goal, rarely are students allowed to learn on an independent basis. Even in graduate school, students still attend classes.

NOTE: In order to clarify a possible misunderstanding, I am defining an independent learner as one who can set goals (product or end objectives) for himself and is capable of taking advantage of available means to achieve these goals and as one who can set up means (process objectives) to follow and is capable of identifying and taking advantage of useful goals achieved as a result of following the means. The student who is involved in independent study may or may not be an independent learner under the above definition. A student could be studying independently in order to achieve process or end objectives set by the teacher which is not within the definition of the independent learner. A student who is studying independently in order to achieve process or end objectives that he or she has set is also an independent learner.

If we want students to be able to study independently and then to

---

[36] Although I am using the one-room school as a model, I am not saying that all one-room schools are great. There were many things lacking in the old one-room schools and eight years of a bad teacher was really a miserable education. But, eight years of a good teacher was fantastic.

become independent learners, we should start as soon as possible to allow students to become effective and efficient at studying independently the teacher objectives and then also to become effective and efficient at learning independently their own objectives. By the time a student is a senior in high school, particularly the terminal student who isn't planning any further formal instruction, he or she should be able to learn almost all of the teacher objectives on an independent learner basis. Responsibility and self-direction are not learned by having opportunities for learning them unavailable. However, responsibility and self-direction are also not necessarily learned by letting the students be completely free to *do their thing.* The cognitive and affective objectives involved in achieving responsibility and self-direction have to be learned by design.

During the past decade, there have been a number of debates on inquiry learning vs. discovery learning. During the past few years, there seems to be an increasing emphasis of discovery learning in the elementary schools and on inquiry learning in higher education. Neither one of these forms of learning used exclusively all or most of the time can accomplish the goals of education. It is necessary to utilize both forms of learning in the development of the independent learner. In inquiry learning, the goals are generally specified, but the student is left up to his own to arrive at the specified goals. In discovery learning, usually the means are specified, and it is left up to the student to discover what the goals are. An over-emphasis of inquiry learning might cripple the student because he has learned the means very well, but hasn't learned much about setting goals. On the other hand, an over-emphasis on discovery learning might cripple the student, in that he would know how to discover goals, but he wouldn't be able to set up the means to get there. Therefore, an over-emphasis of either inquiry learning or discovery learning ultimately becomes a disservice to the student if we truly want the student to become an independent learner.

Actually, there are a series of seven steps in inquiry learning and discovery learning which should be followed if we are truly interested in developing the independent learner. Although some student may be able to intuitively skip some of the steps, if in subsequent steps the student has trouble (learning problems), it may then be necessary to go back through the steps that were skipped.

DEVELOPING THE INDEPENDENT LEARNER

	Means	Goals
First Step	known by the student set by the teacher	known by the student set by the teacher

Some students, depending upon their prior experiences in a given

301

subject area, may have already gone through successful experience in achieving goals that have been set by the teacher by means that have also been set by the teacher. In this first step, it is essential that both the student and the teacher know the specific goals and the specific means necessary to achieve these goals. If the specific objective is to learn the process of discovering goals and the process of identifying means, then the vehicle for learning these objectives can be whatever is of interest to the student. However, it is very possible to combine the learning of these two process objectives with the learning of content objectives in which the vehicle may or may not be prescribed.

DEVELOPING THE INDEPENDENT LEARNER

	Means	Goals
First Step	known by the student *set* by the teacher	known by the student *set* by the teacher
Second Step (Discovery)	known to the student *set* by the teacher	unknown to the student (?) *set* by the teacher
Third Step (Inquiry)	unknown to the student (?) *set* by the teacher	known to the student *set* by the teacher

The order of the second or third step depends on the preference of the teacher involved and/or the motivation of the student involved. Regardless of which step is taken first, both steps should be used in the development of the independent learner. Some educators may feel that discovery or inquiry, if already known to the teacher, are not truly discovery or inquiry for the student. If this is to be a learning experience, it is absolutely necessary for the teacher to know what the student is supposed to discover, and also to know, once the goals have been communicated to the student, more or less what steps the student could go through in order to arrive at the goals. In this way, if the student doesn't discover the right goals, the teacher can help the student to achieve the right goals. If the student doesn't use the right means of inquiry, then the teacher can guide the student along the right pathways of inquiry.

DEVELOPING THE INDEPENDENT LEARNER

	Means	Goals
Fourth Step (Discovery)	*set* by the student known to the teacher	unknown to the student (?) known to the teacher
Fifth Step (Inquiry)	unknown to the student (?) known to the teacher	*set* by the student known to the teacher

In the fourth and fifth steps, the teacher should limit the topics to three or four that the teacher knows very well so that if the student has trouble in discovering the goals in the fourth step and/or in identifying the means in the fifth step, the teacher can help the student have success. Again, the order or sequence of these two steps can be reversed depending upon the preference of the teacher and/or the motivation of the student.

DEVELOPING THE INDEPENDENT LEARNER

	Means	Goals
Sixth Step (Discovery)	*set* by the student unknown to the teacher (?)	unknown to the student (?) unknown to the teacher (?)
Seventh Step (Inquiry)	unknown to the student (?) unknown to the teacher (?)	*set* by the student unknown to the teacher (?)

In the sixth and seventh steps, the student may pick any topic. The teacher's role is as a consultant. If the student picks a topic that the teacher knows very little or nothing about and the student runs into problems, the teacher, as a consultant, will try to find some other teacher or person from the community to help the student solve his learning problems. Again, the order or sequence of these two steps can be reversed depending upon the preference of the teacher and/or the motivation of the student.

DEVELOPING THE INDEPENDENT LEARNER

	Means	Goals
First Step	known to the student *set* by the teacher	known to the student *set* by the teacher
Second Step (Discovery)	known to the student *set* by the teacher	unknown to the student (?) *set* by the teacher
Third Step (Inquiry)	unknown to the student (?) *set* by the teacher	known to the student *set* by the teacher
Fourth Step (Discovery)	*set* by the student known to the teacher	unknown to the student (?) known to the teacher
Fifth Step (Inquiry)	unknown to the student (?) known to the teacher	*set* by the student known to the teacher
Sixth Step (Discovery)	*set* by the student unknown to the teacher (?)	unknown to the student (?) unknown to the teacher (?)
Seventh Step (Inquiry)	unknown to the student (?) unknown to the teacher (?)	*set* by the student unknown to the teacher (?)

Eighth Step (Discovery)	*set* by the student	unknown to the student (?)
Ninth Step (Inquiry)	unknown to the student (?)	*set* by the student

The eighth and ninth steps are concerned with the independent learner and may not be carried out in a school environment although these steps could very well be associated with the students' learning of objectives of his own choosing for a report to other students and teachers under the scholarship function. Just because a student may achieve steps eight and nine in one subject area does not mean that the student can be an independent learner in another subject area.

In all of the continuous progress and non-graded schools which I have visited where students are expected to do independent study, there are students that are not very comfortable trying to learn via independent study. My first choice of a solution to this problem is to check on whether or not the student is given a list of the specific objectives which are to be learned during the independent study time. This is usually the problem for most students: they don't know what they are supposed to be learning. My second choice of a solution to this problem is to check the correlation between the professed specific objectives for the unit or course and the evaluation instrument (test items) used to evaluate student achievement. Of the students who are left where problems were not solved by the first trial solution, many of these will be better motivated to do independent study if they believe that the tests will actually be testing what was supposed to be learned. My third choice of a solution to this problem is to check out the attitudes of the student towards his or her own self-image, towards the course, etc. If the student has had a history of negative experiences in schools, the damaged self-image may very well bring about a defeatist attitude which seriously affects independent study. The solution is then to involve the student in a series of short instructional units in which the student can't help but get 100's which in turn tends to restore the student's self-image.

In following through these steps, it is possible for the schools in the formal teaching-learning situation to train and educate learners so that they can be not only life-long learners, but *successful and independent life-long learners.*

g. THE INSTRUCTIONEER'S ROLE: A LIMITED REALITY ALREADY.

Actually every teacher at one time or another performs the role of the instructioneer. If you are a teacher at present (if not, role play a teacher), think back to the time when a student came up to you at the end of a class and said, *I don't understand* — or *I don't know* —, in reference to a concept you were talking about in class. Would you take out your grade book and grade the student down for asking a question and admitting he or she didn't know or understand something? Of course not. I don't know of a teacher that would do that. What would you do? If you were a typical teacher, you would first try to identify what it was the student didn't understand or know and then you would go back over the concept maybe using different words, illustrations, and/or examples. If you had the time, you would go over and over the problem until you felt that the student did understand or know the concept. Notice, there is no question in your mind about whether or not the student can learn it. You just keep at it until the problem is solved. This is the role of the *instructioneer.*

I want you to role play yourself and imagine that you are walking through the hallway of a school building and you observed a student go up to a teacher and say, *I don't understand* — or, *I don't know* — (the question concerned some concept which had been presented in the teacher's class). In response to the question, the teacher took out the class grade booklet and graded the student down for asking the question! Do you feel and believe that the teacher's behavior in this situation was a negative teaching act? (Answer Yes or No and remember your answer).

Now, let's go back into the classroom. If you are already a teacher, role play yourself. If you are not a teacher, role play a teacher who is sort of a composite of all the teachers you have had as a student. As a teacher you have given a test and you are now scoring the test. As usual, students have made mistakes. When a student makes a mistake on a test, isn't the student saying, *I don't understand* or *I don't know?* (Answer the question with a Yes or No and remember your answer.) Then, as a teacher scoring a test, don't you mark the mistake wrong and end up grading or scoring the student down for making the mistake and saying, *I don't understand* or *I don't know!!!*

NOTE: If you are like the tens of thousands of teachers I've worked with, you believed that the teacher in the hallway committed a negative teaching act and yet in the classroom in the scoring of a test you do what you just said was wrong!!

All I'm really asking teachers to do in writing this series is to bring into the classroom a behavior every one of them already have and perform out in the hallway! When students make mistakes on tests, they don't do it on purpose except in rare situations. Think back to the last time you were driving on a freeway going to a large metropolitan city for the first time. Did you discover that freeway signs are not meant for strangers? They are really meant for people who live there and only need a hint or clue as to when to turn off. Have you ever gone off the wrong exit? Almost everyone has. If you have, did you do it on purpose? Of course not!

The next time you are scoring or grading a test and you come across some student errors, remember, that the student didn't do it on purpose! Consider for a moment, what hint, clue, *freeway sign*, or distractor did you put up that led the student off the wrong exit (to make a mistake)! Student errors are not something wrong with students. The concept of *student errors* is not a negative concept. It is a positive concept.

If people never broke the law, we wouldn't need very many lawyers!

If people never got sick or had accidents, we wouldn't need very many doctors and nurses!

If students never made any mistakes, we wouldn't need very many teachers.

STUDENT ERRORS ARE OPPORTUNITIES TO TEACH NOT SOMETHING WRONG WITH THE STUDENTS!

D. SUPPORTING ROLES TO ASSIST THE INSTRUCTIONEER

Under the traditional approach to education, the primary purpose of schools is a place where teachers can hold classes and as such is very teacher-oriented. Therefore, peripheral roles are also concerned with giving support to the teacher in presenting course content to students. School personnel who either can't get involved in the instructional event or the teachers won't let them get involved with the instructional event usually set up their own little empires within the school and *do their own thing* regardless of how it may or may not affect learning. Under the Behavioral Learning Systems Approach, where the primary purpose of instruction is to maximize student learning, the emphasis on all roles of school personnel is on how that role can have positive affects on student learning.

In describing the following supporting roles, I will only comment on that part of a persons role which actually supports the instructional process which may or may not constitute the persons full responsibility. In some schools, each of the following roles may be held by a different person. In some other smaller schools, one or more of the roles may be held by the same person. In still smaller schools, a teacher may hold one or more of these roles in addition to changing over to an instructioneer.

1. *Master Instructioneers* — these are teachers who hopefully were selected as master instructioneers because they can teach more students and solve more learning problems for more students than other teachers not because they have more seniority, more college credits, or play golf with some administrator. There are three types of master instructioneers:

   a. Specialist in solving learning problems. Given that the process of instruction as described in this book is the same from preschool to graduate school, this person could be called in by a teacher to help solve learning problems at any level and in any subject.

   b. Specialist in solving learning problems in a particular subject matter area at any level. By having extensive experience in the subject matter and also in solving student learning problems in the same subject matter area, this person would be especially useful in identifying alternate vehicles for learning without changing the objectives to be learned.

   c. Specialist in solving learning problems of students at a common grade level or age grouping. By having extensive experience in working with students at a certain grade level or age grouping, this person would be especially useful in identifying and solving communication and motivation problems which might be unique to a particular range of grades or ages.

2. *Principals and Department Heads* — During the past decade, there has been a lot of discussion about what is the best role for principals and department heads. Most principals and some department heads would like to be considered as instructional leaders. Given the traditional educational approach, there isn't too much that can be done except evaluate teachers on their role as presenters of course content which is more the role of the critic than that of a leader. Under the Behavioral Learning Systems approach to instruction, principals and department heads can actually get involved in the instructional game where *the action is*. Their role should be very similar to the instructioneer's role in that they evaluate the teacher on the basis of whether or not the students they are teaching are learning what the students are supposed to. If not, the principal and/or department head doesn't fire the teacher, he or she works with the teacher and helps solve the teacher's instructional problems. The prime function of the principal and/or department head is to facilitate the teacher's facilitating student learning.

3. *Substitute Instructioneers* — Under the traditional approach to education, substitute teachers take over classes when other teachers are

sick, out of town, at a meeting, on strike, etc. The guidelines given to them are essentially that they are to try to follow a lesson plan (if one is left for them) and try to present the material as best they can. If no lesson plan is available, try to keep the kids busy and out of trouble. Neither students, teachers, or administrators really expect much learning to occur unless the substitute teacher stays on for awhile. Under this approach, the substitute teachers often get paid less per day than the regular teachers and may very well be less *qualified* (according to traditional criteria, i.e., degrees and credits, years of experience, etc.).

Under the Behavioral Learning Systems Approach to instruction, the substitute instructioneer may actually get paid more per day than the regular teachers because they will have to be a specialist in instruction-eering at multiple grade levels and in multiple subjects. Given that the courses will all have specific measurable objectives and a record keeping system such that at any time the students, parents, teachers, administrators, and substitute instructioneers know exactly where each student is so the substitute instructioneer can step in and out of the instructional events at any time solving whatever learning problems came up.

4. *Graduate Students as Instructioneers* — In most universities and in many colleges with graduate programs, graduate students are used as teachers. In most of these situations, the graduate student is given one or more classes to meet, a textbook, few objectives if any, and little additional guidelines or help. Yet these graduate students give tests and assign grades and affect the futures of tens of thousands of students just like the so-called professional. Under these conditions, a variety of educational malpractices are being perpetrated against the students being taught by these graduate students. Some schools try to give their graduate students who are teaching some type of training and/or they may also limit their responsibility to just conducting discussion groups, helping in laboratories, etc.

Under the Behavioral Learning Systems Approach to instruction, graduate students can be used very effectively and efficiently. Given the course objectives and the diagnostic tests, the graduate student may very well be able to perform at least parts of the instructioneer's role. In case the graduate student runs across a learning problem that he or she can't solve then there should be a professional instructioneer available to take over and help solve the learning problem. In fact, this could be a very good way to obtain practical experience as an instructioneer.

5. *Layman Teachers* — At the present time, in those schools where the community is looked on as a part of the school, students are supposedly learning *on the job* and their education is in the hands of laymen who are supposed to help the students learn. Since in most of these projects, the specific objectives of what the students should be

learning are not available, the layman teacher tries to help the student understand (?) whatever it is they are doing on the job. Again, the training given the laymen is limited, so although the learning that does take place is more practical and relevant to the learners, it is still a chance learning situation.

Under the Behavioral Learning Systems approach to instruction, the layman would be given some training on how to identify and solve learning problems and would also be given the specific objectives and diagnostic tests concerning what should be learned. As part of the design of the instructional events, the layman would probably work with the instructioneer and/or the curriculum specialists in developing the specific objectives and the diagnostic tests. Just as in the case of the graduate students, the laymen teachers would have a supervising instructioneer to help out in case they encountered student learning problems they couldn't solve.

6. *Associate Teachers* — There are some existing teachers who like working with students, but they don't like the responsibility of being held professionally accountable for student achievement. They would also be much happier working on an hourly basis assisting the professional instructioneer. Although at the present time these teachers have had to go through the same certification requirements as those teachers who as professionals will want to be instructioneers, they really don't have to have the same training because they have much less responsibility. They could handle a lot of the paper work, record keeping, conduct tutoring sessions, and do simple diagnostic and prescriptive functions. In comparison with the medical profession, the associate teachers would be comparable to nurses while the instructioneer would be comparable to doctors.

At the lower elementary levels (including preschool), a similar role has been suggested by HEW's Office of Child Development and is referred to as a Child Development Associate (CDA). A significant change in credential accrediting was also suggested. Rather than give a person a CDA credential as a result of achieving a certain number of credits in certain courses, the suggestion is to have a performance-based certification. This would be similar to some of the efforts in training Teacher Corps students.

7. *Learner's Aids* — The concept of utilizing teacher aids in the classroom has become rather popular in many *modern* schools. They are generally used to actually aid the teacher in doing paperwork such as recording grades, correcting papers, etc. If schools were primarily there to provide employment for teachers, then I think the concept of having teachers' aids might be a very important concept; but since schools are there for learners, I am much more interested in having *learners' aids* than I am in having *teachers' aids.* They might very

309

possibly even carry out the same types of tasks regardless of the name, but it is necessary to keep emphasizing the fact that the ultimate result of having aids in a school should be to facilitate more learning by more students.

As a point of interest, if our goal was really to help more learners learn more, then instead of having the teacher's aid grade papers, the teacher should have to grade the papers in order to identify what it is the students do not know. As a possible compromise, it is alright to have the learners' aid grade the students papers, but all papers that receive less than 100 percent should be checked by the teacher in order to identify and solve the learning problems. Of course, this assumes that the teachers plan to help the students learn what they don't know. As long as the teachers are evaluated on the basis of *Did they present the content of the course*, then this is going to be the teachers' major emphasis in the classroom. Hence, most teachers' aids are used to release the teacher in order that the teachers can prepare their presentations (regardless of whether or not students are learning).

Because most teacher aids aid the teachers without having any measurable affect on student learning and thus increasing the costs of education, my recommendation is that if a teacher can defend the use of a learners' aid based on measurable increases in learning, the teacher should be allowed a learners' aid. However, if a teacher cannot defend the use of a learners' aid based on measurable increases in learning, then I don't believe the teacher should have an aid simply to make the teacher's job easier.

8. *Practice Instructioneers* — At sometime in my seminars with teachers, I always ask the following question, *During your practice teaching experience, how many of you were evaluated on the basis of how much the students (you were teaching) were able to learn?* The number of teachers that answered, *Yes*, would be from zero to three percent. Most students in their practice teaching experience are evaluated on such things as:

Did the student have good eye contact?

Was the student dressed suitably?

Did the student have good classroom control?

How many times did the student use positive and negative reinforcers?

How many times did the student use convergent and divergent questions? etc.

Even though many teacher training institutions are trying to be modern by using Dwight Allen's microteaching concept in which the practice teacher is videotaped, the evaluation is usually the same. Rarely are the students being taught by the practice teacher evaluated to see if they learned what the practice teacher was supposed to teach them.

Any time some kind of checklist is used to evaluate a teacher's or practice teacher's performance in the classroom, the assumption is being made that all teachers or practice teachers are the same. As a result of ignoring individual differences among practice teachers, when they graduate and go to their first job they end up being trained again. Almost every administrator I have talked to states that a new teacher fresh out of colleges needs in-service training before he or she can become an effective classroom teacher.

If the primary function of the schools is learning (rather than teaching), then the best way to evaluate practice teaching is on whether or not the students being taught learned what they were supposed to learn. Also, did the practice teacher identify and solve the students learning problems. With this in mind, one of the best ways to use practice teachers is to have the cooperating teacher identify one or more learning problems (particularly a problem that a majority of the students in a class have) and assign the practice instructioneer to solve the problem such that at least 90 percent or more of the students learn the specified objectives involved with the learning problem. In this way, the practice instructioneer gains the experience necessary to be an instructioneer, the cooperating teacher gains solutions to existing problems, and the students in the class learn more.

9. *Student Tutors* — There are a number of schools throughout the United States and Canada that make use of older students to tutor other students. Although the idea for using students to help their fellow students IN SCHOOLS, is relatively new, anyone who has lived in a large family is quite familiar with the situation where older brothers and sisters will tutor their younger brothers and sisters IN THE HOME. Three of the most important aspects of using students to tutor their classmates or other students are: first, the logic used by the student tutor is liable to be much closer to the logic of the learner; second, the examples used by the student tutor are liable to be much more meaningful; and third, by teaching the subject to other students, the student tutor will get to know it even better.

Another very positive aspect for the use of student tutors is the fact that in most situations, there is very little additional costs, if any, to the school system or to the students who are being tutored. Of interest, is the fact that a number of teachers, departments, and schools at all levels of education have instituted my A, B, and I grading system [37] or

---

[37] A more detailed discussion of the A, B, and I grading system can be found in Chapter VIII, Volume III.

slight variations of it. The "B" grade is given when the student learns 100 percent of all the objectives. The "I" (incomplete) is given if a grade is necessary and the student hasn't achieved the 100 percent yet. The "A" grade is given when the student completes a certain number of hours tutoring other students. The fact that students are encouraged to help one another could also have a very positive fringe benefit in our society.

In spite of the positive aspects of this concept, there are also some negative aspects, as it is being practiced in our schools today. This goes back to the recurrent theme throughout this book, in that if the teachers have not specified what it is the students are supposed to be able to learn, it is rather difficult for a student who is tutoring another student to know what to do to help that student. In cases where teachers have specified what is to be learned, then the students are very capable of tutoring their fellow classmates.

10. *Parents as Tutors* — A very similar situation in many respects would be the utilization of parents as tutors. I have yet to find a parent that does not want his or her child to learn; but since parents are not informed by the teachers as to exactly what it is the students need to learn, it is very difficult for the parents to become involved. Talk to any parent who has gone to schools for parent-teacher conferences (unless you have already participated in some of these conferences yourself), very rarely do teachers specifically point out to the parent exactly what it is his or her child is not learning. If the teachers could point out exactly to the parent what the students were not learning and make some suggestions as to how the parent might help his child learn, it is very possible that every teacher would have a potential of 30 to 60 free learner's aids (the parents of the students).

Traditionally, the parents' role has been limited to parent-teacher conferences about their children, and possibly belonging to the parent-teacher's association. During the past decade, parents have been hired as teacher's aids in classrooms and are presently becoming involved in demands for improved instruction via local or community control over the schools. Since almost every parent wants to help his children learn, there has always been the opportunity of involving parents in the teaching-learning situation. There are actually only two roles the parent could perform; one would be the substitute teacher, and the second would be a substitute learner. In order to carry out the role of a substitute teacher, the parents would either have to have specialized training in order to take over the role of the teacher, or the parents could be given specific temporary training which would allow them to teach a specific skill or piece of knowledge to the learner, based on specific directions given by the teacher. Since the teachers haven't specified what they want the students to learn in their classrooms, it is difficult if not impossible to communicate any kind of suggestions to parents to help them perform the substitute teacher role. In their efforts to help, the parents quite often perform the substitute learner role, in which they help their child do his homework by solving the problems for the students or writing their essays, papers, etc. The substitute learner role may help the student temporarily, but sooner or later the student is going to have to perform by himself at a time when the parents are not going to be available to do it for them. Many parents and students have realized too late that having parents play the role of the substitute learner is not a very effective role and usually ends up in a situation which becomes frustrating for students, parents, and teachers.

Under the traditional approach to education where teachers haven't specified what students are supposed to learn and the emphasis is on the teacher presenting the content of the course, any parental efforts that result in making their child increasingly different from the mythical average student that the teacher is presenting to will end up causing the child more trouble than if they hadn't tried to teach at all.

Under the Behavioral Learning Systems approach to instruction, the instructioneer's role is to identify where the student is intellectually and start the student from there and then to identify and solve any learning problems which may interfere with the student's progress. Because the learning process is individualized anyway, any parental efforts that will help their children learn reduces the amount of work the instructioneer has to do. Whereas at the present time schools receive their state and federal financial aid on the basis of ADA (average daily attendance), once the learning objectives for each course has been identified, it will be possible to receive state and federal financial aid on the basis of the learning which has taken place regardless of whether or not the learning took place at school, at home, or wherever. The more that students can be encouraged to learn on their own and the more that parents can be involved in the teaching-learning process, the fewer students the teacher will have to work with individually. By letting the parents know what the specific objectives are for each course their child is enrolled in and by having sort of in-service sessions to help the interested parents learn how to help their children learn, a lot of learning could be achieved not only during the regular school year but during summers and other vacation periods.

Once schools are given state and federal financial aid based on learning rather than attendance, the compulsory attendance laws will be changed to some minimum learning level that students will have to achieve before being able to drop out of formal school. It won't matter where or when or how a student learns this minimum learning, as long as it is achieved. This minimum learning will consist of the minimum survival skills necessary to exist in our society without becoming a drain on society for most or all of the person's life.

Not all parents will want to actively help their children learn, but for every parent that can help, it is that much less work for the instructioneer. Whereas at the present time, many schools (particularly in the big cities) have daily attendance rates as low as 50 percent of the enrolled students and it is looked on as a bad thing, in the future, it will be normal for a school which is designed for 1000 students to have maybe 1500 students enrolled and only 600-800 students in school at any one time. The major difference will be that at the present time students are absent because they don't like school whereas in the future, students will be out of school because they are learning on the job, at home, at a library or perhaps at a satellite learning center and don't need the instructioneer to identify or solve learning problems.

11. *Guidance and Counseling staff* — In many schools, guidance and counseling staff members would find it very difficult to defend their existence in a school from the point-of-view of the major function of schools: facilitating students learning. Although these staff members generally feel that they are much closer to students than teachers, they all too often assume the teachers are right and try to work with students away from the teaching-learning situation. Since most teachers haven't specified what it is that students should be learning in their courses, it would be very difficult for a guidance or counseling staff member to actually get involved in the educational scene. It doesn't have to stay that way, there are several things that these staff members can do now and in the future in addition to their regular duties or in place of some of their functions to make themselves a critical part of the instructional scene.

In the traditional school:

a. Encourage and/or participate in the setting up of an *Instructional Grievance Committee*. Although one of the first things that groups of teachers and any other organized groups do in getting organized is to set up a Grievance Committee and Grievance Procedures, students rarely have recourse if they don't like a grade. They are at the mercy of the whims of a teacher — particularly in higher education and graduate education. The Instructional Grievance Committee would not get involved in personality conflicts and opinions except where they affect grades. The primary function would be to listen to students and if a charge of unfairness in evaluation can be substantiated, the teacher should be asked to defend the grade. If the grade can't be defended, the Instructional Grievance Committee should have the power to change grades.

b. At the end of each term, obtain a list of all the students who have failed. See the teachers who gave the "F's" and ask them what

314

it was that each student didn't learn. If the teacher can't defend an "F" grade, institute proceedings and get the grade changed. With the lists of whatever it was the students didn't learn, set up tutoring sessions so that the students can learn at least enough not to fail and hopefully enough to eliminate potential cumulative ignorance.[38]

c. Memorize most of the Malpractice Dialogues at the back of my book, *Educational Malpractices: The Big Gamble In Our Schools*, and use these dialogues with teachers in an attempt to reduce the malpractices against students.

In the transition and changed school:

d. Work with the instructioneers in the identification and solving of learning problems which they have found to be especially difficult or are affected by factors which the guidance and counseling staff are more qualified and trained to work with. As these learning problems are identified and solved, the increases in achievement will substantiate the value and contribution of the guidance and counseling staff to the instructional process.

e. Participate in the Instructional Crisis Squad and help teachers to make the change from the traditional approach to education to the Behavioral Learning Systems approach to instruction.

12. *Instructional Crisis Squad* — Very few teachers at the present time were hired because of their ability to help students learn. Until the advent of accountability, very few teachers were evaluated on the basis of their ability to help students learn. Also, very few teacher training institutions actually teach their education majors how to perform the role of the instructioneer. As a result of the foregoing, it would not be fair to teachers if administrators all of a sudden imposed the new criterion for evaluation of student achievement levels without offering help to the teachers needing help. If an administrator evaluates his teachers in accordance with my recommendations in Chapter VIII, Volume III and one or more teachers are evaluated as not doing the job they are supposed to be able to do with their students (student achievement levels are low), then the administrator should send the Instructional Crisis Squad to help the teacher find success. The teachers aren't fired, they are essentially put into an incomplete status just like students when they haven't achieved. The primary function of the Instructional Crisis Squad is to work with teachers in identifying and

---

[38] Since state and federal financial aid is based on average daily attendance, it ends up costing more to fail a student than it does to teach them, particularly if the student drops out of school. By following the suggestion above, many guidance and counseling staff will be able to actually defend their existence in schools on the basis of the number of students still in school who otherwise might have dropped (loss of ADA) and the number of students who completed courses without having to take the courses over again (doubling the costs).

solving their teaching problems in the same manner that the instruction-eer should be doing with students.

The membership of the Instructional Crisis Squad might include most or all of the following:

— Master Instructioneers;
— Librarian;
— Audio-Visual specialist;
— Guidance or Counseling staff member;
— Principal, department head, or other administrator;
— One or more teachers who have had success in performing the instructioneers role;
— One or more students who have proven their ability to tutor other students in the subject matter area involved in the instructional problem; and
— One or more curriculum specialists in the subject matter area involved in the instructional problem.

13. *Curriculum Specialists* — For one reason or another, there may be teachers who are in the teaching profession who do not really like to teach. It is very possible that these teachers could concentrate their energies in the development and handling of instructional materials following the guidelines and results of the teachers who are working directly with students. In addition to these educators, there are other educational materials specialists which should be put into this group because their functions in instruction are so interrelated.

These educators and specialists would fall into three sub-groups: curriculum development, media production, and storage and retrieval systems.[39]

a — Curriculum development specialists would be primarily concerned with updating and evaluating existing curriculum materials from the point of view of what is happening in the real world and the learning problems of the students. As teachers identify learning problems which cannot be solved with available materials, these specialists would develop alternate instructional modules or solutions. They would also be available to meet with students in case the instructioneers didn't have time to develop unique instructional programs based on the student's individual needs or desires.

b — As the instructional modules are developed and it is identified that certain types of media are needed to communicate the instructional message and/or to enable the student to learn on an individual basis, then the media production specialists would be involved. A major

---

[39] Remember that the term *storage and retrieval systems* does not necessarily refer only to automated means of storage and retrieval. It also refers to manual storage and retrieval such as a traditional library.

difference when compared to the present situation is that instead of the development of media being done to fit the needs of a teacher in presenting course content to students, the development and production of media would be because of one or more of three reasons, all related to designed learning:

(1) facilitate the learning of specific objectives which are concerned with other than verbal learning;

(2) facilitate the learning of specific objectives by increasing the level of simulation because of identified learning problems at the lower levels of simulation; and

(3) facilitate the learning of specific objectives via information storage and retrieval systems at the students *own pace,* at the students *best learning time,* and at a place *convenient for learning.*

Media people have suffered a reputation of having had *Mickey Mouse* courses (a little worse than the reputation for most professional education courses) and of being on the periphery of education and a *frill* when it comes to the school budget (first place to make cuts) unless the media people are involved in an innovation which is bringing fame and visibility to the school. As soon as the media *fad* loses the interest of faculty, community, and/or other educators, media people and the media become once again superfluous in the educational scene. The major reason for this problem is that the media people have not been directly involved in the instructional event primarily because of a role identification problem of their own. Both the media production group and the storage and retrieval group have been involved in this role problem. Initially both groups felt their role was as a *custodian* and many individuals in both groups became very possessive over their empires (books, audio-visual equipment, etc.). During the past decade or so, both of these groups and many of the members of each group have changed their role to one that is *service-oriented.* The problem with this role is that as long as education is teacher-oriented, the audio-visual production, storage and retrieval service tends to be for teachers and as such is on the periphery of education. Although the book and print storage and retrieval systems provide service primarily to students, the service is rarely based on the learning of specific objectives (maybe specific activities but not measurable learning objectives). As a result, this group is also on the periphery of education, but because of the student connection and its long history of being associated with academia, the book and print storage and retrieval systems (libraries) are not as dispensable as the audio-visual group. Media production people and librarians do not have to be on the periphery of education. They can jump into the middle of the instructional fray by getting on the Instructional Crisis Squad and by working with the guidance and counseling staff in setting up developmental and tutoring sessions for students having learning problems. If neither of these pathways are available, the media people and librarians can go to the school records and identify teachers that are having maximum unsolved learning problems (teachers with the most "D" and "F" students) and offer their services and help. There are too many students who are suffering from ineffective and inefficient teaching-learning situations for the media production people and the storage and retrieval systems people to sit by on the periphery of education waiting for students and teachers to ask for their services.

There will still be a need for the *presenter-oriented* media under the scholarship function. But instead of this always being done with and for teachers, the media production services will also be available to students who will be presenting in scholarship functions.

c — As learning problems are solved, rather than reinvent the solutions each time the problem is identified, there is a need for storage and retrieval systems of books, pamphlets, programmed instructional materials, instructional modules, films, etc. (including storage and retrieval from computers). In this way, these three groups of the curriculum specialists and particularly this last group become the *prescription pharmacy* of the instructional environment, an Instructional Prescription Center. In addition to the problems mentioned in discussing the last group (media production) which concern the storage and retrieval systems group, this group has been plagued with squabbles between different factions as to who will be in charge of the storage and retrieval system empires. The major problem is that under the traditional approach to education, the various factions were divided up according to the media or product (computers, books, films, etc.). Whereas under the Behavioral Learning Systems approach to instruction, the divisions are determined by function and the relationship of the function to the instructional event. People who are trained under the *product-orientation* may find it uncomfortable to fit in the *function-oriented* environment. However, if student learning is really our major goal, the transition and role changes have to be made. Once made, the storage and retrieval systems will serve the following four groups:

(1) As an Instructional Prescription Center for storage and retrieval of alternate pathways in the learning of required objectives in whatever courses are associated with the instructional environment. (In the storage and retrieval of instructional units and instructional courses, it is possible for a given unit to be a part of the instructional sequence of more than one course.)

(2) As members of the learning problem solving team where the problems deal with the retrieval of solutions, i.e., students learning individually at remote locations away from the normal instructional

environment and at other than *normal* time schedules.

(3) As an Instructional Prescription Center for the storage and retrieval of a wide variety of instructional units which are not required in any courses, but may be requested by an individual because of his or her needs or interest. (It is possible for a student to *want to* learn voluntarily an instructional unit which may happen to be a required unit in a course which the student is not enrolled in.)

(4) As a resource for instructional researchers.

14. *Instructional Researchers* — Under the traditional approach to education where educational research is primarily concerned with the study of educational methods, media, and data, it is not a science because what is being studied is man-made phenomenon. Also, the results of traditional research are of little value to the traditional classroom teacher because neither the researcher nor the teacher are that concerned with what is being specifically and measurably learned by the students. Under the Behavioral Learning Systems approach to instruction, instructional researchers will be first concerned with effectiveness in instruction and will be researching difficult learning problems encountered by the instructioneers in their attempts to get 100 percent of the students to learn 100 percent of the specified objectives. To do this, the researchers will have to work very close with the instructioneers in applied research. As such, the results of this research will not only be very relevant and useful, but it will represent *instructional research as a science* because what is being researched is *how to get the students to learn these objectives* and learning is a natural phenomenon rather than *what happens when students learn this way*, in which the *way* is a man-made phenomenon.

Once effectiveness is not such a serious problem and 90 percent or more of the students are learning 100 percent of all their course objectives, then researchers can turn to concerns of efficiency such as how students can learn what they need to learn in a shorter time, at a lower cost, etc. Again, the instructional research will be relevant and useful to the instructioneers because it concerns real learning of students associated with real learning problems in real courses.

15. *Presenters in the Scholarship Function* — Although the scholarship function is not as important as the learning function in our schools, the presentations under the scholarship function will serve as introductions to the vast areas which can be studied. As a result of these sessions, it may become common to have new courses being developed. These sessions may also provide clues to alternate ways of solving learning problems as motivated students see topics from different points-of-view. Because of the scholarly attitudes in these sessions where everyone is equally a participant and everyone can have an opinion and there are no objectives, no tests, no required attendance,

the spirit of comraderie may very well carry over into the instructional environment to develop an emotional environment where everyone works together to solve learning problems.